THE EARLY TEXTUAL HISTORY OF LUCRETIUS'
DE RERUM NATURA

This is the first detailed analysis of the fate of Lucretius' *De rerum natura* from its composition in the 50s BC to the creation of our earliest extant manuscripts during the Carolingian age. Close investigation of the knowledge of Lucretius' poem among writers throughout the Roman and mediaeval worlds allows fresh insight into the work's readership and reception, and a clear assessment of the indirect tradition's value for editing the poem. The first extended analysis of the 170+ subject headings (*capitula*) that intersperse the text reveals the close engagement of its Roman readers. A fresh inspection and assignation of marginal hands in the poem's most important manuscript (the Oblongus) provides new evidence for the work of Carolingian correctors and offers the basis for a new Lucretian *stemma codicum*. Further clarification of the interrelationship of Lucretius' Renaissance manuscripts gives additional evidence for the poem's reception and circulation in fifteenth-century Italy.

DAVID BUTTERFIELD is a Fellow of Queens' College and Lecturer in Classics at the University of Cambridge.

CAMBRIDGE CLASSICAL STUDIES

General editors

R. L. HUNTER, R. G. OSBORNE, M. MILLETT,
D. N. SEDLEY, G. C. HORROCKS, S. P. OAKLEY,
W. M. BEARD

THE EARLY TEXTUAL HISTORY OF LUCRETIUS'
DE RERUM NATURA

DAVID BUTTERFIELD

CAMBRIDGE
UNIVERSITY PRESS

CAMBRIDGE
UNIVERSITY PRESS

University Printing House, Cambridge CB2 8BS, United Kingdom

Published in the United States of America by Cambridge University Press, New York

Cambridge University Press is part of the University of Cambridge.

It furthers the University's mission by disseminating knowledge in the pursuit of
education, learning and research at the highest international levels of excellence.

www.cambridge.org
Information on this title: www.cambridge.org/9781107037458

© Faculty of Classics, University of Cambridge 2013

First published 2013

Printed and bound in the United Kingdom by CPI Group Ltd, Croydon, CR0 4YY

A catalogue record for this publication is available from the British Library

Library of Congress Cataloguing in Publication data
Butterfield, D. J. (David James), 1985–
The early textual history of Lucretius' De rerum natura / David Butterfield.
pages   cm.
Includes bibliographical references and index.
ISBN 978-1-107-03745-8 (Hardback)
1. Lucretius Carus, Titus. De rerum natura.   2. Didactic poetry,
Latin–History and criticism.   I. Title.
PA6484.B88 2013
187–dc23
2013008189

ISBN 978-1-107-03745-8 Hardback

Additional resources for this publication at www.cambridge.org/butterfield

CONTENTS

List of illustrations   *page* vi
Preface   ix

Introduction   1

1 A sketch of the extant Lucretian manuscripts   5

2 The indirect tradition of Lucretius   46

3 The *capitula* of *De rerum natura*   136

4 The correcting hands of O   203

5 The marginal annotations of Q^I 261

Conclusion   268

Appendices
I Capitula Lucretiana   274
II Apparatus fontium Lucreti *(ante a.d. millesimum)*   286
III The corrections and annotations of O   296
IV The foliation of the Lucretian archetype   299
V The fate of OQS in the early modern period   305
Bibliography   315
Index   340

The colour plates are placed between pages 180 and 181

ILLUSTRATIONS

1	The stemma of the Lucretian tradition posited by Jacob Bernays (1847)	*page* 15
2	A basic stemma of the Lucretian tradition	19
3	A more detailed stemma of the Lucretian tradition	32
4	The stemma of the Italian manuscripts of Lucretius posited by Konrad Müller (1973)	34
Fig. A	*Indices capitulorum libri IV*: O 87^{r-v}. Reproduced with the permission of Leiden University Library	154
Fig. B	*Indices capitulorum libri IV*: Q 30^{v}. Reproduced with the permission of Leiden University Library	155
Fig. C	*Indices capitulorum libri V*: O 120^{v}–121^{v}. Reproduced with the permission of Leiden University Library	157
Fig. D	*Indices capitulorum libri V*: Q 42^{v}–43^{r}. Reproduced with the permission of Leiden University Library	158
Fig. E	*Indices capitulorum libri V* (reconstructed): Ω 96^{r}.	159
Fig. F	*Indices capitulorum libri VI*: O 159^{r-v}. Reproduced with the permission of Leiden University Library	164
Fig. G	*Indices capitulorum libri V*: Q 56^{r}. Reproduced with the permission of Leiden University Library	165
Fig. H	*Indices capitulorum libri VI* (reconstructed): Ω 126^{r}.	166

List of illustrations

Plate I   The first page of the Codex Oblongus (O): *DRN*
           I.1–19. Reproduced with the permission of Leiden
           University Library

Plate II   O 15^r: *DRN* I.545–64 (549–50 added by Dungal
           in rasura). Reproduced with the permission of Leiden
           University Library

Plate III O 19^r: *DRN* I.703–20 (the corrections and glosses
           of O^3 are visible). Reproduced with the permission of
           Leiden University Library

Plate IV   O 192^v: *DRN* VI.1273–86 (the final leaf of O).
           Reproduced with the permission of Leiden University
           Library

Plate V   The first leaf of the Codex Quadratus (Q):
           DRN I.1–51. Reproduced with the permission of
           Leiden University Library

Plate VI   Q 31^r: *DRN* IV.11–65 (the rubrication at 38 is from
           an appreciably later hand). Reproduced with the
           permission of Leiden University Library

Plate VII Q 45^v: *DRN* V.266–83 (the marginal hand is that
           of Q^1). Reproduced with the permission of Leiden
           University Library

Plate VIII The first leaf of the *Schedae Gottorpienses* (G), the
           opening fragment of S. Reproduced with the
           permission of the Royal Library of Copenhagen

PREFACE

This book represents an expanded revision of a doctoral thesis of the same title submitted to Cambridge University in 2010, although questions about the transmission of Lucretius' *De rerum natura* have interested me for the past decade. From my first term as an undergraduate I was spurred on by the warm and generous encouragement of my friends and colleagues David McKie, David Sedley, James Diggle and Ted Kenney, each of whom opened up numerous rich new avenues of learning for me. More directly, the significant researches of Michael Reeve that appeared in *Aevum* for 2005 and 2006 made immediately apparent the sheer breadth of unanswered questions relating to the transmission of the poem. I owe him exceptional gratitude for generously agreeing to supervise this thesis out of retirement and for graciously providing, with exemplary speed and kindness, a remarkably wide array of material to ponder, often when I found myself against what seemed a particularly stubborn brick wall. He continues to provide me with a formidable and inspiring exemplar of what Latin scholarship can be. The close eye and criticism of my doctoral examiners, Stephen Oakley and Marcus Deufert, have allowed me to improve my account in several respects.

I am immensely indebted to Christ's College, Cambridge, where I studied and worked from 2003 to 2011, an institution that has constantly supported my research, and whose Fellowship has genially and enthusiastically welcomed my own diverse scholarly interests. I hope that W. H. D. Rouse, whose Lucretian Loeb (1924) introduced the great Epicurean poem to thousands of students worldwide, would not be displeased with a more narrow study of this kind carried out under his eponymous benefaction. I also owe a financial debt to Christ's, in conjunction with the Faculty of Classics, for generously meeting the funding costs for my doctoral work, for which I will always be profoundly grateful.

Finally, I am very pleased to have entered the Fellowship of Queens' College, Cambridge, a place of serious scholarship that has welcomed me with genuine generosity.

I have analysed and (where appropriate) collated the following manuscripts by autopsy: O (Leiden Voss. Lat. F 30: April 2008, September 2009), Q (Leiden Voss. Lat. Q 94: April 2008, September 2009), G (Copenhagen Kgl. S. 211 2°: December 2008), V (Vienna ÖNB Phil. 107 ff.9–17: December 2007) and the *Florilegium Sangallense* (St Gallen Stiftsbibl. 871: September 2008). I have also derived immense benefit from the high-quality facsimiles of O and Q published by Chatelain (1908; 1913), the scans of G available through the *Codices Haunienses* resource online, and the microfilm of VU kindly provided in January 2008 by the Österreichische Nationalbibliothek. I have depended entirely on my own collations and inspection for these manuscripts and am therefore confident in the veracity of my reports. Readings of the various *Itali* I have obtained from a wide range of digital images, printed resources and the private collations of Michael Reeve. Answers to a number of particular queries were kindly provided by André Bouwman (Curator of Western Manuscripts, Leiden University Library), David Ganz (Professor Emeritus of Palaeography, King's College London), Erik Petersen (Research Librarian, Royal Library, Copenhagen) and Martin Ferguson Smith (Professor Emeritus of Classics, University of Durham). The staff of two incomparable institutions, the Rare Books Room in the University Library of Cambridge and the Wren Library of Trinity College, also deserve my sincere thanks for their patient forbearance of my very regular visits and requests. The splendid staff of Cambridge University Press deserve warm thanks, especially my copy-editor, Jan Chapman.

The work published here is designed to serve as a firm basis for future editions of Lucretius' *De rerum natura*, for which there remains a major need. I am currently preparing a new Oxford Classical Text of Lucretius, to replace Bailey's outdated text of 1922; in its wake I intend to produce a full-scale commentary on *De rerum natura*. In the nearer future I shall publish a full *thesaurus emendationum* for the poem, which will contain a comprehensive appendix that catalogues errors transmitted in the manuscripts, and a collection of my textual adversaria on Lucretius, uniting previously published material and unpublished emendations.

Finally, it is a pleasure and a privilege to have the opportunity to express my gratitude to those who have tolerated me and my researches for their genuine love, encouragement and good humour. My family have continued to provide unstinting support for my scholarship, even if at some geographical remove: their belief in my studies, and faith in my own passions, is more of a blessing than I could have hoped for. Within Cambridge, particular gratitude is owed to Lyndsay Coo (Pembroke and Trinity), Emily Kneebone (Newnham and Trinity Hall), Shaul Tor (St John's, Jesus, King's College London) and Moreed Arbabzadah (Jesus), four contemporary Classicists and close friends who have spurred me on from the beginning of my time at the University and without whom things would have been very different. The sagacity of a historian, Alex Middleton (Pembroke, Cambridge, and Wadham, Oxford), has been a provocative goad throughout my studies. Lastly, I must record the immeasurable debt I owe to my wife Rhiannon (Queens' College), for all of her unbounded support, understanding and inspiration: *sic rerum summa nouatast.*

Queens' College
Summer 2012

INTRODUCTION

Only one work is known to have been composed by Titus Lucretius Carus[1] (*c*. 94–55 BC),[2] the six-book poem of Epicurean philosophy, *De rerum natura* (henceforth *DRN*).[3] Almost nothing is known about Lucretius himself; the biased life summary provided by Jerome[4] cannot be used as a reliable source for his biography.[5] The extant state of *DRN* shows clearly that the work

[1] The praenomen *Titus* is attested in Aulus Gellius and Hrabanus Maurus (see Chapter 1, n. 15) and occurs alongside *Carus* in the subscriptions to each book of O, and Books II and VI (*ari* for *Cari*) of S (= VU).

[2] The dates of Lucretius' life are extremely difficult to resolve from the few data available (for which see Bailey, vol. 1, 2–4). In a paper ('On the chronology of Lucretius' *De rerum natura* and the *Corpus Catullianum*') presented to the First Century BC Philosophy Seminar at the Faculty of Classics, Cambridge, on 6 March 2007, I offered my own arguments for dating Lucretius' life from October/December 94 to late September/early October 55 BC. I discovered later that one significant element of my argument, emending Jerome's figure of Lucretius' lifespan from forty-four years to thirty-nine (i.e. XXXXIIII > XXXVIIII), had been preceded, in his third attempt at solving the problem, by Giovanni D'Anna (2002). Although the date does not affect the arguments of this book, I shall proceed with the hypothesis that no further alteration was carried out on *DRN* from late 55 BC, and that Lucretius died rather than lost interest in his *gigantisches Lebens-werk*. For further discussion of the dates of Lucretius' life, although I disagree strongly with his conclusion, see Hutchinson (2001), to which Volk (2010) has responded.

[3] The title of Lucretius' work is first explicitly attested by Probus (in Keil's *Grammatici Latini* (hereafter *GLK*) IV 225, 29), although Vitruvius had already stated (IX.*pr*.17.1) that one could dispute *de rerum natura* with Lucretius; the title of the work also appears in the subscriptions to the individual books in OS. The phrase occurs in Lucr. I.25, and is perhaps alluded to at IV.969 and V.335. *De rerum natura* was a natural title for a work of Lucretius' genre and can be regarded as a translation of Greek Περὶ φύσεως, the title of Epicurus' major 37-book opus from which Lucretius fashioned his work (cf. Sedley (1998), esp. 21–2).

[4] Hier. *Chron.* s.a. 94/3 BC (Ol. 171.3). I follow most scholars in dismissing the two claims of Jerome not supported elsewhere: (i) that (Marcus Tullius) Cicero *emendauit* the poem, probably a mistaken inference by Jerome or his source from the fact that the earliest mention of Lucretius occurs in a letter from Cicero to his brother (*Ad Q. Fr.* II.9.3); (ii) that through insanity from a love potion Lucretius committed suicide, which probably derives from Lucretius' failure to condemn suicide at III.79–82 and a confusion with the Lucullus said to have died by a love potion (cf. Plin. *HN* XXV.3), negative elements a Christian polemicist like Jerome would happily have applied to Lucretius.

[5] The '*Vita Borgiana*' is now widely accepted to be devoid of authority. For a survey of the very slim evidence regarding Lucretius' life, from which tenuous inferences are drawn, see L. Canfora (1993).

was intended to cover six books alone.[6] It was almost, but not entirely, completed, as demonstrated by the unfinished state and improbable order of several arguments, which cannot be satisfactorily explained by textual corruption.[7] Given that the poem still required additions, deletions and reordering at the time of Lucretius' death, it is natural to suppose that, when he died, much of the work existed on papyrus sheets (*chartae*) rather than in six 'fair copy' book rolls.[8] Because of the poem's incomplete state, editors must acknowledge that the end goal of their textual reconstruction should only be the state of the work as Lucretius left it rather than a fully perfected piece of literature.

The purpose of this book is not to aid the reconstruction of elements of the poem never written by Lucretius, nor indeed to restore the lacunae that have entered the text during its tenuous textual transmission.[9] Rather, it presents a series of studies of the textual fate of Lucretius' work from his death in 55 BC through to the rediscovery of the work by Poggio in 1417. The investigation will be limited to textual and codicological analysis; the philosophical and poetical influence of Lucretius from the classical period through to the modern age, a field that has been closely studied, will be set aside, except where there is scope for inferring the textual state and availability of *DRN* in a given time and place. The difficult question of interpolation in the poem is not considered here: I am extremely wary of positing the wide-scale intervention of interpolating hands in the transmission of *DRN* and, if the text did suffer from the concerted efforts of one or more interpolators, such activity occurred too early in the

---

[6] Lucretius strongly implied that the sixth book was his last at VI.92–5 and referred to the transmitted Book I as his first at VI.937; for a thorough treatment of the question, see Eichstädt (LXIV–LXXVII).

[7] Most notably the survival of dual passages (e.g. IV.26–44 ~ 45–53) and the unfulfilled claim at V.155 that Lucretius would discuss the nature of the gods *largo sermone*. This is very much the *consensus* of editors, with few objectors (most fully, but unconvincingly, van der Valk (1902)). For a more detailed discussion of the question of the work's incompletion and the allegation of interpolation, see Butterfield (2013).

[8] If so, we must assume that someone close to Lucretius and/or experienced in Latin poetry and/or Epicurean philosophy ordered the disparate elements of the work, commissioned the first copies of the poem and put them into circulation.

[9] On this question see, beyond the commentaries, Madvig (1834) 305–22, Raasted (1955) and Owen (1968).

tradition to be elucidated by close analysis of our extant ninth-century witnesses.[10]

There exist two pieces of evidence regarding the editing or commenting of Lucretius' work (in the modern sense of these terms). First, a grammatical tract that survives only in an eighth-century manuscript (the so-called *Anecdotum Parisinum*), which perhaps ultimately drew upon a lost work of Suetonius, seemingly attributes an edition of *DRN*, annotated with critical symbols, to M. Valerius Probus (late first century AD).[11] Second, Jerome testified that, in the late fourth century, at least one commentary upon the poem was available to him (and this could be linked with Probus' work).[12] At any rate, the research behind this book finds no evidence connecting the direct transmission of Lucretius with either of these two works, nor do the *capitula* turn out to be derived from them at all. Although this conclusion is disappointingly negative, it remains the case that, if Probus did indeed 'edit' the text of *DRN*, that recension could nevertheless have influenced a manuscript early in the surviving stream of transmission.

Over the following five chapters I tackle a range of matters relating to the transmission and *Überlieferungsgeschichte* of *DRN*. Chapter 1 reconstructs the history of Lucretius' extant manuscripts and defends a new stemma for the tradition, augmented by the results of Chapter 4. In Chapter 2 I turn to treat Lucretius' indirect tradition, assessing the textual relationships that exist between the various authors who cite him and the direct transmission of *DRN* up to the Carolingian period; on the basis of this study, inferences can be drawn about the availability of Lucretius' poem in Rome and the Empire and the overall value of the indirect tradition for constituting

---

[10] For detailed discussion, which built on K. Müller's edition (1975) in dismissing over three hundred verses from the work as the result of later hands, see Deufert (1996), the sole serious discussion of the problem since Neumann (1875) and Gneisse (1878). For an account of my own view, that interpolation scarcely affected the transmission of *DRN*, see Butterfield (2013).

[11] *Probus qui illas* [sc. *notas*] *in Vergilio et Horatio et Lucretio apposuit, ut in Homero Aristarchus* (Anon. *De notis GLK* VII 534,6 (= Paris. BN Lat. 7530, ff. 28^r–29^r l.6)); for further context see Bonnet (1960), Zetzel (1981) 41–54, Jocelyn (1984, 1985) and Kaster (1995) 257–8.

[12] *puto quod puer legeris ... commentarios ... aliorum in alios, Plautum uidelicet, Lucretium, Flaccum, Persium atque Lucanum* (*Contra Rufin.* I.16, written *c.* 401).

3

its text. The chapter closes with a detailed treatment of the so-called Lucretian 'fragments'. Chapter 3 treats a body of non-Lucretian material that appears throughout the Lucretian manuscript tradition, namely the *capitula*, or subject headings, which are transmitted in the body of the poetic text: the evidence will be refined and then mined for evidence about their origin.[13] Chapter 4 analyses the various (over two thousand) corrections and annotations that occur throughout O, on the basis of a full collation and a new assignation of corrections to different hands; the chapter discusses the activity and methodology of (A) Dungal (early saec. IX), (B) a marginal annotator who highlighted incorrect verses with a series of points (saec. IX), (C) O^2 (saec. $IX^{ex.}$), (D) O^3 (saec. X^2), and various marks by hands of the fifteenth (F) and eighteenth (?) centuries (E: O^4) which have wrongly been given textual significance. Finally, Chapter 5 analyses the few ancient annotations present in Q ($= Q^1$) that offer an insight into a Carolingian reader's approach to the text.[14] The book closes with a Conclusion that integrates the evidence turned up by the preceding chapters relating to questions about the script of the archetype (Ω) and its predecessors; to close, a few methodological recommendations are given for future editors of *DRN*.

Throughout this book I refer to bibliographical material in the shorthand form 'surname (year)', with pagination if appropriate; these works are gathered in the Bibliography, along with others I have consulted but not cited. For Lucretian editions and commentaries, which are listed at the beginning of the Bibliography, I refer merely to the editor's surname where the context provides the relevant information for further investigation. For detailed bibliographical information about all Lucretian editions and commentaries cited in this thesis, please consult the marvellous compendium of Gordon (1985).

---

[13] Since this chapter investigates various matters relating to the processes of producing the three ninth-century manuscripts (OQS), I also discuss matters of rubrication and scribal variation in these codices.

[14] The very great number of corrections made in Q by the mid-fifteenth-century Italian hand are not treated in this thesis, since their basis is entirely conjectural and bears no relevance to the Lucretian stemma. Similarly, the conjectural emendations that occur sporadically in S (saec. IX/X, XVII/XVIII) are not treated, as the former were made by the scribe himself or a contemporary from the exemplar (ψ) alone, and the occasional modern alterations have no manuscript authority.

A SKETCH OF THE EXTANT LUCRETIAN MANUSCRIPTS

There is perhaps no more famous manuscript stemma for the transmission of any ancient text than that of Lucretius' *DRN*.[1] Although its basic form was presented in Karl Lachmann's epoch-making edition of 1850, debate has continued into the twenty-first century about a matter as simple as how many branches it should possess. In this opening chapter, I will demonstrate that the most serious problems should be regarded as solved, even if many scholars have failed to apprehend this. I shall begin with a survey of the primary manuscripts, before turning to their stemmatic relationship.

There is no extant direct witness to *DRN* from the first 850 years of its transmission. The surviving manuscripts fall into two categories, those written in the ninth century, and those in the Renaissance, predominantly in the fifteenth century. Before turning to these, we may briefly consider the proposed existence of a third class, namely papyri. Two decades ago, Knut Kleve (1989) claimed to have found traces of *DRN* in papyrus fragments from the Library of Herculaneum dated to the late first century BC and now preserved in the Officina dei Papiri of the Biblioteca Nazionale in Naples (*PHerc.* 1829–31).[2] Alongside these tiny and tentative snippets of Latin from allegedly four books of *DRN* (I, III, IV, V), Kleve published in 2007 his readings from *PHerc.* 395, first unrolled in 1805, arguing that it contained fragments of Book II.[3] In both cases Kleve conceded that elements not preserved in the direct transmission of the poem must exist in

---

[1] Cf. Reynolds (1983b) 218: 'The stemma of Lucretius has long been one of the great show-pieces of classical scholarship.'

[2] These fragments, though discovered in the late eighteenth century by Sir Humphry Davy (1778–1829), were set aside as unreadable and too fragile for the primitive tools of unrolling available. Images of them can be seen at Kleve (1989) 14–26 and Kleve (2012) 68.

[3] Images of these can be seen in Kleve (2007) and Kleve (2012) 69, 75–6.

these papyri. Although each of his readings presents only a few letters, of which most are uncertain and many differ from any part of Lucretius' extant text (and other surviving literature), his identification was tacitly accepted by several scholars, most recently Ferguson Smith and Flores.[4] In 2001 Mario Capasso (2003) disputed the identification in the case of *PHerc.* 1829–31, revealing amidst a detailed rebuttal that these fragments originate from the same source as *PHerc.* 395.[5] More recently Beate Beer (2009) has succinctly bolstered his arguments, demonstrating that the majority of fragments currently deciphered from *PHerc.* 395 (whose readings Kleve reported without due accuracy) do not coincide with *DRN*, the textual discrepancy being far greater than any supposition of corruption would allow.[6] It may well be that rolls of Lucretius' *DRN* did exist in Philodemus' library at Herculaneum; if so, however, no fragment of that work can yet be shown to have survived the eruption of Mount Vesuvius in AD 79. We can therefore turn to the manuscript witnesses of the ninth century, of which two are complete and one survives in three fragments containing almost half of the poem's text.

(i) O (Leiden, Universiteitsbibliotheek, Voss. Lat. F. 30)

The oldest and most famous Lucretian manuscript is the Codex Oblongus, which has borne this name and the siglum O regularly since Lachmann.[7] This luxurious production, described as 'a most

---

[4] Only Suerbaum (1994), refining his earlier contribution (1992), has sought to develop Kleve's analysis of the text; Nünlist (1997) attempted to improve the rather forced reconstruction of the layout of the original papyrus roll offered by Kleve and Suerbaum.

[5] Doubts about the nature of the script, which Kleve has termed 'Early Roman', had already been expressed by Radiciotti (2000) 366–8.

[6] Obbink (2007, 34 n. 2) recorded his conclusion from autopsy that *PHerc.* 395 was not Lucretian, a view which my own analysis from available images certainly supports. The evidence of Kleve (2010), drawing upon an Oxford *disegno*, does not suggest Lucretian authorship (contrary to the author's tortuous hypotheses of corruption and improbably arranged *sovrapposti*); Kleve (2009), Kleve (2010) and Kleve (2012), which offer no new evidence or arguments, do nothing to strengthen the case of the Lucretian identification, or his dating of them to the mid first century BC.

[7] Munro, Duff and Heinze more methodically termed O 'A' and Q 'B' but no one else has adopted this alphabetical rebranding.

remarkable manuscript' by Ganz (1996, 92),[8] comprises 192 single-columned folios, each averaging twenty verses per page.[9] The manuscript is the product of an early Carolingian scriptorium, bearing the initial signs of that school's scribal reforms,[10] and has been dated to the early ninth century by the primary twentieth-century expert in this field.[11] Since Chapter 4 will treat various features of O, particularly its correcting hands, I here provide a mere outline of the manuscript's history. O was probably copied in a monastery closely linked with Charlemagne's court (then vagrant), either in north-west Germany or north-east France;[12] Bischoff tentatively suggested that the scribe, whose work is also seen in Bern Burgerbibliothek 212 (saec. IX[in.]),[13] was originally trained at Mainz. There is no good reason to suppose that O ever left northern mainland Europe (excepting the period 1670–90, on which see Appendix V). Since no evidence survives that anyone between the tenth century and 1417 read Lucretius directly, there is little scope for tracing the respective fates of Lucretian manuscripts in these intervening centuries.[14] Nevertheless, Bischoff revealed that O was corrected by the Irishman Dungal (who was based at St Denis by 811 until 825); we should presume, therefore, either that Dungal corrected O somewhere in Charlemagne's court soon after its creation, or that it was transferred along with its exemplar to St Denis, to both of which manuscripts Dungal had access

[8] He added that 'it is hard to think of a contemporary non-liturgical volume copied in such large script and with such lavish spacing' (93).

[9] For discussion of O's rubrication and other scribal matters, see Chapter 3, n. 4.

[10] See especially Bischoff in Braunfels (1965) 206 no. 365.

[11] Bischoff (2004) 50 no. 2189: 'IX. Jh., 1./2. Viertel'; cf. also De Meyier (1973) 65: 'saec. IX in.'

[12] Bischoff (2004) 50 no. 2189: 'Etwa Nordwestdeutschland'; cf. also Bischoff (1966–81) vol III, 42, where he placed it more specifically 'in der Nähe des Hofes', having earlier said that it was 'von einem Schreiber geschrieben, der seine Ausbildung in der Hofschule erhalten haben könnte' (1965, 206). Munk Olsen (1985, 87) opted for 'Nord-est de la France'; De Meyier (1973, 67) attributed it to 'Gallia (pars quae inter septentriones et orientem solem spectat)', i.e. north-east France. Metz could tentatively be suggested as a possible place of origin.

[13] See Schaller (1960) for more on this manuscript of Optatianus Porphyrius.

[14] See Appendix II, n. 1. Only one correcting hand can be identified in O between the middle of the ninth century and the seventeenth/eighteenth centuries (i.e. O[3], for whom see Chapter 4 (D)), and it does not help to locate the manuscript (see following note).

(see Chapter 4). O at some stage moved to Mainz,[15] for in 1479 Macarius von Busek, the Canon and Syndic of St Martin's, added his uniform *ex libris* to its first leaf (see Plate I). This note need not signify a new acquisition (*contra* Leonard–Smith (86)), so O could have resided there for some time.[16] Over the next two centuries O was thrust back into the European world: for an account of its circulation until it entered the University of Leiden in 1690, where it has resided ever since, see Appendix V. We may now turn to O's less august sibling.

(ii) Q (Leiden Universiteitsbibliotheek, Voss. Lat. Q 94)

The Codex Quadratus, typically given this name and the siglum Q since Lachmann (but cf. n. 7 above), is a manuscript of sixty-nine two-columned folios, regularly of twenty-eight verses per column.[17] It is dated to the mid ninth century[18] and written, like O, in early Carolingian minuscule. Unlike its older relative, however, Q shows very few signs of having been read before the Renaissance: it did not receive contemporary rubrication, and only two readers left very occasional marks on the text;[19] in the middle of the fifteenth century,[20] by contrast, a north-Italian hand fully annotated the manuscript, not only dividing words and adding

---

[15] As I will argue in Chapter 4, there is no reason to accept the hypothesis of M. Tangl (reported by Diels (XIV)) that O was corrected by Otloh of St Emmeram (*c.* 1010–*c.* 1072) in Fulda in the mid eleventh century or Diels' further contention (XIII) that O was itself written in Fulda. Hrabanus Maurus (*c.* 780–856), who mentioned Lucretius' sigmatic ecthlipsis at *De laud. S. Crucis prol.* (*PL* CVII 146c = *Epp.* 2a (*MGH EKA* V.3, 383,31)), along with the praenomen *Titus* (attested only in the indirect tradition at Gell. XII.10.8), could have encountered *DRN* whilst Archbishop of Mainz (847–56; cf. Falk (1897) 5 (555)). Marginal marks that I discuss in Chapter 4 and attribute to a ninth-century hand have also been associated with Mainz (see Chapter 4 (B)). If so, we can place O in Mainz for some 700 years (mid ninth to mid sixteenth centuries: see below). It was supposed by Lindsay and Lehmann (1925, 15) that O itself was produced in Mainz, which cannot be dismissed as impossible; if so, O seemingly never left Germany until the late seventeenth century. No mediaeval catalogue survives for St Martin's.

[16] De Meyier (1973, 67) suggested plausibly that the shelf-mark *LV.I* is of a fourteenth-/fifteenth-century hand linked with St Martin's, which gives further support to the notion that Mainz possessed the manuscript throughout the Middle Ages.

[17] For a survey of the state of this manuscript, see Chapter 3, n. 9 and Chapter 5.

[18] De Meyier (1975) 215: 'saec. IX¹'; Bischoff (2004) 61: 'IX. Jh, ca. Mitte'.

[19] See Chapter 5.

[20] For this more precise dating, see the citation of Albinia de la Mare's opinion by Reeve (1980) 27 n. 3.

punctuation but inserting his own conjectures.[21] Q was probably produced in north-east France, and Corbie has been suggested as a possible monastery of origin.[22] It may well be that Q was copied in Corbie and transferred to St Bertin at a later date, for a Lucretius is recorded in Corbie in the twelfth century.[23] Alternatively, Q could have been at St Bertin from the ninth century: the unwelcome fact that a Lucretius does not appear in the twelfth-century catalogue of the monastery at St Bertin (see Berthod 1788) can be explained away on the grounds that (i) such catalogues were often incomplete surveys of monastic holdings, (ii) Lucretius' *DRN* was not a work that a monastery would necessarily feel comfortable in recording publicly, and (iii) at an early stage (saec. IX?) the author name '*Lucreti*' was removed from the title on the front leaf of Q (see Plate V).[24] Although no certain evidence survives locating Q between the late ninth and mid sixteenth centuries, a little more is known about its subsequent history before entering Leiden. The Parisian Latinist Lambinus (Denys Lambin, 1520–72) was able to make use of this manuscript of a collation of Q made by Turnebus (Adrien de Tournebou, 1512–65) for his 1563 Lucretian edition. In fact, Lambinus mistakenly made use of this manuscript in two forms: for an account of the fate of Q from its re-emergence in sixteenth-century Paris through to its entry into the Leiden University Library, along with O, in 1690, see Appendix V.

---

[21] See Chapter 5, n. 3.

[22] Cf. Bischoff (2004) 61 no. 2231: 'Nordostfrankreich'; Munk Olsen (1985) 87: 'Nord de la France'; De Meyier (1975) 217: 'Gallia (septentrionalis; an monasterium Corbeiense?)'.

[23] See Coyecque (1893) no. 285 *Titus Lucretius poeta* (= no. 336 *Titi Lucretii de rerum natura*) and Manitius (1935, 42); this view was tentatively held by Leonard–Smith (99, 106). Of course, the manuscript attested in Corbie may well not have been Q, as suggested by Brunhölzl (1962, 103), who supposed that the archetype was copied in Corbie, and that this was the manuscript recorded in the twelfth century. It was mistakenly concluded (from a misunderstanding of the Latin of Diels (XV)) by Leonard–Smith (83), who in turn misled Flores (2006a) 131 and A. Brown (2010) 2, that this St Bertin catalogue contained Lucretius anonymously under its doctored title (see following note).

[24] It seems that an original title, of the form *T. Lucreti Cari De Rerum Natura Liber Primus Incipit*, suffered the erasure of *Lucreti* and the replacement of the title, again in elegant capitals (saec. IX/X), with *de phisica rerum origine vel effectu liber primus incipit f(eliciter)*. Lucretius' name was not restored until a later hand (saec. XIII?) made the addition above (see Plate V).

*(iii)   GVU (S) (Copenhagen Kongelige Bibliotek,
Gl. Kgl. S. 211 2°; Vienna Österreichische
Nationalbibliothek, Lat. 107, ff. 9–18)*

Before outlining the progress made in evaluating OQ in the nineteenth century, we must turn to the third ninth-century manuscript, a codex surviving in three fragments now spread over two locations. The so-called *Schedae Gottorpienses*[25] (whence the siglum G), preserved in Copenhagen, amount to a gathering of eight two-columned folia that typically bear forty-eight verses each;[26] they contain I.1–II.456 but omit I.734–85 and II.253–304 (as well as I.123, 890–1 and 1068–75 with Q).[27] The other two fragments are bound together in a manuscript preserved at Vienna: the *Schedae Vindobonenses priores* (ff. 9–14), typically given the siglum V, contain II.642 to III.621 but omit II.757–806 (with Q); the *Schedae Vindobonenses posteriores* (ff. 15–18[π]), given the siglum U, contain VI.743–1286 (the end of *DRN*), followed by II.757–805, V.928–79, I.734–85 and II.253–304 after the subscription. The form and manner of presentation differ in a number of respects between these two Viennese fragments[28] but they are very probably parts of the same original codex,[29] a conclusion first reached by Lachmann (who worked only from collations) but supported more recently by two experts.[30] Given the identity of these three fragments, future Lucretian editors ought to use for clarity a single siglum for the manuscript – I suggest S (= *Schedae*)[31] – to avoid the misleading collocation 'OQGVU', which suggests a greater array of Lucretian evidence than actually

---

[25] The name of these *schedae* (or sometimes *fragmentum*) was acquired because they were owned by the library of Gottorp Castle in Schleswig, which was transferred to the Royal Library in 1735.

[26] For more details about the physical layout of these fragments see Chapter 3, n. 11.

[27] No facsimile exists for this fragment but high-quality digital images are available through the *Codices Haunienses* project at www.kb.dk/permalink/2006/manus/241/eng/.

[28] See further Chapter 3, n. 11.

[29] The Viennese leaves were first associated with Q and G by Siebelis (1844) 788–9.

[30] Bischoff (1974) 74 n. 30 and Munk Olsen (1985) 87–8. This is much simpler than positing the unification of two separate (and not overlapping) Lucretian manuscripts, both two-columned codices of a very similar age and place of origin, in the same library in Vienna.

[31] Accordingly a new siglum should be used for Laur. 35.29, for which Flores used 'S', if an editor should wish to cite its readings.

The extant Lucretian manuscripts

exists. Most scholars and editors[32] after E. and A.
Goebel (1857) have treated only the *Schedae Vindobonenses priores* as the same
manuscript as G, which is immediately clear from their appearance and the identity of the scribe (from f. 7^{r11} onwards);
this conclusion is also confirmed by the fact that the missing portion
of the text – II.457–641 – would fill a single leaf containing the
regular number of lines.[33] Further, we know that G was still united
with V towards the end of the sixteenth century and that both were
in Vienna, for Hugo Blotius (1534–1608) marked the first folio
of G with 'Q 4784' (see Plate VIII), the same catalogue number
that occurs in his 1576 repertory of the Bibliotheca Regia (i.e. the
Wiener Hofbibliothek, now the ÖNB) for a volume that is said
to contain (among other things) 'Ruff[us] Fest[us]' (= Avienus),
as is the case for the beginning of the current *Sammelband*
(ff. 1–8).[34] The lost leaves between the two sets of *Schedae
Vindobonenses* probably amounted to two and a half quaternios.[35]
For these fragments I shall use the siglum S henceforth.

The creation of S has been assigned to the latter half of the ninth
century[36] and to north Italy, perhaps Bobbio, as suggested by
Lehmann and in due course Bischoff.[37] The monastery of Bobbio

[32] Every editor of Lucretius after Bockemüller has regarded GV and U as fragments of two
different manuscripts, although without treating the matter as one of stemmatic importance, since both are clearly siblings of Q.

[33] See my comments in Butterfield (2008h) 356; this point was first made by Lachmann (9).

[34] See Gordon (1985) 279 n. 1; the purpose of this number had foxed Henrichsen (1846) 9
n. 1. The earliest extant copy of Blotius' catalogue is Ser. Nov. 4451, dated to 1597, see
Menhardt (1957) with p. 37 for G(V); U (with the beginning of Juvenal) was catalogued
separately by Blotius (P 4658) as an anonymous quaternio thought to contain 'poesis
quaedam de variis rebus ad instar epigramatωv' (cf. Menhardt (1957) 82). Clearly then,
S was disbound and broken up by the late sixteenth century.

[35] The lacuna between the two is of 3,866 verses, plus eighty-seven *capitula* and six verses
of subscriptions, i.e. *c.* 3,953 lines. As a very rough calculation, if there were around
fifty verses to a column, then each leaf would have contained two hundred lines, in
which case some twenty leaves are missing: two could have closed the quaternio of the
posteriores, then sixteen made up the next two quaternios, with the remaining two
opening the final gathering.

[36] Bischoff (1998) 411: 'IX. Jh., 2 Hälfte'; Henrichsen (1846, 11) tentatively dated
the fragment to the ninth or tenth centuries, which Diels refined to the ninth century
(XVII, XIX).

[37] See Bischoff (1998) 411: 'Wohl Oberitalien (Bobbio?)' (retracting his earlier statement
(1974, 74 n. 30) that its origin was 'wohl Südwestdeutschland'), a judgment repeated by
Munk Olsen (1985, 89) as '[p]lutôt le nord de l'Italie'). Chatelain (1884–92, I 16)
impossibly suggested that the Corbie and Bobbio *Lucretii* recorded in mediaeval
catalogues (on which see below) survived as G and VU respectively.

11

possessed a Lucretius in the tenth century (see below) but since it recorded *Lucretii vol. I* without mention of Avienus or Juvenal, it is probably distinct from S.

One could tentatively suggest that S was written in St Gallen (after the shift of that scriptorium to a rather standard Carolingian minuscule in 820–30); the compiler of the *Florilegium Sangallense* had access to a text of Lucretius that could have been ψ (the lost parent of QS) as well as Avienus and Juvenal (whom the compiler cited liberally).[38] An interesting feature of S is the fact that it is a poetic miscellany, containing Avienus' *Aratea* (ff. 1–8) and, at the close of the Lucretian section (f. 18^{rII}), Juvenal's first five *satirae* (up to V.96 closing 22^{VII}, after which the text is lost). Oddly, Juvenal begins on the verso of the same leaf, starting eighteen verses from the end of the second column. I presume that the scribe calculated, on the basis of the Juvenal text available, where he should start in order to ensure that the text ended with the close of a gathering. The manuscript, not copied with any particular care, was possibly a collection of rarer poetic texts made by one monastery for use elsewhere, hence their compacted collocation.

The fate of S between being written and residing in Vienna in the late sixteenth century is unknown. Only in the seventeenth century did S begin to attract the attention of scholars, the first eight folia apparently already in separate circulation. For further details on the fate of S in the sixteenth to eighteenth centuries, see Appendix V.

Alongside the effectively complete witnesses OQ, S contains almost 45 per cent of *DRN*. An accurate appraisal of the value of this manuscript was not made until the mid nineteenth century, although G had been highly esteemed by Haverkamp, Wakefield and Madvig, the last of whom 'rediscovered' it when cataloguing the Kongelige Bibliotek in 1842.[39] Until 1787 the readings of VU

---

[38] For more on the *Florilegium Sangallense* see Stephan (1885) and Butterfield (2009c).

[39] See Henrichsen (1846) 6. Haverkamp (vol. I, *Praef.* *4^v) believed the fragment to be lost, since Johann Lorenz Mosheim (1693–1755) told him that it had vanished with other Gottorpian manuscripts during the Great Northern War (1700–21) but provided him with what he took to be Gude's collation of the fragment. G turned up again in the 1786 catalogue of the Kongelige Bibliotek (Erichsen (1786) 32), having entered the library in 1735.

were apparently unknown to scholars; in that year, however, Franz Karl Alter produced a patriotic Lucretian edition based on a fifteenth-century manuscript in his local library (Vienna ÖNB Lat. 170).[40] In an appendix he recorded the perceived 'vitia' of VU as found 'in fragmentis quibusdam Lucretianis codicis Caesarei antiqui chartacei [!] Num. CXXVIII' (*Praef.* IV), a manuscript which he said contained 'fragmenta Lucretii ex lib. 2. 3. 6. a v. 743' and 'in principio seculi XIV. [!] exaratus videtur'.[41] No serious critical regard was paid to its readings, however, by either him or Wakefield, who recorded the readings of G from the appendix to Tonson's 1712 edition, and VU from the testimony of Alter (under the siglum Q). No progress was made in the study of S until a full collation of G was published by Henrichsen (1846)[42] and of VU by the brothers Goebel (1857).[43]

Editorial progress since the nineteenth century

The true age of progress in weighing OQS was the second quarter of the nineteenth century. Many of these advances were recounted in detail by Sebastiano Timpanaro (1963, 56–68 = 2005, 102–41, cf. also Reeve (2005) 115–18), so I record here only the primary points. In 1827 Johann Kaspar von Orelli (1787–1849) observed that all known manuscripts of Lucretius took their origin from the same manuscript 'excepto fortasse fragmento Gottorpiensi' (1827, 86 n.). Five years later, this view was refined by Johan Nicolai Madvig (1804–86), who pointed out that there was also a close relationship between G and Q, for which he cited the shared corruption of *mu* closing I.658 as a particularly obvious example.[44] Turning to the Italian manuscripts, Madvig argued

---

[40] For further details of this manuscript, see Reeve (2006) 166–7.

[41] Alter's tone was unfortunate when he claimed that he offered these readings 'iis hominibus ... qui codicum manuscriptorum vitiis delectari consueverunt' (*Praef.* IV).

[42] In the same year, Purmann (1846, 15–16) published the information about VU that he had obtained on request from Heinrich Pöschl, on the basis of which he concluded '[l]iber ... quod non una re apparet, olim integer fuit' (16).

[43] Some slight further information had already been recorded by Endlicher (1836) 54 no. CXI, who attributed the fragments to the tenth century, stated that they were written 'diversis manibus', and gave the Lucretian line references as I.641 (not II.641) to III.622 and '[a]b alia manu' VI.74–1284 (ignoring the four passages transposed to the end).

[44] Madvig (1834) 308 with n. 2.

(1834, 309) that a 'nova ... apographorum propago' came forth during the Renaissance, a family much corrupted by liberal conjectures that only strayed further from Lucretius' original text; we shall soon return to the thorny matter of the *Itali*. No further investigation into these important observations of Orelli and Madvig occurred until the mid 1840s. In 1845 Friedrich Ritschl (1806–76) founded a competition for the best essay on the text of *DRN* at Bonn University, where he had been Professor of Latin since 1839. This curiously specific prize, perhaps inaugurated when it became known that Karl Lachmann (1793–1851) had begun working on the text of Lucretius in that year,[45] was won by Ritschl's young pupil, Jacob Bernays (1824–81). His essay, 'De emendatione Lucretii' (= Bernays (1847)), was written in 1846 and duly published in *Rheinisches Museum*. The essay was seminal in assessing Lucretian manuscripts in four respects. First and most importantly, Bernays demonstrated that these manuscripts formed two separate branches of the same tradition: he placed QS and the 'Memmianus' in one family, and O in the other.[46] Secondly, he demonstrated that the 'Bertinianus' of Lambinus was actually Q by virtue of its recorded errors and corrections from a later hand. Thirdly, he proved through various persuasive arguments but little textual evidence that the manuscript owned by Franciscus Modius was also Q. Fourthly, he attributed the manuscript discovered by Poggio Bracciolini (1380–1459) in 1417 or early 1418[47] to the same group as O,

---

[45] The rivalry between Ritschl and Lachmann is well documented. Part of Lachmann's failure to appreciate the importance of a number of Bernays' observations (see below) could have arisen from his being Ritschl's star pupil.

[46] For the first fragment of S (G), Bernays depended upon the collation made by Heinsius, which he wrongly took (1847, 536–7) to be a transcription of Gude's (cf. Appendix V). For the fragments VU, he depended upon the brief comments of Pöschl, published by Purmann (see n. 42 above), but despaired about the manuscript (542): 'Donec ... accuratior collatio in publicum edita erit, nullum pene usum habet fragmentum Vindobonense.' OQ he was able to collate by autopsy in Ritschl's house, to which Jacob Geel, Librarian at Leiden (1833–58) sent them in the summer of 1845: see the letter preserved in Leiden (BPL 2426); cf. also Bernays (1847) 533 n.*).

[47] For more on this discovery, made whilst Poggio served as a papal secretary for Pope John XXIII at the Council of Konstanz (1414–18), see Clark (1899) and Sabbadini (1905) 191. One cannot learn much from Poggio's extant letters about the discovery, other than that it was made in a *locus satis longinquus* (Clark (1899) 125) from Konstanz, and that, having found the manuscript, he had someone produce a copy of

Editorial progress since the nineteenth century

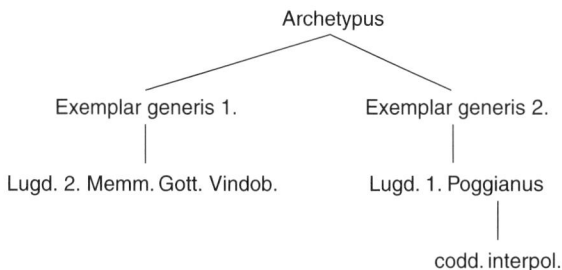

```
                        Archetypus
              /                        \
    Exemplar generis 1.          Exemplar generis 2.
         |                             |
 Lugd. 2. Memm. Gott. Vindob.    Lugd. 1. Poggianus
                                       |
                                 codd. interpol.
```

1. The stemma of the Lucretian tradition posited by Jacob Bernays (1847)

although he concluded that only the evidence of the latter should be taken seriously, as the Italian tradition was too corrupt to allow safe reconstruction of their lost parent.[48] As a result of his close investigation, Bernays was able to offer a stemma that was correct in its fundamentals (see above).[49]

Bernays was correct in his delineation of two branches, and in his wake Munro, Diels and all subsequent editors have accepted the necessity of positing an intermediary between the archetype and QS (= his 'Exemplar generis 1.'), a fact proved by the large number of conjunctive errors in QS,[50] and of treating Q and S as siblings.[51]

it whilst he awaited it anxiously elsewhere. Poggio was convinced, presumably on the basis of Varro's apparent assertion (*L.L.* V.17) that Lucretius (MSS : *Lucilius* coni. Gifanius) published twenty-one books, that he had discovered only *Lucretii pars* (cf. Poggio (1538) 394 = D. Canfora (1998) 11). As for the fate of the Poggianus, Poggio immediately sent it to Niccoli, who selfishly retained it until at least May 1430, when Poggio was still ardently requesting its return (cf. Harth (1984–7) vol. I 103–4); he had already demanded it in 1425, 1426 and 1429 ((1984) 142, 144, 149, 172, 89). Since, however, Niccoli's apograph, L (Florence Laur. 35.30), was probably not made until the mid-1430s, he may not have returned it until 1434, when Poggio reached Florence. This manuscript was possibly the *chartaceus* of Lucretius recorded in Poggio's library on his death in 1459 (cf. Walser (1914) 422 no. 63, and Reeve (2006) 143).

[48] Bernays wrongly argued (1847, 552–3) that O was made up of two parts, the latter section (f. 162, i.e. VI.79ff.) being the older (saec. VIII); rather a similar scribe there took over to finish the manuscript, perhaps after a small pause.

[49] This image is reproduced from Timpanaro (2005) 105, with 'Ludg.' twice corrected. We can see that Bernays, as well as Purmann (1846), used the term 'archetypus' prior to Lachmann; cf. Timpanaro (2005) 103–4 with n. 8.

[50] For instance, since QS share the omission of I.123 and I.890–1 and the repetition of VI.892, not to mention very many shared verbal errors, they clearly descend from a subarchetype.

[51] S cannot derive from Q because it contains the *tituli* (proven legitimate by O) omitted by the latter, nor can Q derive from S because, e.g., Q contains II.806, which S omits.

15

Furthermore, it is clear that the archetype (Ω) had suffered further damage by the time that this apograph (which after Konrad Müller I call ψ) was copied: four leaves had fallen out of the book and been replaced, in an incorrect order, at its end.[52] Beyond the fact that the 'Memm[ianus]' is in fact Q, Bernays' groupings are basically correct ('Lugd. 1' = O, 'Poggianus' = π).

Before turning to Lachmann's further work, we may mention Hugo Purmann of Silesia (1821–87), who in 1846, when Bernays' victorious essay was submitted, published independently a pamphlet that mixed discussion of the stemma with conjectural emendation, and did not develop Madvig's argument for common descent[53] but added a few more pieces of evidence in its support, none particularly significant. Partly on the basis of poor collations, partly because of insufficient investigation of the available evidence, Purmann mistakenly assigned O to the *inferiores* (i.e. the *Itali*).

Immeasurably more significant was the work of Karl Lachmann, whose revolutionary appearance in November 1850 broke Bernays' momentum.[54] Since the great edition was the product of five years of devoted work from October 1845,[55] Lachmann could have been influenced by the contributions of Bernays and Purmann, notwithstanding his claim in a letter to Moriz Haupt that he would not read through Bernays until the first draft of his preface was complete.[56] In fact, Lachmann's own results contained elements that Bernays had not offered and lacked some that he had; Purmann's contribution in stemmatic terms, by contrast, was negligible when set beside those of Bernays and

---

[52] In order: II.757–805, V.928–79, I.734–85, II.253–304: since the first half of the poem lacks lists of the *capitula* (see Chapter 3), a Carolingian reader had no obvious means by which to restore these leaves to their correct place or append them in their correct order.

[53] Purmann stated explicitly (1846, 7) that only one Lucretian manuscript survived into the seventh and eighth centuries; the relevant section of the work is 'Codicum descriptio' (pp. 6–34).

[54] 'Seponendus mihi est Lucretius, donec editionem suam in publicum emiserit Carolus Lachmannus, quocum equidem haud minus temere certarem quam hirundo cum cygnis contenderet' (Bernays to Geel, 1 April 1847 (BPL 2426)). Bernays' own edition of Lucretius (1852) did little to develop Lachmann's researches.

[55] Cf. Hertz (1851) 139. Lachmann wrote to Geel to request the loan of the manuscripts for his work on 31 December 1845 (BPL 2426). For G, Charles Schoenemann sent him Gude's collation; for VU, Heinrich Keil sent a collation made 'rudiuscule', as Keil acknowledged himself.

[56] Vahlen (1892) 180.

Lachmann. The latter chose to dismiss haughtily the efforts of his two younger predecessors, alleging (4) that their inexperience with Lucretius had caused their results to be marred by oversights and corrupted with falsehoods. In the matter of stemmatics, Timpanaro demonstrated (1963, 61–3 = 2005, 106–7) that Lachmann succeeded particularly in two new areas: *eliminatio lectionum singularium* and the reconstruction of the form of the lost archetype.[57] Lachmann's great achievement (disregarding his truly formidable commentary) was to base his text primarily upon OQ, an attitude that most subsequent editors have adopted correctly. He carefully collated the two *Vossiani* from April to September 1846, having had them sent to Berlin, and this painstaking inspection profited him much.[58] He rightly regarded S as less important than both O and Q, although this was largely owing to the poor state of the evidence available (a full collation not being published until 1857).[59]

At any rate, these scholars rightly regarded OQS as descendants of the same manuscript, the archetype Ω (i.e. the latest common ancestor). The most solid proofs of this are the traces of the archetype's physical mutilation in all of its descendants: the loss of the ends of verses at I.1068–75, and the complete absence of I.1094–1101, as well as the reversal of IV.323–46 and 299–322,[60] can only be explained by physical damage to Ω itself. O stands on a separate branch from ψ and has generally been assumed to be a direct descendant of Ω, a fact corroborated by its retention of an eight-verse gap at I.1094–1101, among other things.[61]

---

[57] For more about the reconstruction of the archetype, see the remarks in this book's Conclusion.

[58] Lachmann's collation was so detailed that Munro, who worked through OQ in Leiden in the autumn of 1849 (although he had too much difficulty to finish collating Q, as he confessed to Geel in BPL 2426), typically found it safer to follow Lachmann's readings.

[59] No editor obtained images of all three codices until Hermann Diels (1923–4), who worked on his edition from 1918 until his death in 1923, and only two editors to date, K. Müller (1975) and Flores (2002–9), claim to have collated the manuscripts themselves, although both are inadequate in various respects.

[60] That this transposition had occurred before O was copied could suggest that the archetype was already well read or of some age before transcription.

[61] The onus of proof lies with those who wish to posit an intermediary; the only argument worthy of discussion is treated within Chapter 3, section I (D).

Bernays posited an 'Exemplar generis 2.' not for mere symmetry but because he thought that the manuscript found by Poggio differed from O too much to be a descendant and therefore must have originated from the subarchetype shared with O. Lachmann (in theory, but typically not in practice) and a number of subsequent scholars (see below) likewise treated the Poggianus as being descended from such a subarchetype, although none offered specific arguments for this detail of their genealogy. The only scholar explicitly to argue for an intermediary between the archetype and O was H. Bitterlich-Willmann, a pupil of Karl Büchner at Freiburg, in his 1951 thesis. His single argument (1951, 56–7) was, however, very weak: O was a careful scribe, he maintained, and therefore one should not attribute to him the verse omissions which the 'corrector Saxonicus' was thought to have filled; therefore this deliberate omission of verses was the act of another scribe, that of the supposed intermediary between the archetype and O. As will be argued in Chapter 4, these verses added by O, all of which were actually written in lieu of erased verses (*in rasura*) and not in intentionally blank spaces, are simply restorations from Ω of verses accidentally omitted by O, typically through *saut du même au même*.

The basic stemma relating OQS to the archetype can therefore be sketched as follows (see next page).

The latter of the two states of the archetype (Ω and Ω^{I}) indicates its being damaged by the loss and replacement of four leaves, in an incorrect order, at the close of the manuscript (as n. 52). Before recording a few additional details for this stemma from the end of the ninth century through to the Renaissance, we must tackle the difficult matter of the Italian manuscripts. Fifty-four Lucretian manuscripts copied in Italy between the mid-1430s[62] and 1507, on parchment and paper, are currently known to exist, and the true surviving total can hardly be much higher. Given that these manuscripts were products of the new wave of learning fostered by the Italian Renaissance, they understandably bore a close connection with the early editions of *DRN* (from 1473) and accordingly

---

[62] Cf. de la Mare (1973) 57 no. 10.

800   Ω

O   Ω′

Ψ

850   Q

S

900

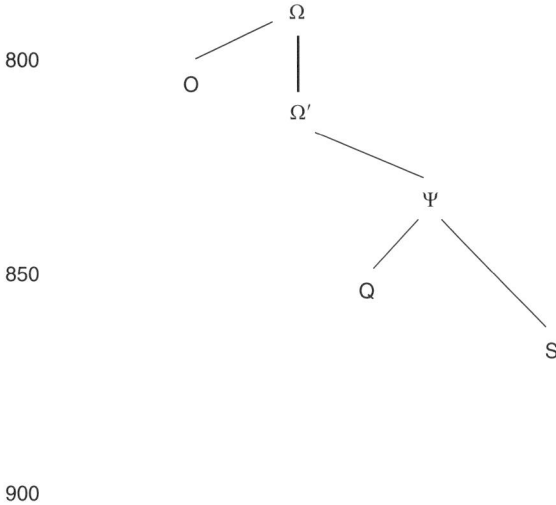

2. A basic stemma of the Lucretian tradition

served as the basis for the various incunabular editions.[63] Indeed, until Lambinus' ground-breaking edition of 1563, all printed editions unmethodically mixed readings from Italian manuscripts, those from preceding editions, and conjectural emendations. Even after Lambinus gained access to Q (by more than one route), editors continued to favour readings from Italian manuscripts until well into the nineteenth century, and recent scholarship has reverted to doing the same (see especially Flores). As is often the case for traditions faced with many Renaissance manuscripts, sorting the wheat from the chaff, and eliminating *codices descripti*, was not a swift process: no real progress was made by Lucretian scholars in evaluating the various *Itali* until Bernays' thesis (1847, 553–64); rather, certain manuscripts had gained informal repute above others, whether through patriotism and scholarly allegiance or merely the fact that certain manuscripts were conveniently available to a given editor and therefore lauded the most.

---

[63] Five incunabular editions of Lucretius are known to have existed: see Gordon (1985) with the correction of Smith and Butterfield (2011). For a detailed account of the Renaissance manuscripts and early editions of Lucretius, and of how their readers responded to them, see Palmer (2012) and (2013); for a briefer survey of modern editorial responses to the challenges presented by Lucretius' poem, see Butterfield (2012a).

As already mentioned, Madvig was the first scholar to regard the *Itali* as derived from a single exemplar, a view that is, save for two minor alterations, correct. This opinion was endorsed by Bernays, who conjectured that this manuscript was the 'Poggianus' – the manuscript found by Poggio – for he did not know that Poggio had commissioned a copy of the manuscript he found (see n. 47 above). For the rest of this thesis, I shall use the term 'Poggianus' and the siglum π for the copy of the mediaeval manuscript commissioned by Poggio and sent to Niccoli. Lachmann's own view about how to treat the Italian manuscripts was shown to be implicitly contradictory by Timpanaro (1963, 63–6 = 2005, 108–10): although he consistently distrusted them, believing that they were corrupted by strata of Renaissance interpolations, sometimes he explicitly regarded them as a third branch of the tradition (and therefore of independent weight), sometimes as descendants of a sibling of O copied from a subarchetype. This latter view, which necessitates a bipartite not a tripartite stemma, seems rather to have been adopted as he engaged in the practical task of editing *DRN*, possibly under the influence of Bernays' researches. Lachmann's general disregard for the Italian manuscripts caused something of a knee-jerk reaction among his contemporaries, and various scholars (including Spengel (1851), Christ (1855) and E. Goebel (1854)) rallied to defend certain fifteenth-century manuscripts, particularly the so-called Codex Victorianus in Munich (Staatsbibl. Lat. 816a). Munro (1864 etc.), however, in his magisterial preface, was happy to follow Lachmann on stemmatic matters, though adopting Bernays' theory in practice, giving the *Itali* some authority, particularly C (Cambridge UL Nn II 40) and F (Florence Laur. 35.31). No serious discussion of the Italic manuscripts occurred again until the second decade of the twentieth century, when Karl Hosius (1914) analysed some of the most famous ones, concluding *a priori* that all the Italian tradition descended from A (Vat. Lat. 2376), B (Vat. Barb. Lat. 154), L and F. In 1926–9 William Merrill published a magpie's nest of many readings from various Italian manuscripts,[64] although he offered almost no analysis of

---

[64] To use the sigla of Flores, Merrill published imperfect collations of ABFLDEHRSTefjz and Aa.

their interrelationships. Faced with an unclear state of affairs, and typically not much interested in the matter, all editors of Lucretius after Lachmann for 125 years, with the sole exception of Diels, gave the Italian manuscripts some credit (particularly ABFCL and P (Paris Lat. 10306)), regarding many of the correct readings of π as authoritative readings rather than skilled emendations. The matter was not seriously reconsidered until the 1970s, which saw two major contributions, those of K. Müller (1973 = his 1975 edition, with additions) and Gian Franco Cini (1976), an abridgement of his Florentine doctoral thesis, to which we will come shortly.

Since it has been demonstrated by the various investigations of the aforementioned scholars that all Italian manuscripts ultimately descend from π, only nine logical possibilities exist as to how π, and therefore all *Itali*, could relate to OQS. They must do one of the following:

(i) constitute a third branch of the tradition descended from Ω
(ii) constitute a second branch of the tradition descended from an archetype anterior to the subarchetype (Ω) of OQS

or descend from:

(iii) a subarchetype shared with O
(iv) O (directly or indirectly)
(v) ψ, the subarchetype shared with QS
(vi) an apograph of ψ shared with Q against S
(vii) Q (directly or indirectly)
(viii) an apograph of ψ shared with S against Q
(ix) S (directly or indirectly).

Given that many corruptions made by ψ, including omissions, do not affect the Italian tradition at all, no scholar has maintained any of possibilities (v)–(ix), and the arguments of Cini (1976, 131–45) are definitive proof of this point.[65] Of the remaining four options,

---

[65] It was supposed by Diels (XXI) (and a few subsequent scholars, including Cinquini (1944), who followed his lead) that Q had some input to the Italian tradition, but there is no reason to believe this beyond the mere fact that Q was thoroughly corrected by an Italian hand of the mid fifteenth century. It is much more probable that an Italian worked in the library at St Bertin than that Q travelled to Italy in the fifteenth century and back again to St Bertin before 1544 (see above).

however, all have found adherents in the twentieth century. Since these conflicting opinions do not allow a chronological discussion of approaches to the problem, I simply list the supporters of each, outline the primary arguments adduced and demonstrate why three of these options are impossible.

(i) Lachmann (in his preface), Munro (1864 etc.), Brieger (1894 etc.), Bailey (1900, 1922, 1947), Lehnerdt (1904), Merrill (1907), Ernout (1920), Fischer (1924), Balcells (1923), Martin (1934 etc.), Leonard and Smith (1942), Bodelon García (1987), García Calvo (1997).

(ii) Chiari (1924), Bitterlich-Willmann (1951), Büchner (1956, 1966), Flores (2002–9).

(iii) Lachmann (in practice), Bernays (1847, 1852), Birt (1913), Hosius (1914).

(iv) Diels (1923), Heinze (1924), Mewaldt (1927), Castiglioni (1937), Cinquini (1944), Pizzani (1959a, 80–7), Valentí (1961), Timpanaro (1963 etc.), K. Müller (1973; 1975 edition), Cini (1976), Reeve (1980, 2005), Deufert (1996, 2005) and Butterfield (various articles).

(i) The first option, that Oψπ each derived independently from the same lost archetype, was advocated by Lachmann (3) after Orelli and Madvig. This view has been adopted by most editors in his wake, although few have probed it in further research. In reality, this view must be disregarded for it is often clear that π contained not only the errors of O[66] (against ψ) but also the alterations of the first two correctors of O, Dungal (the so-called *corrector Saxonicus*) and O², even when they differ from ψ.[67] As will be argued in

---

[66] The clearest examples of π's descent from O are II.198, 1054, V.511, 1019, 1330, VI.563, 1077; see further K. Müller (1975 edn, 301–3) and Cini (1976, 132), who adduced cases where π omitted the same words or syllables as O (e.g. IV.77, 166, V.884, VI.1028, 1040, 1078).

[67] E.g. I.16, 27, 43, 84, 191, 352, 357, 429, 449, 455, 486, 619, 646, 668, 741, 758, 887, 1061; II.147, 192, 197, 233, 265, 278, 326, 827, 982, 1116; III.6, 52, 132, 232, 236, 375, 732, 839, 941, 994, 1034, 1082, 1083; IV.79, 153, 202, 237, 277, 304, 393, 586, 710, 730, 869, 882, 1038, 1083, 1194; V.209, 295, 375, 406, 428, 482, 502, 511, 581, 609, 727, 742, 823, 995, 1001, 1008, 1055, 1071, 1145, 1220, 1253, 1301, 1330, 1416; VI.1, 2, 128, 144, 160, 208, 237, 241, 296, 324, 350, 364, 368, 440, 481, 512, 523, 547, 554, 563, 638, 639, 661, 718, 762, 799, 820, 823, 890, 986, 1088, 1091, 1119, 1126, 1132, 1139, 1167, 1195, 1200, 1251, 1271. I have discussed the oversight of this important body of evidence in reviewing a recent edition of Lucretius (see Butterfield (2011) 598–9).

Chapter 4, although Dungal had access to Ω when correcting O, he made a number of incorrect alterations *ex ope ingeni,* and O^2 operated entirely without an exemplar (very often incorrectly), yet many of these mistakes are likewise found in π.[68] Accordingly, the presence of these two strata of corrections (many of which are manifestly wrong) in π dismisses the possibility of (i), unless we posit that π was fully 'corrected' by collation with O or an apograph made after the work of O^2, a most improbable supposition. Martin (IX) recorded instances where the reading of π is the same as that of QS against O, either correctly or falsely, and, less cogently (X) cases where π divided words differently from the Oblongus, where the latter presents distinct separation. The latter argument, as rightly argued by Castiglioni (1937, 558) and Reeve (2005, 118–19), has almost no authority, and the former is in reality a very small number of substantive cases: only twice do Q(S)π agree in a correct reading that O omits (I.916 *non* ψπ : om. O; Q II.478 *quae* Qπ : om. O) and only twice do Qπ agree in an error that has sufficient weight to be conjunctive (IV.418 *ut* O : om. Qπ; IV.929 *confiat* Aa : *conflat* O : *conflatur* Qπ).[69] However, at I.916 *non* and II.478 *quae* are easy and necessary restorations of sense and metre, at IV.418 *ut* could easily have been omitted before *ui* of *uideare*, and at IV.929 *conflatur* is a natural attempt to correct the faulty metre of *conflat* (if the correction to *confiat* was not apprehended). These few examples, from a work of almost 7,500 hexameter verses, are far too paltry to bear any weight.

(ii) It is equally easy to dismiss the second hypothesis, namely that the Poggianus ultimately descends from a lost manuscript copied not from the archetype (Ω) of OQS but rather from a hyperarchetype; this thesis posits two independent branches,

---

[68] On the basis of the researches of Reeve (1980, 2005), I reconstruct the reading of π from L (Laur. 35.30), the manuscripts which descend from Reeve's μ – d (Laur. Conv. Soppr. 453), Ja (Madrid Nac. 2885), A (Vat. Lat. 3276), B (Vat. Barb. Lat. 154) – o (Vat. Pat. 312) and x (Malatest. Ces. S 20 4); the readings of the φ group (on which see the close of this chapter), which demonstrate frequent emendation and contamination, require more careful analysis.

[69] The agreement at V.871 (*in* Qπ : *ni* O : *nil* Pontanus) is from coincidental conjecture in π.

OQS (itself bipartite) and π. On the basis that Murbach possessed a copy of Lucretius from the ninth century,[70] it was conjectured that the manuscript Poggio found in a *locus ... satis longinquus* (cf. n. 47) was a *codex Murbacensis* of that age.[71] Bitterlich-Willmann (1951), Büchner and Flores adopted this view of tracing the origins of the *Murbacensis* to a pre-archetypal stage after it had been first suggested by Alberto Chiari, in his review of Diels.[72] Chiari maintained that the archetype of the Italian tradition (his α, for which he regarded LF as primary witnesses) was a manuscript in an insular hand of the seventh or eighth centuries, distinct from β, another insular manuscript of the same age from which OQS derive (= Ω); the archetype of the whole tradition (Chiari's 'A') was therefore deemed to be the capital manuscript of the fourth or fifth centuries that Lachmann wrongly took to be his archetype.[73] The theory is not convincing, for the same objection can be given as before, namely that π[74] clearly inherited the corrections of Dungal and O².

A more complicated version of this stemma was offered independently of Chiari by Bitterlich-Willmann (1951), who likewise posited as the archetype ('J') an insular manuscript of the seventh or eighth centuries, from which the *codex Murbacensis* (M) derived on the one hand, and the subarchetype of OQS (his 'R') on the other (1951, 60). He tentatively suggested that the corrections of Dungal (his 'Oˢ') were drawn from M, thereby explaining how those corrections also appeared in the Italian tradition (1951, 53–5). He made two fundamental mistakes, however: first, he disregarded the fact that the corrections of O², which have no manuscript authority, also found their way into π; secondly, he failed to appreciate that the corruption of the archetype at I.1068–75 and 1094–1101 is the result of damage in the

---

[70] Cf. Manitius (1935) 24, and Matter (1846) 4off. no. 303. For further discussion of mediaeval catalogues, see the end of this section.

[71] This suggestion was first made by Bloch (1901) 257.

[72] Chiari (1924); the review was reprinted, with a four-page *Postilla* of 1960 responding to the objections of Pasquali (1952, 112) and Timpanaro (1963, 63–8; 2005, 108–14), in Chiari (1963) 1–27.

[73] For discussion of this theory, see the concluding chapter.

[74] Chiari mistakenly regarded α as the immediate parent of LF, apparently unaware (like Bernays) that Poggio had commissioned a copy of the manuscript discovered.

immediate archetype of OQS, and cannot have occurred in his insular archetype J; therefore, the absence of I.1094–1101 in the *Itali* is left unexplained. His professor Karl Büchner argued five years later (1956, 200) for the same thesis (equally unaware of Chiari's review), repeating these arguments in his own edition of 1966. To explain these corruptions, he had to posit that not only the archetype of OQS, but also that of M, had twenty-six lines per column, although it had two columns, not one, per page.[75] His figure depicting how the damage occurred (XI n. 111; cf. also (1956) 200) cannot be correct: he claimed that it affected the foot of the recto of a page, which removed or made illegible the ends of the verses I.1068–75 and all of I.1094–1101, whereas on the verso the damaged part of the manuscript did not affect the poetic text since the first column contained only the end of the subscription to Book I followed by a space, and the second column contained a list of *tituli* now lost.[76] I will argue in Chapter 3 that no such list of *tituli* ever existed in Books I–III, but was only added for Books IV–VI; therefore, for Büchner's theory to stand, one must credit not only that these same lines occurred at the end of a page as they did in the archetype of OQS but also that the beginnings of various lines in the opening of Book II were somehow left undamaged. Finally, the matter of how all Lucretian manuscripts present IV.299–332 and 323–47 in the wrong order caused Büchner considerable trouble: he supposed that the inversion had already occurred by the time when the archetype of the whole tradition was written. Yet, if this error did occur before the traditional archetype of OQS (Ω), it is a remarkable coincidence that two sections of twenty-six lines were transposed: did a yet earlier hyperarchetype also have twenty-six lines per page with the result that these passages each stood distinctly on the recto and verso of the same leaf? It is improbable almost to the point of impossibility that two scribes (of M and Ω) independently took two correctly ordered columns of twenty-six verses and reversed them in transcription;

---

[75] Büchner implausibly suggested (XI) that the scribe of the archetype kept the same number of verses per page 'sibi hoc modo operam faciliorem redden[s]'!

[76] Büchner thus presumed that the damage meant that this list of *tituli* was subsequently omitted by the apographs of this manuscript but failed to state whether lists of *tituli* preceded (and were later lost from) Books I and III.

further, we must note that it is a remarkable coincidence that these transposed passages can be shown also to have stood neatly and completely on two separate pages in Ω, the 26-line archetype of OQS.[77] Büchner also argued (XXff.) that the scribe of M had access to O in its corrected state, which would mean that M was copied after the time of O², after the late ninth century. His arguments for regarding π, and therefore its parent M, as descendants by a tradition independent of the archetype of OQS rely primarily on the evidence of readings at I.84, 271, 527, 767, 837, 846, II.1020, 1110, V.2 and 679, instances where Mπ 'plus ceteris [= OQS] habent, quod tamen sensum non facit' (XXII).[78] Yet of this meagre haul six are wholly without force,[79] and the remaining four cases involve minor emendation or simple corruption made (presumably) in the Poggianus.[80]

The only subsequent scholar to accept this complicated thesis, Enrico Flores (1978, 1980; 2002–9 edn),[81] adopted Büchner's arguments in principle[82] but with two primary alterations: first, M did not collate O, rather O² obtained his corrections from M (which manuscript Flores (2002, 25) asserted without argument was older than O and much covered with variant readings (1980, 63–8));[83] second, Dungal (his Oˢ) had access to a manuscript independent of the branches of M and the archetype of OQS. Accordingly, Flores believed that he was dealing with a quadripartite stemma: M (reconstructed through π and the corrections of O²),

---

[77] For a more brief rebuttal of this particular argument of Bitterlich-Willmann (1951) and Büchner, see Goold (1958, 25) and Pizzani (1959a, 82–4; 1968, 652–4).

[78] For dismissal of the three instances adduced by Büchner (1956, XXII–XXIII), see Pizzani (1959a, 85–6).

[79] I.84 *triuiai* ad O²π : *triuie* at Oᵃ·ᶜ· : *triuiat* ψ; 527 *pleno* BL : *poena* Ωπ : *poenitus* O²; 837 *sanguenque* ABφ (Charis., Non.) : *sanguemque* Ωπ; 846 *illis iura quod* π : *illis uira quod* (*quo* ψ) Ω : *illi supra quos* recte Laur. 35.32 in marg.; V.2 *maiestatisque* π : *maiestatis atque* Ω (*maiestate hisque* recte Lambinus); V.679 *consequae* π : *consequiae* Ω (fort. recte).

[80] I.271 *portus* π : *cortus* Ω : *tortus* O² : *corpus* Q²; 767 *aeternis* π : *aternis* Ω : *aeternis* recte O³; II.1020 *plagas* π : *plagaes* Ω : *plagae* recte B; 1110 *appareret* π : *appariret* Ω.

[81] Flores (1978) was repeated as chapter 3 in Flores (1980) 45–68.

[82] Flores (vol. 1, 23–4 n. 8) accepted the convoluted arguments of Büchner regarding the text at I.1068–75 and 1093–1101, and IV.299–347, despite their improbability.

[83] As Reeve (2005, 142–4, 155) rightly argued, Flores made this mistaken inference by failing to regard the various readings in the Italian tradition as springing from conjecture.

O, QS, and Dungal's corrections in O. As Reeve (2005, 156) rightly objected, Flores' proposed stemma is actually tripartite (πO^2 : OQS : Dungal's codex), and in the great majority of the text where Dungal had no active involvement, it must be treated as bipartite (for Dungal's failure to correct, as will be shown in Chapter 4, does not guarantee his belief in the text's veracity). Flores failed to explain how M contained the incorrect emendations of Dungal, if they are indeed drawn from an independent source,[84] and how π agrees with O in manifest errors so often against ψ, particularly since it (or Q or S) was not given to emendation. The theory is therefore unacceptable. I shall demonstrate in Chapter 4 that O^2 had no access to any other manuscript source, 'M' or otherwise. On a more complicated matter, Flores assumed that π contained multiple variants; it will be seen at the close of Chapter 4 (D) that the Italian tradition was more probably contaminated in a small number of manuscripts from two later collations, one of a mediaeval copy of O (χ), and one of O itself; any other variations among these manuscripts are the result of transcriptional error and emendation.

(iii) The third hypothesis, namely that π descended from a sub-archetype shared with O, was first advanced by Bernays and seemingly held by Lachmann in practice, although his language was far from explicit: whereas he declared the independence of the *Itali* at the beginning of his preface (3), he spoke of the group later (5, 9–10) as being more closely related to O, which would demand a subarchetype. The essence of Lachmann's argument was simply that the Poggianus shared errors with O against QS which could not be derived from O (a position he did not seek to prove), therefore it drew its origin from a source below the archetype. Without closer scrutiny, this is a perfectly fair supposition to take, although Birt (1913, 21–2) and Hosius (1914, 111) have been the only two twentieth-century scholars to maintain it (without further defence).[85] The theory has to be rejected, however, on the same ground that the mistaken alterations of O^2, who had no access to another manuscript, appear in π (as well as Dungal's conjectures);

---

[84] See K. Müller (1973 = 1975 edn, 305–6), Cini (1976, 147–8), Deufert (2005) 214.
[85] Timpanaro later recorded (2005, 108 n. 23) that it is a natural conclusion *prima facie*.

once more, it is too complicated to regard the mediaeval exemplar of π as a sibling of O corrected from that manuscript between the work of O^2 and O^3 (whose corrections it does not contain: see below), and that π regularly adopted these corrections rather than the original text. Furthermore, there is no reason to posit a manuscript between O and Ω.

(iv) We come then, at last, to the one remaining logical possibility, namely that π derives from O alone, either directly or indirectly. We begin with the first proponent of this view, Hermann Diels, who argued that Poggio found a mediaeval manuscript at Murbach (after Bloch (1901)) copied directly from O. However, Diels supposed (XXI) that the scribe who copied this Murbacensis for Poggio also had access to Q or a similar manuscript. Alternatively, he suggested (XXI, n. 2) that the Murbacensis itself could have received corrections and annotations drawn from QS or another (lost) manuscript of the ψ family. In reality, there is no need to accept such improbable mediaeval contamination from the other branch. Richard Heinze (1924, 41–2) therefore deserves the primary credit for refining Diels' view to what is certainly the correct conclusion,[86] namely that π derived from O alone without contamination. Heinze offered no further evidence for this position, but proofs were eventually adduced by K. Müller (1975 edn, 301–8, 313–17) and Cini (1976, 131–69), including the fact that the alterations of Dungal and O^2 entered π, the incorrect alongside the correct (see n. 67 above).

Müller (1975 edn, 313–17) attempted to show, however, that π was not copied directly from O, for, if it was, it inexplicably disregarded a stratum of corrections in O (those I term O^3 (late saec. X)), whereas it readily accepted corrections from Dungal and O^2. Accordingly, he posited that a mediaeval manuscript was copied from O after it had received the corrections from these two hands but before the work of O^3, which progresses (with glosses) up to I.827.[87]

---

[86] Heinze stated (1924, 41) that 'ich andernorts [es] auszuführen gedenke' but failed to do so before his death in 1929.

[87] This thesis was dismissed by Cini (1976, 162–3), but his arguments are weak and insufficiently defended; see Chapter 4 (D). Having derived the Poggianus from O, Cini also continued to suppose without argument that an intermediary existed between the archetype and O (his 'α').

Further detailed evidence for this thesis, which I accept with various refinements, will be given in Chapter 4 (D). Poggio therefore found in late 1417 a mediaeval manuscript derived from O; although it is theoretically possible that more than one intermediary may stand between O and π, I suggest that he discovered a direct copy of O made in the late ninth or early tenth centuries, which I term χ. There is no need to suppose that this manuscript, or π itself, was contaminated by O in a corrected state after its transcription or by any other codex, extant or lost.

Although such vertical descent of π from O can be proved, it is nevertheless clear that it (and possibly χ itself, via readers' corrections) made various emendations to the text (cf. Müller (1975 edn) 308–12).[88] Often these alterations are simple corrections restoring Lucretius' text, sometimes hopeless attempts at repairing the metre without regard to the argument of the passage or even the immediate syntactic context. Many transcriptional errors were also made, however, as can be seen from a careful perusal of an apparatus, comparing the readings of the primary Italian witnesses (i.e. ABLr) with those of O (including Dungal and O²), a fact more easily explained by positing the intermediary χ.[89]

Accordingly, a more complete stemma of Lucretius' pre-Renaissance manuscripts than that sketched above can now be offered. To provide further context in these dark centuries, I have recorded the locations of lost manuscripts of Lucretius known to exist from manuscript catalogues (cf. Manitius (1935) 42). *DRN*, often referred to only by the name of Lucretius, was attested by Carolingian catalogues in the abbeys of Murbach (saec. IX/X)[90] and Bobbio (saec. X/XI),[91] and by the later mediaeval catalogues

---

[88] In particular, π was clearly given to inserting brief words to restore the metre (e.g. II.104, 331, 1145); for a discussion of such instances, which lack any stemmatic authority, see Butterfield (2008f).

[89] E.g. through the course of the transcription of π (and perhaps χ) verses II.492–4, 1169, III.595–6 and IV.512 were accidentally omitted.

[90] See Bloch (1901) 271 no. 85 *liber Lucrecii* in the section *De poetis gentilium* (= 272 no. 16 *Titus Lucretius de rerum natura volumen unum* in *Breviarium librorum Isghteri abbatis*) with 282–3, and Milde (1968), 48 no. 31.

[91] G. Becker (1885) 32 no. 375, *librum Lucretii unum*.

of the abbeys of Lobbes (saec. XII)[92] and Corbie (saec. XII).[93] We have already conjectured that O spent most of the mediaeval period in Mainz and was perhaps there as early as the first half of the ninth century; it may be that Q resided continually until the mid sixteenth century at St Bertin, although the possibility has been mentioned that it was at Corbie until at least the twelfth century: if not, a manuscript (probably a descendant, or a *gemellus*, of Q) existed at that time at Corbie, 60 miles south.

It is generally agreed, as will be concluded in Chapter 2, that a manuscript of Lucretius existed at St Gallen in the mid ninth century, upon which Ermenrich of Ellwangen (*c.* 814–74) and the compiler of the *Florilegium Sangallense* drew. This codex, as argued above, could have been S, about whose mediaeval tradition no reliable evidence exists; alternatively, it could have borne a close relationship with the codex Murbacensis, 110 miles west.[94] There is no serious objection to accepting *faute de mieux* the argument of Bloch (1901, 101) that Poggio found his manuscript of Lucretius at Murbach, in which case we may suppose that χ, having been copied in the late ninth or early tenth century, found its way to Murbach directly. Given that Murbach is 145 miles south of Mainz, this may seem difficult, but texts are known to have travelled great distances in the Carolingian era; even if O was still at St Denis, or another Carolingian stronghold in the area, when χ was copied from it, it must have swiftly travelled 185 miles (east-south-)east to Murbach. If the Murbacensis is related to the Bobbiensis, located 220 miles to the south, and both descend from Ω, it is a fine indicator of Carolingian scholarship that texts of *DRN* had penetrated to these monasteries by the early tenth century.

As regards the manuscript at Bobbio, Lachmann first suggested tentatively (3) that it could have been a second ancient manuscript that survived the fall of Rome, which, he acknowledged,

---

[92] Dolbeau (1978) 36 no. 347 *Titus Lucretius de natura rerum vol. I*, and (1979) 233 no. 347; cf. also G. Becker (1885) 136 no. 336.

[93] Cf. n. 37 above.

[94] In Geneva BPU MS lat. 6 there are traces of an eleventh-century catalogue of an anonymous abbey library, probably from the Rhine Valley (so Gagnebin (1976) 27), that contained a Lucretius. This could well have referred to Murbach or St Gallen.

subsequently disappeared without trace. Fiesoli (2004, 1–8) recently resurrected Lachmann's suggestion: although he did not believe it to have been the source of any complete manuscript known to exist or have existed, he conjectured (7–8) that the compiler of the *florilegium Sangallense* could have used this Bobbiensis, or a copy of it, thus building upon the tentative suggestion of Diels (VIII) that the compiler used a manuscript of some 'aequal[e] apograph[um]'. Unfortunately, no textual argument is given to support this view, and I dismiss it as most improbable. Perhaps a more likely suggestion is that Dungal took his own copy of Lucretius (presuming that he made or commissioned one of this rare author, no doubt from O or Ω) to Bobbio with him and that this manuscript duly entered that library. We need merely suppose that, at the time of the acquisition of Dungal's books, the monastery did not think it fitting to record so controversial a work among the codices *quos Dunghalus praecipuus Scottorum obtulit beatissimo Columbano*.[95] The subsequent fate of this Bobbiensis is unknown and presumably perished before the Renaissance.[96] The manuscript at Lobbes in the twelfth century, whose library suffered a serious conflagration later in that century, could have been related to Q, being only 90 miles to the (east-south-)east of St Bertin and 85 to the (east-north-)east of Corbie. If Dolbeau (1979, 233) was correct to regard the Lucretius as a late addition to the library at Lobbes, perhaps of the early twelfth century, by virtue of its late position in the catalogue, it could have been copied especially for the abbey around that time from Q, then housed at St Bertin or Corbie.[97]

The stemma on the next page is that maintained throughout this book. An obvious and necessary result of accepting this stemma is that all of the *Itali* bear no independent authority for reconstructing Lucretius' text. I will argue in Chapter 4 that the only corrector of O to have used another manuscript (= Ω) is Dungal. Despite the

---

[95] An absence recorded by Tosi (1984–5, 144) and repeated by Reeve (2007, 206 n. 11).

[96] It would be stemmatically neat (although improbable) to suppose that Dungal took ψ to Bobbio with him, and a copy of this text (S) was made from it in Bobbio, along with other poetic texts. If so, we must imagine that Dungal did not much correct his manuscript, or that the scribes of S generally ignored his corrections.

[97] Sigebert of Gembloux (*c.* 1030–1112) did not read Lucretius directly: see Appendix II, n. 1.

The extant Lucretian manuscripts

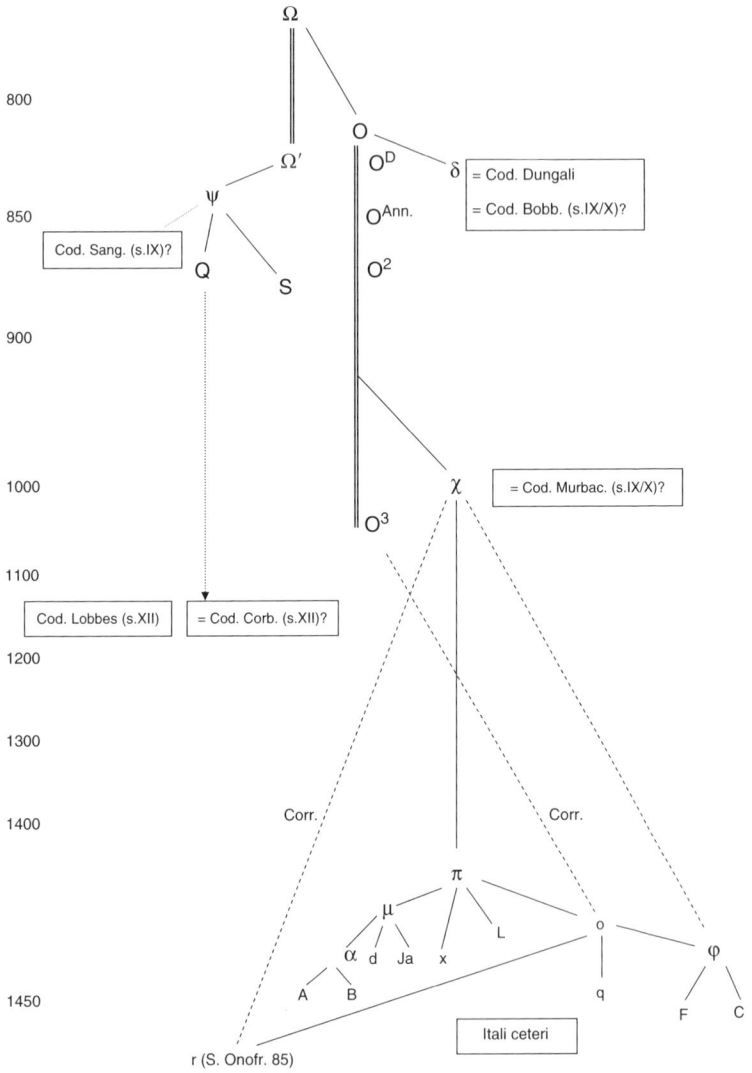

3. A more detailed stemma of the Lucretian tradition

stemmatic irrelevance of the Italian manuscripts, the great labours of Reeve (1980, 2005, 2006), which have improved, revised or refuted the work of Hosius (1914), Merrill (1926), Bertelli (1964, 1965a, 1965b), K. Müller (1973 and his edition), Cini (1976), Flores (1978, 1980, 2006b and his edition), Tomasco (1981) and Paladini (1995, 1996, 2000), have shed much light on the complicated interrelationships between these codices. Further collation is still required to firm up certain areas of the Italian stemma but the conclusions will have no direct bearing on reconstructing the interrelationship of the Lucretian manuscripts that possess independent textual authority. The *Itali* will therefore play no further role in this book, beyond the following discussion of the influence of χ and O in fifteenth-century Italy. I shall defer discussion of the much more tentative matters concerning the nature of the archetype and its antecedents until the concluding chapter, as it has no direct bearing upon the extant Lucretian manuscripts.

Detailed proof will be offered in Chapter 4 of how the Poggianus (π) descended from O by way of its lost copy χ. However, in the wake of the detailed researches of Reeve (1980, 39–40; 2005, 144–50), we must tackle the difficult matter of how certain readings occur in small pockets of the *Itali* that show clear signs of independence of the rest of the Italian tradition, and thus of π. This question is essential to constructing the stemma of Lucretius' Renaissance manuscripts: prior to Reeve's contributions, Müller had suggested a stemma in which a lost apograph of π, named ξ (written between 1418 and *c.* 1435), held a central place between the Poggianus and the majority of *Itali* (see overleaf).

The independent readings considered below entered the text of φ as well as the margins of a few other manuscripts (not recorded in the stemma above). The existence of such readings throws up a dilemma: do they stem from one or more manuscripts anterior to π, in which case Müller's ξ can be conveniently eliminated as identical to π (a suggestion treated by Reeve (1980, 39)), or did the majority of the extant Italian tradition indeed descend from ξ but the supposedly independent readings found in φ descend from π itself, drawing upon readings that were corrupted or eliminated in the writing of ξ? My own investigations strongly support the former of

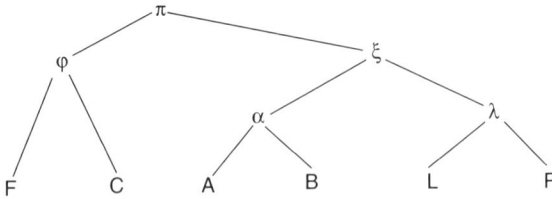

4. The stemma of the Italian manuscripts of Lucretius posited by
Konrad Müller (1973)

these possibilities. The several reasons for adopting this view, for rejecting the existence of ξ, and for asserting that both O and χ underwent further collation in the fifteenth century, will be summarised once the relevant evidence has been introduced.

The textual readings at issue sometimes demonstrate knowledge of O itself (not mediated by χ) and at other times strongly suggest knowledge of χ (not mediated by π). Given that these readings help to confirm the existence of χ and reveal knowledge in the late fifteenth century of both of these mediaeval manuscripts, they deserve careful treatment in this opening chapter. The readings in question are spread among the following witnesses:

– the main text of manuscripts in the φ group, of which F (Laur. 35.31: late 1450s), C (Cambridge UL Nn II 40: c. 1460), e (Vat. Lat. 3275: c. 1460–75) and f (Vat. Ottob. Lat. 1136: early/mid 1460s) are the primary witnesses, along with the second stratum of corrections entered in 1459 by Pomponio Leto (1425–98) into N (Naples IV E 51: 1458)
– corrections up to I.829 in Laur. 35.29 (saec. $XV^{3/4}$), entered in 1487–91 by Politian (Angelo Poliziano, 1454–94)
– manuscript corrections in four incunabula, in the first two expressly linked with a *Codex Pomponianus*: Utrecht X 2° 82 (Verona, 1486) *castigatus cum codice Pomponiano*; Paris Bibl. Nat. Rés. m Yc 397 (Venice, 1495); Milan Ambros. Inc. 186 (Venice, 1495); Vienna ÖNB Ink. 5 H 14 (Venice, 1500)
– later corrections by the scribe up to V.358 (after which the text is lost) of r (S. Onofrio 85: 1467–72)
– a later stratum of corrections (post-1470) up to II.377 in o (Vat. Pat. 312: late 1430s–mid 1450s)
– corrections (late fifteenth century) up to I.492 in q (Vat. Ottob. Lat. 2834: 1465–75).

Before attempting to sort out the possible relationships amongst these disparate readings, I offer succinct proof that direct knowledge of both χ and O is demonstrated by this material. Since, as I conclude later in this book, χ was copied from O at a point after its correction by a ninth-century hand (O^2) but before that by a tenth-/eleventh-century hand (O^3),[98] and since there is no evidence that these later readings of O^3 ever found their way into χ at a later date (and thus could not have been present as variant readings in π), any fifteenth-century evidence of O^3 readings must stem from a fresh collation of O itself. Given that such readings entered before the *editio princeps* (Brescia, 1473), a detailed collation (at least of Book I) of the codex must have been made on an Italian manuscript, but no such manuscript survives.[99] Nevertheless, unequivocal O^3 readings are found as corrections in two of the above manuscripts, namely the corrections up to II.327 in o (Vat. Pat. 312) and those up to I.492 in its apograph q (Vat. Ottob. Lat. 2834), both of which annotating hands must date from the last three decades of the fifteenth century. The most obvious of these readings are as follows (those marked with an asterisk are apparently not found elsewhere in the Italian manuscript tradition):[100] I.70* *effringere*] *frangere* (q), 71* *cupiret*] *uideret* (oq),[101] 77* *quantum*] *quanam* (q), 233 *consumpse ante acta*] *consummere* (*consumere* O^3) *facta* (q), 269* *quae*] *quot* (q : *quod* O^3),[102] 282* *auget*] *urget* (q), 306 *serescunt*] *rigescunt*

---

98 Detailed proof of this is offered in Chapter 4 (D).

99 It is a needless complication to suppose that another mediaeval copy of O was made after the time of the work of O^3, and that the scribe chose to record the variant readings comprehensively, and at least some of the glosses, from the hand of O^3, which manuscript was discovered later in the fifteenth century but lost soon thereafter.

100 Because of the closure of the Vatican (2007–10), and since this information does not impinge upon my primary argument, I have relied on the information published by Reeve in his articles (1980, 2005) and communicated to me from his notes. A closer collation of o will doubtless turn up more interesting variant readings in Book I.

101 The correction of O^3 of this same verb, namely *cupiret*, is also found in o (as well as a few other manuscripts, including $A^1BIC^1r^1$), but since this reading is also preserved in Nonius (507,1 Mercer), Priscian (*Inst. GLK* II 499,10) and thence Dicuil (*De prim. syll.* p. 147,1 (Manitius)), it cannot be used *per se* as a secure sign of contact with O: the correction occurs in a number of other manuscripts (ABCr), none of which I credit with knowledge of O^3.

102 It is unlikely, but not entirely impossible, that the particular form of the abbreviation used by O^3 confused the collator into believing that the correction of *quae* was to *quot*, which is at least grammatical, not *quod*.

(q) and 412* *magnis*] *amnes* (q).[103] These numerous coincidences with the (often bad) conjectures of O³ are too striking to be independent innovations and must originate from a fifteenth-century collation of O.[104] Since secure readings of O³ are not found in any witnesses earlier than these, there is no certain evidence of the collation of O until the last three decades of the Quattrocento.

However, there are a number of reasons to conclude that the readings of χ, the apograph of O found by Poggio and very probably left wherever it was discovered, separately entered the Italian tradition at an earlier point in the fifteenth century. First, the other witnesses that show knowledge of readings independent of π, although they often cite nonsensical or highly improbable readings, inexplicably disregard the better conjectures of O³: his corrections at I.77, 404,[105] 467, 680, 711 and 767, and his plausible suggestions at I.70, 282, 412, 560 and 680, including the deletion of 769, are not (to my knowledge) found elsewhere in the Italian tradition than in oq discussed above.[106] This state of affairs is very difficult to explain when so many other poor and futile variant readings are recorded. Most useful in this regard are the very frequent corrections in r (S. Onofrio 85), several of which show descent from O against QS as well as independence from π.[107] To come to the second reason, however, not only do

---

[103] There is no reason to suppose that the readings of either Q or S (both of which here offer *amnes*) were known in fifteenth-century Italy; this correction instead stems from *amnis* of O³.

[104] A correction that can be dismissed as a confusion of its source occurs in q at I.410: *abscesseris* is given as a variant alongside *recesseris* (O) upon *recesserit* at I.410. I do not believe that this reflects knowledge of either of the two other mediaeval codices (*reabscesseris* Q : *reabcesseris* S). Rather, given that the variant *abs re* (A and presumably other *Itali*) circulated for *ab re* at the end of the line, it is probable that the proximity of the marginal variants *recesseris* and (placed above) *abs* led the corrector of q (or his immediate source) to regard these as two alternative prefixes to *-cesseris*.

[105] This reading has been cogently defended by Deufert (2010) 62–4.

[106] An exception is L's correction *in ras.* of *descedere*(?) to *discendere* at I.680; since these marginalia bear no connection with the other readings I regard as interesting, this is probably a clever conjecture.

[107] The variants recorded at, e.g., I.427 (*haustusquam*), II.493 (*at simili*), III.957 (*abes*), IV.143 (*facile*), 485 (*sonueri*), and V.51 (*diuom*) could only have been taken from O (or χ), and those at, e.g., I.24, 84, 407, 480; II.460, 1078; III.347, 871, 980; IV.40, 53, 66, 449, 501; and V. 61 could not be drawn from QS but only O or a descendant.

the readings of O³ not occur amidst these otherwise rich pickings,[108] but various readings seem to reflect transcription not directly from O but through a mediaeval exemplar, such as χ would have been:[109] at I.590 *ostendant* is recorded by the annotator of r in the form *o͞udant*, a contraction that suggests a mediaeval manuscript, and with a form of the *n* characteristic of ninth- and tenth-century Carolingian minuscule; *qu͞o*, the abbreviation of *quoniam* used by the annotator at I.794, 943, II.810 and 817, where O instead has *quoniam* written in full, suggests likewise a manuscript source other than the Oblongus. It is also evident that an intermediary must lie between these corrections and O itself, since we find almost forty discrepancies:[110] e.g. II.155 *retrahuntur* (*trahuntur* O), II.430 *feculam* (*fecula* O)[111] and IV.442 *flauitare* (*fluitare* O). It therefore seems that readings of a manuscript distinct from O but nonetheless several centuries old entered the Italian tradition at some point in the middle third of the fifteenth century.[112]

Disregarding the incunabula and Politian's annotations in Laur. 35.29 for the time being, we may turn now to the φ group of manuscripts, which present a text that, although ultimately descended from π, is heavily emended and shows clear signs of access to Lucretian readings independent of π: most importantly, the group does not omit lines absent from other descendants of π (II.492–4, III.595–6, IV.512, which thus seem to have been wanting in π).[113] What is clear is that the text of φ, which was

---

[108] In addition to the cases listed above, the corrector of r shows no knowledge of the corrections of O³ at I.87, 639 and 759.

[109] This point was made by Reeve (1980) 41.

[110] Readings that differ from O either materially or in their orthography can be seen at I.43, 166, 225, 590, 794, 885, 943; II.46, 155, 283, 415, 420, 430, 810, 817, 872, 935; III.7, 83, 242, 277, 322, 675, 817, 906, 939; IV.34, 246, 301, 437, 442, 466, 496, 512, 632, 1242; V.122, 171, 316; the manuscript is deficient after V.378.

[111] The fact that we find *fetulam* in π suggests that the reading of χ was *feculam*, an anticipatory error before *iam* in his exemplar (O), which in minuscule was easily miscopied as *fetulam* by the hurrying scribe of π but accurately read by the collator of χ at a later date.

[112] On this theory one can explain away the sort of difficulty touched upon by Reeve (2005) 149–50: χ misread *te* at III.906 in O (f. 82ʳ) as *de* (an uncial *d* with biting), which duly entered π (μx etc.) but was soon corrected to the obvious *te*; *de* nevertheless entered the corrections to r and φ via χ.

[113] However, the group does omit, for no obvious reason, VI.390.

copied from that of o (Vat. Pat. 312),[114] was closely worked on in the 1450s (or perhaps 1440s) by one or more skilled Latinists who somehow had access to Lucretian readings antedating π. There are, however, no definite signs that the corrector(s) of φ had direct access to O: instead, we find a number of significant oversights from that manuscript, even in the earliest stages of codices constituting the φ group.

The most natural explanation for how this cognisance of non-π readings arose is that the mediaeval MS χ was recollated, or less probably re-copied, in the 1420s or 1430s (a possible date will be given below). In order to accept this theory, which would adequately explain the available evidence, we must dismiss the few instances in which the φ group presents emendations coincident with those of O³, which could not have stood in χ. The cases are neither numerous nor of great significance: I.639 *ob obscuram* FCe (also in Vat. Ottob. Lat. 1954, written in 1466) : *ob oscuram* O³ : *oscuram* O^{a.c.} : *obscuram* QS: this correction could have been obtained from Festus (314,3 Lindsay) or offered *ex ope ingeni*; I.659 *uera uiai* FCO³ (also as a variant reading in A) : *ueraula* O^{a.c.}Q^{a.c.}S: this is presumably an intelligent conjecture to restore Lucretian idiom; I.759 *uenena* CFfO³ (also in Conv. Soppr. 453) : *uene* O^{a.c.} : *ueneni* QS: this is a simple emendation to mend the metre.[115] At I.711, φ corrected the reading of the Italian tradition, *longeque errasse*, which itself attempted to correct the unmetrical text of O and χ *longi errasse*: φ restored *longi* from χ but fixed the metre by reading *deerrasse*, a verb introduced with synizesis perhaps from III.860; the suggestion need not be associated with *derrasse* of O³. The only remaining reading of any significance that misleadingly suggests access to O itself (as opposed to χ) is III.1061, where φ restored *quem* for *per quem*, a deletion also made by O² but apparently ignored by χ and thus

---

[114] See Reeve (2005) 133. Michael Reeve has also informed me of another proof of the descent of φ from o: at VI.954 for *caeli* o read *coli* (or *colii*), altered by a later hand to *corii*, which nonsense reading is also found in FC.

[115] See also the four minor cases given at Chapter 4, n. 122, in which coincidental corrections occurred both within and without the φ group. Few emendations outside φ manuscripts restore a reading of O that had been corrupted or ignored by the time of π, the most significant being V.1393 *proptereaque* OQπ : *propter aquae* O²L²Pμab (as well as φ).

found in π: the correction is easy for a competent metrician.[116]
The fact that these few corrections do not enter the collation in r
(which lacks φ emendations) suggests that they were not drawn
from χ but were instead independent innovations of the intelligent
annotator(s) of φ.

Linked with the readings of this group are the three incunabula
(Utr., Mil., Vind.)[117] and the corrections of Politian in Laur. 35.29
('Pol.'): both sets probably draw upon φ itself, and none can be
earlier than 1486, although they probably antedate the close of the
century. φ had by this point been further emended by its keen
owner(s) and seemingly had obtained some of the readings of
O itself. The data that prove descent from O and not χ or π are:
I.16 *tergis* $O^{a.c.}QS$ Pol. : *pergis* recte O^2 (thus χπ), 27 *oralatum*
$O^{a.c.}Q^{a.c.}S$ Pol. : *ornatum* recte O^2Q^2 (thus χπ), and 71 *uideret*
$O^{3\ (u.l.)}$ Utr. Vind. : *cupiret* recte O^3 : *cuperet* $O^{a.c.}QS$ (thus χπ).[118]
As regards the more interesting evidence of Politian's marginal
annotations in Laur. 35.29, the other primitive readings found in
these annotations (see Reeve (2005, 145) for a significant number)
could be derived from χ, although their absence from other sets of
corrections that I attribute to a collation of χ render it more
probable that they were drawn directly from O. Although many
of these readings could have been taken from Q or S, some could
not: I.62*cap. inuentoris*, I.149*cap. de nihil*, I.269*cap. uideantur*
and I.480 *cluere* could not be drawn from Q, which lacks *capitula*
(and offers *luere* at 480); the readings I.16 *tergis* and I.336 *exstat*
could not be drawn from S (*rrgis*, *estat*); the variants I.85 *Iphianassai* (if not drawn from Prisc. *Inst. GLK* II 285,11), 412 *magnes*,
649 *haberet* and 711 *longi*, all but the first of which are manifestly
impossible, could only have been drawn from O or χ. In two
instances the reading of O pre-correction is given: I.27 *oralatum*
(*ornatum* O^2), a reading still visible after erasure to a keen collator

---

[116] Cf. Chapter 4, pp. 250–2.

[117] Further information about the Utrecht and Milan incunabula can be found at Reeve
(2005) 146–7; Dixon (2011) treats in detail the annotations in the Utrecht incunable.

[118] Since it is extremely improbable that χ elected to record variant readings, *tergis* would
not have been visible at I.16; it is effectively impossible that this mediaeval manuscript
recovered *oralatum* as a variant reading from beneath *ornatum* at I.27; it is certainly
impossible that χ knew of the variant/gloss *uideret* at I.71, since this reading was
entered into O by O^3 after the creation of χ.

(as it was to Gronovius: cf. Salmasius (1656) 114), and I.271 *cortus* (corrected by Dungal to *tortus* in O).

It is now possible for me to summarise why one should not assume that, whereas the correctors of o and q were indeed able to draw upon a collation or apograph of O (distinct from χ), the seemingly independent material found in φ and the corrector of r was actually drawn from π itself and not the mediaeval χ. I shall offer arguments against this conclusion in decreasing order of force. First, if Müller's ξ was an apograph of π, and therefore written by the owner of π, Niccolò Niccoli (or an associate), it is very odd that Niccoli, when writing L from ξ, very often misread the text of his exemplar: Reeve (1980, 41; 2005, 153) recorded, among other things, that Niccoli was particularly troubled by the abbreviation for *nisi*, and in ten of the first twenty-two instances wrongly resolved it as *nec*, yet his own handwriting in L or elsewhere shows no sign of this difficulty.[119] In reality it is far easier to assume that the confusing abbreviation occurred in π itself, from which Niccoli made his copy L, and that its various witnesses were troubled by it to differing degrees. Secondly, the corrections of r give us a detailed picture of the source material, and a number of the oddities discussed above suggest a mediaeval exemplar rather than a fifteenth-century Italian manuscript that strangely chose to reproduce these forms. Thirdly, it is rather awkward to assume that Niccoli chose to have L copied not directly from the Poggianus, which he had in his hands for at least a dozen years, but instead from its apograph ξ. Fourthly, it would have to be the case that ξ, despite its importance and distinguished ownership, was rather carelessly made from π, a manuscript we would more naturally assume to be made in haste and with errors (such as the omission of II.492–4, III.595–6 and IV.512). Fifth, it would be strange that the readings of π, the manuscript owned by an influential patron (Niccoli) and then a great scholar (Poggio), should have had so little input into the tradition, there being apparently no direct apograph from it other than ξ: that the collation used by r can show up some forty readings of O (or its early

---

[119] For this reconstruction we must assume that π itself was clear on this point, as the confusion very rarely occurred in φ or the corrections of r.

correctors) not found elsewhere in the Italian tradition (cf. Reeve (2005) 148) is rather remarkable, if π was its source. Sixth, we must suppose that, although no apograph was made of π after the time of ξ (1418–*c*. 1435), it was nevertheless freely available to the owner of φ to use (when Poggio was primarily in Rome). Seventh, we would have to assume that Bartolomeo da Montepulciano's seeking to acquire a copy of Lucretius (on which see below) had no apparent outcome for the Italian tradition of the work. Eighth and finally, the Cesena manuscript (x: Malatest. Ces. S 20 4: 1458–65) could on this hypothesis only be said to be an apograph of ξ: it would therefore have no connection with Poggio and π (on which see Chapter 4, p. 255). Although none of these arguments individually can be considered a knock-down objection, their cumulative effect is to make such a conclusion far less probable than positing the influx of χ: Poggio discovered Lucretius outside Italy, Bartolomeo da Montepulciano and perhaps Aurispa (on whom see below) seem to have encountered manuscripts of Lucretius outside Italy, and someone clearly collated or copied O in Mainz; for a second trip to have occurred to the location where Poggio stunned the learned world by finding χ is hardly a problematic logistical assumption.

We may now turn to a possible reconstruction of how the readings of O and χ entered the Lucretian tradition. o was copied from π in the 1440s/50s, taking some regard of whatever emendations or marginalia Poggio and/or another intelligent reader could have made on it. At some point soon afterwards, φ was copied from o, and the owner of this manuscript evidently had an active interest in Lucretius, for as well as setting about adding his conjectures to the text he somehow obtained access to the readings of χ, which he perhaps knew to have been the manuscript Poggio found. Although Poggio had failed to obtain χ himself, and instead possessed in π a copy made by a commissioned scribe, it is possible that either he or Niccoli bade Bartolomeo da Montepulciano acquire the codex a decade later, perhaps merely to own an old manuscript, perhaps in the hope that collating it would improve the known text. For, in a letter to Niccoli of 17 May 1427, Poggio stated without any contextual background 'Bartholomeus de Monte Politiano dat operam, ut habeamus Lucretium; id si asSequetur, tunc alia aggrediemur ... Paulatim incedendum est, barbari enim sunt et suspitiosi' (Harth (1984–7) vol. I, 73). Given that the preceding and succeeding paragraphs treated German manuscripts, Bartolomeo's attempt to acquire Lucretius may well have been made in Germany, where Poggio and Niccoli already knew a text of *DRN* to be. The most natural assumption is that Bartolomeo was attempting to acquire χ, still in the *locus satis longinquus* where Poggio found it; this mutually known background perhaps allowed Poggio not to record further information about the location and nature of the Lucretius sought by Bartolomeo. At any rate, we learn nothing more of his attempt. It would not be difficult to assume, however, that Bartolomeo did obtain χ, that it returned to Italy, and that, perhaps after his death in 1429, its readings circulated among a small group of scholars; there is no evidence at all that χ itself survived into the sixteenth century, and it perhaps came to its end in a Renaissance Italian library.

Either directly from χ, or by means of a collation, the owner of φ added various readings from it, occasionally recording the origin of these as from a *codex vetustus* (see n. 123 below), sometimes adding them indiscriminately amidst his own emendations. After φ had become marked up with readings of χ and various emendations, copies of it were made – including F (late 1450s), C (*c.* 1460), e (*c.* 1460–75) and f (early/mid 1460s) – whose scribes varied both in how diligent they were in weighing the variants and conjectures against the main text of φ and in how much marginal material they reproduced.[120] φ in its augmented state also served as the basis for the corrections made in 1459 by N[2], namely Pomponio Leto. Detailed knowledge of χ, perhaps more refined than that available to φ, came into the hands of the scribe and corrector of r (S. Onofrio 85), after he had copied the text of o (Vat. Pat. 312) around 1470, when the latter still lacked

[120] One of the figures involved in the correction of φ (as recorded in a few emendations in F and C: see Reeve (1980) 34 n. 2) I have identified as Francisco Vidal de Noya (1430s (?)–1492), who obtained his doctorate in Paris and then became tutor to Ferdinand II of Aragon (1452–1516), being based in Italy from the 1470s onwards; from 1485 he held the Bishopric of Cefalù but continued to travel widely. A few conjectures in FC are attributed to 'Noianus'/'Noya'/'Noia'; these corrections, which must draw on a third source (since neither set could have been copied from the other), cannot have entered circulation in Italy until the late 1470s and thus do not affect my discussion of χ and φ.

the corrections drawn from a collation of O itself. x (Malatest. Ces. S 20 4), by contrast, was copied directly from π over forty years after its transcription, by which time Poggio probably had annotated it to a considerable extent (note the three versions given in x of I.50).[121] Though presumably faced with a smorgasbord of conjectural material, many primitive readings of π were apparently copied by the scribe of x instead of the conjectures that found their way into other descendants of the manuscript, for example I.16 *quoquamque*, II.181 *quamquam*, III.960 *discere*. There is no clear evidence of a new injection into this manuscript of the readings of χ, which, if it did enter Italy through the agency of Bartolomeo, Poggio would presumably have recognised as the direct source of his own manuscript and therefore not have striven to obtain.

So much for χ and π. At some stage later in the fifteenth century, perhaps in the late 1460s or early 1470s, readings of O itself came into circulation. It is probable that the material brought to light by Reeve (2005, 156–7) regarding the apparent connection between A (Vat. Lat. 3276, written at Naples in 1442) and a Lucretian manuscript at Mainz (almost certainly O) is based upon confusion arising from a lost note.[122] Since, as argued

---

[121] For more information about the readings of x, see Reeve (2005) 140–1. Given that π clearly obtained many emendations over the fifteen or so years for which it was in Niccoli's possession, and that L (mid 1430s) appears to be its first copy, it is most improbable that x derives from an early (lost) apograph of π when it still contained few emendations.

[122] The piece of evidence in question was publicised by Augusto Campana in his Rostagno lecture for 1968: in an old catalogue of the manuscripts of Fulvio Orsini (1529–1600) compiled in the early seventeenth century by Domenico Ranaldi (1555–1606), a note is described that does not survive in A in its present form, perhaps having been written on a flyleaf lost in rebinding. Ranaldi recorded that the Lucretian manuscript was copied 'da un'antico codice di Magonza, si come attesta Aurispa nel fine in 4.168'. No such note survives in A, nor does any trace of the hand of Giovanni Aurispa (1376–1459). The note cannot literally be correct, for there is no doubt that it is copied, at two or more removes, from π, which is neither an *antico codice* nor *di Magonza*. The note need not be fully discredited, however, for, since Aurispa was known to have visited Mainz in search of rare texts in 1433 when attending the Council of Basel, we may suppose that he had there learnt of the presence of another manuscript of Lucretius (i.e. O rather than χ) but could not obtain it for himself. Whether or not Aurispa was ultimately responsible for the collation of O that entered the Italian tradition in the late fifteenth century or whether he never had the chance to investigate this manuscript closely is impossible to tell. At any rate, if Ranaldi had some source for his statement, it could simply be a confusion based upon a note of Aurispa's that recorded the existence

above, O did not leave Mainz during the fifteenth century, knowledge of its readings could only have entered the Italian tradition by way of a collation or complete transcript, the latter being less probable. These readings did not much affect the tradition in the dying days of Lucretius' manuscript transmission but found their way into the margins of two closely related manuscripts, o and its descendant q, as demonstrated above. Some of these readings were perhaps added into φ at a later stage, for, by the end of the fifteenth century, the material drawn from φ or a closely related source by the three incunabula and Politian in 1487–91 (when he borrowed φ) shows a certain amount of intermingling of the information drawn from χ, as found in earlier witnesses of φ, with readings drawn from O. It is not particularly difficult to suppose that some interesting readings of O – such as the mysterious I.27 *oralatum* (read in erasure) and 271 *cortus* – were added to φ once it had lost contact with the manuscripts directly copied from it (which contain no such readings), and that, despite the slight variation in the inks he used, Politian obtained all his variant readings in Laur. 35.29 from φ. One could imagine that φ contained two strata of readings, confident corrections *in textu* and interesting (but perhaps improbable) variant readings *in margine*, each of which Politian entered in a different sitting, with a correspondingly different shade of ink. Some of this admixture of material also entered, directly or indirectly, into the Utrecht and Milan incunabula connected with Leto (and presumably φ), and thereafter that at Vienna.[123]

---

of an ancient manuscript of Lucretius at Mainz (a possibility acknowledged by Reeve (2005) 157). Since A is known to have been in the hands of Panormita (1394–1471), he presumably obtained it after Aurispa's death (were he the owner) in 1459. If indeed Aurispa found and collated O in Mainz *c.* 1433, its readings never entered A and took half a century to appear elsewhere (in oq).

[123] The matter of the *codex vetustus* referred to in some of the notes connected with φ must arise from some confusion of the evidence. I suggest that the *codex vetustus* was χ, many of whose readings were entered into φ. Nevertheless, it soon became unclear in that manuscript which marginal readings were drawn from χ and which were mere conjectures, with the result that some of those readings expressly said to have occurred in a *codex vetustus* or *vetus liber* by later witnesses (for instance the absence of I.44–9, I.774 *non animas ex non animo non corpore corpus* and II.919 *ab eortu*) probably never existed in any such manuscript; however, two other readings attributed to the *codex vetustus*, namely II.1110 *appareret* (*appariret* OQ : *appareret* π) and VI.560 *nec minus exultantes dup vis cum que vim* (*nec minus exultant esdupuis cumque uim* OQ), could well have occurred in this form in χ.

The fate of Lucretius' text in the Renaissance is thus more simple and more complicated than has been supposed: all Italian manuscripts do derive their primary text from one manuscript (π), itself an indirect copy (via χ) of the oldest surviving manuscript of the poem (O); however, the efforts of Italian humanists in finding manuscripts and improving texts caused material from both O and χ to be channelled into certain pockets of the Italian tradition throughout the fifteenth century.

2

THE INDIRECT TRADITION OF LUCRETIUS

It is beyond doubt that the transmission of Lucretius' *DRN* is among the more narrow and 'closed' manuscript traditions of classical Latin poets. Nevertheless, after an apparently quiet start, the poem is cited with a comparatively regular frequency, and for a broad range of purposes, in subsequent authors of antiquity. This chapter will treat in detail the transmission of *DRN* until about AD 400, then survey the following four centuries, up to the height of the Carolingian period, which offer comparatively little positive evidence for direct contact with Lucretius; since there is no evidence for first-hand knowledge of Lucretius between the late tenth and early fifteenth centuries,[1] this period – offering almost nothing to the Lucretian scholar – will not figure in this chapter or elsewhere in this book. The second half of this chapter treats the so-called 'Lucretian fragments', verses attributed to the poet and his poem by non-Lucretian authors but not attested in Lucretius' manuscript transmission.

Various foundations have been laid in the study of the indirect tradition, although several authors (e.g. Festus, Isidore and the later grammarians) have received no treatment to date. Only Hadzsits (1935, Chapters IV, IX–XII) and Pizzani (1959a, Chapter II) have offered diachronic interpretations of Lucretius' indirect transmission,[2] and only the latter has investigated textual matters,

---

[1] For corroboration of this statement, see Appendix II, n. 1.

[2] Lists of Lucretian citations and echoes (of varying degrees of accuracy and comprehensiveness) were offered by Jessen (1870: ninth–fourteenth centuries), Manitius (1894: fourth–fifteenth centuries), Philippe (1895; 1896: first century BC–thirteenth century AD), Bignone (1913: fifth–fourteenth centuries), Alfonsi (1978: first century BC–eighteenth century) and, most fully, Solaro (2000, 93–122: seventh–fifteenth centuries), although all lack close textual analysis. The survey of Bodelon García (1988) is too vague to be of any use. It is regrettable that the detailed analysis of prose citations of Lucretius up to the age of Lactantius offered by Gatzemeier (2013) appeared too recently to be incorporated into my own research.

albeit selectively. My purpose is to ascertain how available and how diverse the tradition of Lucretius was from late antiquity onwards, not to treat the broader questions of his cultural reception, namely the general attitudes of citing authors towards the philosophical and literary content of *DRN*.[3] It will be demonstrated that, despite a good amount of material on offer, the evidence for significantly divergent traditions or 'recensions' of *DRN* is slim and to be treated with caution.

There are four ways in which a discrepancy between the text of Lucretius' manuscripts and that of a citing author can occur: the citing author (a) had access to a manuscript tradition different from the extant direct tradition; (b) cited the Lucretian passage from memory (whatever its source) and in so doing inadvertently introduced errors; (c) actively altered the text he cited; (d) cited the Lucretian passage in its correct form, as also transmitted by the direct tradition, but subsequent scribal error in his own manuscript tradition introduced corruptions. It will be seen that (d) is relatively common and easily detectable (especially if the result is truly nonsensical); although (c) is relatively rare, distinguishing between (a), (b) and (c) is difficult, and authors must be treated case by case.

I shall treat the citations in eleven groups: (A) authors up to *c.* AD 200, (B) Festus, (C) the Church Fathers, (D) Nonius, (E) Macrobius, (F) Virgilian commentators, (G) other grammarians, (H) remaining minor authors (saec. III–VI), (I) Isidore, (J) citations in florilegia, (K) late citations (saec. VII–X).

(A)   Authors up to AD 200.

There is no doubt that Lucretius' work was freely available to Roman poets in the immediate wake of his death: Horace,[4]

---

[3] For a summary of Lucretian citations in the indirect tradition, see Appendix II. Full use of textual discrepancies will be made in my Oxford Classical Text.

[4] The occasional citation of Lucretius occurs in (pseudo-)Acro and Porphyrio but without any explicit statement concerning his general influence; modern Horatian commentators from the time of Lambinus and Bentley, however, made great redress in the field. The most important treatments are Goebel (1857b), Reisacker (1873), Weingärtner (1874), Wöhler (1876), Merrill (1905), Brakman (1921); cf. also Munro (*ad* III.938, V.1029).

Virgil,[5] Propertius,[6] Tibullus,[7] Ovid,[8] Manilius,[9] and seemingly his contemporary Catullus already in the mid-50s,[10] among other more minor figures,[11] all offered clear echoes and/or responses to the poem;[12] nevertheless, only Ovid among poets before Statius referred to Lucretius by name. Echoes in prose writers of the first century BC are notably rarer,[13] most suggested imitations being unconvincing.[14] It is highly probable, however,

[5] Gellius (I.21.7) and Servius (*ad* Verg. *Geo.* III.293), among other Virgilian commentators, were conscious of Lucretius' influence upon Virgil, particularly in the *Georgica*. Conington claimed to have found some two hundred Lucretian echoes in Virgil, but the total no doubt rises far higher. For discussion, see primarily Regel (1907) 39–52, Merrill (1918), Bailey (1931), Rostagni (1931), Paratore (1939), Klepl (1940), Hanon (1943), Farrington (1958; 1963), Castelli (1966; 1967), Cleary (1970), Nethercut (1973), Hardie (1986) esp. Chapter 5, Farrell (1991) 169–207, Fernadelli (1998), Gale (2000); cf. also Munro (*ad* I.253).

[6] I know of no individual study of Lucretian influence upon Propertius; for brief remarks on Epicureanism and Propertius and Tibullus, see Ferguson (1990) 2270. Incidentally, I disregard Turnebus' conjecture *Lucreti* in lieu of the transmitted *crethei* at II.34.29.

[7] See, e.g., Pillinger (1971) and Ferguson (1990) 2270.

[8] Ovid devoted a couplet to Lucretius in his list of literary immortals (*Am.* I.15.23–4: *carmina sublimis tunc sunt peritura Lucreti,* | *exitio terras cum dabit una dies*), reflecting the permanent fame *DRN* had attracted already in its first few decades; in the catalogue of great poets in the second book of his *Tristia* he gave Lucretius a distich between Ennius and Catullus (II.425–6: *explicat ut causas rapidi Lucretius ignis,* | *casurumque triplex uaticinatur opus*). For further discussion, see Zingerle (1869–71) vol. II, 12–47, Washietl (1883) 43–115, Migliorini (1980), Sommariva (1980), Shulman (1981), Korpanty (1990), Flores (1999), Lecocq (1999).

[9] Manilius evidently saw the production of his *Astronomicon* as something of a Stoic *Anti-Lucrèce*: for further discussion, see Woltjer (1881a) 53ff., Rösch (1911), Brakman (1922), Farrington (1954), Flores (1993), Abry (1999), Volk (2002) 225–33 and (2009) *passim*.

[10] It is probable both that Catullus echoes Lucretius (rather than vice versa) and that Catullus learned of Lucretius' poetry in its *post-mortem* circulation, not through personal connection prior to that. See Jessen (1870), Frank (1933), Herrmann (1956), Grimal (1978) 258–60, Skinner (1976), Perutelli (1996), Gómez Pallarès (1998), Morisi (2002), Biondi (2003); cf. also Munro (*ad* III.57) and Bailey (*ad* II.618–20; vol. III, 1753–4). If more than two verses of Egnatius' *De rerum natura* survived, it would be interesting to know its relationship with Lucretius; for discussion of the fragments, see Traglia (1962) 60, 128–9, Marinone (1974), Courtney (1993) 47–8, Hollis (2007) 87–9.

[11] See for the *Culex*, Paratore (1947); for Lucan, Verdière (1971); for Persius, La Bua (1997); for Petronius, Munro (*ad* IV.361, 966); for the *Aetna*, Anziger (1896) 3; for Statius, Helm (1892) 67ff., Serrao (1982) and Taisné (1999); for Juvenal, Highet (1951) 392 n. 54 and Watts (1972); for Lucretian elements in epigraphic poetry, see Tolkiehn (1912) and Löfstedt (1913).

[12] For more general treatments of Lucretian influence upon poets, see Woll (1907), Disch (1921) and Giesecke (1992).

[13] See below for a dismissal of the appearance of Lucretius' name in two Varronian quotations (*L.L.* V.17 = fr. **XII**; VII.4 = fr. **XIII**).

[14] For possible Livian reminiscences of Lucretius see Stacey (1898).

that Cicero knew the poem in full,[15] and possible that Caesar had read it.[16] A few decades later, Vitruvius (IX.*pr*.17–18) praised Lucretius, as did Nepos (*Att.* 12.4) and Velleius Paterculus (II.36), all *en passant*. In the first century AD Pliny the Elder cited Lucretius as a source for the tenth book of his *Historia naturalis* (recorded as *T. Lucreti[us]* in the list of contents presented at the close of Book I).[17]

Yet, to assess the textual development of Lucretius' transmission, we must focus squarely upon direct citations of *DRN*, leaving mere allusions and imitations aside. Quite surprisingly, given his broad influence and range, no author quoted Lucretius in the first century BC, although this may be a distortion thrown up by the prose authors that do survive from the period; for the first direct quotation of *DRN*, we must wait until the 50s AD, over one hundred years after the poet's death.[18]

We come then to Seneca the Younger (*c.* 3/2 BC–AD 65),[19] who explicitly quoted six passages of Lucretius (ten verses in full or in part), drawn from at least two books of *DRN*.[20] *Carthaginis horror*, applied to Scipio at *Epp.* 86.5, certainly echoes the same phrase from Lucr. III.1034, and a number of more doubtful

---

[15] Cicero's famous judgment on the Lucretian work he read (*Ad Q. Fr.* II.4) has been treated briefly in the Introduction (n. 4), as has his spurious editorial involvement with *DRN*, reported by Jerome. Notwithstanding his apparent appreciation of Lucretius' literary merits, Cicero made no mention of Lucretius elsewhere in his writings, although his later philosophical corpus, which regularly treats Epicureanism, gave him ample cause to do so. For further discussion of Lucretius' influence on Cicero (largely *argumenta ex silentio*), see Merrill (1909), Howe (1951), Trencsényi-Waldapel (1958), Pucci (1966), Fontaine (1966), André (1974), Auvray-Assayas (1999); cf. also Munro (*ad* V.619).

[16] See Dale (1958) and Németh (1983).

[17] It is curious that Lucretius is cited as a source only for this book (presumably for X.69 and 197, drawing on Lucr. IV.640-1), when more obvious indebtedness to *DRN* occurs in Pliny's second and seventh books.

[18] I disregard Ou. *Tr.* II.261–2 (*c.* AD 9), which shows knowledge of the first two words of the opening couplet of the poem: *sumpscrit 'Aeneadum genetrix' ubi prima, requiret,* | *Aeneadum genetrix unde sit alma Venus*; choriambic *alma Venus* also occurs at *Met.* X.230, XIV.478, XV.844, Verg. *Aen.* I.618, X.332, Germ. fr. 4.50 and Stat. *Silu.* I.2.52, 159 (the adjective had already been used of Venus by Plautus and Laevius).

[19] Various general studies have been written on the influence of Lucretius and Epicureanism upon Seneca the Younger: see especially Hadzsits (1935) 167–72, Mazzoli (1970) 206-9, Innocenti (1972), Chambert (1999), Althoff (2005).

[20] I.57 (*Epp.* 95.11), 304 (*Epp.* 106.8), 313 (*Quaest. nat.* IVb.3.4), II.55–6 = III.87-8 = VI.35–6 (*Epp.* 110.6), III.1034 (*Epp.* 86.5, in a passage demonstrating wider knowledge of III.37–86), 1068 (*Tranq. an.* 2.14).

reminiscences or imitations have been suggested.[21] The direct citations are found in *De tranquillitate animi* (composed in the 50s), the *Epistulae morales* (early 60s) and the *Quaestiones naturales* (*c.* 65). Seneca himself, learned, influential and active in Rome, certainly had access to a full manuscript of the work, presumably his own copy, with each book in its individual roll (although he provided no book references).[22] Among the citations there are few divergences from the Lucretian tradition: *quoque* for *quoue* in I.57 at *Ep.* 95.11; *ita* for *sic* in II.56 (or III.87 = VI.36) at *Epp.* 110.6; *semper fugit* for *fugit* in III.1068 at *Tranq. an.* 2.14.[23] These three errors suggest neither corruption in Seneca's source nor corruption in his own manuscript tradition but rather that he knew certain passages of Lucretius relatively well[24] and could quote from memory: in so doing, words of minor force were altered (*-ue* > *-que* and *sic* > *ita*) and the intensifying *semper* was easily added to the generalising present tense of the original wording of III.1068, still metrical in Seneca's partial citation of the verse.

Leaving aside the passing mentions of Lucretius as a celebrated poet in Statius' *Siluae*[25] and Tacitus' *Dialogus*,[26] we may turn to the evidence presented by Quintilian (*c.* 35–*c.* 95/100), who cited Lucretius only twice, both citations drawn from the famous passage[27] I.926–50 = IV.1–25.[28] In the first (I.936–8 = IV.11–13

---

[21] Quite probable instances were raised by La Penna (1994) and Ronnick (1995).

[22] It is a strange fact that, when positing three common names (analogous to English 'Tom, Dick and Harry') at *Epp.* 58.12, Seneca chose Lucretius alongside the major political names of Cato and Cicero.

[23] Nothing can be concluded from the agreement of the orthographical error *stillicidii* with QS (*stilicidii* O : corr. It.) in I.313 at *Quaest. nat.* IVb.3.4.

[24] It is worth observing that these verses occur either in much-praised (and much-read) parts of the work (the prefaces to Books I and II (or III), and the close to Book III) or towards the beginning of the first scientific discussion (149ff.) of Book I.

[25] In the *Genethliacon Lucani* (*Silu.* II.7.76) he famously – and influentially – praised the *docti furor arduus Lucreti*.

[26] Aper records the preference of archaising *littérateurs* for Lucretius over Virgil (*Dial.* 23.1). The passage is interesting evidence for a partial revival of interest in the antique style of pre-Virgilian authors, either in the late first century AD (the dialogue being set in 75) or at the turn of the second century (when it was very probably written).

[27] I believe, *pace* the arguments of several scholars (see Deufert (1996) 32–40 for thorough treatment), that both passages existed in Lucretius' manuscript at his death, regardless of whether he intended to leave both standing in a final version (cf. n. 30 below).

[28] For brief discussion on the attitude of Quintilian to Lucretius (but without treatment of textual matters), see Giri (1911), Savage (1952) and Poignault (1999c).

at III.1.4), he argued for the importance of making one's ora-
tory pleasant to listen to: *qua ratione se Lucretius dicit prae-
cepta philosophiae carmine esse complexum*; *namque hac, ut
est notum, similitudine utitur*: ac ... liquore. The parenthesis *ut
est notum* is again indicative: Lucretius' simile had evidently,
by the 90s AD, received the status of a *locus classicus* that
Quintilian fully expected his readers, even learners (the natural
audience of the work), to know.[29] Quintilian's own citation
contains the easy error of *ac* in the unimportant opening conjunction of the passage (*nam* transmitted in Lucretius' manuscripts at IV.11, but *sed* at I.936);[30] the more grave error of
inspirant (*adspirant* B) for Lucretius' *contingunt* at I.938 =
IV.13 probably reflects in origin a slip of his memory: since
inspirare is an odd verb to supplant *contingere* by mistake, and
there is no classical usage to support it, it is possible, as suggested by Haupt (see Lachmann *ad loc.*), that Quintilian wrote
inspergunt (if not *aspergunt*), reflecting his incorrect recollection
and not an otherwise unknown authorial variant, and that this
verb was banalised in Quintilian's tranmission to *inspirant*.[31]
Given the nature of these errors, it is probable that Quintilian
cited the passage from memory; if so, it is idle to speculate
whether he based the quotation upon Book I or IV. The same
author mentioned Lucretius thrice elsewhere, as a natural philosopher alongside Varro *in Latinis* (I.4.4), as a poet whose
achievements Virgil was brave enough to surpass (XII.11.27),
and as an author who is *difficilis* for the student (X.1.87).

---

[29] For a succinct survey of this simile throughout Latin writers from Lucretius to Sisebut
(*c* 565–620), see Madoz (1947; 1952).

[30] Kenney's First Law posits that any monosyllabic particle opening a poetic verse can be
corrupted into any other, and it seems perfectly possible that *sed* is a corruption of *nam*
(causal, not adversative, force being appropriate after I.935 = IV.10); of the nine times
where *uel uti* follows an opening monosyllable in Lucretius, six follow *nam* (and none
sed), with *sed*, *et* and *quae* each having one instance. That Jerome and Nonius both
support *ac* will be discussed below. For further discussion of Lucretian repetition and
the question of interpolation in the poem, see Butterfield (2013).

[31] An alternative suggestion, motivated by Jerome's paraphrase of this quotation with
inlinimus (see section C below), would be that Quintilian wrongly wrote *inliniunt*,
perhaps having interpreted *contingunt* as a compound of *tingere* not *tangere* (as
Lucretius probably intended), which was corrupted to the much commoner verb
inspirant.

We now move into the second century AD, to the *Epistulae* of Pliny the Younger (*c.* 61–*c.* 112), in which we find only one Lucretian citation. At *Epp.* IV.18.1 he produced a casual paraphrase of three Lucretian words that close I.832 and III.260: Pliny spoke of the *inopia ac potius, ut Lucretius ait, egestate patrii sermonis.* As with three of Seneca's citations (*Tranq. an.* 2.14, *Epp.* 95.11, 106.8), Pliny used the bare *ut Lucretius ait* (or *ut a. L.*), which suggests that Lucretius' turn of phrase was too well known to require further context for an educated readership. Nothing of weight can be inferred from Pliny's rearrangement of word order, save perhaps his distancing himself from a direct poetic quotation of a poet he seemingly did not hold in high esteem (and mentioned nowhere else).

Marcus Cornelius Fronto (*c.* 96–*c.* 166) does not mention Lucretius in his extant writings but provided a partial citation of I.926–7 = IV.1–2 (*auia Pieridum peragro loca nullius ante | trita solo*) without mention of Lucretius:[32] *nullius ante, nisi unius Caii Sallusti, trita solo, sensum dictu periculosum et paene obstetricium pulcherrimo cultu et honestissimo ornatu protulisti* (*De eloquentia* 3.2). Nothing of textual significance can be concluded from this. Two other minor echoes can be cited from his fragmentary treatise *De feriis Alsiensibus*.[33] We know, however, that Fronto had an active interest in Lucretius' poem, not least its language,[34] for he was asked by his tutee, the Emperor Marcus Aurelius, for excerpts of Lucretius' work (*Ad Antoninum* IV.1.3), as though he could easily provide them; given the Emperor's general wording,[35] I do not think that a known 'edited' selection of Lucretius is envisaged. Fronto termed Lucretius *sublimis* (*De eloq.* 1.2), included him among praiseworthy poets (*Epp. ad M. Caes.* IV.3.2) and mentioned him as relaxing holiday reading (*De fer. Als.* 3.1); at *De eloq.* 4.4 he stated that audiences are

---

[32] This apparent omission of Lucretius' name may be owing rather to the lacuna preceding the letter's text before *nullius*.

[33] 232.10–11 ~ Lucr. VI.140–1; 233,11–12 ~ Lucr. IV.962.

[34] For Lucretian reminiscences in Fronto (and Gellius) see Marache (1956).

[35] *mitte mihi aliquid, quod tibi disertissimum uideatur, quod legam, uel tuum aut Catonis aut Ciceronis aut Sallustii aut Gracchi aut poetae alicuius … etiam si qua Lucretii aut Enni excerpta habes* εὐφωνότατα, ἁδρά *et sicubi* ἤθους ἐμφάσεις.

inconsistent to moan about the sound of Sallustian passages: *Ennium ... et Accium et Lucretium ampliore iam mugitu personantis tamen tolerant.*

Aulus Gellius (*c.* 125/8–*c.* 200), like all authors treated so far, spent most of his life amidst the upper echelons of Rome. He cited five passages from *DRN* directly (seven verses in full or in part),[36] drawing on Books I, II, IV and VI; in two further instances[37] he demonstrates knowledge of Lucretian vocabulary from Book I and apparently Book IV. There are few significant deviations from the text of the direct Lucretian tradition: *aut* for *et* in I.304 at V.15.4 (an easy slip of memory),[38] omission of *ut* in II.1153–4 at XIII.21.21 (probably an error of Gellius' transmission, given that the resultant verse is unmetrical), corruption of *radit* to the meaningless *tradit* in IV.528–9 at X.26.9 (probably again corrupted in Gellius' transmission, perhaps influenced by the preceding *praeterea*). However, Gellius' citation of II.1153–4 presents the earliest independently correct reading found in the indirect tradition, *enim mortalia* against the corrupt *et inmortalia* of the direct tradition. This could suggest that *enim* was corrupted to *et in* in the direct tradition in or after the third century AD, or – perhaps more probably – that Gellius had contact with a branch of the tradition that had separated from that which survives to the ninth century during the first two centuries of the poem's transmission and prior to the occurrence of this particular corruption in the latter.

Last in this section stands Lucius Apuleius 'Platonicus' (*c.* 125–late second century), who mostly lived outside Rome (where he temporarily studied in his youth), primarily on the North African coast in Numidia. He cited Lucretius only twice

---

[36] I.304 (V.15.4), II.1153–4 (XIII.21.21), IV.223–4 (I.21.6), 528–9 (X.26.9), VI.1275 (XII.10.8).

[37] At XVI.5.7 Gellius showed knowledge of Lucretius' employing *uescus* (of *sal*) at I.326, without obvious dependence upon Festus' source (Verrius Flaccus?). At II.26.19 he perhaps alluded to Lucretius' use of *caesia* at IV.1161: although the adjective was used by Cicero (*De nat. deo.* I.83, of the eyes of Minerva) and Hyginus (*Fab.* 165.2, of Minerva), Lucretius' collocation of the feminine with *Palladium* ('little Minerva/ Athena') suggests that he was Gellius' probable source.

[38] Although Gellius could have cited this verse because of Seneca's prominent quotation of it, we should not suppose that he could not have accessed a text of Book I otherwise (see previous note).

in his extant works but other echoes are evident.[39] His most relevant work is *De deo Socratis* (late second century): at 1.7 he drew explicitly on Lucr. V.575–6 in discussing the theory of the moon's luminescence: [sc. *luna*] *tota proprii candoris expers, alienae lucis indigua, denso corpore sed leui ceu quodam speculo radios solis obstitit uel aduersi usurpat et, ut uerbis utar Lucreti, notham iactat de corpore lucem.*[40] Nothing should be concluded from the transfer of *nothus* from *lumine* to *lucem* (in lieu of the omitted *suam*) given Apuleius' casual prose citation. Later in the same work, at 10.7, he directly cited the three verses VI.96–8: his manuscripts record the unmetrical *propter alia* for *propterea quia* of 97, undoubtedly a later scribal corruption in Apuleius' transmission; the appearance of the hypermetric *propugnantibus* for *pugnantibus* in 98 could also be the result of scribal dittography of the initial *p* of that verb, misread as the abbreviation for *pro* (ꝓ). Apuleius preceded this second citation with *nonne audis quid super tonitru Lucretius facundissime disserat?*, a question in a tone expecting his audience to be sufficiently familiar with a discussion buried deep within *DRN* VI. We can tentatively conclude, then, that by the late second century, educated speakers of Latin in certain areas outside Italy, even on the North African coast, were expected to have ready access to *DRN* prior to Apuleius' own writings.

Finally, we come to the chronologically insecure fabulist Hyginus, who in his 57th fable (Istheneboea) cited Lucr. V.905 (*prima leo, postrema draco, media ipsa, Chimera*), later paraphrasing it in his 151st (offspring of Typhon and Echidna).[41] In both instances the poetic quotation is introduced abruptly and without Lucretius' name. Hyginus nowhere else cited Lucretius or showed any obvious traces of Lucretian influence, which suggests that he obtained this one-verse summary of the Chimaera at second hand, from a work now lost (an earlier mythological encyclopaedia?) that perhaps neglected to name its poetic source.

---

[39] See Barra (1960–1) 100ff., di Giovine (1981), Bajoni (1994), Lucarini (1999); broader discussion is provided by Mattiaci (1986) and Harrison (2000) Chapters 4–5.

[40] The thorny text of this Apuleian passage is discussed by Tomasco (1980).

[41] *Chimaera in Lycia quae priorem partem leonis, figuram posteriorem draconis habebat, media ipsa Chimaera.*

(B) Sextus Pompeius Festus (Verrius Flaccus and Paulus Diaconus)

In the late second century AD the grammarian Sextus Pompeius Festus (dates uncertain) abridged the lexicon *De uerborum significatu* of Verrius Flaccus (*c.* 55 BC–*c.* AD 20), which does not survive. The first half of Festus' compilation was lost in the late mediaeval period and the primary extant manuscript (the codex Farnesianus = Naples IV.A.3) is badly damaged by fire; for the remainder of the text there exists the further summary of Festus' abridgement by Paulus Diaconus (*c.* 720–99). In what survives of Festus between these two witnesses, we find sixteen Lucretian citations (seventeen verses cited in full or in part) drawn from all books except V (no doubt a coincidental absence).[42] Since Festus' quotations of Lucretius were seemingly drawn at second hand from Verrius Flaccus (who certainly had direct access to *DRN*), and in Paulus' case at a further remove,[43] the scope for manuscript error is greater, reducing the chances that deviations reflect error in a Lucretian manuscript. Since, however, the focus of all three scholars fell upon words of lexical interest, there is more security regarding the quoted words cognate with the given lemma.

Although deviations from the direct Lucretian tradition (usually in error) are relatively common, the majority are mistakes of Festus' (or Paulus') transmission, if we credit Festus with an intelligent mind that could construe Latin. The examples of misdivision, loss and/or confusion of letters are: *tu es corsales* (= *cor sales?*) for -*t uesco sale* in I.326 at Fest. Paul. 506,10–12 (s.u. *impendent*; preceding text damaged); *tergaios* for *inter graios* in I.640 at Fest. 314,2–4 (s.u. *quamde*); *narde florem nectare qui flaribus halet* for *nardi florem nectar qui naribus halat* in II.848 at Fest. 160,20–1 (s.u. *nectar*); *momento si* for *momine uti* in III.188 at Fest. Paul. 123,17=18 (s.u. *momen*), where the lemma guarantees that Flaccus and Festus at least originally recorded a form of *momen*;

---

[42] No previous analysis has tackled Festus' quotations of Lucretius, even in brief.

[43] Paulus was based primarily in Benevento but possibly had connections with Charlemagne; although he could have known Lucretius' text directly, there is no evidence that he applied such knowledge when abridging Festus. For more on his life and works see Chiesa (2000).

obstita (X : *obsita* W) for the correct *obstipa* (Ω) in IV.516 at Fest. 210,15–17 (s.u. *obstipum*), where once again the lemma suggests that the corruption of -*p*- to -*t*- postdates Festus;[44] *nexari* for *nixari* (Ω) in VI.836 at Fest. 182,32–3 (s.u. *nictari*). In the last case it is possible, given that the Lucretian instance is the first cited after the lemma, that Flaccus/Festus had access to a codex that presented *nictari* for *nexari*, a reading subsequently corrupted to *nexari* in Festus' transmission. There are two errors which, by contrast, could be owing to Flaccus' (rather than Festus' or Paulus') mistaken memory: the banalisation *terra* for *tellus* in the last two words of I.7 = I.228 at Fest. Paul. 59,27 (s.u. *daedalam*), and (less probably) *halet* for *halat* in II.848 at Fest. 160,20–1. It is unlikely that either of these errors represents an error in the Lucretian manuscript that Flaccus or Festus used. Finally, Festus twice presents a correct reading against the erring direct tradition: the retention of *ob* (omitted by easy haplography before *obscuram* in Ω)[45] in I.639 at Fest. 314,2–4, and *nec* for the corrupt *ne* of Ω in II.840 at Fest. 426,9–11. Although it is possible that the direct tradition of Lucretius already exhibited these corruptions, and that Flaccus/Festus had access to a manuscript from a different branch of the tradition, it is more economic to posit that, in a time when Lucretius was still widely read, these errors did not exist in higher-quality manuscripts of Lucretius, and that they are subsequent mistakes of the direct tradition. Festus, then, whose own geographical location is unknown, can tell us very little indeed about the state of Lucretius' text in his own time, not least since his knowledge of Lucretius is probably drawn from Verrius Flaccus alone.

(C)   The Church Fathers (Tertullian, Lactantius, Arnobius, Augustine, Hieronymus)

Epicureanism's vigorously anti-religious stance and stout rejection of an incorporeal and immortal soul could hardly escape hostile discussion at the hands of the Christian Latin Fathers.

---

[44] I follow most editors in accepting *necesse* (Q, Festus) over *necessu* (O).
[45] The easy restoration of *ob* by O³ was very probably independent of Festus.

Nevertheless, direct quotations of the poet occur in just three writers in this fecund field of literature: Tertullian, Lactantius and Hieronymus. In addition, a unique paraphrase of a Lucretian verse can be found in Arnobius of Sicca and a single mention of his name in Augustine. These Christian authors' use of Lucretius (or Epicureanism more generally) has been studied with some interest, albeit very rarely with focus on textual matters.[46]

We begin with Quintus Septimius Florens Tertullianus (c. 160– c. 220), who only cited a single Lucretian verse (I.304) but twice (De anima 5.6, Adu. Marc. IV.8.3). Given that this was Tertullian's sole direct citation of Lucretius, and that the verse was also quoted by Seneca the Younger (Epp. 106.8) and Gellius (V.15.4), he probably had no ready access to Lucretius as he wrote in Carthage (although he could have read it already) and employed this one quotation indirectly. None of the Lucretian parallels and reminiscences elsewhere adduced in Tertullian's writings shows any close familiarity with Lucretius' text.[47] Despite Apuleius' concurrent close knowledge of the text, its availability on the North African coast may have been patchy.

Lucius Caelius Firmianus Lactantius (c. 240–c. 320) offers certainly the most concerted anti-Epicurean attack surviving from antiquity. Further, Lactantius' knowledge of Epicureanism plainly came from close engagement with DRN (as well as with Cicero and Epicurus directly). Lucretian influence pervades much of his work,[48] but for our present purposes we find twenty-five passages (sixty verses in part or in full) cited in thirty-one instances throughout the Institutiones diuinae and its Epitome, De ira and De opificio Dei, and drawn from all six books of DRN. The textual divergences from the direct tradition are few.[49] Several errors are

---

[46] The best general treatments remain Philippe (1895; 1896) and Hagendahl (1958), although some more specific material is available in Dal Pane (1905–6; 1906–7). For a broader survey of Epicureanism and the Church Fathers see Ferguson (1990) 2298– 2326 and Jones (1992) Chapter 4.

[47] See Borleffs (1932), Otón Sobrino (1989), Uglione (2001).

[48] See Brandt (1891a; 1891b), Rossetti (1928) 137–50, Niccolosi (1946), Rapisarda (1947), Bufano (1951), Giancotti (1980), Smolak (1995), Althoff (1997), Goulon (1999), Schrijvers (1999).

[49] I ignore errors of individual branches of the Lactantian tradition and irrelevant ortho- graphical variations (e.g. nil ~ nihil).

probably natural mistakes of Lactantius' memory: the less striking pronoun *sese* for *caput* and the frequentative *ostentabat* for *ostendebat* in I.64 at *Inst.* III.27.10; *putandum* for *fatendum* in I.205 at *De ira* 10.16; *ipse* for *saepe* in II.1102 at *Inst.* III.17.10;[50] *uertere se* for *uertier* and *et* for *nec* (1200) in V.1198–1202 at *Inst.* II.3.11; *hominum* for *igitur* (perhaps prompted by recollection of Lucr. II.14: *o miseras hominum mentes, o pectora caeca!*) and the unlucretian *limite* for *tramite* in VI.24–8 at *Inst.* VII.27.6. The strange error *fulgentia* (modifying *templa*) for *relatum* in II.1001 at *Inst.* VII.12.5 presumably springs from a mistaken reminiscence of *fulgentia templa* at V.491. The substitution of *agere* for *gerere* in V.167 at *Inst.* VII.3.13 could be Lactantius' own error, if he accepted the resultant hiatus *causā | agere*; if not, this discrepancy must reflect corruption in Lactantius' transmission. It is merely his casual manner of reference that explains his citing I.83 at *Inst.* I.21.14 as if it immediately followed I.101:[51] he therefore wrote *quae peperit* at the beginning of I.83 for continuous syntax, since Lucretius' *religio peperit* would have required repetition of *religio*, already in 101; his additional insertion of *saepe* after *peperit* represents nothing more than a weak adverb filling the metre,[52] although it can only scan if its latter syllable suffers *productio in arsi* (which Lactantius might have allowed given the Virgilian parallels and, if he knew them, the two illusory examples of such diastole presented by Lucretius' manuscripts at II.27 and V.1049).[53] The confusion among Lactantian manuscripts between *miseras* (R : *miserae* B) and *stultas* (SPG) in II.14 at *Inst.* I.21.48 probably stems from his wrongly remembering *stultas*, subsequently corrected by a more educated reader, thereby affecting part of the transmission (cf. esp. *miseras o stultas* of H). Two less

---

[50] It is noteworthy that, later in this same paragraph, Lactantius (or his manuscripts) misquote the beginning of a Ciceronian verse (*Poem.* 6.37 *ipse suos*) with the same two words as the Lucretian misquotation, *ipse suas*.

[51] The same looseness probably explains *lumen ... ut ait poeta, liquidum atque clarum* (*Inst.* VI.2.6), which intermingles Lucr. III.1 and V.281, although *poeta* is not used of Lucretius elsewhere by Lactantius. Similarly, he drew loosely upon II.992 at *Inst.* V.6.12 (*pater idem omnibus*) and 14.17 (*cunctis idem pater*).

[52] Given Lactantius' conception of Lucretius as most virulently anti-religious, it is somewhat surprising that he did not insert the more forceful, and metrically simple, *semper*

[53] See Butterfield (2006–7b) 99–100 with n. 90.

marked divergences from the direct tradition could be corruptions in Lactantius' source or his own transmission rather than trivial slips of the memory: *animos* for *animum* in IV.7 at *Inst.* I.16.3 and *primum* for *primus* in V.336 at *Inst.* III.16.14. Probable corruptions in Lactantius' own manuscript tradition (*contra* Bodelon García (1988) 40) are the unmetrical and/or unmeaning errors *quoque quae* for *quo quaeque* and *proferri per* for *proferrier* in I.205–7 at *De ira* 10.16, and *cupidinis* for *cuppedinis* (O : *cupedinis* Q) in VI.24–8 at *Inst.* VII.27.6. All of this provides abundant evidence for Lactantius' intimate knowledge of the complete text of *DRN*, allowing him to cite from memory.

By contrast, in a few instances, Lactantius' readings are correct against the direct tradition: *possint* against *possent* (Ω) in I.207 at *De ira* 10.16; *periclis* against *perictis* (Ω : *periclis* Q^2) in II.15 at *Inst.* I.21.48; *terram* [SP^2 : *terra* BH] *sed quod missum est* against *terras et sed quod missus* (Ω) in II.1000 at *Inst.* VII.12.5; the retention of *in* (om. Ω) before *deserta* and *recedens* for *decedens* (O : *decendens* V) in II.1102 at *Inst.* III.17.10; *immortalis* for *immortales* ($O^{a.c.}Q^{a.c.}$) in III.612 at *Inst.* VII.12.26; *aetherius* against *aerius* (*haerius* $O^{a.c.}$) in III.1044 at *Inst.* III.17.28; *restet transire* against *re & transirest* (Ω) in V.227 at *De opif.* 3.2; *recto* against *recta* (Ω : *recto* O^2) in VI.28 at *Inst.* VII.27.6. On the strength of this evidence – several examples from a relatively small corpus – it seems very probable that the manuscript Lactantius accessed in North Africa was not an antecedent of the direct tradition but had diverged at a prior stage.

Proceeding chronologically, we must mention the Lucretian echo in Arnobius (†*c.* 330), probably an associate of Lactantius.[54] In his *Aduersus nationes* at III.10 he evidently alluded to Lucr. IV.1168 (*at tumida*[55] *et mammosa Ceres est ipsa ab Iaccho*): *auet animus atque ardet, in Chalcidicis illis magnis atque in palatiis caeli deos deasque conspicere intectis corporibus atque nudis, ab* <u>*Iuccho Cererem*</u>, *Musa ut praedicat Lucretia,* <u>*mammosam*</u>.[56]

---

[54] See Klussmann (1867) and Hagendahl (1958) 9–88.

[55] So Bernays for the meaningless *iamina* Ω.

[56] The curious parenthesis *Musa ut praedicat Lucretia* can be defended by taking the last word adjectivally ('as the Lucretian (poetic) Muse terms [her]'), dismissing Sabbaeus' emendation *Lucretii*.

The Lucretian echoes pervading the work evince that Arnobius was well immersed in Lucretius' poem, although there is no evidence that he lived or worked outside his native Sicca in Numidia. This serves as further evidence, then, of Lucretius' availability along the North African coast around the turn of the fourth century.

Eusebius Sophronius Hieronymus (Jerome, c. 347–420) cited Lucretius only twice, and in two further instances offered a close echo.[57] At *Epp.* 133.3 he recorded the three verses cited by Quintilian, I.936–8 = IV.11–13 with numerous divergences from Ω: *ac* in lieu of *sed* / *nam* (an error also found in Quintilian and Nonius), the unmetrical banalisation *damus* for *dare conantur*, omission of *pocula* before *circum*, and *inlinimus dulci mellis* for *contingunt mellis dulci*. These errors evidently spring from Jerome's casual citation of the verse from memory: that *ac* is also found in Quintilian, as well as a verb (compounded with *in-*) in lieu of *contingunt*, suggest that Jerome learnt of these famous verses through an indirect route, perhaps from Quintilian's popular work itself; if Quintilian did write *inliniunt* for *contingunt* (see n. 31 above), this connection would be certain.[58] The other citation was also probably drawn indirectly: at *Epp.* 125.18 Jerome cited, without error, Lucr. V.905 (introduced by *iuxta illud poeticum*, omitting Lucretius' name), a verse quoted twice in Hyginus' *Fabulae* (see above) that was presumably widely known, although its authorship could not have been (even to Jerome). At *Epp.* 77.11, Jerome imitated II.28 (*nec citharae reboant laqueata aurataque templa*): *aurata tecta templorum reboans in sublime alleluia quatiebat*. The phrase *tecta templorum* ('temple ceilings'; for the collocation, cf. Isid. *Etym.* XV.8), as distinct from the simple *templa* of Lucretius' direct tradition, shows some similarity to Macrobius (see section E below), who cites the verse with *tecta* at *Sat.* VI.4.21, but *tempe* at *Sat.* VI.2.5. Finally, discussing the translation of Greek in his commentary upon Paul's *Epistola ad Ephesianos* (I.1.4) he

---

[57] See Opelt (1972).

[58] If the chronology supports dating Nonius' work prior to this letter of Jerome (which cannot be guaranteed), we would still not posit him as a possible source of the citation, because he quoted only IV.11–12 (to *conantur*) at both 190,25–7 and 413,17–19.

effectively cited I.139 (*propter egestatem linguae et rerum nouit-atem*): *unde et nos propter paupertatem linguae et rerum nouitatem, et sicut quidam ait, quod sit Graecorum et sermo latior et lingua felicior, conabimur … uim uerbi quodam explicare circuitu*. He therefore changed only *egestatem* to the unmetrical *paupertatem* (a noun nevertheless found thrice in Lucretius), perhaps to disguise the fact that this was a hexameter cited from a controversial author.[59] Bare mention of Lucretius was made twice elsewhere: Jerome claimed to have read one or more commentaries on him at *Apol. adu. libr. Ruf.* I.16 (cited in the Introduction n. 12) and at III.29 he mentioned that, *de natura rerum*, he could *si esset locus … uel Lucretii opiniones iuxta Epicurum, uel Aristotelis iuxta Peripa-teticos, uel Platonis atque Zenonis secundum Academicos et Stoicos dicere*, a claim not supported by the scant knowledge of Epicurean-ism shown elsewhere in his corpus.

Finally, we come to Aurelius Augustinus Hipponensis (354–430), who in his vast corpus never quoted Lucretius and men-tioned him in only one passage: at *De util. cred.* 4.10 he instanced Lucretius' assertion that the soul is corporeal and perishes on death as an example of one believing the incredible, polemic potentially drawn indirectly from Lactantius alone. Otherwise, Augustine was silent, perhaps reflecting his claim (*Ep.* 118.12) that Epicurean (and Stoic) schools had by his time reached a state of comparative inactivity.[60]

(D) Nonius

We move to the work of a second scholar devoted to elucidating ancient Latin, the twenty-book *De compendiosa doctrina* of Non-ius Marcellus (*fl. c.* 400).[61] Some solid work on Nonius' Lucretian

---

[59] It is not impossible that *et sicut quidam ait* is a corruption of *sicut quidam ait et* following the quasi-hexameter, with Jerome understandably reluctant to underline the Lucretian appropriation in the preceding words.

[60] The case made by Pizzolato (1971) is not convincing. For Lucretius' influence on Cyprian (†258) and Prudentius (348–c. 413), neither of whom mentioned Lucretius, see respectively Pascal (1903), and Lohmann (1882) 50–9, Brakman (1920), Rapisarda (1950).

[61] The dating of Nonius is notoriously difficult; for a valuable discussion, concluding with a tentative dating of *De compendiosa doctrina* to around 400, see Deufert (2001).

citations was done over a century ago by Lindsay,[62] who formed a potential list of Nonius' various sources, concluding that the grammarian had access to a complete text of *DRN*. In his wake, and that of Strzelecki (1936, 23–9),[63] Rychlewska (1964; cf. (1954) 123) developed the argument that some Lucretian citations were nevertheless drawn from indirect sources (scholia, glossaries, other grammarians) and therefore limited her study to analysing the nature of Nonius' manuscript for the sixty-one citations she deemed to be direct. Nevertheless her treatment is unsatisfactory, and White (1980) demonstrated that there is no good reason to suppose that the majority, if not all, of the Lucretian citations were not all obtained directly. Rychlewska therefore ignored a large body of the available evidence, judging with dubious legitimacy (1964, 281–3) that Nonius had access to a quite separate and more complete recension of the poem from the direct tradition (as it stood in the fourth century), an assertion based on a number of divergences that can generally be treated as simple corruptions of transmission. Mazzacane (1984), in an incomplete and inaccurate survey, re-examined the Lucretian citations, concluding that 'Nonio avrebbe avuto cioè a disposizione un esemplare di Lucrezio diverso da quello, a noi noto, della tradizione diretta' (175), which may well be true, although the suggestion (176) that Nonius could have had access to the tradition of Probius (if such there was), distinct from that which she believed Cicero edited, is mere guess-work.

Nonius cited 134 Lucretian verses (in 111 instances) in part or in full, drawn from 101 passages distributed, relatively regularly, throughout the work.[64] Remarkably, only three of these quotations are also cited by extant pre-Nonian authors.[65] Of Nonius' citations, forty-one are quoted as the primary definition of the lemma; the rest are secondary quotations thereafter. The

---

[62] Lindsay (1901; 1905).

[63] The major point of his argument was that Nonius used Flavius Caper as the primary basis for his citations in Book III, a theory that White (1980) showed to be without force.

[64] The citations are distributed thus (total number of verses: of instances cited: of distinct passages): I (21:17:14), II (27:25:23), III (23:18:17), IV (25:19:16), V (23:20:19), VI (15:12:12).

[65] I.304 (Seneca, Gellius, Tertullian), II.576 (Festus), IV.528–9 (Gellius).

(D) Nonius

transmitted accuracy of these citations is not particularly impressive:[66] sixty-one of the 111 instances (55 per cent) present a definite error; thirty-four (31 per cent) preserve the text as found in the direct tradition, only once exhibiting a conjunctive error (V.1094).[67] However, in twenty-four instances (some of which also exhibit an error elsewhere in the citation, and are therefore included in the preceding sixty-one) Nonius recorded correct readings against the erring direct tradition. The various discrepancies can tentatively be classified as follows:

(a) Mistakes either of Nonius' memory or of the manuscript tradition he drew upon: *perfringere* in I.70 (*effringere* Priscian : *confringere* Ω) at 506,37–507,1 (s.u. *cupiret*); *degimus* for *degitur* in II.16 at 278,17 (s.u. *degere*); *adulescendi* for *alescendi* in II.1130 at 248,3–4 (s.u. *adolere/adolescere*); *ac* for *et* in III.8 at 420,37–9 (*et* cited correctly at 306,8–10) (s.u. *uis*); *perculsa est exin* for *percussast exim* in III.160 at 420,37–9 (s.u. *icit*); *longiter* for *longius* in III.676 at 515,16–17 (s.uu. *longinque, longiter*); *inuadi* for *insinuari* in III.722 at 159,32–5 (s.u. *priua*); *eorum* for *corpora* in III.723 at 159,32–5 (s.u. *priua*); *expleri* for *explere* in III.1004 at 424,28–30 (s.u. *expleri*); *ac* for *nam* in IV.11 at 190,25–7 (s.u. *taetrum*); *pauit* for *radit* (Ω : *tradit* Gell.) in IV.528 at 453,7–9 (s.u. *transgressus*); *parturiendi* for *partum* in V.865 at 13,7–8 (s.u. *ueterina*); *tremunt* for *fremunt* (Marullus : *premunt* Ω) in V.1064 at 221,21–2 (s.u. *rictus*); *ruina ... geli* for *geli ... ruina* in VI.156 at 487,4–5 (s.u. *gelu*). I regard all of these as errors of Nonius' memory, or as mistakes of his transcription from his source, excepting III.676, 1004 and IV.11, the first two of which exhibit incorrect readings that are defended by their respective lemmata, the last of which may well be drawn from Quintilian or a manuscript family displaying that same reading.[68]

(b) Mistakes presumably of Nonius' transmission are: *nouus dictor* for *nobis uictor* in I.75 at 381,30–1; *ceratam* for *certam* and *uident* for *uiderent* in I.107 at 205,8–9; *surdae* for *sua de* and *aliqua* for *alique* in I.191 at 115,7–8; *ici* for *dici* and *quodcumque* for *quocumque* in I.470 at 204,3–4; *et terrae* for *e terra* in II.2 at

---

[66] One should note, however, that, excepting the corrections of F³, who seemingly had access to a manuscript markedly better than the archetype, the number of errors would be far greater.

[67] I disregard *nihil* (Nonius Ω) for *nil* at II.815, since this orthographical variation, pervasive in manuscripts, bears no textual significance.

[68] The apparent mistake of *classem lateque creari* for *belli simulacra cientis* in citing II.41 at 503,24–5 is treated below as fr. **XVI**.

63

The indirect tradition of Lucretius

402,13–14; *abet* for *auet* (O(?)S : *habet* in ras. O²) in II.265 at
517,24–5; *squamigerae* for *squamigerum* in II.343 at 158,38–40;
neque adam for *ne quaedam* in II.498 at 136,8–9; *nec* for *neque*
(correctly cited at 252,38–9) in II.651 at 408,24; *lanigene* for
lanigerae (correctly cited at 208,24–5) in II.661 at 80,27–9; the
addition of *in* before *principiis* in II.815 at 482,5–6; *actus* for
auctumst (*auctum est* S : *autumst* O); *una se* for *unica sed* and
innumera for *innumerali* in II.1086 at 131,5–6; *conuerterit amnes*
for *conuertere omnes*, *aetheris* for *aetheriis* and *suffere* for *suffire*
in II.1097–8 at 197,2–4; *naturae* for *natura* in II.1116–17 at
160,13–15; *aureas* for *aurea* in II.1154 at 205,21–2; *acuta* for
aucta in II.1160 at 115,5–6; *et* (306,8–10) and *aeui* (420,37–9) for
haedi and *ui* for *uis* (420,37–9; correctly cited at 306,8–10) in
III.7–8 at 306,8–10 and 420,37–9; *magnibus* for *manibus* in III.52
at 446,4–5; *eicit* for *et icit* in III.160 at 420,37–9; *principis* for
principiis in III.318 at 184,10–11; *rati* for *errat* in III.676 at
515,16–17; *horritico* for *horrifico* and *cobus* for *busto* in III.906
at 94,2–3; *Helicaoniadum* for *Heliconiadum* in III.1037 at 481,25–
7; *uere* for *uepres* in IV.62 at 458,13–15 (*uepres* is correctly cited
s.h.u. at 231,17–19); *eis* for *esse* in IV.118 at 209,15–16; *sedere*
for *edere* in IV.1010 at 192.26–8; *iocis* for *locis* in IV.1242 at
73,6–7; *diluuium* for *diluuiem* in V.225 at 203,26–8 (s.u. *diluium*
… *feminino*); *torte* for *forte* and the omission of *ne*, *ex* and *et* in
V.890 at 13,9–10; *ratiore* for *ratione* in V.910 at 103,22–3;
ychimnique for *scymnique* in V.1036 at 457,14–15; *cannit u* for
gannitu in V.1070 at 17,7–8 (*gannitu* correctly cited at 450,7–8);
uocis for *uoces* in V.1070 at 450,7–8; *uare* for *uapore* in V.1095 at
506,15–17; *infestu* for *infesto* in VI.782 at 394,18–20; *ados* for
odos (Lambinus : *odor* Ω) in VI.952 at 487,7–8; *spurcitiis idem
subrutunda* for *spurcities eadem subus haec iucunda* (It. : *ciuunda*
O : *inunda* Q : *iuunda* S) in VI.977 at 394,21–3. The prevalence of
error shows the negligence that had corrupted the Nonian manuscript tradition by the time of its archetype (saec. VI/VII?).
(c) Ambiguous instances, which cannot be confidently attributed to (a)
or (b), are: *uiuendi* for *uidendi* in II.1038 at 172,17–18; *denique* for
donique in II.1116–17 at 160,13–15 and for *donec* in II.1130
at 248,3–4; *consimili* for *consimile* in III.8 at 306,8–10 and
420,37–9; *obrutiscat* for *obbrutescat* in III.545 at 77,26–7; *mentes*
for *mentem* in III.765 at 181,3–4; *potitur* for *potitus* in III.1038 at
481,25–7; *iuuantque* for *iuuatque* in IV.3 at 252,19–20; *pluuiis* for
fluuiis in IV.219 at 247,12–14 (cited correctly at 311,1–2); *aspera*
for *asperiora* in IV.529 at 453,7–9; *cauanti* for *cubanti* in IV.952
at 218,25–6; *patri* for *patrio* in IV.1212 at 230,12–14; *nos* for *post*
and *partus posset* for *partu possent* in IV.1252–3 at 158,19–21;

64

(D) Nonius

similis for *simili* in V.910 at 103,22–3; *tum* for *alituum* and the
omission of *alis* in V.1039 at 74,16–18; *adulat* (17,7–8) and
adulent (450,7–8) for *adulant* in V.1070 at 17,7–8 and 450,7–8;
auri topet (A^A : *auris et* LB^A) for *auris terget* in VI.119 at
245,7–8; *gladis* (L^1C^A : *gladiis* A^AB^A : *cladis* D^A) in VI.339
at 482,23–4; omission of *sit* before *paruula* in VI.651 at
136,10–12; omission of *sint* before *homini* and of *-que* before
grauisque in VI.781–2 at 394,18–20; *peruolitas* (*peruolitans* D^A)
in VI.952 at 487,7–8; omission of *ea* before *uis* and *omnium*
for *omnis* in VI.1098 at 158,1–2.

(d) Correct readings against the direct tradition are: *tendere* against
tollere (Ω) in I.66 at 411,2–4 (s.u. *tendere*);[69] *cupiret* for *cuperet*
(Ω : corr. O^3) in I.71 at 506,37–507,1; *materie* against *materiae*
(QS : *materia* O) in I.191 at 115,7–8; *candenti* for *dispansae in* in
I.306 at 175,5–7; *cluent* against *ciuent* (Ω Flor. Sang. : corr. O^2)
and *coniuncta duabus* for *coniuncto duobus* (O^a.c.·Q^a.c. : corr.
O^2Q^2) in I.449 at 203,33–204,2; *sanguenque* for *sanguemque*
(O : *sangueque* ψ) in I.837 at 184,12–13 and 224,13; *praeterea*
against *praetere* (Ω : corr. O^2) in II.342 at 158,38–40; *lauit* against
pauit Ω in II.376 at 503,45–6 (s.u. *lauit*);[70] *colores* against *colore*
(Ω) in II.815 at 482,5–6; *creatrix* against *cracreatrix* (Ω : corr.
O^2Q^2) in II.1117 at 160,13–15; *quae* against *qua* (Ω) in II.1160 at
115,5–6; *ut pletate* against *ut pietate* (O : *suppletate* Q : *suppleta*
S) in II.1170 at 225,18–19; *uis* for *ui* (Marullus : om. Ω) in III.159
at 124,9–11; *priuas in* against *priua si* (Ω : corr. Q^2) in III.723 at
159,32–5; *alguque* against *algoque* (Ω) in III.732 at 72,13–14 (s.u.
algu); *quae quasi* against *qui quasi* (O : *quasi* Q^a.c. : *quas si* Q^2) in
IV.51 at 199,35–200,1; *cinefactum* against *cinem factum* (Ω) in
III.906 at 94,2–3; *horum* against *harum* (Ω) in IV.118 at 209,15–
16; *in* (om. Ω) before *his* in IV.636 at 95,28–9; *patribus* against
partibus (Ω : corr. Q^2) in IV.1212 at 230,12–14; *quoque* against
quoue (Ω) in V.71 at 415,31–3; *adsiduosque* against *adsiduusque*
(Ω) in V.205 at 487,2–3; *fluuios* against *fluuius* (Ω) in V.516 at

---

[69] Although *tollere* may seem the more striking reading, the raising of one's eyes
conveying the insubordination of Epicurus, three factors recommend Nonius' *tendere*:
(i) the verse is cited under this verb (cf. Housman (1972) vol. III, 801), (ii) the verb
suggests the bending or straining of a bow, which is appropriate to the imagery of the
passage, (iii) the usage is supported by Lucr. IV.325 (*sol etiam caecat, contra si tendere
pergas*) and Verg. *Aen.* II.405 (*ad caelum tendens ardentia lumina frustra*; for *tendere
contra* see *Aen.* V.27, IX.377, 795), which outweigh Ou. *Met.* I.86 (*erectos ad sidera
tollere uultus*). Bernays, Diels, Martin, Leonard–Smith and D. West (1969, 57–63) have
followed Lachmann in accepting Nonius' variant.

[70] Although *pauit* (Ω) is undoubtedly the *lectio difficilior*, Deufert (2010) 58–61 has
demonstrated that *lauit* is correct, despite its not appearing in any edition since du
Fay (1680).

65

13,4–5; *ueterino* against *ueteri non* (Ω) in V.865 at 13,7–8 (s.u. *ueterina*); *porro* against *proporro* (Ω) in V.1039 at 74,16–18; *deserti baubantur* against *desertibus aubantur* (Ω) in V.1071 at 80,30–1 (s.u. *baubari*); *ad* (om. Ω) in VI.364 at 205,25–6; *flammea* against *flammae* (Ω) in VI.642 at 495,15–16; *in ore iacens rictu . . . manebat* for *inoret* (*inhoret* O : *inhorret* Dungal) *iacet rectum . . . mebat* (Ω : *meabat* Dungal) in VI.1195 at 181,24–5. Among these instances, the correct readings at I.306 and VI.1195 are the only significant divergences; the remaining corruptions could well have occurred in the direct tradition in the three or more centuries intervening between Nonius' work and the writing of Ω.[71]

(e) Only in one instance do Nonius and the Lucretian tradition present a shared error that cannot be dismissed as an orthographic triviality: *insita* (thus Ω) against *incita* (Marullus) in citing V.1094 at 506,15–17. However, given the ease of a pronunciational or palaeographical error (in minuscule), this instance cannot bear much evidential weight.

It is clear, then, from the foregoing data that Nonius had direct and seemingly complete access to *DRN*; from (a) it seems probable that his Lucretian manuscript belonged to a branch of the tradition with numerous divergences from that which survives, and presumably multiple intermediaries lie between it and the common ancestor it ultimately shared with OQS. This Lucretian source seems to have been of a generally poor quality: the errors it avoided against the direct tradition (as listed in (d)) are typically very trivial. It is clear from the work of White (1980, 118–26) that Nonius probably worked from lists compiled from his sources, which introduced an intermediary between his reading Lucretius and recording quotations in *De compendiosa doctrina*, thus providing greater scope for error.

Despite these shortcomings, Nonius is the first author to provide readings of genuine benefit to the direct tradition, although his scale of error (especially if the remaining errors of (a) are mistakes of memory) should be borne in mind. More can be said about the two significant instances in which Nonius preserved the

---

[71] *uis* could have been easily lost at line-end at III.159 and *deserti baubantur*, once misdivided as *desertib aub-* would have led to the natural expansion of *-b* to *-bus* (as if *-b'*).

correct reading against the direct tradition, I.306 and VI.1195. At I.306 the correct *candenti* has been displaced in Ω by *dispansae in*,[72] no doubt resulting from accidental copying of *suspensae in*, which appears in the same *sedes* of the previous line, with *dis* perhaps arising from the influence of *dispergitur* in I.309. The *Florilegium Sangallense*, as will be argued in section K below, probably had access to a manuscript descended from the Lucretian archetype, and does not therefore provide independent weight in also offering *dispansae in*. The form *dispansus* is otherwise found in classical authors only in Suetonius,[73] Lucretius rather writing *dispessus* (II.1126, III.988), and the repetition from the preceding line is without force; *candenti*, however, is perfectly Lucretian (cf. *candenti lumine* of the sun at V.721 and VI.1197). At VI.1195, by contrast, we rather see the confusion into which the direct tradition has been led: Nonius preserved *in ore iacens rictu frons tenta manebant*, an intelligible text unlike *in(h)oretiacet rectum frons tenta mebat* (*meabat* Dungal) of Ω. The correct reading of the line has been much disputed,[74] but after some deliberation I am inclined to preserve Nonius' text, with Lambinus' *rictum* and Heinsius' *tumebat*.

(E) Macrobius

We turn now to Ambrosius Theodosius Macrobius (dates uncertain), who in the sixth book of his *Saturnalia* (*c.* 395–430)[75] came to treat echoes and parallelisms of various Republican poets in Virgil's works. The citations of Lucretius have been studied in detail by Pieri (1977),[76] with due attention given to points of textual discrepancy. The two major results of his study can be

---

[72] The Nonian variant was unconvincingly adopted by Lachmann (who conceded that *candenti* 'fortasse verius est altero'), Bernays, Munro, Housman (1972, vol. III, 801), Bailey and Martin.

[73] Gellius (XV.15.4) stated that in early Latin (citing Plaut. *Mil.* 360) *dispessus* was preferable to the expected *dispassus*.

[74] See, alongside the discussion of the commentaries, Sinclair (1981).

[75] The date of Macrobius is a contested matter: Cameron (1966) has argued for a date markedly later than the generally posited 395, around 430; in his wake, Döpp (1978) has suggested that the first decade of the fifth century is more likely.

[76] Prior to Pieri, Bentley had clearly sought to investigate the matter of Macrobius' citations of Lucretius, for he engaged William Wotton to inspect a Cambridge

briefly summarised as follows: there is no clear evidence that
Macrobius made direct use of Lucretius, since he rather drew
upon various works of Virgilian scholarship that cited him (a fact
that neatly explains how Macrobius can cite the same verse in
different places with differing texts); the constant focus upon
Virgil during Macrobius' composition has often resulted in a
'Virgilisation' of the Lucretian text to the detriment of its transmission. Macrobius cites 102 Lucretian verses (in forty-two
instances) in part or in full, drawn from forty passages taken from
all books, with focus on the second, fifth and sixth (and particularly, given the similarities with Virgil's third *Georgic*, the close
of the last).[77] The following discrepancies occur in Macrobius'
citations:

(a) Errors of Macrobius' memory or his manuscript source: *fulgens*
and *renidens* for *fulget* (*s.u.l.*) and *renidet* (*s.u.l.*) in II.27 at
VI.2.5;[78] *cum primum aurora respergit* for *primum aurora nouo
cum spargit* in II.144 at VI.2.5; *componunt ... cientur* for *cam-
porum ... cientes* in II.324 at VI.1.28; *uirentes* for *uigentes* in
II.361 at VI.2.6; *in* for *cum* and *corniferas* for *cornigeras* in
II.367–8 at VI.5.3; *sed* for *et* in V.213 at VI.2.29; *claro* for *largo*
in VI.432 at VI.2.23; *magnum* for *altum* in V.446 at VI.2.24;
obscenum for *opprobrium* in V.1294 at VI.1.63; *sedibus* for *soli-
bus* and *exuperant* for *exibant* in I.1219–21 at VI.2.14.[79]

(b) Errors in transmission: unmetrical *mihi* for *mi* in I.924 at VI.2.3;
citharam for *citharae* and *tempe* for *templa* in II.28 at VI.2.5;
cithara for *citharae* in II.28 at VI.4.21; *lumina* for *lumine* in
II.144 at VI.4.21; *Scipiades* for *Scipiadas* in III.1034 at VI.1.46;
ad for *at* in V.945 at VI.1.64; *liceret* for *licere* in VI.1228 at
VI.2.12.

(c) Ambiguous between (a) and (b): *eas* for *eos* in I.134 at VI.1.48;
abruptis for *abrupti* in II.214 at VI.1.27; *inrigat* for *inriget* in
IV.908 at VI.1.44; *torrens* for *torret* in V.215 at VI.2.29; *his* for
hic in VI.432 at VI.2.23; *artae* for *atrae* in VI.1157 at VI.2.9; *tunc*
and *perturbati* for *tum* and *perturbata* in VI.1182–3 at VI.2.11;

manuscript (Corpus Christi 71, saec. XII) of the author and to transcribe all relevant
passages (cf. Wordsworth (1842) vol. I, 1–5, written in May 1689).
[77] I: 10 verses; II: 24; III: 5; IV: 4; V: 25; VI: 34.
[78] For brief discussion of these instances see Butterfield (2006–7b) 99–100 with n. 90.
[79] I disregard Macrobius' *tristia* against the deficient *tia* (Ω) in citing VI.1220 at VI.2.14
since I deem it corrupt: see Butterfield (2008b) 21–2.

raucas . . . tussis for *rauca . . . tussi* in VI.1189 at VI.2.11; *alis* for *ali* in VI.1227 at VI.2.12.

(d) Macrobius presents the correct reading against Ω in the following instances: *reboant laqueata* against *reboantia queat* OS (*queata* Qᵃ·ᶜ·) in II.28 at VI.2.5 and VI.4.21; *ulla* against *illa* Ω in II.362 at VI.2.6; *fratris* against *fratres* Ω in III.72 at VI.2.15; *modis . . . quietem* against *modi . . . quiete* Ω in IV.907 at VI.1.44; *lychni (s.u. l.)* against *lychini* Ω in V.295 at VI.4.18; *altiuolans* against *alte uolans* Ω in V.433 at VI.2.23; *inde* against *indue* Ω in V.437 at VI.2.23 and VI.4.11; *magna* against *magnas* Ω in V.439 at VI.2.23; *umore* against *umor* Ω in V.447 at VI.2.24; *crearat* against *crearant* OQ (*creant* S) in V.937 at VI.1.65; *ulla* against *uita* and *sonitu* against *sonitus* Ω· in VI.154–5 at VI.4.5; *radiis* against *radis* O (*radi* QS) in VI.874 at VI.4.7; *mortifer aestus* against *mortiferae* Ω and *Cecropis* against *Cecropit* Ω in VI.1138–9 at VI.2.7; *ulceribus*, *coibat* and *tactu* against *uiceribus* OS (*uiscer-* Q), *coibet* Ω and *tacta* Ω in VI.1148–50 at VI.2.9; *mali* against *mari* Ω in VI.1177 at VI.2.13; *spiritus* and *humor* against *spiritum* Ω and *umum* Ω in VI.1186–7 at VI.2.11. It is possible that, in citing *tecta* in II.28 at VI.4.21 (*tempe* at VI.2.5), Macrobius reflects the correct tradition, against the transmitted *templa* of OQS: *templa* could be a simple banalisation in the direct tradition, and Macrobius' *tempe* at VI.2.5 probably reflects an unwelcome recollection of *tempe* at the close of Verg. *Geo.* II.469, cited just above at VI.2.4; further support for *tecta* arrives from the same period in Jerome's verbal borrowing (*aurata tecta*) discussed in section C above.[80]

(e) There is again only one example of a conjunctive error, *calor* for *color* in VI.205 at VI.5.4, an error, owing to the easy confusion of *a* and *o* and Lucretius' frequent use of both nouns, on which little weight can be placed.

From this evidence it seems to me clear enough that Macrobius had indirect access to a less corrupt text (or, more likely, texts) of Lucretius than Nonius and that his own transmission has subjected the poetic quotations to less corruption than that of the lexicographer. The nature of Macrobius' work suggests strongly that his Lucretian citations are drawn from works of Virgilian scholarship rather than a given text of Lucretius; accordingly, with this added intermediary, it is impossible to conclude anything about the

---

[80] For further discussion, prompted by a new fragment of Diogenes of Oenoanda, see Smith (2004) 41–2.

nature of this/these Lucretian text(s) in the remote distance. Amidst Macrobius' citations we find a significant number of correct readings against the direct tradition; however, all of these discrepancies clearly result from minor palaeographical errors affecting the direct tradition, many of which would naturally occur in minuscule: *i* for *l*, *t* for *l*, *r* for *l*, *e* for *i*, *a* for *u*, the loss of final *m* (as a macron). There is therefore no reason to suppose that Macrobius had indirect access to a manuscript tradition (or traditions) that differed notably from the state of Lucretius' direct tradition around the fourth century.

(F) Virgilian commentators

(i) Servius

We may progress now to the other major Virgilian source for Lucretian citations, the commentary of Macrobius' near contemporary Maurus Servius Honoratus. I include here the larger form of this work, the *soi-disant* Servius Danielis (SD), even if it may represent a later stratum of material; other Virgilian scholars I leave until the subsequent section (F(ii)). Throughout this corpus we find twenty-three Lucretian verses cited (in full or in part) in thirty instances, drawn from all books except the third.[81] Of the direct citations, six occur in Servius Danielis; three occur in the commentary on *Bucolica*, eleven on *Georgica* and the rest on *Aeneis*. Further to these citations, we find three paraphrases that reveal partial knowledge of Lucretius' Latinity (*DRN* I.571, IV.244 = VI.930, VI.630) and twenty-five further mentions of Lucretius' name without any textual significance.[82]

The following discrepancies occur:

(a) Errors of Servius or his manuscript of Lucretius: *hic pecudes fessae* for *hinc fessae pecudes* in I.257 (SD) *ad Geo.* III.124; *aruo*

---

[81] That is, unless the citation of *continuo hoc mors est illius, quod fuit ante* in his discussion *ad* Verg. *Aen.* I.123 refers specifically to III.520, not I.671, I.793 or II.754.

[82] I exclude the supposed Lucretian fragments (on which see frs. **I**, **IV** and **VII** below). The Servian citiations of Lucretius were surveyed by Deschamps (1999) but without consideration of textual issues or the question of whether Servius had direct access to *DRN*.

for *aruis* in I.314 *ad Geo.* I.46; *nascuntur* for *procrescere* in I.715 *ad Aen.* I.123; *ad* for *et* and *ueniamus* for *scrutemur* in I.830 *ad Aen.* IV.625; *primordia* for *uestigia* in II.476 *ad Geo.* I.129; *penitus* for *placidi* in II.559 (SD) *ad Geo.* IV.442; *curae* for *nostri* in II.650 *ad Aen.* XII.794; *cum* for *dum* (citing VI.630 by implication) *ad Aen.* X.807; *effundere* for *descendere* in VI.736 *ad Aen.* IV.250. More complex are the corruptions *et iam prima nouo* (by implication) for *primum aurora nouo* (II.144) (SD) *ad Aen.* IX.457, *supra spoliatus lumine aer* for *nisi lumine cassus aer* (IV.368–9) *ad Aen.* IV.654 and *florebat nauibus pontus* for *florebat propter odores* (V.1442; text uncertain)[83] *ad Aen.* VII.804.

(b) There is no corruption certainly resulting from Servius' manuscript tradition.

(c) Ambiguous in their origin are: *frondiferosque* for *frondiferasque* in I.18 *ad Geo.* II.372; *occulto* for *occulte* in I.314 *ad Geo.* I.46; *imbri* for *igni* and *igni* for *imbri* in I.715 *ad Buc.* VI.31 (correctly cited *ad Aen.* I.123); *ipsa* for *ipse* in II.650 *ad Aen.* XII.794.

(d) Correct readings against the direct tradition: *quouis* against *quoduis* Ω in I.102 (SD) *ad Aen.* IV.606; *pingui* against *pinguis* OQS[1] (om. S); *sanguenque* against *sanguemque* Ω in I.837 *ad Aen.* I.211 and *Geo.* I.139; *color* for *calor* Ω in VI.205 (SD) *ad Buc.* VI.33; *albas* against *albos* Ω in VI.736 *ad Aen.* IV.250.

(e) If we ignore the orthographical triviality of Servius' presenting along with Ω the unmetrical *nihil* of Ω for *nil* in II.650 at *Aen.* XII.794, we find no conjunctive error.

The manuscript tradition of Servius, even more so than that of Macrobius, has inflicted limited damage upon the text of Lucretius; indeed if the four basic (and in quotation not ungrammatical) errors in (c) are mistakes of Servius himself, or his sources, no such corruption appears to have occurred in transmission. As regards Servius' *modus operandi*, it has been concluded that he had no direct access to a manuscript of Lucretius but was rather working from the citations built up in various works of Virgilian scholarship that would have been available to him in abundance.[84]

---

[83] For discussion of the problem, see, e.g., Murgia (2000) and Butterfield (2009a) 188–9.

[84] This was apparently the conclusion reached by Hadzsits in his unpublished work on 'Lucretius and Servius' summarised in *TAPhA* 69 (1938), li–lii, which never appeared in full. This conclusion is supported not only by the fact that in certain mentions of Lucretius' name Servius appears not to know the true contents of Lucretius' work but also from his attributing to Lucretius fragments which are almost certainly non-Lucretian (cf. n. 82).

This additional remove from a manuscript of Lucretius complicates the task of assessing the state of Lucretius' transmission at the turn of the fifth century. For, although errors in (a) are numerous, and often significant (e.g. I.715 (hardly a banalisation), 830, II.144, 476, 559, 650 and IV.368–9), they could be the mistake of Servius' source, or that author's transmission, rather than errors of Servius himself or, more interestingly, the Lucretian manuscript at root in the citation. In fact, there seem to be only two errors which could possibly spring from a Lucretian manuscript: the metrically possible transposition *pecudes fessae* for *fessae pecudes* at I.257 and singular *aruo* for plural *aruis* at I.314. Nothing can be concluded from this. The numerous mentions of Lucretius' name do not reflect intimate knowledge of his poem.[85] There is thus not enough secure evidence to conclude anything of interest about the state of the Lucretian tradition, other than the observation that Servius perhaps could not obtain his own copy of the text in Rome around the turn of the fifth century.

(ii)   Other Virgilian scholia

Alongside the commentaries of Servius, Lucretius is cited in other extant works of Virgilian scholarship: the *Scholia Veronensia*, the *Breuis expositio*, the *Scholia Bernensia* and pseudo-Probus on the *Bucolica*. Although in three instances the same passages are cited as in Servius (I.314, IV.132) or Macrobius (I.123), for the most part these works provide the sole citations of certain Lucretian lines. I shall consider these commentaries individually.

The *Scholia Veronensia*, composed roughly around the fourth century, cite Lucretius four times (in full or in part), and in one

---

[85] Basic knowledge of Lucretius' devotion to Epicureanism (*Aen.* V.81, X.467), the Athenian plague (*Aen.* III.138, *Geo.* III.478, III.481), unity of *mens* and *animus* (*Aen.* VI.11), minuteness of atoms (*Buc.* VI.31), non-existence of the Underworld, a false extrapolation of worldly suffering (*Aen.* VI.127, VI.596), movement of the earth's surface by water (*Geo.* II.479), use of the word *semina* (*Geo.* II.151), nature of superstition (*Aen.* VIII.187), corporeal structure of air/wind (*Aen.* VI.239, *Geo.* IV.219), goats' resistance to hemlock (*Aen.* IV.486), choice of Memmius as addressee (*Geo.* I.pr.), vague knowledge of I.926–50 = IV.1–25 (*Geo.* III.293) and the close of Book IV (*Geo.* III.135); we often find misunderstanding or misreporting (*Aen.* III.587, V.81, V.527, VII.37, XII.87, *Geo.* II.329, IV.51).

instance (*ad Aen.* II.649) provide a rough paraphrase of VI.297–8. One mistake is easily explicable: the error from memory of writing *petiuit* for the imperfect *petebat* of I.92 (*ad Aen.* XII.718); the other is more complicated. After explaining *ad Geo.* III.3 that Virgil's *uacuas ... mentes* refers to the minds of writers, the author cites as a Lucretian phrase *uacuas aures animumque sagacem.* Yet these words do not occur in the direct tradition; the closest passages we find are *tu mihi da tenues aures animumque sagacem* at IV.912 and, in the line transmitted as I.50, *quod superest uacuas aures* (the rest of the line being lost). On the basis of this evidence, most scholars in the wake of Bernays have interpreted the citation in the *scholia* as the close of I.50 rather than as a quotation of IV.912 with accidental imposition of a different (but nonetheless Lucretian) adjective. Although certainty is unattainable, this is probably correct. Since I do not credit the introduction of any complete line from the indirect tradition into Lucretius,[86] if this incorporation is correct, it represents the most significant addition of lost Lucretian material from a secondary author. At any rate, it seems that the composer of these *scholia* had read Lucretius but was largely citing from memory.[87]

The *Scholia Bernensia*, a collection of exegetical material of the ninth century that drew heavily on earlier commentators, particularly Junius Philargyrius (fourth/fifth century), cite five verses of Lucretius (in full or in part) drawn from Books I, II and V, and mention his name *ad Geo.* IV.51. Among these citations the sole error is *occulto* for *occulte* in I.314; this error also occurs in Servius and the *Breuis expositio*, along with *De dubiis nominibus* and Isidore; such a prevalence of the error suggests either its occurring in an influential work of Virgilian scholarship, which later spread to related works, or its existence in a number of Lucretian manuscripts. Given the second- or third-hand fashion

---

[86] For a detailed analysis of the problem of multi-word Lucretian 'fragments', see the latter half of this chapter.

[87] The reading *nisibus* for *uisibus* at V.819 has been attributed to the manuscript of these *scholia* since Diels, despite its not being recorded in Hagen's generally thorough apparatus. Given that *uiribus* is very commonly found in Lucretius (eighteen times, but never the form *nisibus*), that the confusion of *n* and *u* is so easy in minuscule, and that *magnis* precedes, I very much doubt that, if *nisibus* is actually transmitted in these *scholia*, it can tell us anything about the Lucretian tradition.

in which these Virgilian scholastic works drew upon other poetic texts, the former assumption is markedly more probable. The apparent misunderstanding of Lucretius' doctrine *ad* Verg. *Geo.* IV.51 is discussed below.

Closely related to these *scholia*, and perhaps drawing upon material of a similar date, is the *Breuis expositio*, a summary of Virgil's first two *Georgica* that cites five Lucretian verses (in full or in part) in three instances from Books I, II and V. These verses, the first of which (I.314) is also cited by Servius and the *Scholia Bernensia*, are cited without error and therefore can likewise tell us little about Lucretius' development, beyond the accurate preservation of these verses in certain works of Virgilian scholarship. The uncertainty about Lucretius' poem, presumably resulting from no direct contact, is well attested by the comment (195,4–5 Hosius) that *DRN* is addressed *ad Mettium uel Memmium uel Remmium*, with further corruption of these names in many manuscripts: no such corruptions of Memmius' name occur in the direct tradition.

We come finally to Pseudo-Probus' commentary, a work of very uncertain date and origin but perhaps learned enough to antedate the fifth century.[88] In the long note upon *Buc.* VI.31 the author cites four Lucretian verses (in full or in part) in two instances from Books IV and V.[89] That at IV.132 could well be drawn from Servius (who regularly repeats it) or a mutual Virgilian source; the three verses given without error at V.92–4 could be taken directly from a (here uncorrupt) manuscript of Lucretius but, whether true or not, the uncertainty surrounding the work's place and date of origin renders any conclusion inept.

Alongside these works, the name of Lucretius is mentioned twice elsewhere in Virgilian scholarship but without textual significance: once in Donatus' *Vita Vergilii* (6, which claims that Lucretius died on Virgil's fifteenth birthday) and once in Junius Philargyrius' *Explicatio in* Verg. *Buc.* (4,col.2,14 H, which simply records Memmius as the addressee).

---

[88] Two other works attributed to pseudo-Probus are treated in section G below.

[89] IV.132, V.92–4. I disregard the repetition of Lucretius' name in the same note (343 H), where a fragment is mistakenly attributed to him rather than Ennius (see fr. **IX** below).

(G) Other Grammarians (second–eighth centuries) (Terentius Scaurus, Marius Plotius, Marius Victorinus, Donatus, Charisius, Audax, Diomedes, Consentius, Cledonius, Pompeius, Priscian, 'Maxim(in)us Victorinus', pseudo-Probus, Eutyches, anonymous works)

Under this heading I unify various grammatical writers, whose dates range from the second to eighth centuries AD but whose sources are deeply interconnected. Given that we are faced with so diverse a body of authors, some of whom cite Lucretius only once or twice, I tabulate the figures below (see Table 1) and discuss only those instances where Lucretius is cited often or with significant error.

Despite this broad range of material, little of interest can be concluded from the evidence presented by certain authors. I shall survey the authors chronologically in brief, leaving the two most interesting cases – Charisius and Priscian – to the end. Terentius Scaurus cited Lucretius only once (I.259–61), the first two lines of which are recorded without error but the third, having been reduced to an acronymic form (as often found in the scholiastic tradition to other authors, most notably Virgil) has suffered some corruption: *t l n m p n* appears in lieu of *l(udit) l(acte) m(ero) m(entes) p(erculsa) n(ouellas)*. I am confident that Scaurus originally penned the correct order, and it is natural to assume that he is also responsible for the shorthand, the unmeaning string of letters later being corrupted. If so, this suggests that he regarded his second-century audience as being familiar with the text of Lucretius, or at any rate this passage.

Marius Plotius Sacerdos cites Lucretius seven times from the first three books (and also Book IV, if IV.16, not I.941, is the source of his citation at *Gramm. GLK* VI 504,28). The unmetrical *animantium* (perhaps a scribal corruption for the rarer *animantum*) for *animalis* in II.927 is probably an error of memory, whereas *uitae* for *uitai* at III.1093 is more likely a mistake of his own transmission. I attribute little weight to the sole preservation of *alituum* in II.928 against *alitum* of the direct tradition, as the latter corruption is so trivial as to have occurred by chance late in transmission. The preservation of *sanguen* at I.837 (if not I.853

75

Table 1

Grammarian	Number of Lucretian citations	Lines cited	Number of divergences from direct tradition
Terentius Scaurus (early 2nd cent.)	1	I.259–61 (*Orth. GLK* VII 25.4–7 (43.8–10 Biddau))	2
Marius Plotius Sacerdos (3rd cent.)	7 (excl. fr. **II**)	I.186 (*Gramm. GLK* VI 448,9), I.837/ I.853/I.860 (*Gramm. GLK* VI 474,21–2), I.941 = IV.16 (*Gramm. GLK* VI 504,28), I.1063 (*Gramm. GLK* VI 450,20–1), II.927–8 (*Gramm. GLK* VI 445,19–21), II.1097 (*Gramm. GLK* VI 450,12), III.1093 (*Gramm. GLK* VI 503,5–6)	4 (+1 erroneous fragment)
Marius Victorinus (3rd cent.)*	3	II.2 (*Gramm. GLK* VI 31,28), III.1035 (*Gramm. GLK* VI 56,9–10), IV.1207 (*Gramm. GLK* VI 28,6)	1
Donatus (4th cent.)	11	I.2 (*ad* Ter. *Eun.* 325), I.124 (*ad* Ter. *Andr.* 175), I.186 (*Gramm. GLK* IV 392,14), I.326 (*ad* Ter. *Phorm.* 180), I.571 (*Gramm. GLK* IV 393,31), II.16 (*ad* Ter. *Phorm.* 232), II.30 = V.1393 (*ad* Ter. *Ad.* 576), II.476 (*Gramm. GLK* IV 432,27–8), II.531 (*Ad* Ter. *Phorm.* 213), II.1097 (*Gramm. GLK* IV 431,33), III.385–6 (*ad* Ter. *Eun.* 688)	3

Charisius (late 4th cent.)	9 (excl. frs. **III** and **VI**)	I.227 (77,18 Barwick, 150,19 B), I.837 (114,20 B), II.637 (119,6 B, 154.29 B), II.662 (118,2 B), III.94 (272.2–8 B), III.676 (265,11 B), VI.736 (116,8 B)	5 (+2 erroneous 'fragments')
Audax (late 4th(?) cent.)	2	II.265 = III.643 (*Exc. GLK* VII 348,29), VI.868 (*Exc. GLK* VII 329,2–3)	1
'Victorinus' (late 4th(?) cent.)	1	II.265 = III.643 (*De arte gramm. GL* 202,19)	
Diomedes (4th/5th cent.)	3	I.186 (*Inst. GLK* I 430,2), I.587 (*Inst. GLK* I 371,20–1), III.765 (*Ars GLK* I 343,8–10)	0
Consentius (5th cent.)	1	I.84 (*Ars GLK* V 389,15–16)	1
Cledonius (5th cent.)	1	II.476 (*Ars GLK* V 42.29–30)	0
Pompeius (5th/6th cent.)	4	I.186 (*Comm. GLK* V 109,18), I.571 = II.449 = V.313 (*Comm. GLK* V 291,15), II.1097 (*Comm. GLK* V 162,32–163,1), III.1010 (*Comm. GLK* V 297,1–2)	2
Priscian (5th/6th cent.)	28	I.1 (*Inst. GLK* II 292,18–19), I.27 (*Inst. GLK* II 444.24–445.1, 527.7), I.29 (*Inst. GLK* II 285,8), I.70–1 (*Inst. GLK* II 499,8–10), I.84–5 (*Inst. GLK* II 285,10–11), I.102 (*Inst. GLK* II 591,10–11), I.212 = V.211 (*Inst.*	29

Table 1 (cont.)

Grammarian	Number of Lucretian citations	Lines cited	Number of divergences from direct tradition
		GLK II 476,24–477,1), I.269 (Inst. GLK II 591,7–9), I.587 (Inst. GLK II 542,19–20), I.720 (Inst. GLK II 27,2–3), I.806 (Inst. GLK II 349,22–3), II.155–6 (Inst. GLK II 401,12–14), II.476 (Inst. GLK II 275,3–5, Part. GLK III 493,15), II.586–7 (Inst. GLK II 249,10–12), II.888 (Inst. GLK II 132,21–2), III.156 (Inst. GLK II 445,9–10, 474,6–7), III.160 (Inst. GLK III 510,3), III.796–7 (Inst. GLK II 528,28–529,1–2), III.978 (Inst. GLK II 27,4–5), III.984 (Inst. GLK II 27,6–7), VI.179/VI.307 (Inst. GLK II 281,18, 319,11–12), VI.290 (Inst. GLK II 152,13–15), VI.876–8 (Inst. GLK II 211,20–3), VI.929–30 (Inst. GLK II 444,14–16)	
'Maxim(in)us Victorinus' (date uncertain)	3	I.147 = II.60 = III.92 = VI.40 (De rat. metr. GLK VI 221,10–12), I.186 (De	0

'pseudo-Probus' (two works of perhaps distinct composition) (dates uncertain)	7	*rat. metr. GLK* VI 216,9–11), II.25 (*De rat. metr. GLK* VI 220,11–12) I.82 (*De ult. syll. GLK* IV 262,34–263,1), I.186 (*De ult. syll. GLK* IV 263,13–14), I.837/I.853/I.860 (*Cath. GLK* IV 9,21–2), II.586 = III.265 (*Cath. GLK* IV 19,22–4, 31,1), V.96 (*De ult. syll. GLK* IV 225,29–31), VI.6 (*De ult. syll. GLK* IV 255,10–11)	1
Eutyches (6th cent.)	1	V.598 (*Ars GLK* V 484,7–8)	0
Anon. *De dub. nom.* (7th cent.)	1	I.314 (867 = *GLK* V 593,9–10)	0
Anon. Bob. *De uerbo*	2	II.1122 (*GLK* V 650,29), III.106 (*GLK* V 650,33–4)	3
Anon. *Ars Bernensis* (8th(?) cent.)	1	VI.877–8 (*GLK* VIII 127,27–8)	0

* The instances at II.2 at III.1035 may originally be the work of Aelius Festus Apthonius (4th century?).

or I.860) we have encountered in discussion already. The two allegedly Lucretian 'fragments' (**II** and **VI**) are discussed at the close of this chapter.

Marius Victorinus cites Lucretius three times from Books II–IV. The correct citation of II.2 could be drawn from Nonius (before the corruption in the latter's tradition of *e terra* to *et terrae*), and the omission of *atque etiam* after *etiam* in IV.1207 is no doubt the result of a scribal *saut* owing to homoeoteleuton rather than Victorinus' having a corrupt Lucretian text as his source. The two mentions of Lucretius in Victorinus' commentary upon Cicero's *De inuentione* briefly refer to Lucretius' denying the existence of the five senses (*ad* I.6) and the assertion of Lucretius and others that *inane totum locus est* (*ad* I.26).

Donatus cited Lucretius seven times in his Terentian commentary and four times in his grammatical treatise *Ars grammatica*; the citations come from the first three books (and Book V, if V.1393 not II.30 is cited), which could mean that he had access to an incomplete text of the work. Errors are typically rare: the defective manuscripts at I.326 present *tu es corsales* for (*impenden*)*t uesco sale*, a simple scribal misdivision, with the doubling of the *s* of *saxa* that follows. As with Terentius Scaurus, we find the acronymic preservation of part of I.2 (a line surely known to all educated readers): *alma Venus c(aeli) s(ubter) l(abentia) s(ignis)*. In citing II.1097 we find the strange error of *quis totidem uertit caelos* for *quis pariter caelos* (... *conuertere* [sc. *potis est*]);[90] this same mistake, presumably the result of inaccurate memory (aided by the natural desire to have a finite verb), occurs later in Pompeius (with the further corruption of *uertit* to *uertat*), who presumably drew the citation from Donatus. In two cases Donatus makes brief reference to Lucretian doctrine: to I.936–47 = IV.11–22 (*ad* Ter. *Eun.* 515) and to IV.1265–72 (*ad* Ter. *Eun.* 424), once mistakenly thought to support the existence of *crissare* in Lucretius. Given that Donatus appears to have had direct access to a text of Lucretius, his citation of I.186 and II.476, the earliest extant instance of each case, may be

---

[90] *totidem* occurs in Lucretius only at I.870, a passage which has no verbal similarities to the present instance.

responsible for the accession of these commonly cited lines into the grammatical canon.

The citation of the Lucretian idiom *de subito* by Audax (II.265 or III.643) is no doubt drawn from Nonius, 'Victorinus' or a similar source; the citation of VI.868 with the banalisation *aquae* for *laticis* is an interesting error (and repeated from this source by Bede), for Audax claims that Lucretius here employed the trisyllabic (i.e. anapaestic) scansion of *aquae*. The mistake probably arises from misapplying Lucretius' use of this licence at VI.552 and 1072 to this (self-contained and easily memorable) line; that the direct tradition replaced *aquae* with *laticis*, as Diels believes, is highly unlikely. The sole citation from '*Victorini De arte grammatica*' is identical to that of Audax (II.265 or III.643).[91]

Diomedes probably did not have direct access to *DRN*: he cites I.186 (certainly at second hand), the citation of III.765 may well be drawn from Nonius, and I.571 (later cited by Priscian) could be drawn from an indirect source in the grammatical tradition. Consentius cites Lucretius only at I.84, with the correct *Triuiai* against the probable *Triuiaet* of the archetype (*triuiaet* O : *triuiat* ψ), a correct reading also found in Priscian (whom Consentius is certainly copying here) and perhaps other lost grammatical works. Cledonius' correct preservation of *primordia* at II.476 against *mordia* of the direct tradition cannot tell us much, for this part of the line had already been cited by Donatus and Servius (and, if chronologically earlier, Priscian).

Pompeius cites Lucretius four times from the first three books: I.186 again could come from a number of indirect sources, and II.1097 from Donatus or Plotius Sacerdos; the striking error *magna fieri* for *expleri nulla* in citing III.1010 suggests, however, that in that instance his source (or he himself) quoted Lucretius from memory.

The work under the name 'Maxim(in)us Victorinus' cites Lucretius thrice (from Books I and II) and without error: the

---

[91] The recording by Dositheus (late fourth (?) century; *Ars gramm. GLK* VII 428,11) of *Lucretii carmina* as an example, alongside the first three books of Virgil's *Georgica*, of the *genus enarratiuum* of poetry does not necessarily show any specific knowlege of the poet's work.

citation of I.186, a line clearly canonical in grammatical literature for elucidating the metrical phenomenon of sigmatic ecthlipsis, could have been drawn from the pseudo-Probian *De ultimis syllabis* or another early grammatical work.

The two grammatical works spuriously attributed to Probus are of uncertain date and quite probably different authors/compilers. Four Lucretian citations from Books I, V and VI occur without error[92] in *De ultimis syllabis*. The two citations of single words (*sanguen* and *uis*) in the *Catholica* are probably drawn from the grammatical tradition and do not reflect direct knowledge of Lucretius' text; the mistaken attribution of fr. **VIII** (see the close of this chapter) to Lucretius at *Cath. GLK* IV 10,31–2 also supports this conclusion. The sixth-century Eutyches, working at Constantinople, cites only V.598: although the line is transmitted without error, it is wrongly attributed to Book VI, which suggests either that the grammarian had no direct access to Lucretius' text or that his text has been subsequently corrupted.

The remaining anonymous citations of a later date tell us very little: the corruption of *adauctu* to *hauctu* in the citation of II.1122 in the *Fragmentum Bobiense de nomine* is probably scribal, as are *proptu* and *cernemus* for *promptu* and *cermimus* in III.106; the preservation of *aegret* against *aegrum* of the direct tradition in the same line, however, raises the possibility that if the author was working from a Lucretian manuscript, it was part of a family distinct from that of the direct branch. The anonymous *De dubiis nominibus* probably cites I.314 from Servius (before corruption of *aruis* to *aruo*), if not the same source as the *Scholia Bernensia*. The anonymous *Ars Bernensis* (an Irish compilation of several grammatical sources, preserved in Bern. 123) is able to cite without error, its only use of Lucretius, two incomplete lines from Book VI (877–8), which are not otherwise quoted in the indirect tradition. Given the insular nature of the compiler, and the absence of Lucretian material from the rest of the work, I would posit a lost grammatical tract rather than a manuscript of *DRN* as the source for this unremarkable couplet.

---

[92] I except the mistaken attribution of V.96 to Book VI.

We are left with the two more interesting and informative testi-monies of Charisius and Priscian. The late-fourth-century gram-marian Fl. Sosipater Charisius, probably of African origin but based professionally in Constantinople, cites Lucretius nine times (from Books I, II, IV and VI) throughout his *Ars grammatica*. The misattribution of *nauiter* of I.525 to Book III (spuriously giving rise to fr. **III**, for which see the close of this chapter) may be a scribal error. The citation of I.837 could be drawn from Nonius, who cites the line twice. The error *pulsabant* for *pulsarent* in both citations of II.637 is more probably in both instances a banalisation in Char-isius' mind rather than the corrupt reading of his Lucretian exem-plar. The mistakes of *acribus* in citing the line at 119,6 B and *ducere has* for *bucerias(que)* at II.662 are clearly scribal. Neverthe-less Charisius rightly presents *quam* against the *lectio facilior* of *quem* at III.94. Finally, he betrays either direct use of Nonius or their shared use of the same source in citing III.676 with the ἅπαξ *longiter* in lieu of the very probably correct *longius*.[93] Given the above, and especially the two incorrect attributions of words to Lucretius where they do not belong, it is likely that Charisius did not enjoy direct access to *DRN*. Instead, his knowledge of the poem could have been drawn wholesale from works such as those of Remmius Palaemon (first century AD) and Iulius Romanus (third century AD) from whom he regularly drew material.

We come finally to Priscian, by far the most prolific citer of Lucretius among these grammarians: he quotes the poem twenty-eight times (from Books I–III and VI), all but one instance (II.476 at *Part. GLK* III 493,15) occurring in his *Institutiones grammaticae*. It seems beyond doubt that Priscian had direct access to a text of Lucretius, which explains how many of his citations lack any extant precedent in the indirect tradition; the prevalence of instances from the first half of the work also supports their being the result of his own researches, as he progressed from the poem's opening until the desired example was found.[94] Many discrepancies from the direct

---

[93] The lucid discussion of the problem by Timpanaro (1978, 140–6) concludes in favour of *longiter* against most twentieth-century editors.

[94] It is possible that the four instances not in these first three books are limited to the last owing to his scanning for apposite citations occasionally backwards from the end of a codex.

tradition occur among these citations. Two that are certain scribal errors require no further discussion.[95] In a number of instances Priscian's memory led him astray: *terrarum* for *portarum* in I.71; *aurarum* for *terraique* (with the subsequent *solum subigentes* omitted) in I.212 = V.212, a corruption (*pace* Bollack (1976) 263–70) perhaps inspired by *in auras* that closes V.213; *quod . . . nequeas* for *quid . . . nequeant* in I.587; *supra . . . uestigia* for *supera . . . primordia* in II.476 at *Inst. GLK* II 275,3–5; at *Part. GLK* III 493,15, by contrast, Priscian's memory corrupts a different word, giving *diri primordia* for *taetri primordia*; at II.586 *sed quam multarum rerum uis* stands instead of *et quodcumque magis uis multas*, a discrepancy showing Priscian's occasional disregard for the irrelevant details of the line (acc. pl. *uis* being the purpose of citation). We also find *nasci* for *gigni* in II.888, the banalising addition of *est* at the close of III.796, *quia* for *quod* in VI.877. In none of these instances does Priscian's alternative version hold a candle up to the reading of the direct tradition. Nevertheless, in a few cases he does preserve the correct reading: *ornatum* against *oralatum* (Ω) in I.27 (cited twice); *militiai* against *militia* (Ω) in I.29; *effringere* against *confringere* (Ω) (*perfringere* Nonius) in I.70;[96] *cupiret* (also Nonius) against *cuperet* of the archetype in I.71; *Triuiai* and *Iphianassai* against *Triuiaeat* (Ω?) and *Iphianassa* (Ω) in I.84–5; *quouis* (also Servius) against *quoduis* (Ω) in I.102; *ut* against *et* in I.806;[97] *retrahuntur* against *trahuntur* (Ω) in II.155. Finally, in one certain and one possible case Priscian shares errors with the direct tradition of Lucretius: at VI.877 *demittat* is wrongly transmitted for *dimittat*; I.720 is cited with *undis* at line-end,

<hr/>

[95] *phoedi* for *foede* in I.85 and *sonare* for *sonere* in III.156 at *Inst. GLK* II 474,6–7 (correctly preserved at 445,9–10).

[96] Presumably by the third century AD *effringere* became (via *efringere*) the simplex ˣ*fringere* in a given branch of the tradition, which was expanded to the incorrect compounded forms *confringere* and *perfringere* in separate descendants of that manuscript, the former of which became the branch of the direct tradition; the alteration to i.e. *frangere* in O³ is certainly an independent change. This supposition, more probable than that *effringere* was corrupted to *perfringere* and thereafter *confringere*, suggests a relatively narrow line of transmission in late antiquity.

[97] It is unclear to what author Kaspar Barth was referring when he made mention of the close of this Lucretian line (with the corrupt *uacillant* for *uacillent*) in a 'membraneu[s] cod[ex]' at *Adv.* 37.XIII (Frankfurt, 1624) 1691. At any rate, nothing of value can be concluded from this comment about the Lucretian tradition.

against which several scholars have argued.[98] The former error could have been made independently in the direct tradition and by Priscian or his scribes; the latter error suggests that, at least by the turn of the sixth century, a branch of the manuscript tradition in which *undis* had wrongly entered the close of I.720 from the previous line existed. Many of the further instances where the direct tradition differs from Priscian can be explained away by its own scribal corruption in later stages of transmission.

Alongside Priscian, therefore, it seems that only Terentius Scaurus and Donatus had direct cognisance of Lucretius; for the rest of these wide-ranging grammarians (largely from the turn of the fifth century onwards) such contact does not seem probable, texts of Lucretius now perhaps being few and far between in Rome and beyond.

(H) Remaining authors (third–sixth centuries) (Serenus, Censorinus, Ausonius, Porphyrio, pseudo-Acro, Sidonius, Martianus Capella, Lactantius Placidus, Boethius)

In this section are treated the few citations that are not easily categorised in the analyses above, namely non-grammatical authors postdating the second century AD and anonymous author-specific *scholia*. Again, a table (Table 2) will most easily set out the data.

Many of these citations tell us little. Censorinus' *De die natali*, written in AD 238, contains a citation without error of the Lucretian verse I.733; it is reasonable to assume that he had access to a good text of the poem in Rome. Decimus Magnus Ausonius shows knowledge of the first two lines of *DRN* in two instances, for *Aeneadum genetrix* is collocated with (*alma*) *Venus* in two instances – in one of his *Epigrammata* (XIII.36.2) and one of his *Eclogae* (XIV.3.7) – although no explicit mention of Lucretius is made. Since the openings of classical poems were so well known, we cannot necessarily conclude that texts of Lucretius were available in Ausonius' native Burdigala (Bordeaux) or his later residence of Augusta Treverorum (Trier), although well-connected

---

[98] After Lachmann, Bernays and Diels, among others, I have offered a new emendation: see Butterfield (2008e) 117–18, with Butterfield (2009d) 86–9.

Table 2

Grammarian	Number of Lucretian citations	Lines cited	Number of divergences from direct tradition
Censorinus (3rd cent.)	I	I.733 (*De die nat.* 4.7).	0
Ausonius (mid. 4th cent.)	(2)	I.1–2 (cf. *Epp.* XIII.36.2, *Ecl.* XIV.3.7).	0
Porphyrio (early 3rd cent., revised in 5th (?) cent.)	2	IV.450 (*ad* Hor. *S.* II.1.25), VI.1222 (*ad* Hor. *C.* I.1.27).	0
ps.-Acro (compiled in 5th cent.)	4	II.1–2 (*ad* Hor. *Epp.* I.11,9), II.651 (*ad* Hor. *S.* I.5.101), VI.97 (*ad* Hor. *C.* II.12.14), VI.1222 (*ad* Hor. *C.* I.1.27).	I
Martianus Capella (late 5th cent.)	2	II.476 (III.305), VI.233 (III.295).	I
Lactantius Placidus comm. *in* Stat. *Theb.* (5th/6th cent.)	4	I.31–4 (*ad* III.296), I.292–3 (*ad* VII.585), II.646–51 (*sine* 649–50) (*ad* III.659), V.913–15 (*ad* VII.585).	II
Boethius (*c.* 480–*c.* 524)	I	I.715 (*Inst. arith.* II.1).	I

elites presumably could acquire copies through contacts based elsewhere. We cannot say anything of weight regarding the citations of Lucretius by the Horatian scholiasts Porphyrio and Acro, who are probably responsible for the quotations of Lucretius in the fifth-century compilations linked with their names. At any rate, their citations contain no errors (save for *motantibus* in lieu of *turbantibus* in I.2 (ps.-Acr. *ad* Hor. *Epp.* I.11,9), an error of memory influenced by Virgil)[99] and matters of chronology and geography are too obscure to allow any firm conclusions.[100]

Martianus Minneus Felix Capella compiled his *De nuptiis Philologiae et Mercurii* in Carthage (under Vandalic rule) towards the end of the fifth century. We have already seen that there is no compelling reason to conclude that Tertullian in Carthage had direct knowledge of Lucretius; the same can probably be said of Martianus. His citation of the single word *uiri* at II.476 could be drawn from Donatus, Servius or Cledonius (if not another lost grammarian). He is the only author, by contrast, to cite part of VI.233, which he does (with the corruption of *rarique* for *rareque*) to illustrate the rare genitive form *uasi*. In fact, OQ here present the expected third-declension genitive *uasis*. Of the ten other times Lucretius employs *uas*, it is third-declension in form, save for the two second-declension ablative plurals *uasis* at III.434 and just before at VI.231 (in both cases *uasibus* being impossible). I think it more probable that Martianus had access to a (lost) grammatical tract that wrongly associated genitival *uasi* with Lucretius than that a nevertheless intelligible *uasi* in VI.233 was corrupted to the also rare form *uasis*.[101] His statement (III.266) that *A et I* [sc. *in genetiuo*] *et Lucretius crebro et noster Maro 'aurai pictai'*, suggests direct familiarity only with the latter author. I thus see no reason to believe that Martianus had read Lucretius.

The commentary upon Statius' *Thebais* attributed to a Lactantius Placidus (about whom nothing is known) cites Lucretius in four instances, covering twelve verses from Books I, II and V. These quotations, more extended than is typical of roughly contemporaneous authors, suggest direct knowledge of *DRN*. Although they show a large number of corruptions of Lucretius'

---

[99] Cf. *Buc.* V.5 (VI.28); the dependence of Shuckburgh (1888, 90) upon such commentaries (*ad* Hor. *Epp.* I.11.10) is unfortunate.

[100] That we find the citation of VI.1222 in the *Schol. in codd. Par. Horat. ad* Hor. *C.* I.I.27 merely shows dependence upon pseudo-Acro, where the same verse is quoted.

[101] One eagerly awaits the arrival of the *TLL* article on *uas* but it seems that genitival *uasi* is only attested by Festus (169 L. s.u. *nassiterna*), if one adopts *uasis* from the *recentiores* for the transmitted *uasi* at col. XII.20.2, an author who regularly employed *uas* as a third-declension noun in the singular.

text,[102] in three instances we find the correct reading against Ω: *regit* for the anticipatory error *regium* (before *in gremium*) of Ω and *qui* for *que* Ω in I.33, and *ponere* against *pondere* of Ω at V.313. These corruptions of the direct tradition are so slight, however, that they could certainly have been made in the wake of Lactantius Placidus' work. In three further instances, mention is made of Lucretius without direct citation: *ad* I.206 (a reference to *DRN* VI.476–80 and the water cycle), *ad* III.97–8 (an allusion to Lucretius' belief that souls perish with the body), and *ad* VI.363–4 (a rather opaque reference to the earth's being suspended at the bottom of all elements, with which Jahnke in his Teubner (1898) tentatively compares V.449ff. and 509ff.). Although it is possible that Lactantius was working through intermediary works of scholarship that cited *DRN* in order to elucidate the *Thebais*, it is perhaps more probable that he had access to a text of Lucretius (distinct from the direct branch), which was in a rather corrupt state by the fifth century.

The Neoplatonic-cum-Stoic tract of Anicius Manlius Severinus Boethius, *De consolatione philosophiae*, composed soon after 520, cites Lucretius just once. Although Boethius wrote while under arrest, he could have retained access to certain books. At any rate, his version of I.715, perhaps reproduced from memory, presents *gignuntur* in lieu of *procrescere*, and probably stemmed from Servius' commentaries, who twice (*Aen.* I.123, *Buc.* VI.31) gives the semantically and syntactically similar verb *nascuntur*. Boethius does not add the name of Lucretius to his citation and perhaps had never read *DRN*.

Finally, we may record two brief mentions of the poet. The medical poet Quintus Serenus (early third century?) added, when discussing human conception, the parenthetic distich *femineo fiat uitio res necne, silebo*: | *hoc poterit magni quartus monstrare Lucreti* (605–6). From this we can conclude nothing beyond the fact that Serenus as well as his audience were

---

[102] Banalisations or rewordings: *quia* for *quoniam* in I.32; *diuum per se* for *p. s. d.* in II.646; *cum pace summa* for *s. c. p.* in II.647; presumably scribal corruptions: *moenia* for *moenera* in I.32; the repetition of *Mauors* at line-end (from I.32) in lieu of *amoris* at the close of I.34; *iunctaque* for *seiunctaque* in II.648; ambiguous are *deuinctus* for *deuictus* in I.34 and the unmeaning *iussit* for *posset* in V.914.

expected to know (and admire?) *DRN* IV. Sidonius Apollinaris (*fl.* 450–90), the politician and writer from Lugdunum (Lyons), who spent much of his career within Gaul, mentioned Lucretius within his *Carmina* (published in 469) when recording the many poets who will not be found in his own poetry: *nec Lucilius hic Lucretiusque est* (IX.265). Perhaps Sidonius had read Lucretius in full at some stage but this could have occurred during his time in Rome (*c.* 455–61 and 468) rather than in any Gallic city.[103]

(I) Isidore

We return now to the territory of a single author, Isidorus Hispalensis, Bishop of Seville, who flourished at the turn of the seventh century. Although Isidore was of Roman descent, there is no firm evidence that he ever left Spain, so his interaction with Lucretius, at this late date and presumably in Iberia, is potentially of great interest. Only two scholars have tackled the question of Isidore's engagement with Lucretius to any serious degree, namely Dressel (1874) and Gasparotto (1965–6a, 1965–6b, 1966–7, 1983).[104] From the many verbal reminiscences and obvious adaptations of Lucretian theories in his tellingly titled *De natura rerum* and the unfinished, twenty-book enyclopaedic *Etymologiae*, it is highly likely that Isidore had direct access to the Lucretian text.[105] The same conclusion is strongly suggested by the fact that, as we shall see, Isidore cites many Lucretian lines that are not found in other extant authors.

Isidore quotes Lucretius explicitly twelve times (sixteen verses) drawn from all books except III; in five further instances (all in Books V–VI) Isidore paraphrases Lucretius so closely that I have deemed these instances worthy of discussion.[106] To focus on the

[103] For possible Lucretian influence on the anonymous *Peruigilium Veneris* (early fourth century), see Wilhelm (1965) 48–9.
[104] Gasparotto (1983), which collects and augments his preceding articles on the topic, has almost no interest in textual matters and suffers from the lack of a detailed introduction to his method and the absence of any unifying conclusion to his five 'chapters'.
[105] Cf. esp. Dressel (1874) 49: 'Dubium non est, quin Lucreti carmine re vera usus sit Isidorus.'
[106] V.1192 (cf. *Etym.* I.36.13), V.1273–4 (cf. *Etym.* XVI.20.1), VI.165–6 (cf. *Etym.* XIII.8.2), VI.538 (cf. *De nat. rer.* 41.1), VI.1128–30 (cf. *De nat. rer.* 39.2).

direct citations, we may first observe that Isidore's interest in natural phenomena means that most of the citations relate to the terrestrial or celestial processes of nature, and accordingly most come from Book VI. In these citations we find comparatively few errors. In two instances faulty recollection by Isidore appears to be the case: in *fluuio* for *ut fluuios* in V.516 (XX.15.1);[107] *summo cessit honore* for *in summum cessit honorem* in V.1275 (XVI.20.1). The mistake of *nascuntur* for *procrescere* in citing I.715 at XIII.10.4 is drawn directly from Servius (*Aen.* I.123, *Buc.* VI.31), with whom Isidore was evidently very familiar.[108] A complete misremembering of a Lucretian line explains his metrical misquotation of V.1192 (*nubila sol imbres nix uenti fulmina grando*, albeit without explicit mention of Lucretius) at I.36.13: *nubila nix grando procellae fulmina uenti*. Certain errors are ambiguous in origin: the unconstruable *occulto* for *occulte* in I.314 at XX.14.1, possibly drawn from Servius (who, however, does not cite *uncus aratri* of 313), and *caelum* for *caelo* in IV.132 at XIII.4.3. *patra* for *parta* in citing IV.1129 at IX.5.3 is a simple error of transmission. Isidore provides no reading that is correct against a corruption in the direct tradition. The few close paraphrases of Lucretius' doctrine in *De natura rerum* as well as the *Etymologiae* – which do not impinge on any reading of the direct tradition – are probably drawn secondhand from Servius or Jerome.[109] Nevertheless, given the number of citations for which Isidore is our only source, the statement of Brunhölzl in the *Lexikon des Mittelalters* (vol. V, 2164) – 'Dass in Spanien Isidor v. Sevilla noch ein Exemplar zur Verfügung stand, ist mögl., aber nicht beweisbar' – is probably incorrect: unless we posit the existence of a lost encyclopaedic text that cited Lucretius in all of these places, Isidore's access to the poem seems eminently provable. A member of the Spanish ecclesiastical elite could therefore, in the early 600s, find access to a complete

---

[107] Unless otherwise stated, Isidorian textual references are to the *Etymologiae*.

[108] Cf., e.g., XIII.9.1, where Isidore repeats *uerbatim* Servius' discussion of fire created by friction (*ad* Verg. *Aen.* I.473, *nam omnium … arborum*), although with no acknowledgement of his source.

[109] The four more general mentions of Lucretius or his doctrine are also mostly drawn from Servius or Jerome: *Etym.* VIII.3.7 (from Servius), XIV.1.3 (from Servius), *De nat. rer.* XXX.4 (possibly a summary from direct access to Lucretius?), *Chron.* 222.1 (from Jerome's *Chron.*).

manuscript of Lucretius, albeit one which seems to differ not too much from the branch of the direct tradition.

To this discussion of Isidore we may append Hrabanus Maurus: in his *De uniuerso*, composed *c.* 842–6, a number of Lucretian citations occur but there is no doubt that these were drawn directly from Isidore: in his citation of I.313–14 (22.14 = *PL* CXI 610D) and IV.1129 (7.2 = *PL* CXI 185D), we also find the same errors *occulto* and *patra*; it is unclear whether *in fluuios*, found in Hrabanus' citation of V.516 (22.15 = *PL* CXI 612B), reflects a further corruption of Isidore's *in fluuio* (for Lucretius' *ut fluuios*) or rather that Isidore wrote *in fluuios*, which Hrabanus found in his text of that author, but it became corrupted to *fluuio* in Isidore's transmission. At any rate, Hrabanus can tell us nothing about the fate of Lucretius' own text.[110]

(J)   Citations in florilegia

We come now to four metrical florilegia that preserve Lucretian verses; by virtue of the purpose of these works, that is, to elucidate the scansion or more recondite Latin words, we typically find the full Lucretian hexameter cited. I take the four instances in rough chronological order:

(a) The poetic florilegium of 413 verses known as the *Opus prosodiacum* was compiled by Mico Centulensis (†853) in the middle of the ninth century, and was edited by Ludwig Traube in the third volume of the *Poetae Latini Aevi Carolini* series for *Monumenta Germaniae Historica* (Berlin, 1896, pp. 279–94), from which edition I provide line references.[111] In it we find thirteen Lucretian verses, and the single-word trace of what could have been a fourteenth. These lines are drawn from all Lucretian books save the third, no doubt a chance absence. Errors in citation are relatively few

---

[110] His citation of II.25 in *Exc. de arte Prisc.* (*PL* CXI 644C) is drawn from 'Maxim(in)us Victorinus'. The mention of Lucretius at *De laud. S. Crucis prol.* (*PL* CVII 146C = *Epp.* 2a (*MGH EKA* V.3, 383,31)): *feci quoque et synaloepham, aliquando in scriptu in opportunis locis synaloepharum, quod et Titus Lucretius non raro fecisse inuenitur* could stem from direct access to Lucretius at some stage or could reflect one of the numerous records of the poet's sigmatic ecthlipsis in the writings of Roman grammarians and/or metricians.

[111] For further discussion of this florilegium, see Sivo (1987) and Butterfield (2009e).

and rarely significant: *saluifragis* for *siluifragis* in citing I.275 (278); *transitat* for *transit at* in II.388 (398), where the lemma is the frequentative verb *transito*;[112] the omission of *in* before *primis* in II.447 (9); *soboles* for *suboles* and *mulieris* for *muliebris* (s.u. *mulieris*) in citing IV.1232 (242). In many instances the error is attested in only one of the primary witnesses (B P b) and I ignore these anomalies. The verses are typically attributed to Lucretius but V.1221 (72) is misattributed to P(rudentius) and I.275 (278), II.966 (315) and VI.752 (76) lack any authorial attribution. In one instance we find a correct reading against the erring direct tradition: *curamque* for *curaque* at II.365.[113] Finally, once (V.1221) we find that the *Opus prosodiacum* agrees in error with the direct tradition, namely in presenting *murmure* for *murmura*. The fact that ten of these verses (if we take the *Opus prosodiacum* as the oldest of these four florilegia) do not occur elsewhere in the indirect tradition, suggests that Mico had access at some point to a manuscript of Lucretius. Given that Mico is thought to have compiled his collection by obtaining at St Riquier an apograph of a florilegium sent from Reichenau in Lake Konstanz, twenty miles north-west of St Gallen, where we know a manuscript of Lucretius to have been (see below), his Lucretian citations probably descended ultimately from the archetype Ω.

(b) The collection entitled *Exempla diuersorum auctorum* was compiled anonymously, also in the mid ninth century, and was edited by Keil (1872) and Chatelain (1883).[114] Amidst the 220 verses recorded we find three drawn from Lucretius: II.128 (198, unattributed and without lemma, i.e. *clandestinos*), II.888 (111, attributed to 'Livi[us]', s.u. *sensile*) and V.6 (33, attributed to 'Luca[nus]' (R) or 'Luc[anus/retius]' (P), s.u. *opinor*). II.128 and V.6 are recorded without error but in II.888 we find *ex insensibili* for *ex insensilibus* and *nasci* for *gigni*. Since Priscian cites this verse (*Inst. GLK* II 132,21–2) with the corruption in some manuscripts into various

---

[112] *transitat* stands for *transit at* in OQS, from which we can assume that the archetype read *transitat*, which was wrongly taken (directly or indirectly) as a single verb by Mico in compiling his florilegium.

[113] *curaque* is retained by many editors but, as I have argued in Butterfield (2012b) 2–3, *curamque*, which could have been easily corrupted in the form *curāque*, is a much more natural expression.

[114] For further discussion of this florilegium, see Butterfield (2009b).

forms of *insensibili*, and also with *nasci* in lieu of *gigni*, it seems probable that the verse entered the florilegium, directly or indirectly, from this grammarian (*ex insensibili* easily being misdivided, in a verse chosen to exhibit *sensile*, to *exin sensibili*). We may also observe that it is clearly the case that *DRN* II.128 gained a somewhat canonical status in metrical florilegia, as, uniquely, it occurs in all four florilegia under discussion (without corruption). We can therefore be confident that the compiler of this florilegium had no text of Lucretius before him.

(c) In the Abbey Library of St Gallen there survives a late-ninth-century poetic miscellany (Stiftsbibl. 870), usually termed the *Florilegium Sangallense*.[115] Within this collection of verses Lucretius is cited twenty-eight times, alongside various poetic authors, among whom Juvenal plays by far the primary role in terms of frequency of citation. The majority of Lucretian quotations occur in a block of eighteen verses from the first two books, arranged largely in order (but with II.201 occuring between I.396 and I.448–9, and the last five occurring in reverse order: II.551, II.525, II.429, II.351, II.128); the others are spread beween the single citations of I.155 and III.207 as well as eight verses, cited in the order IV.639, II.447, III.1013, I.934, V.559, V.949, VI.896, VI.725. The general chronological and methodological citation of these verses suggests that the compiler of the florilegium was working first-hand with a text of Lucretius at his side, to which he returned during the collection of exempla. Given that connections evidently existed between St Gallen and Murbach (some thirty miles north-east), where there is known to have been a manuscript of *DRN* in the ninth century (see Chapter 1, pp. 29–30 with nn. 90 and 94), this is not a difficult supposition. Errors in citation are not especially common (I ignore the orthographical variations of the period): *iuuentes* for *iuuenes* and *parui* for *paruis* in I.186 (p. 10); *umescunt edem* for *uuescunt eaedem* in I.306 (p. 10); *nam* for *nec* in I.396 and I.448 (p. 10); *ciuent* for *cluent* and *conuincit* for *coniuncta duabus* in I.449 (p. 10); *ciuent* for *clueant* in I.580 (p. 11); *uideamus* for *uideamur* in II.245 (p. 11); *clueret enim* for *cluere. etenim* in II.525 (p. 11); *uota* for *nota* in

---

[115] For further discussion of this florilegium, see Butterfield (2009c)

II.351 (p. 11); *augent* for *auget* in IV.641 (p. 11); *adamantia* for *adamantina* in II.447 (p. 12); *pernitio . . . copus* (^a.c.) for *pernici . . . corpus* in V.559 (p. 12). All of these betray simple errors in copying a minuscule hand; given that we know Stiftsbibl. 870 to be a copy at least one remove from the original florilegium (cf. Butterfield (2009c) 352 n. 21), it remains possible that we simply have careless reporting of a manuscript related to the Lucretian archetype.

(d) Finally, we find two citations (three verses) of Lucretius in the brief metrical florilegium compiled by the short-lived Benedictine Heiric of Auxerre (841–76) and preserved in B.L. Harl. 2375 (ff. 207^r–208^v):[116] II.128 (f. 207^v) and IV.528–9 (f. 208^r). As mentioned above, II.128 was a verse that appears to have become a standard feature of metrical florilegia; the pair of lines IV.528–9, by contrast, was cited by both Aulus Gellius (X.26.9) and Nonius (453,7–9). Although these two authors present the corruptions of *radit* to *tradit* and *pauit* respectively, it remains possible that one of them is the source, directly or indirectly, of Heiric's quotation, which nevertheless preserves the correct *radit*. Since Nonius cites the line for *pauit*, and his manuscripts exhibit the further corruption of *aspera* for *asperiora*, Gellius seems the more probable source for Heiric.[117] Thus we need not assume that Heiric in compiling this florilegium had direct access to *DRN*. However, we should also note the two instances in which the same author seemingly echoes Lucretius in his *De uita Sancti Germani*: at I.96 (*uestibat teneras molli lanugine malas*) we find a close reminiscence of V.889 (*officit et molli uestit lanugine malas*); although the phrase *lanugine malas* (or *mala/malae*) closes a number of hexameters in Latin literature,[118] the presence of a form of *uestire* as well as *mollis* renders the imitation likely; and at VI.456 (*emersisse solet. modica ditescere praeda*) the Lucretian close *ditescere praeda* of V.1249 (*siue feras interficere et*

---

[116] For publication of this florilegium, see Ganz (1991) 307–9.

[117] Martin of Laon (Hiberniensis) is supposed to have had contact in the ninth century with Gellius (see Reynolds (1983a) 177 n. 6), so it is not impossible that Heiric did too, although the evidence is confessedly slim.

[118] Verg. *Buc.* II.51, *Aen.* X.324; Ou. *Met.* IX.398, XII.291, XIII.754; Luc. X.135; Sil. II.319, VII.691, XVI.468; Stat. *Theb.* VII.655, IX.703; Mart. II.61.1; Nemes. *Ecl.* II.77; Claud. *Carm. dubia* 5.14, Drac. *Romulea* 492.

ditescere praeda) is repeated.[119] Given that neither of these verses survives in the indirect tradition, it is probable that Heiric had at least read through *DRN* at some stage.[120] One could suggest therefore that IV.528–9, which appear at the end of Heiric's small florilegium, were added from his own reading; if so, nothing of interest can be concluded about Lucretius' text, since the sole error of *clauis* ('with nails/sticks'?) for *clamor* (529) is much more likely to be an odd recollection of the verse's close than the reading of a corrupt exemplar. If Heiric had access to *DRN* in Auxerre, the ninth-century circulation of the poem becomes broader.

(K)   Late citations (seventh–tenth centuries) (Aldhelm, Bede, Julian of Toledo, Sergius, Dicuil, Ermenrich, Hincmar, *Codd. Vat. Reg. Lat.* 598 and 1587, anonymous glossaries)

We at last come to citations from the seventh to tenth centuries AD, excluding the grammatical excerpts and metrical florilegia already considered.[121] We begin with Saint Aldhelm (*c.* 639–709), the scholar-poet and Bishop of Sherborne, who cited Lucretius once (but without mention of his name): *DRN* II.661 is reported in his *De dactilo* (p. 165,10 (Ehwald)) without error. It is probable, despite the rarity of the lexicographer's text, that this citation was drawn directly or indirectly from Nonius, who cited II.661–2 twice, rather than from direct access to Lucretius, as Rudolph Ehwald first suggested in his edition of Aldhelm (*MGH AA* 15 (1919)).[122]

---

[119] The only other similar collocation in Latin literature is Anon. *Carm. de bello Sax.* III.246 (*pluribus extractis gaudent ditescere praedis*).

[120] The one echo of Lucretius (IV.221 *nec uariae cessant uoces uolitare per auras*) in the anonymous *Vita Beati Leudegardii Martyris* (*tu ne uerba putes uacuas uolitare per aures*) could instead reflect knowledge of Mart. I.3.11 (*aetherias, lasciue, cupis uolitare per auras*); the collocation *uacuae aures*, as well as being Lucretian (I.50), is found in Horace (*Epp.* I.16.26), Ovid (*Am.* III.1.62, *Met.* IV.41, XII.56) and Martial (XI.3.2).

[121] Since there is no scope for their being independent authorities, I disregard the citation of I.186 in the following places: *Ars Laur. exp. in* Donat. I.158.3; *in* Donat. III.192.63; Murethach *in* Donat. III.195; Sed. Scott. *In Don.* III p. 327 (Löfstedt); Cruindmelus, *De arte metr.* p. 14.

[122] For brief discussion of the question of Aldhelm's access to Lucretius, see Lapidge (2006) 101–5, who closes with the improbable conclusion that Lucretius could have been read directly by the Saint. Further context can be obtained from Manitius (1886) 544.

The Venerable Bede (672/3–735) also quoted Lucretius once, citing VI.868 without error in his *De arte metrica* (I.16.18 = *GLK* VII 253,18–19); the corruption *aquae* for *laticis* and general context prove that Bede took this citation directly from Audax (*GLK* VII 329,2–3).[123]

Julian of Toledo (642–90), Archbishop of his Spanish birth city, cited two phrases of Lucretius in three instances. His mentioning *ualidi silices* (I.571/II.449) at *Ars* XV.12 is certainly drawn from Donatus (*Gramm. GLK* IV 393,31), and his twice recording V.1192 in the heavily corrupt form that Isidore presents shows that the fellow Spaniard was his source.[124]

The Irish monk and scholar Dicuil (fl. *c.* 800) cited Lucretius three times in his treatise *De primis syllabis* (sometimes *De prima syllaba*), composed around 825;[125] it transpires, however, that all of these citations are almost certainly drawn from the indirect tradition. The quoting of I.70–1 at p. 146,29–147,1 (Manitius) (= ff. 20^r–20^v) could have come from Nonius or Priscian; that of I.186 at p. 176,16–17 (= f. 34^v) (with *fuerant* for *fierent*) from a very large number of grammatical writers, as we have seen; that of III.156 at p. 146,13–14 (= f. 20^r) (with *et* wrongly inserted after *oculos*) from Nonius or Priscian. The mention of Lucretius alongside Lucan (incorrectly) at p. 140,14–15 (= f. 18^r) merely shows knowledge of the fact that the *paenultima* of *clandestinus* is long in these poets (which, in the case of Lucretius, could have been drawn from the citation of I.779 in the *Florilegium Sangallense* or, more probably, II.128 in all four florilegia discussed above).

In the short treatise *De grammatica*, attributed to a 'Sergius' and preserved in a manuscript dated to the early ninth century (Cod. Vat. Reg. Lat. 1587, ff. 16^v-21^v), we find the citation of two Lucretian verses. These citations, discussed by Finch (1967),[126] appear

---

[123] The mention of Lucretius at *De arte metr.* I.25.14 (*GLK* VII 259,25) is drawn wholesale from Dositheus (cf. n. 91 above), as is that by Cruindmelus at *De arte metr.* p. 45 (Heumer).

[124] Its form is identical to Isidore's at *Ars* XVIII.29 but bears the further corruption of *flumina* for *fulmina* at *De uitiis et fig.* V.32.

[125] This work, first edited by Manitius (1912), who wrongly attributed it to Mico of St Riquier, has been convincingly shown to be Dicuil's by Van de Vyver (1935).

[126] The work has not been fully published; the section *De litera* was edited by Keil at *GLK* VII 537–9.

towards the close of the section *De syllabis* (f. 19ᵛ). Ignoring trivial orthographic differences, this manuscript presents the errors *putatis* for *putamus* in VI.1106, and in VI.1135 *ultra* and *corrupit* for *uitro* and *corruptum*.¹²⁷ Mistaken recollection, quite possibly at second hand, seems the most likely explanation for these divergences from the direct tradition.

Ermenrich of Ellwangen (*c.* 817–74) was able to quote seven consecutive verses of Lucretius (I.150–6) in his letter to Abbot Grimaldus of *c.* 854 (*MGH* V.3 554,7–13). Ignoring the presumably scribal errors of *diuitiis* for *diuinitus* in 150 and *quocumque* for *quaeque* (before its correction by a later hand), the verses are given as we find them in the direct tradition. Ermenrich thus offered the passage with the same mistaken ordering of Ω, with 155 (*et quo quaeque modo fiant opera sine diuom*) appearing between 154 and 156; editors since Marullus have moved the line to its correct place after 158. It can be concluded with some certainty, therefore, that Ermenrich had access to a text of Lucretius very similar to the witnesses of the extant branch of the direct tradition. Given that Ermenrich was a guest in the early 850s at St Gallen, where the rich content of the *Florilegium Sangallense* has shown a manuscript of Lucretius was available, we can assume that Ermenrich there had direct exposure to a text of *DRN* which was evidently related to Ω.

Hincmar (806–82), the Archbishop of Reims, twice (*PL* CXXV 114A (AD 860), CXXVI 118A (AD 870)) cited without error the Lucretian verse upon the chimaera (V.905), which he could have found in Hyginus, Jerome or Isidore. Given that he attributes the phrase simply to *antiquus poeta* and that he makes no other mention of Lucretius, it is as good as certain that he obtained this citation indirectly from one of these widely read authors.

We come now to the anonymous *Annotationes* on Lucan whose date is most difficult to pin down. These *scholia*, which cannot be securely dated but probably contain vestiges of commentaries from antiquity, show basic knowledge of Lucretius' employment of the words *exemplare* (II.124) and *auere* (II.265/III.643) but no direct citation *per se*. Both facts of vocabulary could have been drawn from

---

¹²⁷ I have argued elsewhere (Butterfield (2006–7a) 90–1) that we should here read *uitio*, from which Sergius' *ultra* is more removed than *uitro* of the direct tradition.

the grammatical or lexicographical tradition. In the so-called *Commenta Bernensia Lucania* a citation of six Lucretian verses (VI.633–8) occurs, quite on its own; this passage is large enough to suggest that the scholiast (whenever and wherever he was working) had direct access to a text of Lucretius. We find only two errors in these lines, the vulgarised orthography of *ecore* for *aequore* (634) and the meaningless *undae* for *undas* (638). That these errors are so small could suggest that our tenth-century manuscript of these *scholia* (Bern. 370), if it did not copy from a text of Lucretius directly, was not many transcriptions removed from such a manuscript. It is very probable that the original scholiast (of whatever date) had direct access to a Lucretian manuscript, perhaps (if later) bearing a relationship with the Lucretian archetype (Ω).

Two sets of Lucretian verses (I.152–8, excluding I.155, and I.281–5)[128] are found in a Vatican manuscript of Serenus (Cod. Vat. Reg. Lat. 598, early saec. IX, at f. 33^r), under the designations *Titi* and *Item eiusdem*.[129] We may first note that verse I.155, misplaced as just discussed in the direct tradition, is omitted from the citation of I.152–8; we must therefore suppose either that the scribe had access to an entirely different tradition from that of Ω, or that he deliberately omitted the verse on the ground that it was manifestly out of place.[130] Given the additional corruptions of *munere* for *numine* (154, no doubt encouraged by the Christian concept of *diuinum donum/munus*), *dum* for *tum* (157) and *perspiemus ut* for *perspiciemus et*, it seems likely that these errors reflect mistaken transcription of these appended lines. In the other citation (I.281–6) we find the shared error *quem* in 282 with Ω (for *quam*), but in 282 and 284 the corruptions *aug* and *conitiens* for *auget* and *coniciens*. I suggest, therefore, that the verses were added to an earlier manuscript of Serenus by a reader who had access to a text of Lucretius without I.155 misplaced; whether or not this text contained any of the

---

[128] The later hand that has added the beginning of verse 286 (*uim subitam tolerare*) shows, by its recording page references for the Lucretian verses, that it is so late as to be working from a printed text of Lucretius.

[129] These citations were treated succinctly and lucidly by Pizzani (1959b); the existence of these verses had already been signalled by Lehmann (1929) 26.

[130] The third possibility, that the verse was lost by chance in transcription of this appended passage in Serenus' transmission, is too improbable to merit serious consideration.

corruptions just mentioned, or rather subsequent errors of memory engendered them, is impossible to say.

Among direct citations, we come finally to the anonymous and chronologically dubious glossaries. We may say at the outset that no glossographer seems to have had direct access to Lucretius' text. Lucretian verses are quoted in the *Excerpta e Libro glossarum*, the *Glossarium Placidi*, the *Excerpta e Cod. Vat. 1469* and the *Excerpta e Cod. Cass. 90*. The *Excerpta e Libro glossarum* cite the close of II.28 (*Corpus Glossariorum Latinorum* (hereafter *CGL*) V 215,21, s.u. *laquearibus*) in a corrupt form: *laqueata aure ad aque tecta* for *laqueata aurataque templa*: the banalisation *tecta* suggests that Macrobius (*Sat.* VI.4.21) is the source, whereas *aure ad aque* is a clear scribal error; *laqueata* is, by contrast, a correct survival (as in Macrobius) against *-ia queata* ($Q^{a.c.}$: *-ia queat* OS) of the direct tradition. The *Glossarium Placidi* cites (s.u. *extima*) the opening of IV.647 (*extima membrorum circumcaesura*) with the near-insignificant corruption of *casura* for *caesura*. We find in the *Excerpta e Cod. Vat. 1469* (*CGL* V 525,26, s.u. *puppus*) and *Excerpta e Cod. Cass. 90* (*CGL* V 574,52, s.u. *pappus*), both dating to the tenth century and both drawing upon a shared source, citation of III.386 (*uestem nec plumas auium papposque uolantes*); the former has the corruption *pupposque* (cf. also its mistaken lemma), the latter *nestem* and *pluuias*, all probably mere scribal errors. The source of the verse's citation is presumably Festus (cf. Paul. 246,6–7), directly or indirectly.

In the *Excerpta e Glossis A A*, a collection which survives in manuscripts from the tenth century onwards, we find the appearance of the word *ordia* (*CGL* V 471,56); despite the lack of explicit attribution to Lucretius (IV.28), it can be referred to him with confidence, since it occurs in no other (extant) Latin author. Similarly, in the *Glossarium Placidi* (*CGL* V 78,23) we find the lemma *interfiat*, a form that only survives in Lucretius (III.872). Finally, in the *Excerpta e Libro glossarum*, the glossographer records that Lucretius uses *triquetra* (I.717) of the island of which Virgil says *litore Trinacrio* (*Aen.* I.196), namely Sicily.

To close this final section of the survey, two late mentions of Lucretius' name, and allusions to his doctrines, remain to be recorded. In the second Vatican Latin mythology (of the ninth/tenth century), Lucretius is mentioned in discussion of Sisyphus (II.105), which is certainly drawn from Servius (*ad* Verg. *Aen.* VI.596): *dicit etiam Lucretius per eos, super quos iam casurus imminet lapis, superstitiosos* [*superstando* RPW] *designari qui inaniter semper uerentur, et de diis et caelo male opinantur.*[131] We also find mention of Lucretius in the anonymous *Fragmentum Parisinum de notis*, a passage which I had occasion to cite in the Introduction (n. 11) but which also does not show evince direct knowledge of the poet.

We have seen that, until the fifth century AD, Lucretius' *DRN* seems to have been available to those who troubled to seek him out at Rome; his presence in North Africa is likewise evident for the second to fourth centuries. Thereafter his circulation appears to have become much more attenuated: his text was seemingly available to the composers of the *Scholia Veronensia* for Virgil, and to Isidore in Iberia but scarcely any other figure in such a literary dark age. Once Lucretius started to circulate in the more favourable climate of the Carolingian Age, direct access to *DRN* was enjoyed in the ninth century at St Gallen by Ermenrich of Ellwangen (*c.* 817–74) and the compiler of the *Florilegium Sangallense*, and possibly Heiric of Auxerre (841–76), which shows the remarkable speed of the work's diffusion (see Chapter 1). The revival was short-lived: from the tenth century until Lucretius' rediscovery in 1417/18, direct access to a text of *DRN* is nowhere in evidence.

Statistical summary of the indirect tradition

Fifty-five different Latin[132] authors cited 492 different Lucretian verses in full or in part. The number of citations of each book is: I: 124; II: 107; III: 50; IV: 48; V: 83; VI: 80.[133] Book I is understandably given particular attention; more puzzling, however, is the comparative disregard of Books III and IV: perhaps the controversial subjects of their closing sections (the non-existence of Hell and irrelevance of death;

---

[131] For mention of Lucretius in the third Vatican mythology (of the twelfth century), see Appendix II, n. 1.
[132] Lucretius is not cited or mentioned by any Greek author; for dismissal of the equation of Lucretius with τοῦ ... θαυμασίου Κάρου in the inscription of Diogenes of Oenoanda (fr. 122 Smith), see Smith (1993a; 1997, 68–71).
[133] When weighted according to book lengths, the list of most cited to least cited books runs: I, II, VI, V, III, IV.

Table 3

Book	Festus	Charisius	Lactantius	Nonius	Macrobius	Servius	Priscian	Isidore	Florilegia	Other
I	5	3	8	20	11	10	13	3	9	78
II	5	3	20	30	25	7	12	1	16	37
III	2	2	6	25	5	0	6	0	2	12
IV	4	0	1	30	5	8	0	2	3	13
V	0	0	20	24	27	1	1	10	6	20
VI	2	1	9	19	34	3	5	2	3	21
Total	18	9	64	148	107	29	37	18	39	181

sexual intercourse) rendered them less amenable to authors of Christian beliefs, perhaps their being buried in the midst of the work (when unified in a codex) made them less prone to citation. The 650 instances of citations in Table 3 show the distribution of the 492 Lucretian verses quoted from *DRN* by authors of the indirect tradition.[134]

Despite this fluctuating stream of citations from the mid first to the tenth centuries AD, the *disiecta membra* of *DRN* generally bring disappointment. The value of the indirect tradition is limited for the Lucretian editor: few authors treated in this chapter command reverence in their authority when citing *DRN*, often because of their apparent reliance upon a flawed memory or a secondary source. The editor must instead pick and choose readings from the indirect tradition where he sees fit, although the comparative veracity of the direct tradition should restrict his preference for the indirect to more minor cases of discrepancy. Yet in certain cases where the indirect tradition finds its own voice an editor must stop in his tracks. We now turn to this special class of citations.

The so-called fragments of Lucretius

The most interesting species of citation are the sixteen purported elements of Lucretius' *DRN* not found in extant Lucretian manu-scripts,[135] most of which can conveniently be found in Diels'

---

[134] Since the table counts repeated citations of the same verse as separate verses numeric-ally, the totals are in some cases (especially Nonius) higher than those given for the discussion above.

[135] If genuine, these verses were lost from the direct tradition by the time the archetype (saec. VIII) was written.

edition (386–90). Although some were treated briefly and haphaz-
ardly in early commentaries, their first detailed analysis came in a
chapter of Forbiger's 1824 dissertation.[136] J. Becker (1847) succinctly discussed the majority, and Lachmann made due mention
of most throughout his magisterial but sprawling commentary.
Pascal (1906 = 1920, 69–81) overturned the general scepticism
about Lucretian authorship by attributing almost all of these
fragments to lost elements (including whole books beyond the
transmitted six)[137] of *DRN*. Relevant scholarship in Diels' wake
has been scanty, the sole detailed treatment being that of Pizzani
(1959a, 96–128), who judiciously whittled down the number of
plausibly Lucretian fragments.[138] Building upon his work, I will
argue that the majority of these assignations are indeed not Lucretian and analyse the possibly genuine ones that remain. We may
begin with those that can be dismissed with comparative certainty
as unlucretian.[139]

Fr. **I** Seru. *ad* Verg. *Aen.* VI.625:

non mihi si linguae centum sint oraque centum] Lucretii uersus sublatus de
Homero, sed *aerea* [Forbiger : *aenea* MSS contra metrum] *uox* ait

        non ego cuncta meis amplecti uersibus opto.
        non mihi si linguae centum sint oraque centum
        aerea uox

cf. also Seru. *ad.* Verg. *Geo.* II.42: *non ego cuncta*] Lucretii versus, sed ille *aerea*
uox ait, non *ferrea*.

In his note upon Verg. *Geo.* II.42–4, Servius alleged that Virgil
drew two lines and two words wholesale from Lucretius,
changing only *aerea* (as recorded in Servius' *Georgica* note
and rightly introduced by emendation[140] into that concerning
the *Aeneis*) to *ferrea* in the third line.[141] In his note upon Verg.
Aen. VI.625(–6), where Virgil repeated *Geo.* II.43 and the first

---

[136] Forbiger (1824) 75–89.   [137] See discussion of fr. **XII** below.
[138] Remarkably, Bailey (1947) did not treat these fragments beyond a single uninterested
sentence (vol. III 1682 with n. 1).
[139] My numeration up to XIII is that of Diels.
[140] The emendation is typically attributed to Lachmann but is Forbiger's (1824, 78–9).
[141] That the beginning of v. 42 is the lemma and the text opening 44 is also discussed
strongly suggests that *uersus* is plural.

choriamb of 44, VI.625–6 is attributed to Lucretius as a Homeric appropriation.[142] The crucial question therefore arises: did Virgil repeat without alteration such a large fragment from a Lucretian passage entirely lost in its direct transmission? We may first observe that Virgil seems nowhere else to have drawn a full hexameter from any poetic predecessor.[143] This borrowing, therefore, employed separately in his two greatest poetic works, would be quite unparalleled: it would also be surprising for such a major literary appropriation to go unmentioned in Virgilian commentators outside Servius, not even in Macrobius, for whom it would have been the prize specimen of his discussion of such borrowings at *Sat.* VI.

We can easily verify Servius' observation that the conceit can be traced back to Homer, for *Il.* II.489–90 is here closely imitated: οὐδ᾽ εἴ μοι δέκα μὲν γλῶσσαι δέκα δὲ στόματ᾽ εἶεν | φωνὴ δ᾽ ἄρρηκτος, χαλκέον δέ μοι ἦτορ ἐνείη. Yet two other parallels prior to Lucretius and Virgil are cited elsewhere in late-antique commentaries: we learn from the *Breuis expositio ad* Verg. *Geo.* II.43 that Ennius had already drawn the idea from Homer: *Homericus sensus Graeci poetae,*[144] *sicut et Ennius 'non si lingua loqui saperet quibus, ora decem sint* | *in me, tum* [L. Mueller : *metrum* codd. contra metrum] *ferro cor sit pectusque reuinctum'* (= *Ann.* 469–50 Skutsch).[145] In comparison with the

---

[142] It is of course possible that Servius' note should rather have *Geo.* II.43 as its lemma, in which case the verse beginning *non ego* is omitted from the alleged Lucretian fragment (so Lachmann, Diels and Büchner, among others).

[143] *Pace* Ferrando (1473, 106ʳ: '[Lucretium] ita suis descriptionibus [pœte] imitentur et Virgilius praesertim pœtarum princeps ut ipsis cum uerbis tria interdum & amplius metra suscipiant)', his largest borrowings are of four and a half feet: *Aen.* VI.622 (Var. Ruf. 1.2 Blänsdorf) and 846 (Enn. *Ann.* 363 Sk, although if *qui* is correct in the Virgilian line, the borrowing is reduced in size). See Jocelyn (1965) 142, for convincing arguments against the full attribution of Verg. *Geo.* II.404 and *Aen.* X.396 to Varro Atacinius; the case of *Geo.* I.377, which Seru. Dan. *ad loc.* declared to have occurred in the same form in a larger Varronian passage, is more complicated; nevertheless, Jocelyn's suggestion (1965, 141–2) that the Virgilian verse was artificially conflated with the Varronian seems probable. Finally, Servius' testimony (*ad* Verg. *Buc.* X.46: *hi autem omnes uersus Galli sunt, de ipsius translati carminibus*) should not be taken literally, and Gellius' assertion (I.21.7: *non uerba autem sola, sed uersus prope totos et locos quoque Lucreti plurimos sectatum esse Vergilium uidemus*) should be read with due emphasis upon *prope.*

[144] The banal *Graeci poetae* could perhaps be a nominative plural gloss (rather than genitive sc. *Homeri*), reflecting a widening of Homer to other Greek sources.

[145] The same information is conveyed by the *Schol. Bern. ad loc.* (*Homericus sensus*).

Aeneis lines, Macrobius (*Sat.* VI.3.6) adduced alongside the Homeric passage a quotation from Book II of the *Bellum Histricum* II (fr. 3 Blänsdorf) of Hostius (date uncertain: saec. II BC?): *non si mihi linguae | centum, atque ora sient totidem, uocesque liquatae*. He therefore made no mention of Lucretius, despite citing *DRN* thirty-seven times elsewhere in *Sat.* VI (Hostius, by contrast, is only cited by Macrobius once elsewhere); it is also true, however, that Macrobius here ignored the Ennian parallel, which he presumably knew.[146] Alongside these passages, the conceit would also have been known to Virgil from Caecilius (126: *si linguas decem | habeam, uix habeam satis te qui laudem, Lache*). Therefore, whereas Homer, Ennius and Caecilius employed the notion of ten tongues, Hostius augmented it to a hundred, as did Virgil (leaving aside his possible source), with Valerius Flaccus (VI.37) introducing a thousand.[147]

Beyond the unlikelihood of Virgil's drawing so large a passage from *DRN*, the Lucretian attribution of the quotation is improbable for other reasons. First, we may consider its linguistic features. Lucretius nowhere else employed the verb *opto*, either of his own poetic choices or in any other context. The adjective *aereus* (first found at Var. *Men.* 169 and Laber. *Com.* 50.3 Panayotakis) is also unattested in Lucretius; his word for 'brazen' is *a(h)enus*,[148] regularly used without synizesis (I.316, V.1294, VI.1045) and at verse-end. Further, despite its metrical utility, Lucretius restricted his use of nominative *ego*:[149] of the six transmitted instances, two (I.943 = IV.18) open the line with the phrase *sic ego nunc* (serving to explain his own philosophical methodology), three occur in relative clauses with verbs of striving (*persequor*), trying (*conor*) and inability (*nequeo*), and the sixth forms part of his proud claim to be the first to transmute Epicureanism into Latin (V.337); all except the first line of these (I.943 = IV.18) occur in

[146] Skutsch (1985, 628 n. 14) fairly compared Macrobius' practice at *Sat.* VI.3.5, where he mentioned Homer, Furius and Virgil but not Enn. *Ann.* 584 Sk.
[147] Pascucci (1959) discussed the trope's amplification from Ennius onwards; Courcelle (1955), after Weinreich (1918), charted its development from Greek literature to the Middle Ages.
[148] The form *ahenus* is attested at VI.1045: at I.316 and V.1294 Ω read *aena* and *athen(a)e* respectively.
[149] Cf. Giancotti (1976) 74–5.

subordinate clauses. Finally, the anaphora of *non* at the beginning of two adjacent hexameters is attested only once in *DRN*, at VI.1075–6 (where *non si* is repeated within the same sentence).

Secondly, we must consider the force of the fragment. If Lucretian, it would be manifestly programmatic, declaring that Lucretius, as a poet, did not wish to be comprehensive. This is the case in both Virgilian contexts: *Geo.* II.42–4, where Virgil confesses that his poetic narrative is not all-encompassing, and *Aen.* VI.625–6, where the Sibyl, lamenting the scale of suffering in the Underworld, rejects recounting the misery completely. Such an apologia for an incomplete account is redolent of an astounded narrator – particularly in an epic context – rather than of Lucretius' confident, all-embracing didactic programme: we could expect him perhaps to state that it is impossible for everything to be treated in the scope of his work, but his declaring that he has purposefully chosen (*opto*) to omit material seems most uncharacteristic.[150]

Thirdly, the fragment would have to precede an in-depth account covering a large section of the work. Yet, of the various lacunae generally posited in *DRN*, there is no truly plausible candidate to contain such a remarkable authorial announcement. Nonetheless, scholars have offered various suggestions: although Forbiger (1824, 79 n. 44)[151] did not specify a location, and J. Becker (1847, 49–51) only observed that it could have concerned the Attic plague in Book VI, four specific suggestions have been offered, which I treat in their textual order. (i) Giancotti (1976, 83ff.) argued that the attribution of the fragment to Lucretius is credible, although his arguments are inconclusive and provide little positive defence of Servius' attribution. He improbably contextualised it as part of an invocation of the Muses(!) in the lacuna (first identified by Pontanus) after II.164, which was evidently of some size but presumably treated the speed and motion of atoms:[152] there is no clear topic to which this

---

[150] We may instructively compare Lucretius' lucid and tactful discussion at I.400–14 of how many arguments he needs for Memmius.

[151] He argued that because Macrobius did not mention this passage, he had access to a corrupt tradition of the poem (like, if not the same as, that which survives) that had lost this passage.

[152] For discussion of this lacuna outside commentaries, see Raasted (1955) and Owen (1968).

programmatic assertion could refer, and the ensuing extant discussion seems comparatively comprehensive.[153] (ii) Boeck (1958, 245–6) suggested that the lines stood before VI.92 (and in his view after VI.47, so transposed by Martin). The subject matter Lucretius rejected discussing in full would therefore be the full gamut of terrestrial and celestial phenomena. Although this is the most plausible place to insert fr. **I**, it would sit oddly after the clear list of topics outlined at VI.48–55. It would be curious for Lucretius here to confess that there are innumerable distinct phenomena, tantamount to acknowledging that one's *ratio*, even when perfected like Lucretius' or Epicurus', cannot embrace the full workings of earth and sky. (iii) Madvig (1834, 16) placed the fragment in the lacuna he posited before VI.608; this suggestion, which would place the lines strangely amidst arguments concerning earthquakes (535–608) and why the sea does not increase (609–38), has understandably lacked subsequent favour. (iv) Finally, Lachmann inserted these verses, among others, in the lacuna of fifty-two lines he diagnosed after VI.839. Even if one grants the existence of this textual loss (on which see my discussion of fr. **II** below), it would be remarkable for Lucretius to make such a grandiose programmatic statement so late in *DRN*, when turning to the pedestrian matter of the temperatures of wells throughout the year.[154]

A more positive line than taking Servius, who wrote some 450 years after Lucretius' death and did not have direct access to *DRN*,[155] at his word and speculating at what point this unlucretian fragment should be inserted, is to suspect the commentator of error. We may first wonder whether he misattributed the passage to Lucretius, after Virgil had drawn it from elsewhere. Becker (1847, 49–51) first assigned the fragment to another poet, namely Lucilius, a suggestion followed by Mueller (1872a) and discussed in further detail by Scaffai (2008). It is certainly possible that

---

[153] García Calvo (unaware of Giancotti (1976)) also inserted fr. **I** after II.164, although he placed it within forty verses of his own composition!

[154] Marx (1904–5, *ad* Lucil. 1364–5 M) rightly objected 'uix credibile est tanto hiatu nouum carmen Lucretium illo loco fuisse exorsum'.

[155] See above at section F(i). For Servius' often inaccurate citations of Lucretius, see Pizzani (1959a) 120–2; the survey of Poignault (1999b) is more general. No weight can be attributed to Servius' vague assertions *ad Geo.* II.329 and IV.219.

Lucretius sprang from *Lucilius*, perhaps through an incorrect expansion of *Luc.* (or *Lucīus*),[156] in one of the two Servian passages, an error that could easily have engendered the corruption in the other by contamination in a work so carefully read. Were we to emend to *Lucilius*, however, we would have to respond to Marx's objection that Virgil would not have appropriated so large a passage from a satirist.[157] Although Virgil occasionally did imitate Lucilius,[158] the complaint retains genuine force, for such a stark, unaltered and unparalleled borrowing in two significant parts of both poems would be an exceedingly emphatic and disproportionately distinct homage to a writer of satire. Marx instead explained the appearance of Lucretius by conjecturing that 'falso et temere Servium Lucretii nomen supposuisse'. The suggestion is possible, given that Servius would have known of Virgil's frequent Lucretian imitations but could not verify imitations by personal access to *DRN*.[159]

Virgil, I submit, did not borrow such a large passage unchanged from a predecessor; it is also improbable that he only doctored to a small degree some such passage. I rather suppose that Servius, without access to *DRN*, was well aware of Latin precedents of the Homeric motif, yet in writing the note he had no such quotation to hand so instead attributed the verses loosely (cf. his statement at the close of n. 143 above) to a particular poet. Perhaps he wrote *Lucilius*, who could also have taken up this conceit (as would have been fitting for a hyperbolic satirist); perhaps he confused Ennius with Lucretius, on the basis that Virgil commonly echoed both poets. Whatever the truth, the sheer irregularity of Virgil's lifting unchanged so much text from Lucretius, the coincidence of the

---

[156] Much evidence can be supplied to document the scribal confusion between *Lucretius* and *Lucilius*, along with other names beginning with *Luc-*; for such material see below at n. 168.

[157] Marx (1904–5, *ad* Lucil. 1364 M): 'ridiculus fuerit Vergilius si integrum saturae uersum heroo inseruit carmini.'

[158] Cf. Wigodsky (1972) 105–8.

[159] Brieger (*Prol.* LXXX) alleged that Munro attributed the fragment to Ennius but the latter actually stated (app. crit. *ad* VI.839) that it seemed sufficiently Lucretian; I have found no discussion of the fragment in Munro's shorter writings; Brieger probably confused Munro's remark on fr. **IX** (app. crit. *ad* IV.126; see below). At any rate, the attribution to Ennius is rendered most unlikely by his using so similar a trope elsewhere (cited above).

passage's complete absence from the direct and indirect tradition of *DRN*, the evident frequency of the conceit in other poets, and the unlucretian nature of the phraseology render attribution to Lucretius most improbable. This so-called fragment, the longest of those that survive (even if the first line is to be excluded), thus deserves no place in critical editions of *DRN*.[160]

Fr. **IV** Seru. Dan. *ad* Verg. *Geo.* III.136:

sulcos oblimet] claudat meatus. et hoc similiter per translationem dixit. nam legimus supra *et obducto late tenet omnia limo* [= I.116]. et aliter: Lucretius

ne oblimet

pro 'obturet' et 'obcludat'. alibi [*mss* : alii *tent. Thilo*] *oblimet* 'tcrat', perdat'. Horatius [= *S.* I.2.62].

A number of scholars since Lachmann have deemed this fragment Lucretian and inserted it in the lacuna posited after VI.839. I rather regard it as a citation of Virgil himself:[161] we should unite *et aliter Lucretius*, and treat *ne oblimet* as the lemma drawn from Verg. *Geo.* III.135–6 (*nimio ne luxu obtunsior usus | sit genitali aruo et sulcos oblimet inertes*), with *ne* repeated to elucidate the form as present subjunctive and thereby reveal its conjugation.[162] How then was the verb's usage attributed to Lucretius? The most probable explanation is that proposed by Broughton (1939, 239), namely that the transmitted text corrupted *et aliter Lucanus* (possibly abbreviated *Luc.*); the mention of Lucretius in the preceding note (*ad Geo.* III.135) could have prompted the scribal error.[163]

---

[160] That Servius in both instances as well as the *Breuis expositio* and the *Schol. Bern.* stated that Virgil wrote *ferrea* rather than *aerea* of his exemplar points towards a common source in which bronze not iron was mentioned. The underlying origin of this statement was probably the fact that Homer used χαλκέον at *Il.* II.490; although it modified ἦτορ and not φωνή (qualified rather by ἄρρηκτος; yet cf. χαλκεόφωνος of Stentor at *Il.* V.785), Virgil's *ferrea uox* could still be thought to have replaced it with the concept of iron.

[161] This observation was first made by Mueller (1872b), who noted that Lucretius was also mentioned in the previous scholion.

[162] Donatus in his *Ars maior ad loc.* (V f. 124) cited *ne oblimet* as his lemma.

[163] At Seru. *ad* Verg. *Geo.* I.139, Servius attributed a passage of Lucan (III.658) to Lucretius before citing a genuine Lucretian passage (I.837); this point escaped Forbiger (1824, 81), who treated the former as a lost fragment of Lucretius. We may also compare the reverse error of *Lucanus* for *Lucretius* at Seru. *ad.* Verg. *Geo.* III.481; for confusion of other names beginning *Luc.*, see below at n. 168.

Although Broughton believed that the two words are a fragment taken from a lost Lucanian work, I rather suppose that his *oblimat* at *Bellum ciuile* VI.364 (of 'covering' islands with mud) served as the basis for the reference. Alternatively, it is possible that Lucilius once employed the verb, was duly cited and, as a casualty of the ever-present danger of scribal error, his name was banalised into Lucretius (cf. n. 168 below).[164]

Fr. **VII** Seru. *ad* Verg. *Aen.* XII.419:

panaceam] genus herbae; sciendum tamen Lucretium

panaceam

ubique salem dicere, unde possumus et hoc loco salem intellegere; nam omnem pellit dolorem.

The nature of this testimonium renders unclear in what case(s) Lucretius supposedly wrote *panacea* in plural instances.[165] In the direct tradition, the only cognate form of *panacea* occurs at IV.123–4: *odorem | expirant acrem, panaces absinthia taetra*, where *panaces*, 'prunella' or 'selfheal', is probably masculine plural (of *panaces/panax*).[166] Although this passage could have inspired Virgil to use *odoriferam panaceam* (*Aen.* XII.419), there is no evidence that Lucretius ever wrote *panacea*. Furthermore, the use of *ubique* in Servius' note would demand plural (i.e. at least three?) instances of its employment for *sal*.[167] The likelihood that all such passages where Lucretius so employed the word have

---

[164] Thilo (1887 *ad loc.*) suggested that Lucretius could be the corruption of the name of a Virgilian scholar but offered no suggestion.

[165] We may reject the possibility that the fragment is instead the three words *panaceam ubique salem*. Such a phrase could only scan in dactylic metres if the final syllable of *panaceam* was in prosodic hiatus, a licence unattested in Lucretius with words ending in -*m*. Pizzani (1959a, 114–15), who implausibly thought that all three words stood in the lacuna after IV.126, ignored the metrical problem. If, however, *panacea* was written with a Greek termination (*panacean*, as first suggested by Marx (1904–5, *ad* Lucil. 1367 M)), the metre could be dactylic. However, Servius' subsequent words (*unde . . . intellegere*) clearly treat *panacea* and *sal* as equivalent, which demonstrates that he did not envisage a three-word fragment.

[166] The Greeks employed ἡ πανάκεια, ὁ πάναξ and τὸ πάνακες. Bailey (*ad loc.*) asserted that it is neuter on the basis of Pliny the Elder's various neuter singular citations of the word, but, alongside *absinthia*, the plural seems the easier interpretation.

[167] Servius used *ubique* almost a hundred times, typically referring to a universal, or almost universal, occurrence.

been lost in lacunae is so slim that we can safely reject the Lucretian associations of this testimonium.

To what author, then, did Servius refer? Or rather, if Servius actually wrote *Lucretius*, with what author had he confused him? Lucilius again seems the most probable suggestion. This testimonium was attributed to him as early as Baptista Pius (*ad* IV.123 (f. CV^r)), who stated that the error of names could have occurred 'facili et consueto scribentium lapsu',[168] and Forbiger (1824, 77 n. 42), J. Becker (1847, 48–9) and Marx (as n. 165) have prudently followed him. With so much of Lucilius' poetry lost, it is not a particularly difficult supposition to believe that he used *panacea* as a synonym, euphemism or mock term for salt.[169] We need not follow Becker in supposing that Lucilius employed *salem* here in the sense of 'wit'.

Remaining theories can be swiftly dismissed as less attractive. Scaliger[170] instead attributed the fragment to Licinius Macer (i.e. Aemilius Macer?), a suggestion that has not found subsequent

---

[168] It has long been observed that the confusion of *Lucretius* with similar names, particularly *Lucilius*, was common in Latin manuscripts. In a Lucretian context, we can cite the third preface of Avancius in the first Aldine: 'multa etiam deprauata correximus ex uersibus citatis a Prisciano Macrobio & ante omnes Marcello, apud quem tamen saepius pro Lucretio, Lucilius est suppositus' (π3^v). Gifanius (**7^v) later observed: 'Saepe Lucilius, Lucretius et Lucullus, ut Coelius ac Cecilius, alius in alterius locum vitiose subiecti sunt.' Note also Mueller (1872a, 193): 'nomen Lucili frequenter in libris scriptis grammaticorum per abbreviationem exaratur Lucil. vel Lucl, transfixo ut plurimum *l* lineola curva . . . omnium quidem frequentissime *Lucius* legitur pro *Lucilio*, sicuti e contrario . . . praeterea confusa cum huius nomina quae sunt *Lucretius, Lucillus, Lucullus, Lucanus, Licinius, Caecilius*, alia; quorum passim errorum exempla in apparatu critico invenies.' Cf. also Forbiger (1824) 77–8 n. 42, J. Becker (1847) 42–3, Lachmann (1849) 3 (= 1876, 62), Regel (1907) 81–2. For *Lucilius* wrongly transmitted for *Lucretius*, see Charis. 116,8 B (N), 118,2 B (NC), Non. 181,3 M; perhaps also *schol. ad* Pers. I.2 (if not I.1; see Zetzel (1977), Bo (1991), Sosin (1999) 281–4). *Luc.* was used for *Lucretius* at Charis. 268,5 B (= fr. VI). For *Lucretius* wrongly transmitted for *Lucilius*, see (alongside frs. I (very probably), III (perhaps), VII, IX–XIV): Macr. *Sat.* VI.1.35 [*Lucretius* RF], *schol ad* Iuu. X.66 (= Lucil. 1145 M); Fest. Paul. 495,13 L (= Lucil. 1195 M; *Lucilius* rightly given by Fest. Paul. 494,32 L); Non. 117,18 M (= Lucil. 16 M). Wilkinson (1949) plausibly suggested that the fates of Lucretius and Lucullus were confused by Jerome or his source when asserting that Lucretius died from a love potion. The possible instance in ps.-Apuleius' *De orthographia* (2: *ex nostris Nasone et Caluo, Lucilio* [*Lucretio* coni. Osann] *uero primo libro*) is best disregarded owing to the work's doubtful origin and the possibility that the error was the author's own (cf. Osann (1826) 3).

[169] Pizzani (1959a, 114) cited Apicius I.13 for the wide range of medical usages salt was thought to have.

[170] Under the guise of 'Yvo Villiomarus': Scaliger (1586) VIII.5 (= cap. 13, 152–3).

favour. Lachmann (*ad* V.1273) instead asserted with more probability that the passage was drawn by Servius from a Lucretian commentary, such as those mentioned by Jerome (cf. Introduction p. 3 with n. 12). Broughton (1939, 239) suggested Lucan (as with fr. **IV**), who indeed employed *panacea* (*potens*) at IX.918 and with whom Lucretius was confused by Servius or his scribes (cf. n. 163 above). Yet, Lucan presumably used *panacea* because of the Virgilian instance and, since his employment of the word concerns neither salt nor wit, we would still have to credit the loss of plural instances in which he so used the word.[171]

In conclusion, we should posit grave error either by Servius in attributing Lucilius' (if not a comic writer's?) habitual usage of *panacea* for *sal* to Lucretius (perhaps through mistaken reminiscence of the cognate *panaces* at IV.124) or by a scribe in writing Lucretius for *Lucilius* (perhaps abbreviated *Luc.*).

Fr. **VIII** ps.-Prob. *Cath. GLK* IV.10,30–2:

PO syllaba terminata producuntur, *uappo*, *uapponis*, animal est uolans, quod uulgo ammas [animas *corr. Lachmann*][172] uocant; lectum est apud Lucretium

hos uappones

This fragment should probably only read *uappones*, the rather prosaic *hos* being added to elucidate the gender of *uappo*,[173] a noun not attested in literature before this citation (saec. IV?). It was first attributed to Lucilius (= 1358 Marx) by Dousa (1597, no. 161 of *incertae*).[174] Lindemann,[175] tentatively supported by Pizzani

---

[171] Lucan used *sales* only twice, of jesting (II.368) and brine (X.257).

[172] Although Jahn (1847, 137 n. 67) provided evidence that *pupillo* and ψυχή were associated in Greek thought, Lachmann's emendation to *ammas* is highly probable; alongside his citation of the glossary entries in Mai (1828–38, VI 506 *ama, auis nocturna*; VII 551 *amma, auis nocturna*), we may add the entry in the *Liber glossarum* (saec. VIII; see Lindsay *et al.* (1926, AM 1 (= p 47 col. 2) *amma: auis nocturna*). I tentatively suggest that *ammam* could be read instead of *animam*, corruption to a plural here being easy. After the citation of Luc. VI.689, Isidore wrote *haec auis uulgo amma dicitur, ab amando paruulos* (*Etym.* XII.7.42). The only other emendation of this citation, Krenkel's *animans*, is inherently implausible.

[173] This is perfectly standard among the Latin grammarians: cf., e.g., the opening of fr. **X** below.

[174] Dousa likewise disregarded *hos*. I cannot identify the 'multi' referenced in his comment *ad loc.* who had already rejected the Lucretian attribution.

[175] Lindemann (1831–40) I 1450.

(1959a, 124–5), more probably regarded the fragment as emerging from a confusion of Lucr. III.386 (*uestem, nec plumas auium papposque uolantes*, a verse cited by Paul. Fest. 246,6–7 s.u. *pappo* and *CGL* V 525,26; 574,52).[176] Although the variant *uapposque* (*uel sim.*) is not attested in Lucretius' extant manuscripts, the collocation of a noun modified by *uolantes* and *plumae auium* could have suggested that this word was another form of flying creature so light that our skin cannot perceive its touch. Further, that the grammarian wrote *hos* not *hi* suggests that he or his source recalled the noun as accusative in its context. So rare a noun as *pappus* could have led the writer (or his source) to misremember the line as containing a form of *uappo*. This seems a neater solution than positing that either Lucretius or Lucilius ever used the most rare *uappo* in a lost passage.

Fr. **IX** Prob. *ad* Verg. *Buc.* VI.131 (343,4 H):

plane trinam esse mundi originem et Lucretius confitetur dicens [Lucr. V.92–4] et alio loco:

> omnia per sonitus arcet terram mare caelum

Probus' words imply, but do not explicitly state, that this verse was Lucretian in origin. It is much more probably Ennian (= *Ann.* 556 Sk), for Seru. Dan. *ad* Verg. *Aen.* I.31 recorded *Ennius 'qui fulmine claro | omnia per sonitus arcet'*, *id est continet*.[177] Lachmann (*ad* Lucr. IV.126) thought that the line could have been drawn wholesale from Ennius (comparing the lesser borrowings at III.1025, 1035, IV.409 and VI.195)[178] and lost in the lacuna after IV.126. But Munro (app. crit. *ad loc.*) fairly replied that 'it has nothing of [Lucretius'] style about it' but is rather Ennian in nature.[179]

The mistake is far more probably Probus' than a curious scribal error. The suggestion of Diels (*ad loc.*) and Pizzani (1959a,

[176] Lachmann (*ad loc.*) expressed his doubt: 'mihi quam recte grammaticus *vappones* Lucretio adscripserit non liquet.'
[177] We may note that for the citation of Enn. *Ann.* 510 Sk (*terrai frugiferai*) at *Frag. Bob. de nom. et pronom. GLK* II 555,3, we find *apud Lucretium* for *apud Ennium*, although this error was probably influenced by Lucr. I.3 (*terras frugiferentes*).
[178] The verse that Lachmann envisaged (cited anonymously by Cicero at *Tusc.* I.37.5) is not now generally attributed to Ennius.
[179] We do however find the asyndeton of *mare, caelum* and *terra/-ae* at II.1015 and V.68 (for their collocation in a single line, see V.434 and 592 [594]).

125–6) that it could have arisen from Probus' using a source in which the Ennian verse followed the Lucretian (e.g. IV.738 *si mare, si terram cordist, si denique caelum?*) is certainly plausible. More likely, however, is Bernays' simple suggestion (1848 = 1885, vol. II, 68–9) that *et alio loco*, if not corrupt, introduced the Ennian citation. Baehrens (1886, 111 fr. 411) offered the alternative supplement *Ennius etiam in Medea 'quique tuo cum lumine mare terram caelum contines'* (= *Scen.* 235 Jocelyn).

Fr. **X** ps.-Prob. *De nom. GLK* IV 212,10:

nasus hic an hoc nasum? antiqui neutraliter dicebant; itaque Lucretius

nasum deductius [diductius *coni. Marx*] quam pandius paulo uellem

This verse, which is evidently not hexametric,[180] is certainly from the hand of Lucilius (= 942–3 M), as Keil (*GLK ad loc.*) first suggested,[181] a poet who employed neuter *nasum* at 267 M and 582 M (where we find *nasum rectius*), both cited by Non. 215,2–5 M.[182] The fragment is therefore merely of interest to us in providing further evidence of how either grammarians or ancient scribes confused the names of Lucretius and Lucilius (cf. n. 168 above).[183]

Fr. **XI** Macr. *Sat.* VI.1.43:

magna ossa lacertosque
exuit [= Verg. *Aen.* V.422–3]

Lucilius [Lucius *PN* : Lucretius *RFA*] in septimo decimo

magna ossa lacertique
apparent homini

---

[180] Marx (*ad loc.*) attempted to recreate the beginning and end of iambic senarii: *nasum deductius | quam pandius si paulo uellem.*

[181] However, he wrongly added 'nasus nec masculino nec neutro genere in Lucretii libris legitur', for *nasi* (Q : *nisi* O) is correctly transmitted at VI.1193, although its gender cannot in this instance be discerned.

[182] We may also compare *GLK* V 584,24: *nasum generis neutri, ut Lucilius 'nasum hoc corpusque scutum'.*

[183] The carelessness of the author of *De nomine* is evident in his mistaking Horace's usage for Lucretius': *sed Lucretius, metrum custodiens, rationem regulae excessit, qui ait 'anciliorum' non 'ancilium'* (= Hor. *C.* III.5.10) (*GLK* IV 208,25–6).

This instance again requires almost no discussion, since it is Lucilian (= 547–8 M), as the reference to a seventeenth book clearly indicates.[184] *Lucretius* is merely a scribal error in one of the two manuscript families[185] for *Lucilius*, as also slightly earlier in the same book (Macr. *Sat.* VI.1.35, where RF wrongly present *Lucretius*), as well as in frs. **X** and (quite probably) **VII**. I have sought elsewhere to remove the single transmitted instance of hypermetre in Lucretius, a licence seemingly not taken up by him.[186]

Fr. **XII** Var. *L.L.* V.17:

sic caelum et pars eius, summum ubi stellae, et id quod Pacuuius cum demonstrat dicit: 'hoc uide circum supraque quod complexu continet terram': cui subiungit: 'id quod nostri caelum memorant.' a qua bipertita diuisione Lucretius suorum unius et uiginti librorum initium fecit hoc

aetheris et terrae genitabile quaerere tempus

Although *genitabilis* is attested only in Lucretius (I.11) in classical Latin,[187] there is no good reason to suppose that this verse is Lucretian. First, its context is highly problematic, since it is said to be the beginning of a Lucretian work of twenty-one books. Lucretius' *DRN* was certainly no longer than six books,[188] and no evidence suggests that he composed another poetic work.[189] Secondly, the line

---

[184] See the discussion of fr. **XII** below.
[185] RFA; J, the fourth witness of this family, lacks *Sat.* V–VI.
[186] Butterfield (2008a) 118–20.
[187] But cf. its appearance at Aug. *Contra ep. Man.* 30 (*CPL* 320 232,3) and Arnob. IV.28.
[188] Cf. Introduction p. 2 with nn. 6 and 7. The '*Vita Borgiana*' first recorded disbelief in Varro's testimony (see Solaro (2000) 34); Pascal (1906, 264 n. 1) tentatively suggested that Varro was referring to Lucretius but that *suorum IX librorum (uel sim.)* was corrupted into *suorum I et XX* [!] *librorum*; yet even if *VII* were transmitted in Varro's manuscripts, I would set little store by its evidence. The suggestion of García Calvo ([575]) that XXI is a corruption of VI is inept.
[189] Pascal (1906) suggested that Lucretius wrote other works than *DRN* but offered no evidence beyond crediting the fragments currently under discussion; Hermann (1956, 472–3) later supported Pascal's idea that Lucretius also wrote a satirical work. Hutchinson (2001, 154 and n. 11) supported the notion, and argued that Cicero referred to such lost works when writing to his brother (cf. Introduction p. 1 n. 4). Romano (1993–4, 27–36) argued that frs. **II, III, IV, VII, VIII** and **XI** (as well as Servius' comments *ad* Verg. *Aen.* XII.87 and the reading *acribus iris* drawn from a papyrus (cf. Bassi (1926) 209)) were drawn from another Lucretian poem. This rather groundless inference of lost Lucretian poems had been made earlier by Wakefield (vol. I, *Praef.* XXIV), and yet earlier by the '*Vita Borgiana*' (cf. Solaro (2000) 36).

transmitted as I.1 in Lucretian manuscripts was evidently regarded as the opening line of Lucretius' work in antiquity (cf. Ou. *Tr.* II.261 and Prisc. *Inst. GLK* II 292,18). Thirdly, as Girolamo Borgia rightly objected,[190] it is difficult to imagine a context in which Lucretius would have said that he (or anyone else) sought out the 'generative time(s)' of the aether and earth.[191] Finally, we may note (dismissing fr. **XIII** as unlucretian below) that Varro never cited any contemporary poet, Lucretius included.[192]

Gifanius in 1565 therefore wisely suggested that *Lucilius* be read for *Lucretius*,[193] a change later made without acknowledgement by Lambinus in his third edition (1570, *ad loc.*)[194] and by Scaliger in his Festus (1575).[195] The corruption was probably aided by the prominent place of the same adjective *genitabilis* in *DRN*'s proem and the fragment's apparently philosophical nature. Rather, this line presumably opened Lucilius' corpus; that Varro wrote twenty-one rather than thirty, if XXX has not been corrupted into XXI, perhaps reflects the existence of a smaller edition of his work, perhaps restricted by metre (Books I–XXI being in hexameters). Varro cited Lucilius thirteen times elsewhere in what survives of *De lingua Latina*; the corruption to Lucretius could here have been facilitated, as Giancotti (1976, 57) suggested, by the Pacuvian citation immediately preceding, which would have called to mind Lucr. V.318–19. I ignore the curious suggestion

---

[190] This text, a fifteenth-century compilation bearing no individual authority, was first published by Masson (1895) 222–5 (cf. Solaro (2000) 31–6). The strange attribution in this life of *Neptuni lacunas* and *caeli cauernas* to Lucretius, phrases originating from *Rhet. ad Herenn.* IV.10.15 and Cic. *Arat.* 252 (if not Var. *Men.* 270.2), need not be treated here (cf. Rostagni (1939) 124–6).

[191] Lachmann strangely sought to insert this line into the lacuna after II.164.

[192] The mention of the common phrase *Vesper adest* at *L.L.* VII.50 is not, *pace* Thomson (1997), a partial citation of Cat. 62.1.

[193] Bergk (1850, 13 n. 6 = 1884, vol. I, 68 n. 6) rather attributed the verse to Pacuvius, since he claimed that it echoed Eur. fr. 1023 Nauck.

[194] Lambinus also suggested that the name of an unknown poet could stand in lieu of *Lucretius*.

[195] Scaliger (1575) *Castigationes ad loc.*: 'Perperam Lucretius pro Lucilius, ut apud Varronem.' The correction is attributed to Scaliger *passim* but unjustly: in his Varro (1565) and other *Scaligeriana* the corruption goes unmentioned. Turnebus (1566, 12) simply believed that Lucretius wrote more books but Vetranius (1563, 221–2) suspected either that this passage was corrupt or that another Lucretius was meant, suggesting also that Lucretius wrote twenty-one books which were divided into six by a later epitomiser.

recorded by his *'Vita Borgiana'* that the 'lost' fifteen books should stand between I.3 and I.4.[196]

Fr. **XIII** Var. *L.L.* VII.94:

apud Lucretium

          atque aliquos ibi ab rebus clepsere foro qui

clepsere dixit, unde etiam alii *clepere*, id est corripere, quorum origo a *clam*, ut sit dictum *clapere*, unde *clepere*, *e* ex *a* commutato, ut multa. potest uel a Graeco dictum κλέπτειν *clepere*.

aliquos *codd.* : aliquo *Turnebus* : aliquas *Warmington* : aliquot *Kent* ibi *codd.* : ibus *Scaliger* : ibi si *Marx* : subito *Turnebus* : sibi *Goetz-Schoell* : se illi *Spengel* : sibi si *Kent* : ibidem *conieci* foro qui *codd.* : foroque *Scaliger* : modo qui *Turnebus*

The verse is Lucilian (= 1118 M), for the line, however emended,[197] could have no place in Lucretius' work, the subject matter being alien to any part of the poem. The scribes of Varro have again corrupted *Lucilium* to *Lucretium* (cf. n. 168 above), a correction first made by Vetranius (1563, 309) but soon followed by Scaliger (1565), who is again wrongly credited with the emendation.

I dismiss fragment **VI** (Charis. 268,5 B (= *GLK* I 207,1) as insignificant: *'nauiter'* ... *Lucretius quoque de rebus naturalibus III*). Once we see that *rebus naturalibus* is a corruption (via *rerx* [= -*rum*] *naturalib.* [= -*bus*]) of *rerum natura lib.* [= *liber*], it is no difficult supposition to see III as a corruption of I: the sole transmitted instance of *nauiter* in Lucretius occurs at I.525. An easy alternative supposition is that Charisius mistakenly recorded the wrong book number. I therefore regard the insertion of the word into a verse lost after III.97 by Diels[198] and after III.834

---

[196] 'Sunt qui putent unum et viginti libros composuisse et poematis principium hoc esse *Aetheris et terrae genitabile quaerere tempus*; et usque ad eum locum *Concelebras* quindecim carmina intercidisse.' Borgia proceeded to dismiss this suggestion.

[197] The hiatus I have emended elsewhere (2008a, 113 n. 13) by reading *ibidem* ('at that time', 'then and there'), taking *qui* as relative, but this does not affect the present argument.

[198] <*at quidam contra haec haud nauiter exposuerunt*> | *sensum animi certa non esse in parte locatum* (III.97a–8).

most tentatively by J. Becker (1847, 42)[199] as misguided attempts to accommodate the transmitted evidence.[200]

Three further fragments still require discussion here, the first of which has been overlooked by twentieth-century critics:

Fr. **XIV** Fest. 212,7–13 L:

Oufentinae tribus initio causa fuit nomen fluminis Ofens, quod est in agro Priuernate mare intra et Tarracinam, Lucretius:

> Priuerno Oufentina uenit, fluuioque Oufente.

postea deinde a censoribus alii quoque diuersarum ciuitatum eidem tribui sunt adscripti.

This *spondeiazon*, certainly not Lucretian, was first attributed to Lucilius (= 1260 M) by Lambinus (1570, d3ᵛ) and only later by Scaliger in 1575 (cf. n. 195). The scribes of Festus therefore made the same mistake as those of Varro, Charisius, Macrobius, Nonius, and Servius.

I also disregard the curious four words appended to the citation of I.313–14 (*uncus aratri* ...) by Isidore (*Etym.* XX.14.1): *sumitque per detrimenta fulgorem* (= fr. **XV**).[201] This unmetrical phrase, not evidently deficient in grammar or syntax, is not a corruption of a lost Lucretian verse). Yet they have been variously emended on the supposition that they were once hexametric. Comparison, however, of Seru. *ad Geo.* I.46 is instructive:

ADTRITVS SPLENDESCERE VOMER] Lucretius *occulto decrescit uomer in aruo*, quod euenire frequenti aratione nouimus, ut et splendidior fiat et teratur.

As Purmann (1847, 73–6) well argued, it is clear that, having cited this phrase from Lucretius, Servius provided a simple explanation of the gleam that can come from a well-used ploughshare. Isidore's own addition, *sumitque per detrimenta fulgorem*, is simply

---

[199] In his subsequent discussion he rather supported corruption of III to I.
[200] Forbiger (1824, 81–3) believed *florebat nauibus pontus* to be the end of a verse deleted by a later editor of the work. I follow the majority view, that it is a mistaken citation of V.1442, and I have argued elsewhere for my own emendation of the line (Butterfield (2009a) 188–9).
[201] Cf. also Hrabanus Maurus (who drew upon Isidore): *uomer dictus, quod ui humum eruat seu ab euomendo terram. de quo Lucretius 'uncus aratri occulte decrescit uomeri marius' sumpsitque detrimenta fulgorem (De uniuers. XXII.14).*

a loose paraphrase of this same appendix.[202] Evidence that Isidore worked from either Servius or a common source is the corruption of *occulte* to *occulto*, found in both authors but not in Lucretius' manuscripts (*occulte* Ω). As was seen in section I, although Isidore often worked from Servius, he did have direct access to *DRN*, to which he may or may not have been led by Servius' prompting.

I must also express my strong scepticism about the only Lucretian fragment typically accepted into the text of Lucretius itself:

Fr. **XVI** Non. 503,16–25 Mercer:

ab eo quod est feruit breuiato accentu feruere facit, ut spernit, spernere. Afranius *Epistula* [= 127–8 Ribbeck], Lucilius *Satyrarum* lib. IX [= 54 Marx], Vergilius *Aeneidos* lib. IV [567], Lucretius lib. II

> feruere cum uideas classem lateque uagari

Naeuius *Lycurgo* [49 Klotz], Accius *Telepho* [631–2 Klotz], Varro *Desultorio* περὶ τοῦ γράφειν [86 Buecheler].

This citation of a Lucretian verse by the usually reliable Nonius (cf. section D above) bears a number of hallmarks that suggest it is genuine, not least in its recording a specific book. Accordingly, most editors since Lambinus have added the verse into their texts of Book II. There is, however, considerable scope for doubt.

We may first note that the verse is very reminiscent of the transmitted II.41 *feruere cum uideas belli simulacra cientes*. Indeed Nonius could have cited this verse (generally agreed to be from earlier in Book II) for the very same purpose, unless *feruere* had become corrupted to *fruere* in the manuscript(s) available to him, as evidently was the case in the Lucretian archetype.[203] Owing to this similarity of content and phrasing, all scholars who have accepted the Nonian verse as Lucretian have inserted it near II.41. Furthermore, since lines II.42–3 were evidently very corrupt in Ω (and perhaps at earlier stages),[204] the

---

[202] For Isidore's own use of *detrimentum* (not attested in Lucretius), cf. *De diff. uerb.* 169,28 (*bis*), *Sent.* 207, 69 (III.5.12), 327,19–20 (*bis*), *De nat. rer.* 19.2, 21,3, *Etym.* XVII.2.1.

[203] *fruere* OS : *eruere* Q (corr. Q²).

[204] 42–3: *subsidiis magnis epicuri constabilitas | ornatas armis itastuas* (*itastuas* Oᵃ·ᶜ·) *tariterque animatas* litteris uncialibus rubricatis OS : om. sp. trium uu. rel. Q.

same scholars have considered the loss of a verse in this area to have been more probable. It is important to note, however, that among many editors there has been the general misconception concerning II.42–3, which were evidently presented as a rubricated *capitulum* in the archetype, that a gap of three verses was left in Q for II.42–3 and a missing third verse. Rather, Q left such a gap solely to accommodate the large number of letters in what it took to be a *capitulum* (see Chapter 3, n. 10). Therefore no Lucretian manuscript suggests the omission of a lost verse in the vicinity of II.42–3.

Lambinus first placed this verse in Lucretian texts to supplant the difficult II.42–3, yet most subsequent editors, though accepting that location, have retained these two preceding verses before it. Diels did so but also deleted II.41 as an authorial doublet of the line. Leonard–Smith, by contrast, regarded II.43a 'as part of an alternative or further treatment of war games which Lucretius failed to eliminate from, or incorporate in, his manuscript' (*ad loc.*),[205] similar to the suggestion of Forbiger (1824, 85–7) that the verse reflects a double recension of Lucretius in antiquity. Du Fay rather placed Nonius' verse before II.40, Bignone (1909, 59–60) followed by Martin and de Plinval (1942), after II.42, and Roos (1847, 32–3) and Munro after II.46.

Yet there is certainly scope for suspecting that the verse cited by Nonius is not genuine but a mistaken reminiscence or corrupt form of II.41. First, a single-line reference to a wandering fleet would be somewhat weak when set alongside the evidently longer description of an army (however lines II.42–3 are emended). Further, the *-que* appended to *late* is extremely difficult to construe in almost all locations where the line is inserted. Fowler (2002 edn, 116) rightly observed that it is suspicious that Nonius' next quotation under this lemma (Naevius 49 Kl) begins with *late*; more suspect is the anaphora of *ferucre cum uideas* at such close quarters. If the error is in Nonius' recalling II.41, into which he inserted more general material after the important verse opening,

[205] Flores (1965, 127–8) also thought that the verse should be inserted after II.43, arguing fallaciously that Q had a gap of three lines 'per la inserzione di 42–43–43b' (128 n. 34), a view followed without argument by Mazzacane (1984) 164–5.

The indirect tradition of Lucretius

two passages from later prominent poets could have catalysed the mistake: Verg. *Aen.* I.583 *omnia tuta* uides, classem *sociosque repertos* and Luc. II.101–2 *nobilitas cum plebe perit,* lateque uagatus | *ensis*.

Finally, I am not persuaded by the arguments of Eichstädt (*Praef.* LXXVI), Forbiger (1824, 79), Purmann (1847, 66–70), J. Becker (1847, 36–7) and Jocelyn (1986, 49–51) that the closing comment of Seru. *ad* Verg. *Aen.* VI.595 is evidence that a description of Ixion's suffering in the Underworld has been lost from the close of Book III: *ipse etiam Lucretius dicit per eos, super quos iam iam casurus imminet lapis, superstitiosos significari, qui inaniter semper uerentur et de diis et caelo et superioribus male opinantur: nam religiosi sunt qui per reuerentiam timent. per eos autem qui saxum uoluunt ambitum uult et repulsam significari, quia semel repulsi petitores ambire non desinunt.* per rotam *autem [sc. Lucretius] ostendit negotiatores, qui semper tempestatibus turbinibusque uoluuntur.*[206] Although the first statements accurately reflect some of the contents of Lucr. III (Tityus (prior to this quotation), Tantalus, and Sisyphus), it is more probable that Servius' final comment, strangely specific in its attack on shipping magnates, arose from the commentary tradition and not from direct access to *DRN*; it could have originally referred to *Aen.* VI.601 (where Ixion is mentioned), if not 616–17 (*radiisque rotarum districti pendent*), and was wrongly incorporated with the Lucretian material *ad* VI.595.[207]

The three fragments that still remain cannot be dismissed as unlucretian so readily and will require more detailed discussion.

Fr. II Mar. Plot. Sacerdos *GLK* VI 448,7–9:

---

[206] Kenney (1971, *ad* III.1010) provided strong counter-arguments, including the fact that Lucretius' three sinners (Tantalus, Tityus, Sisyphus) are mentioned in Homer's *Odyssey* but Ixion is not.
[207] I also disregard the description of Barth (1624, XXXII *cap.* 1, col. 1465) of another fragment: 'Hoc quod nunc sequitur non intelligo quid sibi velit: *Mortuum corpus, iam exanime, emortuum morti proximum.* Lucretius. *Mortua si dicas jampridem emortua molis.* Toto Lucretio nihil tale exstat, nescio an somniaverit Rhapsodus, an vero sit Lucilianum aliquid isthic corruptum.' If the fragment does come from an ancient author, Lucilius is indeed rather probable (although his editors have been silent).

s uero eliditur sola si a consonanti incipiat altera pars orationis, ut Lucretius

mensibus frigus

et alibi *ex infantibus paruis* [= Lucr. I.186].

The Lucretian paternity of this fragment has never been explicitly rejected.[208] The fact that this adonean is cited along with the end of a certainly Lucretian hexameter could support its veracity. There is nothing unlucretian in the two words: sigmatic ecthlipsis before more than one consonant has parallels in Lucretius (e.g. before *st-* VI.943 and *str-* VI.195), this (very probably) fifth-foot instance[209] coheres with his typical practice,[210] and the vocabulary is not unlucretian, although *mensis* occurs only twice elsewhere in *DRN*.[211] Lucretius was often cited by antique grammarians as a primary source for sigmatic ecthlipsis, but it is understandably the first instance in the work, I.186 (*ex infantibus paruis*, if not the whole line), that is typically cited.[212] The pairing *mensibus frigus* is not found elsewhere in Latin literature. Marius Plotius Sacerdos cited Lucretius in six other instances,[213] with general accuracy, and on three occasions is the sole extant indirect source for Lucretian lines (I.227, II.637, III.94). His few errors probably reflect his own manuscript transmission rather than personal errors,[214] with the possible exception of *animantium* for *animales* at II.927 (*GLK* VI 445,20). It cannot therefore be ruled

---

[208] Munro (app. crit. *ad* VI.839) called this fragment and **III–IV** 'very doubtful', although he accepted fr. **I** into his text.

[209] The comparative rarity of ecthlipsis at the close of a foot elsewhere in Lucretius' hexameters renders it improbable that *mensibus frigus* did not close the verse: cf. Butterfield (2008d) 198 with Table 2.

[210] See Butterfield (2008d).

[211] III.1094 and V.618 *lunaque*; cf. also *menstrua* at V.764 (of the moon) and VI.796 (of women).

[212] See Appendix II *ad loc.*

[213] Alongside the two passages quoted in the testimonium above we find: *sanguen* (I.837/853/860 = *GLK* VI 474,22), I.941 = IV.16 (*GLK* VI 504,28), *inferiora magis* (I.1063 = *GLK* VI 450,20–1), II.927–8 (... *alituum* = *GLK* VI 445,19–21), *caelos* (II.1097), III.1093 (*GLK* VI 503,6). In two instances the book number is given with the author's name (II.927–8, III.1093); in the remainder, only 'Lucretius' is recorded, although I.941 = IV.16 lacks any authorial attribution.

[214] E.g. *deceptique* (B) and *capiant* (ABC) for *deceptaque* and *capiantur* in the citation of I.941 = IV.16.

out that *mensibus frigus* is indeed the close of a genuine Lucretian hexameter. Accordingly, Lachmann inserted the phrase into the lacuna of fifty-two lines (i.e. one leaf of Ω) he posited after VI.839, conjecturing that the adjective *aestiuis* stood earlier in the line before *mensibus frigus*.[215] Many critics have accepted his suggestion, albeit with some hesitation. We must first consider the likelihood of a lacuna after VI.839, which Lachmann stipulated not only because it ended an archetypal page[216] but also for two further reasons:

(i) The testimony of Seru. *ad* Verg. *Geo.* IV.51–2 suggests that Lucretius treated the matter of differing temperatures on opposite sides of the world, although no such discussion survives in his text.

(ii) The presence of *porro* in VI.840, which verse, immediately after the treatment of Avernian lakes, opens up a quite new discussion concerning the varying temperatures of wells in different seasons, strongly implies that it continued a preceding argument, but none such survives.

Let us first take a closer look at Servius' own wording. The note upon *pulsam hiemem sol aureus egit | sub terris* (= Verg. *Geo.* IV.51–2) runs as follows:

secundum physicos qui dicunt, quo tempore hic hiems est, aestatem esse sub terris et uersa uice, cum hic aestas, illic hiemem. quod etiam Lucretius exsequitur, et trahit in argumentum putealem aquam, quae aestate frigidissima est, hieme uere tepidior.

From this statement it has been supposed that Lucretius treated the question of the relative climate or temperature of the Antipodes, in which he discussed wells as part of his argument. Yet not only is Lucretius' treatment of Antipodean climates lacking but nowhere does he give an indication that this is a matter for discussion. After the second account of Avernian places (VI.818–39), the topics that survive from VI.840 to VI.906 (where discussion of the

---

[215] *aestiuus* is also found only twice in Lucretius, at V.615 and 639 (both describing the sun's course).

[216] It can be discerned from Lachmann's reconstruction that he correctly regarded this as the 142nd page of the archetype; see Appendix IV for my reconstruction of the archetype's foliation.

magnet begins) are specific in focus: wells cold in summer and warm in winter (840–7); the spring by the shrine of Ammon, cold by day and warm by night (848–60); why that spring operates in this unusual manner (861–78); a spring over and in which tow sets alight (879–89); why this occurs (890–9), including comparison of the spring of Aradus, which issues fresh water into the sea (890–4); comparison of other things set alight at a distance (900–5). Since none of these phenomena has an explanation potentially linked with differing climates on opposite sides of the planet, none can be a specific example adduced to support a preceding (lost) discussion of this phenomenon.

Yet more objections can be made against Servius' assertion. First, Lucretius earlier (I.1058–67) argued explicitly against the existence of the Antipodes, including the notion that they *alternis nobiscum tempora caeli | diuid[unt]*.[217] Therefore, although Lucretius was aware of theories about the Antipodes, his sole mention of the topic is in the context of an explicit rejection of it (I.1068–1113). We may also add that, since the Antipodean climate was not something known to a Roman, let alone its relationship to the European climate at a particular time of the year, a discussion of the matter would have sat oddly in a discussion of visible and empirically known phenomena. Secondly, Broughton (1939, 240) made the valid observation that, if another fifty-two lines were added to Lucretius' discussion of temperature (840–905), it would be over one hundred lines in length and therefore disproportionately long amidst Lucretius' discussion of terrestrial phenomena, with the exception of the much more arresting matter of electrical storms (VI.160–442). Thirdly, we may note the improbability of a random 52-line section's being lost from the poem but doing no harm either to the grammar of the preceding and following sections or to the development of each given argument: we would have to suppose that the fifty-two lines represented in totality one self-contained argument (or perhaps two or three).[218] Fourthly, I will demonstrate in Chapter 3 that the

[217] I.1066–7; Munro and Bailey rightly took *tempora caeli* in this context as 'seasons' (cf. VI.362).
[218] This objection was made by Büchner (app. crit. *ad loc.*).

lists of subject headings (*indices capitulorum*) extant in Books IV–
VI necessarily existed before the writing of the archetype (having
been introduced either two or three manuscripts earlier). Therefore, if
Lachmann's supposition is correct, we must believe that the author
of the *capitula* chose not to give any title at all to the large (52-verse)
section concerning Antipodean climates. Yet we find *capitula* in the
environs summarising most of the topics covered, many of which are
significantly smaller than the hypothetical lost argument: on Aetna
(639–702), the Nile (712–37), the Avernian lake (738–48), crows'
avoidance of the Temple of Athena in Athens (749–55), Syrian
quadrupeds (756–9), the unexpected temperature of wells (840–7),
the spring by the shrine of Ammon (848–78), tow being kindled in
water (879–89), the spring of Aradus (890–4), and the magnet (906–
16). The alternative supposition, that a heading for the passage that
was lost in the lacuna was overlooked by the compiler of the *index*, or
independently lost from that list, only renders Lachmann's suggestion more unlikely through its improbability.

If these foregoing objections are convincing, we must consider
why Servius implied (but did not state) that Lucretius treated such a
topic. Two interconnected reasons can be given. The first is that
Servius had no direct contact with Lucretius' *DRN* but worked at
second hand (if not at further remove) by means of earlier commentaries upon Virgil.[219] Therefore he seemingly had no means of
ascertaining exactly what Lucretius said on Antipodean climates
(if anything), even if he desired to do so. His vague comment that
Lucretius merely 'follows up' (*exsequitur*) the assertion of other
natural scientists (inspecifically termed *physici*) in his discussion
about wells' contrasting temperatures presumably reflects Servius'
vague conception of the evidence. Secondly, since this doctrine
was held by other philosophers than Lucretius – and indeed by
those outside (and antecedent to) the Epicurean school, as Servius'
own note makes clear – there was ample scope for Servius or his
source to confuse which philosophers or scientists devised the
whole theory and which only maintained parts of it.[220]

---

[219] See section F(i) in the first half of this chapter.
[220] Both of these considerations are more probable than the attempt of Bollack (1976)
270–7 to reconcile the evidence with Lucretius' transmitted text.

We should now consider the *scholia Bernensia* upon this Virgilian passage (at the lemma *pulsam hiemem*), where we find further information:

nunc secundum physicos dicit, qui dicunt, quo tempore hiemps hic <est> [*suppl. Hagen*], aestatem esse sub terris et uersa uice; ut Lucretius ostendit, putealem aquam aestate frigidissimam, hieme uero tepidiorem. hoc Suetonius [*Reifferscheid* : sentit *codd.*][221] et Iunilius dicit.

The *Scholia Bernensia*, which evidently drew upon a similar tradition to that of Servius, here offer an important attribution of this note's origin. For the compiler (or his source) states that Suetonius (*s.u.l.*) and Junilius[222] provided the information. For our present purposes, the actual identities of these names are unimportant; more significant is the fact that some pre-Servian commentators on this Virgilian passage had already recorded that *physici* and Lucretius treated matters in this field. Such a collocation of material explains how Lucretius' specific views could easily have been confused by Servius with the more general views of others.

We can cite at least two figures who treated the relationship between heat within the earth and without: Oenopides of Chios (fifth century BC), whose views are cited by Diodorus Siculus (I.41.1–2) and Seneca (*Quaest. nat.* IV.2.26–7), and Strato of Lampsacus the Peripatetic (*fl. c.* 300 BC), whose views Seneca also recorded (*Quaest. nat.* VI.13.2–3). Oenopides believed that heat is contained within the earth in winter, which duly warms caves and wells, located as they are deeper in the earth's crust. Strato asserted similarly that cold and heat cannot exist together in the same place, but the former overpowers the latter, with the result that heat is forcibly crowded into the earth in winter, from where it heats caves and wells. It therefore seems that Servius confused Lucretius' tackling a topic that these other physicists treated (the surprising temperature of wells) with the fiction that

---

[221] Mommsen (1861, 447 n.**) emended the word to *Gaudentius*, a figure cited elsewhere in the *scholia*, but the corruption is difficult to explain; an abbreviation of *Suetonius*, however, could easily have been expanded to *sentit* (*Suet.* > *Sent./Seut.* > *sentit*).

[222] The name of Junilius, about whom we know nothing, appears some sixty times throughout the *scholia*; cf. Daintree and Geymonat (1988) 714.

he actually maintained that different sides of the planet simultaneously experienced opposing seasons. Whether or not Servius knew that Lucretius mentioned the Antipodes at the close of Book I, he mistakenly attributed this theory to him, albeit in the rather non-committal fashion that his wording suggests.[223]

To return to Lucretius' text and Lachmann's second additional reason for positing a lacuna, how can one explain the presence of *porro* in 840, a word Lucretius often employed when moving to a further argument within the same macro-argument?[224] The best solution appears to be that tentatively suggested by Brieger (*Prol.* LXXX) and independently by Broughton (1939, 240–2), namely transposing the paragraph 840–7 to after 878. This transposition undeniably provides a very neat progression of thought: the new section of argument begins with the discussion of the shrine of Ammon (848–60), which is then explained (877); we then move to discussion of wells' similarly variable temperatures, in which the opening *frigidior* (840) naturally follows the *frigidus* of six lines before (873); after these wells comes the spring that kindles tow (879–89), opening with *frigidus est etiam fons*. If the error was palaeographically motivated, the mode of error is simple enough: a scribe accidentally wrote 879ff. (*frigidus est etiam fons* ...) before the preceding 840–7 (*frigidior porro* ...); once the error was apprehended, a marginal annotation signifying that the verses should be added earlier misled a later scribe to insert 840–7 after 839, rather than after 878. A necessary consequence of accepting that a transposition occurred is that the error preceded

---

[223] This error would not be unique. Lachmann himself highlighted (as had Purmann (1847, 70–1) before him) Servius' potential for recording Lucretius' views inaccurately, observing (*ad* Lucr. V.1273) that he strongly implied *ad* Verg. *Aen.* XII.87 that, according to Lucretius, *orichalchum* was discovered after bronze; yet the relevant passage (V.1241ff.) makes no mention of *orichalcum* or an equivalent. Pizzani (1959a, 111) also cited his note *ad* Verg. *Aen.* V.527, where Servius incorrectly alleged that Lucretius spoke of wind having a role in the movement of stars (cf. II.206–8).

[224] We may instantly dismiss the two unsatisfactory emendations: E. Goebel (1854, 14) conjectured *frigidior fit ut in puteis aestate sit umor*, which, though not unlucretian, provides a very abrupt transition to a new line of argument and is difficult to explain as a corruption; Woltjer (1881b, 782) added a verse before 840 that ran *frigore cum premitur terra est calidus magis atque*, which introduces awkward syntax, the strange anaphora of *frigore cum premitur* (here and at 845) and the stylistic irregularity of *atque* at the close of a verse: the only other example of *atque* in the sixth foot I have dismissed as corrupt elsewhere (2008a, 123–5; cf. also Butterfield (2008c) 390–2).

the collection of *capitula* in the *index* at the front of Book VI, which list corresponds with the transmitted text by placing the *capitulum* concerning 840ff. before that concerning 848ff. As Pizzani (1959a, 104) observed, it is not problematic to suppose that the transposition occurred at a stage prior to the transference of the *capitula* into the *indices*. My conclusions in Chapter 3 suggest that the transposition must therefore have occurred at least prior to the hyperarchetype.

Alternatively, since the transposition is of a whole paragraph, it could well be that Lucretius had on his death not ordered these verses in their finite form, and that, when the work was circulated, 840–7 appeared in their transmitted place, earlier than Lucretius had intended. Much the same could be said of VI.608ff., at which *principio* should signal the first element of a newly introduced argument, not the very beginning of a new section. Many critics have supposed (since Giussani) that a lacuna should be posited before this verse but we would once more be faced with the (*prima facie* surprising) loss of the exact beginning and end of one argumentative passage or more.

We may deal finally with a point raised by Clark (1918, 309 n. 1; 453), who suggested that the ninth-century variants of the superfluous word transmitted at the beginning of VI.840 before *frigidior* (*Quae* O : *uae* Q [= *Quae* without rubricated initial] : *que* S) are the mistaken expansions of $\overline{Q}$, a marginal annotation for *quaere*, signifying a supposed fault in the transmission. Although Clark mistakenly attempted to explain the insignificant *cur* among the *Itali* by the same means (it being rather an attempted correction of O's *Quae*), his diagnosis of the corruption could be correct; if so, that the symbol is not attested before the eighth century suggests that it was entered then, presumably straight into the archetype Ω. Even if correct, the presence of such a marginal addition has no authority; rather, it serves as interesting evidence of a closer reader of Ω, or more probably the hyperarchetype, since OQS treat *Quae* as a legitimate part of 840, O rubricating the initial letter and Q intending to do so.

Having dismissed the existence of any lacuna after VI.839, careful reflection does not suggest another plausible location from which this fragment could have been lost. Pizzani (1959a, 108), who showed considerable scepticism about a lacuna after VI.839, instead suggested that, if *mensibus frigus* could stand in a verse such as *terras, hibernis permanat mensibus frigus*, it could be placed in the lacuna (posited by Brieger) after VI.954. Yet discussion of cold, something internal to the atmosphere, hardly serves to emphasise the porous nature of the sky and heavens (which the sentence is expected to demonstrate).

mensibus frigus, therefore, may well not be a Lucretian fragment at all. How then could we explain Marius Plotius Sacerdos' attribution of this fragment to the poet? Despite his relatively strong track record, we should note that, as his first quotation, he failed to cite an extant instance exhibiting ecthlipsis at the close of the fifth foot when twenty-eight are available in our transmitted text, itself an implausible statistic. Further, it is odd that his second citation, by contrast, should be the grammarians' canonical example (I.186, which occurs first in Lucretius' work), as though it was appended as an afterthought. Supposing the fragment *mensibus frigus* not to be Lucretian, four possibilities arise: that Plotius (a) misremembered a genuine Lucretian phrase; (b) correctly recorded a phrase from another poet; (c) misremembered a genuine phrase of another poet; (d) fabricated the instance as a convenient example for the relevant point. I do not know of a parallel fiction for (d) in Plotius' work and, in view of his then citing a genuine example, I shy away from such an accusation; (c) is perfectly possible, not least since we learn from one of the two fragments of Egnatius' *De rerum natura* (which could have been confused with Lucretius' work by virtue of its date and title) that he employed sigmatic ecthlipsis.[225] The strongest candidate for (b) is a subconscious semantic reversal of Verg. *Geo.* II.149, which closes with *mensibus aestas*. Finally, if a genuine passage of Lucretius was misremembered (a), we may be dealing with the likes of *mentibus capti* (IV.1022), *manibus diuis* (III.52), *montibus passim* (V.824) or *mentibus saepe* (VI.51) being corrupted under the influence of a verse-close such as *manabile frigus* (I.534) or *corpora frigus* (V.1015).

---

[225] See Egnatius, *DRN* fr. 2.1 Blänsdorf (see also Hollis (2007) 87–9).

If (a) or (d) reflects the truth, the context of the quotation requires no emendation; if rather (b) or (c), we should suppose that a different author's name preceded *mensibus frigus*, and it was followed by *et Lucretius 'ex infantibus paruis'*, from which the name of Lucretius came to be moved before the first quotation, replacing the original author's name, *alibi* being added later. It is certainly odd that *alibi* is found nowhere else in the grammarian's work. Whichever of these four options stands, the fragment has no place in Lucretius' text, although it cannot be proven to be unlucretian with certainty. Since I do not believe in a lacuna after VI.839,[226] I of course reject Lachmann's insertion of frs. **I–IV** (and potentially **V**) at this point.[227]

Fr. **III** Charis. 73,10 B (*GLK* I 58,23); Beda, *Orth. GLK* VII 266,12–14:

camara dicitur, ut Verrius Flaccus affirmat, non *camera* per *e*. sed Lucretius,

cameraeque caminis

†ecterritibus

[dicendo *Beda*] etiam *cameram* dici posse ostendit.

cameraeque [cameraque *a.c. N*] caminis N *ed. princ. Neap.* (1532), *recc.* : cameraeque cameris *Beda, Exc. orth. Montep.*, Barth (1624, XXXVII.14 (col. 1693), LII.4 (col. 2433)) : cameraque camini *Marx* ecTritibus [= ecterritibus] *N* : ecteritibus *C* : ex teretibus *Exc. orth. Montep., Beda* : ex cratibus *ed. princ. Neap.* (1532), *recc.* : ex crateribus *Forbiger* : ex tereti (cum calor ex fornace meat camerque camini *antea suppletis*) *Marx* : ex torrentibus *Diels* : experti rebus *Boeck* : ex trucibus *García Calvo* flamma *ante* cameraque *suppl. Krenkel*.[228]

These three or four words, unmetrical as transmitted and probably spanning two lines if originally dactylic, were attributed to

---

[226] I am equally unmoved by the arguments of Washietl (1883, 82–3), who welcomed Lachmann's suggestion of a lacuna but, on the tentative basis of Ou. *Pont.* IV.2.17–20, which he took to be an imitation of a lost Lucretian passage, conjectured that the missing text discussed the seasonal variation of gushing springs (*scaturrigines*, a word metrical only in the nom. sg.).

[227] Compare Diels' comment (app. crit. *ad loc.*) 'frustra ... Lachm[annus] lacunam fragmentis 4 aliquo modo sarciebat.'

[228] It is an odd fact that Niccolò Perotti (1429–80) reported this fragment in a form containing the word *tepidis*. At *Cornu copiae* 70,42 he recorded 'unde interdum pro calido accipitur [sc. *tepidus*]. Lucretius: *tepidisque caminis*.' That he cited a form of *camina* indicates, as Stok (2000, 65) noted, that Charisius was his source, not Bede or a text similar to Barth's. He presumably read *cameraeque caminis* | *ex tepidis*, although I have not found this particular reading transmitted elsewhere.

Lucretius by Charisius, whose testimony is followed by Bede and (if we trust the assertion) the author of a manuscript cited by Kaspar Barth. Since Cramer,[229] the fragment has been tentatively attributed to Lucilius (= 1351–2 M). The sense of this brief quotation is difficult to gauge, since the corrupt final word and the doubts about the case of the first leave little solid basis. If *cameraeque* is correct, it is presumably genitive; *ex teretibus*, in effect the phrase transmitted, could be read only in a non-dactylic metre,[230] 'and from the rounded furnaces of the vaulted ceiling'. Marx retained a similar sense but restored dactylic metre by making *camini* genitive and reading *cameraque ... tereti*, 'and by/from the smooth vaulted ceiling of the furnace'. The corruption is not particularly difficult (the introduction of an -*s* to *caminis* leading to the expansion of *tereti* in order to agree with its plural counterpart). Forbiger's *ex crateribus* is a valid hexametric opening (and Lucretius employed *crateres* at VI.701) but the sense remains puzzling, even in the context (as he suggested (1824, 85)) of Lucretius' treatment of the workings of Etna (VI.639–702).

Lachmann himself demonstrated rare restraint in asserting that he could not emend the fragment; he nevertheless supposed it to be Lucretian and inserted it in his improbable lacuna after VI.839. Boeck (1958, 243–4) altered the final word to *experti rebus*, completed the hexameter with *tantis uoluere maiora* (apparently unaware that the suggestion was unmetrical)[231] and posited that the fragment stood after V.1107. The resultant sense is undeniably weak after the clear assertion of 1105–7; furthermore, the introduction of *cameraeque caminis* is a curiously specific addition to *igni* closing 1106, a word which itself may well be corrupt.[232] Yet worse is García Calvo's insertion of the fragment within VI.668 (*excussit calidam <uoluens*

---

[229] Cramer (1823, 509–10) rejected the fragment as unlucretian 'propter legem Pediam', instead suggesting that Charisius meant to refer to Lucilius but that he or a later scribe corrupted that citation.

[230] Barth's hopes of defending the metre (1624, LII.4, col. 2433) were futile: 'Neque sane tam relligiosus metrorum etiam Lucretius est quin aliquo modo verba isthic producta [= *cameris ex teretibus*] eum auctorem possint agnoscere.'

[231] Pizzani (1959a, 107 n. 47) failed to point out the metrical problem of *maiora*.

[232] For my own emendation of *igni*, see Butterfield (2009a) 186.

cameraeque caminis | ex trucibus rapuit> flammas uelocibus ignem), which produces a remarkably inelegant pair of lines.

Neither *camera* nor *caminus* is attested in Lucretius. The adjective *teres* (which could be read following Marx's emendation) is not found in a certainly pre-Lucretian context but occurs thrice in *DRN* (I.35, IV.58, V.803, of living creatures' bodies); nevertheless, it is found at Var. *Men.* 132.3 B, composed between 80 and 50 BC, occurs four times in Catullus 64 (65, 262, 314, 363) and at 61.174, a poem probably composed in the early 50s BC, and also in Cicero's *De oratore* (III.199) of 55 BC, as well as Caes. *B.Gal.* VII.73.6 from the close of that same decade. It is therefore probable that one or more literary writers had employed the adjective before this particularly fertile period for Latin literature. If the fragment truly is Lucretian, I would suggest emending it by reading *ex terris*, retaining *cameraeque caminis*, '[a flame surges?] from the furnaces of the vaulted ceiling out of the earth'. For *e(x) terris* in Lucretius we can compare I.1062 and VI.788. Perhaps the following *etiam* catalysed the corruption to *ex terretis*, which was then expanded to the closest available grammatical form (*ter[r]etibus*).

It seems more probable, however, that Charisius misattributed the fragment to Lucretius. The grammarian (on whom see section G in the first half of this chapter) recorded quotations from the poet eleven times, but he cited a full verse only thrice (I.837 at *Inst.* 114,20 B, III.94 at *Inst.* 272,7–8 B, III.676 at *Inst.* 265,11 B). Among his few errors of citation or transmission, we find *longiter* for *longius* in III.676,[233] and *pulsabant* twice for *pulsarent* in II.637 (119,6 B, 154,29 B); the mistake of writing *III* for *I* at 268,5 B (= fr. **VI**, discussed above) is probably scribal rather than Charisian. It is perfectly possible on this basis that Charisius lacked direct access to a text of *DRN*, and a number of the passages he cited (I.837, II.662, III.676, VI.736) are found in other grammatical writers either antecedent to or independent of him. Nevertheless, Charisius' testimony

---

[233] Like most Lucretian editors, I am confident that *longius* (Ω) is to be preferred over the grammarians' *longiter*, for further discussion see Timpanaro (1970) and Mazzacane (1984) 168–9.

is otherwise comparatively reliable, and if we do posit a confusion over the author's name, scribal error is perhaps more likely.

Given that the subject matter of the fragment, however emended, does not relate to a section of *DRN* where a lacuna could reliably be located, it seems probable that we are faced with another scribal corruption where Lucretius has been written for *Lucilius* (cf. n. 168 above), a poet who could have mentioned furnaces in his varied work, availed himself of assonance like *cam- cam-*,[234] and was cited by Charisius over forty times. Alternatively, it remains possible that these words come from a more technical poet whose works do not survive to us.

Fr. V Non. 229,1 M:

torpor generis masculini. Lucretius:

tantus conduxerat omnia torpor

'And such a numbness/shock had brought all things together.' This close of a dactylic hexameter, the second longest of the fragments here discussed, was cited by Nonius (without reference to a specific book) to elucidate the gender of *torpor*. Although this noun is not attested in *DRN*, the line was generally deemed to be Lucretian[235] until Roth[236] first attributed it to Lucilius, a view that Marx (*ad* Lucil. 1306 M) supported on the ground that he was the only pre-Catullian author to use *torpor* (391 M). It is certainly striking that Nonius, very shortly before this passage, cited the Lucilian fragment in which *torpor* occurs (219,12–13M s.u. *pigror*).[237] The correction of *Lucretius* to *Lucilius* therefore has much to commend it, although Nonius did not misattribute verses

---

[234] The only instance of this particular repetition in classical Latin poetry is Ou. *Fast.* IV.691, where we find the polyptoton of *in campo* (*campumque ostendit*), whose parenthesis renders it inappropriate as a comparison.

[235] Creech (*ad* I.469) declared Lucretius' poem to be 'lacer', i.e. missing parts, because he could not find this particular citation in the transmitted text. Forbiger (1824, 83) also deemed the fragment's language Lucretian and thought that it could have occurred in a lost passage of *DRN*.

[236] Gerlach and Roth (1842) *ad loc.*

[237] *torpor* is also found among poets in Catullus, Virgil, Ovid, Lucan, Seneca, Silius and Statius.

to Lucretius elsewhere – if we regard fr. **XVI** above instead as a mistaken conflation.

Weil (1847, 311) was the first scholar to suggest a context for the fragment when defending it as Lucretian, namely the account of the symptoms of the Athenian plague: he conjectured that the words stood before *frigida pellis* of VI.1194, although it is unclear whether he meant that they also followed *caua tempora* of 1194, how he envisaged creating a metrical line, and to what *omnia* refers. Diels later maintained that the quotation is Lucretian (*torpet* III.305 and *torpens* III.981 supporting Lucretius' use of the noun),[238] again suggesting that the fragment relates to the Athenian plague, that *omnia* understands *saecla hominum*, and that it could be inserted after VI.1225 (transposed by Lachmann to after 1246), a view that Pizzani (1959a, 124),[239] Rychlewska (1964, 282) and Mazzacane (1984, 172–3) regarded as the most probable option available. Boeck (1958, 244–5) supported placing the verse with Diels after VI.1225, or alternatively in 1277 so that the passage would read:

nec iam religio diuom nec numina magni	1276
pendebant: <tantus conduxerat omnia torpor>	1276a
<pectora. cladis> enim praesens dolor exsuperabat.[240]	1277

With this arrangement he compared Thuc. II.52.3, a passage that in reality bears no close resemblance to these reconstructed lines. Lachmann tentatively suggested that, if the fragment originally read *conduxerit*, it could stand, along with frs. **I–IV**, in the lacuna he posited after VI.839 and refer to the effect of wintry conditions. Yet to emend a perfectly intelligible passage in order that it cohere with the conjectured content of a lacuna is not an attractive option.

---

[238] Both of these two Lucretian usages refer to the numbness of fear, which would suggest that *torpor* would bear the same force for the poet.

[239] Pizzani rightly reprimanded (1959a, 123 n. 72) Martin's careless misreading of Diels' note upon this fragment.

[240] For my emendation of VI.1277, and rejection of the possibility that *pendebantur* was followed by a consonant, see Butterfield (2008g) 642.

Since it is hard to think of a context in which the fragment could stand (if unemended) in Lucretius,[241] we may rather follow the line first taken by Becker (1847, 54–5), who considered Lucan a possible author, not least because he employed *torpor* seven times in his *Bellum ciuile*, including the collocation *tamen omnia torpor | pectora constrinxit* (VI.466–7), where *constrinxit* is certainly reminiscent of *conduxerat* (a verbal form not attested in any extant classical Latin poet). He dismissed the suggestion, however, on the ground that Nonius never cited Lucan. Broughton (1939, 239 with n. 8) independently suggested that the verse could originate from a lost work of Lucan (such as his *Orestes*). It seems possible to support the fragment's attribution to Lucan only if we posit that it was wrongly considered Lucretian by the source of Nonius' work, for Lucan could hardly have been deemed suitable for his dictionary of 'Republican' Latin, which limits post-Augustan citations to secondary authorities.[242]

An alternative supposition would be that Nonius, or more probably his source, was already confident about the masculine gender of *torpor* (like most nouns in -*or*, -*ōris*) and recollected this ultimately Lucanian passage (VI.466–7). Consciously or not, he emended *tamen* into *tantus*[243] in order to mark the gender, and *constrinxit* was brought into the same hexametrical line in a banalised (*conduco* for *constringo*) and metrically tractable (pluperfect) form. After due consideration, I would rather consider the similarity between the fragment and Luc. VI.466–7 coincidental, and, although it remains possible that it was lost from Lucretius (V or VI), I prefer to suppose that the verse is not Lucretian but Lucilian, Lucanian or another's.

---

[241] If Lucretian, the pluperfect possibly limits the likelihood of the fragment's appearing in Books I–IV: of the twenty-three active pluperfect indicatives in *DRN*, all but one (IV.320 [345]) occur in Books V–VI, and only four (V.174, 414, 809, VI.23) occur outside V.925–1457 and VI.1145–1276, where distinct narratives of past events occur.

[242] For broader context about linguistic authorities for ancient grammarians and lexicographers, see Schmidt (1993).

[243] Cf. Verg. *Aen.* XI.357 *quod si tantus habet mentes et pectora terror.*

Having now worked through sixteen alleged fragments of Lucretius, I believe that none can confidently be judged to be Lucretian. However, in decreasing order of probability, fragments **V**, **III** and **II** could possibly come from lost portions of *DRN*, although no obvious locations present themselves. This trio accordingly deserves, unlike the remainder, to be recorded in an appendix at the close of future critical editions of the work, with a concise summary of the difficulties treated above.

3

THE *CAPITULA* OF *DE RERUM NATURA*

Although Lucretius has enjoyed the attention of a long series of formidable scholars, a significant feature of his poem as transmitted has received remarkably short shrift. I refer to the *capitula*[1] interspersed throughout the work, subject headings also recorded in indices preceding Books IV–VI.[2] This dearth of discussion is presumably due to the general assumption that these *capitula* are not Lucretian but spring from some later hand(s). As will become evident, I agree that they are later accretions but refute the notion that this renders them irrelevant to Lucretian scholarship. Rather, since they can certainly be tracked back significantly before the extant manuscripts, they can provide information about the *Überlieferungsgeschichte* of *DRN*.

In this chapter I will provide answers to two major questions: (i) what can be learnt about the work's transmission from the nature of the *capitula*'s survival? (ii) what can be discerned about the authorship and purpose(s) of these headings? It will be seen

---

[1] I shall use the term *capitulum* rather than *titulus*, since the former approximates more to 'heading' than the latter. For a discussion of these terms and their ancient significance, see Schröder (1999) *passim*.

[2] Discussion of Lucretian *capitula* occurs in the following editions and commentaries: Lachmann (*ad* I.734, 1093, II.253–304, 757–806, IV.126, V.928–79, VI.840, and pp. 426–8), Diels (XIff.), Leonard–Smith (97 n. 13; also *ad* I.43a) and Bailey (vol. I, 39–41). Only three works have treated the *capitula* specifically: Fischer (1924), Pasetto (1962–3) and Sconocchia (2002), of which only the first analyses textual matters; the other two discuss almost exclusively the *capitula*'s composition and authorship, the latter even promoting the perverse theory that they were composed by Lucretius. A list of *capitula* drawn from Italic manuscripts, with some additions, was given in the editions of Gifanius and thereafter Haverkamp and Merrill (1917); Lachmann (249–52) reported the *capitula* as given in O(S), as do most subsequent editors, with Müller (289–93) and Flores (vol. III, 255–66) also relegating them to an appendix. Merrill, Diels and Leonard–Smith were the only twentieth-century editors to record these *capitula* in the main body of the text. Diels also printed *indices capitulorum* before Books IV–VI, a practice that Leonard–Smith extended to all six books. Martin's Teubner, Bailey's three-volume edition, Orth and Büchner, by contrast, collected the *capitula* in an index before each book, with Orth being the sole scholar to have translated them (into German).

that my conclusions shed light upon two significantly different phases of the transmission of Lucretius.[3]

(I)   The Lucretian *capitula* and their manuscript tradition

The preservation of *capitula* in the ninth-century manuscripts may be summarised as follows. O exhibits 182 *capitula*, typically marked distinctly from the text in rubricated capitals.[4] These

---

[3] A full collation of the ninth-century *capitula*, including cases where headings were misinterpreted as Lucretian verses and vice versa, is included in Appendix I.

[4] O's rubrication is variable (see Plates I–III): it presents no opening title but leaves the first line blank. Each book opens with an enlarged and rubricated initial that typically displaces the initial of the second line. Enlarged initials of the same nature also follow genuine *capitula* throughout the poem from I.830 (22^r) onwards; perhaps the archetype lacked such enlarged initials throughout and someone external to the scribe(s) advised O, between 19^r and 22^r, to add this adornment to an already most lavish manuscript. A number of these subsequent initials, particularly those in Book II connected with verses wrongly written as *capitula*, are not rubricated (II.711, 888, 910, 963, 1013, 1105(?), 1144, V.1161(?)), some only partially enlarged (I.566, II.711, 730, 810, 1013, 1105, 1144, V.1161), some not at all (II.609, 888, 910, 963, 1024, 1113). The anomaly at I.566 follows a Lucretian verse falsely taken as a *capitulum*, and V.1161 begins a new leaf and follows a *capitulum* at the bottom of the preceding page that was not rubricated. The *capitula* themselves are typically indented from the margin in alignment with the second letters of the main poem, except in nineteen centralised cases (often shorter *capitula*), and the false *capitula* that are not indented at all (save II.522 and 733, which are anomalous in being on a rewritten leaf (see n. 56) and amidst a number of false *capitula* respectively). The subscriptions in O are in rubricated capitals placed immediately after the last line of each Book: *Titi Lucretii Cari De Rerum Natura Liber X Explicit. Incipit Liber X+1*, with the addition in Book VI of *Lege feliciter Amen* after *explicit* (see Plate IV). These subscriptions typically cover two lines, but after Books I and III three lines and, with the freedom afforded by the final leaf (192^r, on which VI ends), four. In a number of cases (II.2, 465, III.446, IV.117, 178, 328, 477, 837, 877, 963, V.133, 252, 420, 590, 775, 879, 902, 1243, VI.220, 286, 841, 889, 922) it is clear that the rubricated initial preceded the writing of the following poetic verse: most notably, the initial of IV.117 (90^v) is written over the ink of the descender of the enlarged *P* of 116 (cf. also V.590 (136^v) and VI.841 (181^v)); the appearance of the initials at V.420 (132^v), 775 (141^v) and 1243 (153^v) has obviously been affected by the preceding rubricated initials. Given that the consistency and hue of the *capitula* match the rubricated initials that immediately follow, and that certain scribal features of the *capitula* are particularly similar to enlarged initials, I confidently regard both as concurrent additions by the text scribe(s) (which would explain the traces of red ink that appear on non-rubricated pages, e.g. 93^r, 93^v, 157^r). The scribe's neglect of the *capitula* but addition of the subsequent initial letters at V.892, 901, 916 and 1161 (144^v–151^r) could be explained if the mix of minium for rubrication had become too weak in red, i.e. too black, for appropriate use in writing the *capitula*, and indeed the last *capitulum* that occurs (V.878) and the enlarged initials from 144^v to 151^v are extremely dark, almost nearing black: at V.1161, the scribe neglected even to add an enlarged initial. Presumably he intended to return to add the *capitula*, more deserving of proper rubrication, once a new mix had been made but failed to do so. The next rubricated *capitulum* that

capitula usually cover one line but on occasion two.[5] In two instances (I.705, IV.1) the *capitulum* is written as if part of the poem, that is, in black minuscule.[6] In two other instances (II.608, III.905) the *capitulum* is rubricated but in minuscule; twice elsewhere (III.673, 949) the *capitulum* is rubricated but partly majuscule, partly minuscule. No fewer than twenty of these apparent *capitula* are in reality Lucretius' hexameters written as if *capitula*.[7] In three places (I.112, 418, V.91) O transcribed the *capitulum* one verse too late; in two others the *capitula* are arguably misplaced (III.388 should probably be at 381, V.526 at V.524). An index of *capitula* precedes Books IV–VI but not I–III; since no space is left before those books, the scribe(s) of O seemingly had no knowledge of *indices* for these books. It is from these *indices*, however, that we learn that O lacks nine *capitula* in the main body of the manuscript,[8] an error which will likewise be found in ψ (QS). O thus preserves 162 of the 171 *capitula* commonly attributed to Lucretius in the main body of its text, typically marking them as *capitula* (although four were not entered in Book V: see n. 4).

Q was evidently familiar with the existence of *capitula* and duly left spaces for the rubricator, allocating up to three lines for them (II.42–3, III.445, 842, IV.312). As with O, *indices capitulorum* precede Books IV–VI but no trace of them survives for I–III. Q's rubrication was not carried out as projected, and almost all *capitula* are wanting in the blank spaces left for them; in ten instances in Book IV, however, rubricated and majuscule *capitula* are inserted in these titular interstices, having been drawn, correctly or incorrectly, from the preceding *index capitulorum* in that manuscript.[9] In three instances where OS offer *capitula* (I.418,

appears (V.1240 (153ᵛ)) is of a typical colour, and probably belongs to a new scribal session.
[5] II.184, 842, III.445, IV.1, 312, V.471, VI.50.
[6] At I.705, however, O³ has written *capitulum* in the left margin.
[7] I.11, 411, II.42–3, 94, 502, 508, 608, 711, 809, 887, 909, 962, 1012, 1023, 1112, III.673, 759, 805, 905, 949.
[8] IV.127, 230, V.1, 575, 892, 901, VI.50, 906, 936.
[9] For the most part, Q's rubrication is absent (cf. Plates V and VII): no subscriptions are extant (disregarding the haphazard fifteenth-century additions of Q²), and rubrication is found only in the work's title and the sporadic (and often misplaced) *capitula* and subsequent initial letters in Book IV (1, 29, 269, 353, 364, 476, 571, 595, 722, 836, 962). Apart from the title, only one other spell of rubrication occurred, and certainly some

II.62, 89), Q has neglected to leave a gap. Twice a *capitulum* has been written by Q as if it were Lucretius' poetry (I.705, as in OS, and I.565). Seven gaps are left for *capitula* that were in reality parts of the poem and accordingly these verses are absent in Q;[10] all these verses O likewise treated as typical *capitula* with the exception of III.905, which, though rubricated, was written by O in minuscule. Accordingly, other than for the *indices capitulorum* to the last three books, Q is a limited source of information about the *capitula*, only signalling when a *capitulum* was thought to be desirable by leaving a gap. These interstices suggest that 159 of the 172 *capitula* were known to Q; as before (cf. n. 8), nine further can be supplied from the *indices* to Books IV–VI.

In S, *capitula* have typically been written in a majuscule rubricated script as in O (which mixes rustic capitals with uncial).[11]

time later; inspection reveals that the enlarged initials up to I.951 were written concurrently (cf. esp. I.1, 107, 311, 635, 715) with the text itself and also in black ink. Typically, Q left space for the enlarged initial without indenting (the sole exception being I.1052, the first instance where the scribe did not add the letter as he worked); from III.806 to IV.130–1, IV.513–95 and with II.756, 801, V.928, I.734 at the end of the manuscript, the second subsequent line is indented along with the first. In Book IV, by contrast, where we find the primary patch of rubrication, the hand is evidently different from that of the scribe (s): his addition of *capitula* and enlarged initials is sporadic and his ornamentation is not paralleled elsewhere in the manuscript (see Plate VI). Rather, at a later stage, probably in the tenth or eleventh centuries, someone saw an opportunity to practise his rubrication on a manuscript evidently not held in high esteem. Unfortunately, he had no access to another codex and therefore could not insert *capitula* in Books I–III (which lack *indices*) and could not or would not invent his own. Book IV, however, provided the opportunity to transfer headings sporadically from the *index* (with its faulty numeration) into the spaces left for them, misplacing the *capitula* by one space from IV.269 onwards: IV.127 (?) (*esse item maiora*), though preserved in the *index*, was lost in a lacuna prior to the archetype (and therefore has no gap in the text proper), yet the scribe mistook the gap at 132 as its proper place. As a result, his counting was out of step thereafter, although corrected at IV.364 and in a number of later instances. The fact that the decoration of the *capitula* increases suggests that the annotations are the work of a practising scribe rather than a reader who wished to adorn his copy for personal use. Although Q may have left the *capitula* for an expert rubricator, the manuscript could have been copied from ψ before the latter had been rubricated (but was by the time S was copied some decades later).

10 The following are verses omitted in the belief that they were *capitula* requiring rubrication (the number of verses left blank noted in brackets): II.42–3 (3), 707 (2), III.673 (2), 759 (2), 805 (1), 905 (2), 949 (1); II.508, wrongly written as a *capitulum* in O, was omitted by the oversight of Q along with II.507 and 509.

11 In its first section (G) we find not only rubricated *capitula* and subsequent enlarged initials throughout but also rubricated initials opening many normal verses (see Plate VIII). *capitula* appear in rubricated capitals, although after the change of scribe (from 7[n] onwards) they are primarily in minuscule. Subsequent initials alternate between

In one instance (II.184), the *capitulum* has been written in rubricated minuscule; in another (I.411), the words of the poet (which O presents as if a *capitulum* but Q wrote correctly) have been written in rubricated minuscule. In three instances (I.419 as in O, 705 as in OQ, II.112), *capitula* are not understood as such and are written as if Lucretian verses. Twice the *capitulum* is misplaced, once slightly (I.418 being placed above 419, as in O), once greatly (I.565 being placed above 523). The manuscript is not a witness for those instances where we would expect an *index capitulorum* (the beginning of Books IV–VI); at the beginning of Books I–III, as with OQ, no trace of such *indices* survives. In the fragments of S, we find a total of sixty-nine *capitula*; for the same portion of text O also preserves sixty-nine *capitula* and Q leaves gaps for sixty-five. S only thrice (I.411, II.42–3, 707) errs with O in writing Lucretius' text as *capitula*; for the other instances in which O made this error, S is accurate.

being rubricated and being written in the text ink, before this practice is abandoned for plain black ink from 7^r onwards (the rubrication of the adjacent I.269 and 277 arises from the turning of the page). As commonly in Latin manuscripts, the level of decoration decreased as the work progressed (rubrication in every initial 1^{rI}–1^{vII}, 2^{vII}, 3^{rI}, 3^{vII}; alternate initials 2^r; no initials 1^r, 2^{vI}, 3^r, 3^{vI}, 4^r–8^{vII}; Henrichsen (1846, 9) is imprecise on this point). The surprising fact that the first column of the first leaf lacks rubrication accords with leaves 2^v, 3^r and 3^v, whose first-column initials are in black ink, with those of the second rubricated. *capitula* are slightly indented from the left margin (except the more centrally positioned I.334, 498 and 1052); subsequent initials are enlarged but to a lesser degree than in O(Q). It is clear (cf. I.215–16 (2^{rI}), 334–5 (2^{vII}), 550–1 (4^{rI}), 830–1 (5^{rII}), II.14–15 (6^{vII})) that the rubrication of the enlarged and subsequent initials was carried out at the same time as the writing of the text: most strikingly, on 7^{vI}, the scribe began to write verse II.142 before the *capitulum* (for which he left no gap) but, having transcribed half the line (*Nunc qu<a>e mobilitas*), realised his mistake and finished the verse (*sit reddita materiai*) at the beginning of the next line. He then marked his mistake with an *x* and added the *capitulum* to fill the latter half of the line beginning with the opening of II.142. The long *capitulum* at II.184, squeezed into one line, suggests that the scribe added the heading as he worked, without forethought. V repeats most of G's format, with forty-seven ruled lines per page (14^{rI} having forty-eight, 14^{vI} forty-six). The *capitula* are similarly not indented but placed in line with the body of text (except II.1058 (central), III.94 and 241 (both left of the text block)). Enlarged and rubricated initials are generally found throughout (save II.730, 801, 806, 842, 1144, III.136, 381); III.369 demonstrates that, as before, rubrication was contemporaneous. U presents two immediately obvious differences from GV: it typically has fifty-five ruled lines per column (16^{vI} presents fifty-four, immediately rectified by the fifty-six of 16^{vII}) and the initial letter of each verse is separated from the rest of the text by a vertical rule, as in OQ, no doubt from another change in scribe. The *capitula* are also indented to a more marked degree, although rarely central; their following letters, however, are neither enlarged nor rubricated.

Clearly the presence of *capitula* in OQS is not negligible. Since these manuscripts record them in the main body of the text in rubricated capitals (OS), or intended to (Q), the archetype Ω presumably presented them in a similar form.[12] We may therefore enquire whether these *capitula* held such a prominent place in the text from their introduction; if it can be shown in what form they entered the text, and indeed what subsequent changes occurred, we will have valuable further insight into the history of Lucretius' transmission. In the ensuing section, I tackle five separate tasks: (A) to assess the extent of corruption in the text *capitula*; (B) to investigate the relationship between the *indices capitulorum* and the text *capitula*; (C) to reconstruct the form of the *indices capitulorum* in the archetype; (D) to analyse the instances where original *capitula* have been written as the text of the poem, or *uice uersa*; finally, (E) to gauge the extent of the dislocation and loss of the text *capitula*.

(A) The extent of corruption in the text capitula

The text *capitula* are relatively well preserved: the extent of corruption is slight and certainly more minor than would be expected for the same number of words of Lucretius' poetry.[13] Three possible reasons for this discrepancy exist, and all are probably true: (i) the *capitula* passed through fewer stages of transmission (and were therefore later additions to the manuscript tradition); (ii) they were written in a larger and clearer script;

---

[12] As will be demonstrated later (Appendix IV), the archetype was spaced with *capitula* in the text proper. The form of the *subscripta*, which must have appeared in Ω between each book and at the close of the work, is securely reconstructable – *Titi Lucreti Cari De Rerum Natura Liber X Explicit. Incipit Liber X* – and may take its origin from antiquity. Regarding a title at the work's beginning, there is no certainty: in O a single line is left blank, which was never filled, whereas in Q the first three have been filled with a longer title (*T. Lucreti Cari de phisica rerum origine vel effectu liber primus incipit*) by a later hand (saec. X(?)), loosely paraphrasing the incriminating *natura*, perhaps to suggest that the poem treated the physical creation of the world (cf. *natura* at I.21 and 25) and was therefore not overtly anti-Christian. As mentioned in Chapter 1, the added name of *Lucretius* was later erased, no doubt to disguise the work's controversial author. S lacks any opening title or interstice.

[13] As a comparison, I find twenty-nine archetypal corruptions in the 698 words of the (genuine) text *capitula*; in the same number of words of the poem drawn at random (VI.1–106) there are forty-eight.

(iii) the syntactic structure of these brief phrases is typically shorter than clauses in the poem and was therefore less susceptible to corruption. Of the minor corruptions of *capitula* that existed in Ω, few can tell us much. We find the loss of final,[14] as well as medial,[15] letters, one instance of a final *e* being read as &,[16] the occasional loss of nasals, probably owing to oversight of the virgula above vowels,[17] *i* or *l* for *e*,[18] and *t* for *l*,[19] which last errors probably occurred in *capitalis*, as perhaps did the corruption of *priuatam* to *paratam* (III.711).[20] *u* is twice written for *a*,[21] typically an error in minuscule from the sixth century onwards, and *o* is once written for *u*.[22] The mistaken writing of *uocemus* for *uocem* at IV.526 by O (and perhaps Ω) suggests a minuscule error, *m* being read as if *m'* (= *mus*) (the same abbreviation used by *ind.* Q at IV.779), an abbreviation not attested in ancient *capitalis* and but rarely in uncial. The loss of words at the beginning of *capitula* is evidenced in at least three cases;[23] perhaps in three instances a word has been transposed from one part of the *capitulum* to

---

[14] I.150 *nihil* for *nihilo*; II.1105 *e* for *et*; VI.840 *frigidio* for *frigidior*; VI.536 *arq//* (*arci* Dungal) could also reflect the loss of final *-o* or *-uo* in the archetype.

[15] VI.932 *omnibus* O : *abminibus* S : *abminibus* Ω(?); VI.1138 *Athenienium* for *Atheniensium* (as in the *index*).

[16] II.809 *poss&* for *posse* (a Lucretian verse misunderstood as a *capitulum*); I therefore reject Fischer's insertion of *et* after *potuisse*.

[17] V.91 *terra* for *terram*, V.376 *sit* for *sint*.

[18] I.951 *pepirasmenon* for *peperasmenon*, III.805 *saluas* for *saeuas*, IV.312 *uidere* for *uideri*.

[19] I.411 *ptano* for *plano* (a Lucretian verse wrongly written as a *capitulum*).

[20] The corruption could, however, have been motivated by the close of III.710, *partita per artus*.

[21] IV.1 *clarum* for *claram* (a *Perseverationsfehler* after *iucundissimum* three words before is much less probable), V.471 *nascuntur* for *nascantur* (see n. 60 below).

[22] II.1058 *mundos* for *mundus* (perhaps an error through assimilation to *apiros*).

[23] At IV.221 *declinatione motus* could well be the result of haplography of *de declinatione motus*, since *clinatio* is otherwise unattested and, if the phraseology is drawn from Lucretius, we would expect *clinamine* (for more on this point, see section II(B) below). At IV.233 *tactu uideri* is difficult alone: we may supply (before *tactu*) either *res*, as tentatively suggested by Fischer, or alternatively *omnia* (nevertheless, the use of the bare passive in the following *capitulum*, IV.269 *ultra speculum cur uideatur* demands caution: *tactu uideri* could be rough-and-ready Latin for 'sight occurs by touch'). At VI.921 (*fluere ab omnibus rebus*) we surely require a subject for the infinitive, and Fischer's *corpora*, which could easily have been lost via *c̄oā* (an abbreviation whose vestiges can be seen elsewhere in OQ and (particularly) S), is a good suggestion. At VI.1090 the structure of the *capitulum* (*pestilentia unde creatur*) is anomalous and may be a corruption of *de pestilentia unde creetur*. A word could have been lost at IV.127 (*esse item maiora*): since, however, the *capitulum* is preserved only in the *index*

another.[24] Other minor errors (II.589, V.526, VI.749, VI.879) need not be mentioned at this stage; treatment of *ultimum saeculum* at IV.269, along with other possible corruptions that require further discussion, I defer until below.[25] There is only one instance of serious corruption:

II.522 in terra †insemina† inesse
(*sic* O : *sp. duorum uu. rel. om.* Q : inter se similia infinita esse *Lachmann*)

The text cannot be emended with certainty. It is immediately apparent that the wording has arisen under the influence of the following correct *capitulum* (II.589 *in terra semina insunt*),[26] for the present passage (522–31) treats neither *terra* nor the *semina* in it. Rather, the paragraph states that atoms of a similar shape are infinite in number. Lachmann's conjecture is admirably close to the *ductus* but this is largely irrelevant if the following *capitulum* was copied here by anticipation. The supplement is also inappropriate in force, for it is atoms *inter se simili ... figura* (524) that are infinite, and the bare neuter *similia* could scarcely

and its particular context is not known, it is difficult to supply a noun with certainty. Lachmann argued (*ad loc.*) that *simulacra* could be inserted or simply understood. I regard the *capitulum* as complete but *animalia* must be supplied from the previous heading (IV.116 *quam parua sint animalia*), to which it is closely bound by *item*; for the consequences of this supposition, see section II(C) below.

[24] At V.780 (*de nouitate mundi et dispositione rerum quae in eo sunt*) *rerum* has moved from after *dispositione* (or possibly from immediately before it) to after *nouitate* (but retains its correct place in the *indices*); at I.184 *nihil sursum ferri corpusculorum* is curiously ordered (not reflected by Lucretius' wording) and may be a corruption of *nihil corpusculorum sursum ferri*; at IV.312 it could well be that *ex tenebris in luce quae sint* was originally written as *ex tenebris quae sint in luce* (or *q. i. l. s.*). The *capitulum* at II.1105 (*mundum natum et* [*e* Ω] *multos similes*) is probably not corrupt, rather *multos similis* understands *mundos natos esse* and the latter half of the *capitulum* is not specifically drawn from the text that follows. The heading at III.228 (*tertiam animam esse mentem*) could only mean 'the third soul [= its third part?] is mind', which neither Lucretius' text nor Epicurean theory supports; the generous translation of Orth ([195]), 'Die dritte Seele ist die Kraft des Denkens (= der Verstand)', does not resolve the problem. Although I formerly posited corruption here (of, e.g., *etiam animam esse mentem*), it is more probable that this *capitulum* proceeds from misunderstanding the text, failing to see that *aura* and *aer* are treated as distinct elements of the soul in 232–4, such that *mens* need be posited as the third element, before the nameless fourth (241ff.). The other two corruptions occur in the *capitula* as recorded in the *index* (V.680, VI.50), treated below in (B).

[25] I exclude minor errors made by O and corrected by Dungal or O²: II.478, III.379, IV.1, 595, V.324, VI.50, 225, 246, 879.

[26] I shall argue in section II that *insunt* is almost certainly a corruption of *inesse*.

bear that sense. I think it certain that *infinita* has been lost but restoring the remainder of the *capitulum* is mere guesswork. Some indication is given by the fact that Q has left a space of two lines, which suggests a slightly longer *capitulum*, at least of twenty-four characters.[27] We could tentatively suggest *infinita esse corpuscula simili figura perfecta.* I will offer an explanation of how this error occurred, based upon other criteria, in section (E) below.

(B)   The relationship between the indices *and text* capitula

In Books IV, V and VI it is possible to compare the states of preservation of the *capitula* owing to their dual presence in the *index* prefixed to these books and in the main body of the poetic text. In considering the textual merits of our witnesses, I limit myself to cases where both O and Q differ from the text in the *indices*; for the text our sole evidence is O, sometimes with the support of S. I ignore instances where *capitula* appear in Book IV in Q, since they have been copied from the *index* and are thus of no independent textual value.[28] The following textual discrepancies exist, in which the reading underlined is the superior one, although preference is sometimes unclear;[29] I have neglected to record mistaken word division unless it is evidently of some import):

---

[27] For the relationship of the gaps of more than one verse in Q with the size of the *capitula* extant in O (and S), see n. 57 below. The present number of characters in the *capitulum* to 522 is 25, whereas the smallest number of characters for which Q leaves a two-line gap is twenty-four (VI.1090); the second smallest is twenty-seven (II.1105, though twenty-nine after emendation); the average is forty.

[28] For instance, no weight can be attributed to the spelling *iocundissimum* found in the *capitulum* preceding the opening of Book IV in Q; it is simply a slip in the copying of the text from the beginning of the *index*, which (like the *index* and text of O) presents *iucundissimum*; the use of various abbreviations is identical to those employed in the *index* version (see, e.g., IV.836); at IV.269 we find the mistaken fusion of *de celeritate tactu uideri*, as in the *index*; at IV.353, 384 and 476, we find the wrong *capitulum* recorded; at IV.595 the incorrect *quo* (as found in the *index*) is written for *qua* (preserved by the text *capitulum* of O). It is scribal error or a rare correction at 962 that brought about the correct *somnis* from *somniis* of the *index*.

[29] In two instances (V.780, VI.840) it is not possible to select one form of the *capitulum* and I have combined parts of each.

(I) The transmission of the *capitula*

Liber IV

127 esse item maiora *ind*. O *ind*. Q : *om. sine sp. text*. O *text*. Q

131 de nubibus *ind*. O *ind*. Q : de nubibus et simulacra gigni *text*. O

176 de celeritate *ind*. O *ind*. Q : de celeritate simulacrorum *text*. O

230 tactu uideri *ind*. O *ind*. Q : *om. sine sp. text*. O *text*. Q

269 ultra speculum cur uideatur *ind*. O *ind*. Q : ultimum saeculum cur uideatur *text*. O

312 ex tenebris in luce quae sint uideri *ind*. O *ind*. Q : ex tenebris in luce quae sint uideri et rusum ex luce quae sunt[30] in tenebris uidere non posse *text*. O

353 de turbis *ind*. O *ind*. Q : de turribus *text*. O

476 de uero sensu quae cognoscatur *ind*. O *ind*. Q : de uero sensu quare cognoscatur *text*. O

526 corpoream esse uocem *ind*. O *ind*. Q : corpoream esse uocemus *text*. O

877 de ambulando *ind*. O *ind*. Q : de motu membrorum hoc est de ambulando *text*. O

907 de somno *ind*. O *ind*. Q : de somno quem ad modum fiat *text*. O

Liber V

1 plus hominibus profuisse qui sapientiam inuenerit quam Cererem Liberum Herculem *ind*. O *ind*. Q : *om. sine sp. text*. O *text*. Q

64 de mundo *ind*. O *ind*. Q : mundum et natum et mortalem esse *text*. O

91 mare caelum terram interitura *ind*. Q : mare caelum terra interitura *ind*. O : mare celum terra interitura *text*. O (*ante* 93)

200 *om. ind*. O *ind*. Q : diuisio terre uel uitium *text*. O

240 cui pars natiua sit totum natiuum esse *ind*. O *ind*. Q : quo pars natiua sit totum natiuum esse *text*. O

---

[30] *sint* should be read.

145

324 quare natiua (nata *ind.* O) omnia dicta *ind.* O *ind.* Q : quare natiua (O^D i.e. Dungal : natia *a.c.*) omnia dicat *text.* O

376 et natiua esse *ind.* O *ind.* Q : et natiua (O^D : natiu& *a.c.*) esse cum sit[31] mortalia *text.* O

471 de solis et lunae magnitudine *ind.* O *ind.* Q : de solis et lunae magnitudine et motu eorum et quem ad modum nascuntur[32] *text.* O

575 de luna *ind.* O *ind.* Q : *om. sine sp. text.* O *text.* Q

629 de lunae cursu *ind.* Q : de lune cursu *ind.* O : de lunae (O^D : lune *a.c.*) cursu *text.* O

663 ex Ida (Ia *ind.* Q) uiseo solis *ind.* O *ind.* Q : ex Ida uisio solis *text.* O

680 de die longo et breui nocte *ind.* O *ind.* Q : de die longo et nocte breui *text.* O

705 de lunae (O^{D}Q^2 : lune *a.c.*) lumine *ind.* O *ind.* Q : de lune lumine *text.* O

751 de eclipsi *ind.* O : de eclypsi *ind.* Q : *om. sine sp. text.* O

780 de natiuitate mundi et dispositione rerum quae in eo sunt *ind.* O *ind.* Q : de nouitate rerum mundi et dispositione quae in eo sunt *text.* O

878 de scylla *ind.* Q : de sculla *ind.* O : *om. sp. rel. text.* O

901 de chimeera *ind.* O *ind.* Q : *om. sp. rel. text.* O *text.* Q

916 non potuisset (posse *ind.* Q) chimeram et scyllam et similia eorum gigni *ind.* O *ind.* Q : *om. sp. rel. text.* O *sp. duorum uu. rel. text.* Q

1161 quomodo hominibus innata sit deorum opinio *ind.* O *ind.* Q : *om. sp. rel. text.* O *text.* Q

Liber VI

50 qui procurationem dis attribuit mundi, sibi ipsum de dis immortalibus sollicitudines constituere *ind.* O *ind.* Q : *om. sine sp. rel. text.* O *text.* Q

204 in nubibus seminet (eminet *ind.* O) ignes inesse *ind.* O *ind.* Q : in nubibus semina ignita inesse *text.* Q

---

[31] *sint* should be read.   [32] *nascantur* should probably be read: see n. 60 below.

225 <u>ignis ex fulmine natura</u> *ind.* O *ind.* Q : ignis et fulmine (O^D : fulminis *a.c.*) natura *text.* O

526 <u>de arquo</u> *ind.* O *ind.* Q : de arci (O^D : arq// *a.c.*) *text.* O

839 <u>cur aqua in puteis frigidior sit aestate</u> *ind.* O *ind.* Q : cur aqua in puteis aestate frigidio sit *text.* O : cor aqua in puteis estate frigidio sit *text.* S

906 <u>de lapide magnete</u> *ind.* O *ind.* Q : *om. sine sp. text.* O *text.* Q *text.* S

921 <u>fluere ab omnibus rebus</u> *ind.* O *ind.* Q : fluere omnibus rebus *text.* O : fluere abminibus rebus *text.* S

936 <u>raras res omnis esse</u> *ind.* O *ind.* Q : *om. sine sp. text.* O *text.* Q *text.* S

1138 <u>de pestilentia Atheniensium</u> *ind.* O : de pestilentia Athenienium *text.* O *text.* S

First, it should be noted that the better reading is typically found in the text *capitula* rather than the *indices*. If we ignore the thirteen instances where the reading is lacking in one of the two witnesses, in sixteen of twenty-five cases (i.e. almost two-thirds) the *capitula* written in the text provide the better reading. Of the cases where the reading of the *indices* is superior, the text of O typically demonstrates a minor corruption (the few exceptions will be treated below).[33] When the text of O offers a better reading, however, it is often manifestly superior (and considerably longer) than that found in the *index*.[34] Most notable is IV.312, where the text of O provides *ex tenebris in luce quae sint uideri et rusum quae sint in tenebris uidere* (a slip for *uideri*) *non posse* against

---

[33] E.g., for the loss of one or two letters, IV.476, V.9, VI.921, 1131. The only problematic error is the presence of the correct *cui* in the *indices* at V.240 but *quo* in the text *capitulum* of O. It is true, as Lachmann first observed, that the most economical way to explain this error would be to posit that *quoi* was in the main *capitulum*, which was normalised to *cui* by the compiler of the *index* but mistakenly transcribed as *quo* in the main text. For reasons that will become clear in section II of this chapter, however, I do not believe that these headings were written in the period (before the middle of the first century AD) when *quoi* would have been a possible (and not affected) orthographic alternative to *cui*. It is perhaps better to posit that *cui* was correctly transcribed by, and transmitted in, the *index* but that it was corrupted to *quo* in a one- or two-stage corruption: *cui* > *qui* (pronunciational error) > *quo* (to provide at least possible sense). The more natural *cuius* (perhaps written *cui'*) could originally have opened the *capitulum*.

[34] More serious instances of corruption can be seen at IV.176, 353, V.780, VI.150, 204.

the mere *ex tenebris in luce quae sint uideri* of the *index*; likewise, at V.471 the text of O offers *de solis et lunae magnitudine et motu eorum et quem ad modum nascuntur* but the *index* only *de solis et lunae magnitudine*; at V.64 we find more detail with the text of O's *mundum et natum et mortalem esse* than with *de mundo* of the *index*. In these and a number of other instances (IV.131, 176, 877, 907, V.376) it seems that the *indices* deliberately curtail the versions of the *capitula* found in the text; in the unique instance at V.64 just cited, it appears that *de mundo* is rather a summary reworking, not an abridgement, of the longer form found in the *capitulum*. It is most improbable that these particular differences between the *indices* and the text *capitula* are the result either of severe loss in the transmission of the *indices* or subsequent additions to the text *capitula* after the *indices* had been established. As one would expect, then, the *index capitulorum* seems to be not only a summary of the contents of the following book but a slightly condensed catalogue of the summary already provided by the *capitula* in the main body of the text.[35] The origin of the *indices* therefore seems to have been the transcription, and appropriate abbreviation, of the *capitula* scattered throughout the books: they were not composed independently of the text *capitula* but rather created from them. (For why *indices* are lacking for the first three books, see n. 39 below.)

Before turning to the six instances where the *indices* present a *capitulum* but no trace of it exists in the main text,[36] it is worth noting a particularly instructive error. At IV.269, the text of O presents the corrupt *ultimum saeculum cur uideatur*, whereas the *index* preserves the certainly correct *ultra speculum cur uideatur*. Although it is possible that an intelligent reader or scribe corrected *ultimum* to *ultra* whilst collecting the *indices*, one would naturally assume that *ultimum* would be likewise corrected in the main *capitulum* by so diligent a reader. What instead seems far more likely is that the *indices* were copied from the *capitulum* when it still correctly read *ultra speculum* and that the corruption

---

[35] Some curtailings can involve the loss of detail, as at IV.131, V.376, 471.
[36] I disregard a few instances in O towards the end of Book V, which was left unrubricated (cf. n. 4).

in the text *capitulum* occurred thereafter. Yet *ultra speculum* >
ultimum saeculum is not, *prima facie*, a particularly simple error.
Indeed, it is hard to understand how the error could have occurred
in *capitalis*: VLTRA SPE- is at some remove from VLTIMVM
(or VLTIMV̄) S(A)E-.[37] Yet rather than posit a series of corruptions, it seems more economical to infer that the error occurred, in
one step, in minuscule: if *ultra* was written with an *r* whose bar
was slightly detached from the descender, and *a* was *u*-shaped,
one could have easily read *ultīu* or even, if the bar of the *r* were
rather long, *ultīū*, that is, *ultimum*. The corruption of *sae* to *spe* is
more difficult: since the only real similarity between *a* and *p* is in
Roman cursive of the third to fifth centuries (when *p* is often
bowl-less), a most unlikely script for the poem's transmission, it
may be safer to conclude either that *p* was omitted in transmission
and *seculum* easily provided with the diphthong in its first syllable
by the same or a later hand or that the error was a one-stage
banalisation. If it is accepted that this corruption could only have
occurred in minuscule, an interesting conclusion is that in the
manuscript from which the *indices* were first written, the text
capitula (if consistent) were apparently still in minuscule.
The writer of the *indices*, unlike the scribe of the next manuscript,
read *ultra* correctly. By the time of the archetype, however, the
text *capitula* were evidently capitalised.[38]

A quick survey of corruptions in the *capitula* of both the text
and the *indices* provides an insight into phases of their transmission. A minuscule phase is strongly attested by the confusion of *u*
and *a* (IV.1, V.471), *t* and *x* (VI.225), *-mus* (*-m'*) and *-m* (IV.526),
and in the case of *ultra* > *ultimum* at IV.269 just discussed.
We have observed that the practice of OS strongly suggests that

---

[37] Ecclesiastical Latin does turn up the phrase *ultimum saeculum* but in no particular
frequency or famous text: Jerome's commentary on Zach. II.v.6–7, Augustine on *Psalm*
LXIV.13 and at *Serm.* 239.6, Nicetius *Epp.* 11, and Peter Comestor's sixth sermon.
Outside the religious sphere we find only Servius *ad* Verg. *Buc.* IV.10, on the age of
Apollo. Although I consequently think it unlikely that *ultra speculum* was written as the
phrase *ultimum saeculum* for psychological reasons, I welcome the idea that, if *ultimum*
was mistakenly read for *ultra*, the scribe thought that *saeculum* was a more natural word
to follow than *speculum*, and consciously or unconsciously made that alteration.

[38] Corruptions in the *capitula* of S show that ψ also wrote its *capitula* in capitals (as the use
of capitals by S, and Q's generous allocation of space (cf. n. 57 below), itself suggests),
e.g. AGROE for ACROE (I.951) and *Hedem* for *Aedem* (O) (VI.749).

the *capitula* were written in capitals in the archetype; errors such as *t* for *l* (I.411) and *l* for *e* (III.805) could be a further indication of a prior capital phase, but since both are Lucretian verses rather than *capitula*, these errors could well have occurred when they were still treated as the Lucretian text. I can find no evidence that decisively proves a capital phase anterior to the archetype.

If we begin by assuming what I argue in section II of this chapter, that the *capitula* began their life as marginal notes, we would expect that they were written in a cursive hand in a relatively constricted space. Such a peripheral location helps to explain the loss of initial words from *capitula* (e.g. II.221(?), IV.230(?), VI.921, 1090), which would have been particularly susceptible to loss in the margins; these words were evidently lost before the *indices* were copied from the text *capitula*. An initial marginal location – and therefore the writing of longer *capitula* on several lines – also helps to explain the transpositions of words that cannot be understood as having occurred on syntactic grounds (e.g. *rerum* at V.780 and *mundi* at VI.50).

If these arguments are accepted, as I shall argue below, we can posit at least four manuscript phases for the *capitula*:

(i)   A manuscript in which the *capitula* were added, in minuscule, to the margins. This manuscript suffered some damage or trimming, including the loss of certain initial words.
(ii) A manuscript in which the *capitula* were copied into *indices* for the last three books[39] and the *capitula* were copied in minuscule (either in the margin or the main body).

---

[39] I deem it most unlikely, as Diels (1918, 937–9; 1923–4 edn, X) and Birt (1919, 713–14) maintained, that the individual leaves on which the *indices capitulorum* for Books I–III were written were wholly lost; Diels' supposition that they stood at the beginning of three different rolls for the first three books would require threefold damage to these *uolumina* and would push the *capitula* back to a period markedly earlier (saec. II?) than is probable (see below). The single most likely explanation is that someone who commissioned a manuscript (or wrote it himself) realised that, for the longer – and perhaps more interesting – books with many *capitula* (IV, V and VI), it would be a useful resource to have a list of the *capitula* recorded at the beginning. The first half of the manuscript could have already been copied by this point. It is an artificial innovation, therefore, for Leonard–Smith to supply *indices* for Books I–III 'for the sake of uniformity with Books IV–VI' (196); the confident assertions of Flores (vol. III, 17) are likewise fundamentally flawed. It is also most improbable that the absence of indices for Books I–III suggests that this half of the work had a different source from Books IV–VI.

(iii)   The archetype (Ω), in which the *capitula* stood in the text, rubricated and capitalised.
(iv)   O and ψ, which sought to replicate Ω.

Further light can be shed on the manuscript tradition by considering the eight instances (IV.127, 230, V.1, 575, 751, VI.50, 906, 930) where a *capitulum* is preserved in the *indices* but no trace of it (neither a blank space nor following rubricated initial) remains in the body of the text. Although it is possible that the *capitulum* at V.1 was omitted in the general confusion between the end of the dense *index* and the beginning of the poetic book, for the other five instances there seem to be only two explanations that can be offered, although both may be right, in combination. Five or six *capitula* could be absent from the main body of the text because either (a) these *capitula* were later additions made to the *indices* but not to the main body of the text or (b) after the *indices* had been formed, they were accidentally omitted by a subsequent scribe (or scribes) when transcribing the main body of the text. Of these options (a) seems to me unlikely, for if a reader wished to add further *capitula*, they would presumably appear not only in the *index* but also in the main text – where they are certainly of more practical use (the index only providing an order of topics and not their location); furthermore, there would be little likelihood of a reader's later additions to the cramped *index* being preserved in their correct place in transmission.

Therefore, for want of any other alternative, (b) is probably correct. Yet since the loss of five of ninety-nine *capitula* is a relatively large proportion, we ought to consider the positioning of the *capitula* at an earlier stage of the tradition. It is unlikely that they were written in the main column of the text (whether in black or red) for, if black, such a capital heading would be difficult to miss,[40] and, if red, a clear space would have been left for the rubricator. Although it is possible that such spaces were left, that the rubricator failed to copy out the *capitula* in five such gaps and that a subsequent scribe merely closed the gap (and, if present,

---

[40] I think the possibility that such *capitula* were ignored purposefully according to the wish of the scribe can be dismissed.

replaced the following rubricated initial with a normal letter), I think it considerably neater to posit that the *capitula* were initially marginal. Therefore the compiler of the *indices* to Books IV–VI could diligently have sought out these marginal *capitula* and added them to the *indices*; yet a subsequent scribe of the main text, concentrating on the columns of poetry, could easily have overlooked small marginal *capitula* (and perhaps did so in Books I–III without our being able to realise it), thereby omitting them from the tradition without trace: if, as argued below, the marginal annotations were not intended to serve as formal headings, they may well have been small in size. I therefore believe it can be concluded that when the *indices* were created, and perhaps also in a later manuscript or manuscripts, the text *capitula* were recorded in the margin and (as argued above) in minuscule.

Finally, a few words should be said about V.200, the sole instance where the *capitulum* is found in the main text alone and not in the *indices*. Three possibilities present themselves: the *capitulum* (a) was a later addition to the main text after the *indices* had been transcribed and was never added to the *index* to Book V; (b) was transcribed into the *index* of Book V when it was compiled but accidentally omitted in transmission of the *index*; or (c) was present before the creation of the *index* but the compiler of that to Book V failed to notice or record this particular *capitulum*. Since we have only one instance to consider, it is clear that any of these three options is possible. Nevertheless, (a) is perhaps unlikely if, as seems self-evident, the *indices* were formed after the *capitula* had been written fully; (c) appears more likely than (b) but either is entirely possible.

(C)   The reconstruction of the forms of the indices capitulorum in Ω

The *indices* to Books V and VI are confusedly arranged in our ninth-century manuscripts, which is primarily attributable to two distinct columns of *capitula* being roughly conflated into one. Nonetheless, the situation is complicated and it will prove profitable to reconstruct the precise layout of the *indices* in the archetype.[41]

The *index* to Book IV requires little discussion; Figures A and B show the form of the *indices* in, respectively, O and Q (the *capitula* are numbered sequentially).[42] All thirty *capitula* are in the correct order; in four instances in O and in two instances in Q, two *capitula* have been written on the same line. Since there is no significant division between these *capitula* (cf. esp. 7 and 8 in O), it is probable that they were already written on the same line in a manuscript prior to the archetype, then in the archetype they were transcribed closely together (with an interpunct only being added or preserved between 27 and 28 in O). It should be noted (so Lachmann *ad* IV.126) that in O the *index* covered twenty-six lines and thus certainly took up one full page (= 69$^{\rm v}$) of the archetype. Therefore either ψ or Q elected to separate the two pairs of *capitula* that were apparently (based upon their layout in O) easily separable, namely 12–13 and 27–8. That Q conceived its *index* with numeration from the beginning but it does not relate to evidently separate *capitula* suggests that such numbers are the *ad hoc* creation of Q (if not ψ).[43]

The situation with Book V is considerably more difficult. As can be seen in Figures C and D, serious dislocation has taken place. It is evident that an earlier form of the *index* was written, moving vertically, in two columns, which were later conflated into one, thereby either bringing later *capitula* between earlier ones, or creating hybrid entries from the two. The second column began with the 28th *capitulum* (*de lunae lumine*). The two *capitula* at the bottom of the *indices* in O and Q (*de die longo et breui nocte* and *ex Ida uiseo solis*) are in the wrong order, probably because the scribe of the archetype, having reached the base (i.e. line 26) of

---

[41] The reconstruction of the archetype is discussed briefly in Appendix IV.

[42] There has been no other depiction of the *indices* of Books IV–VI in OQ, save for Fischer's (1924, 34–5) of the latter part of the *index* to Book V, which is necessarily inaccurate owing to typographical strictures combined with numerous typographical errors. Fischer himself did not attempt to follow Lachmann in reconstructing the archetype's *indices*: 'Archetypum reconstruere non conor, cum nihil nisi coniicere in his rebus liceat' (38), with which assertion I disagree.

[43] It is evident that the addition of *eorum usum* in Q two lines above its *capitulum* (XXIIII) is a result of the scribe's running out of space, marked by '/'.

The *capitula* of *De rerum natura*

1 S ibi iucundissimum esse quod claram lucem mortalib; ostendat
2 ð esimulacris
3 ð eimaginibus
4 Q uam paruae sint animalia
5 & ssectem maiora
6 ð enubibus
7 ð ecelerrataetactu uideri [8]
9 u beaspeculum curuideatur
10 p luresimagines cur fiant
11 & xtenebris inluce quae sint uideri
12 ð eaurbis deumbra hominis [13]
14 ð euisu
15 ð euerosensu quae cognoscatur
16 ð efalso sensu
17 ð eaudieris corpoream esse uocem [18]
19 ð euoeis imaginibus
20 q uauisus nomtanea uocemranare
21 ð esapore
22 q uare alia aliis contraria sint
23 ð eodore
24 ð eanimi motu
25 Q uare quodlibuerit facili cognemus
26 p ruisoculos linguam auris tenatam quam eorum unusim
27 ð eambulando · desomno [28]
29 ð esomnis
30 ð erebus uenerios

Fig. A: *Indices capitulorum libri IV*: O 87[r-v]

154

1 I Sibiiucundissimueaqddaralucemostalib'ostendat·
2 II Desimulacris
3 III Demaginibus
4 IIII Quamparuasint animalia
5 V Essetem maiora
6 VI Denubibus
7 VII Deceleritate tactuuidem [8]
9 VIII Vltra speculum curuideatur
10 VIIII plures imaginescurfiant
11 X Extenebrisinlucemquaesintuideri
12 XI Deturbis
13 XII Deumbrahominis
14 XIII Deuisu

XIIII [15] Deuerosensu quaecognoscatur
XV [16] Defalso sensu
XVI [17] Deauditascorpoream esseuocem [18]
XVII [19] Deuocis imaginibus [20]
XVIII [20] Quouisusnontrans&uocetrana
XVIIII [21] Desapore
XX [22] Quarealia aliiscontrariasint
XXI [23] Deodore [25]
XXII [24] Deanimimotu eaqusum
XXIII [25] Quarequodlibueritstaticognem?
XXIIII [26] Pruisoculoslinguaauresesenataqua
XXV [27] Deambulando
XXVI [28] Desomno
XXVII [29] Desomniis
XXVIII [30] Derebusuenerris f1.

Fig. B: *Indices capitulorum libri IV*: Q 30^v

the page for the *indices* (i.e. 96ʳ) with the 26th *capitulum* (*ex Ida uiseo solis*), began a second column as far up the right-hand side of the page as he could but in so doing accidentally overlooked the 27th *capitulum* (*de die longo et breui nocte*). Either he or another realised the error and therefore added this *capitulum* at the bottom of the page alongside the 26th but such that it was subsequently thought to precede it. Nonetheless, the 26th and 27th *capitula* were evidently sufficiently distinct for O to transcribe them separately; presumably in ψ they were more closely placed, as Q, for no other obvious reason, has written both on the same line and numbered them as if united.[44] Again, we find numbering throughout the *index* of Q, although a good number of separate *capitula* have not been noticed or counted; in O the numbering progresses to XII but when faced with the obvious difficulties of the next entry (*stitutum in eo sunt*), the rubricator apparently threw in the towel.

Notwithstanding this confusion, however, from close observation of the forms of these two *indices* we may reconstruct the form of the *index* in the archetype (Ω) as in Figure E, which can easily explain the forms of the *index* found in OQ. It is probable that the scribe of the archetype was working from a list of *capitula* that progressed vertically alone. Beginning a new leaf for the list, he proceeded in the same manner, writing as far across the page as each *capitulum* took him, and in some instances (ll. 3, 11, 17) he placed plural *capitula* on the same line; the first and sixth *capitula* were of a length that brought them onto two lines; the seventh and fourteenth had seemingly been divided onto two lines[45] already with *stitutum* and *intereant* beginning new lines. However, having reached the bottom of the page (a 26-line page again being reconstructed, as posited throughout the archetype), he thought it better to include the remaining third of the *capitula* on the same page. Since the first two lines had been filled by the initial *capitulum*, the first available space for the 28th *capitulum* was at

---

[44] It is unclear whether Q or ψ miscopied *ida* as *ia*.

[45] Such a division was probably the arrangement in the hyperarchetype, from which the scribe of Ω was working. It is possible that numerous *capitula* were on each line and he failed to realise that *stitutum* and *intereant* belonged with items in their preceding lines.

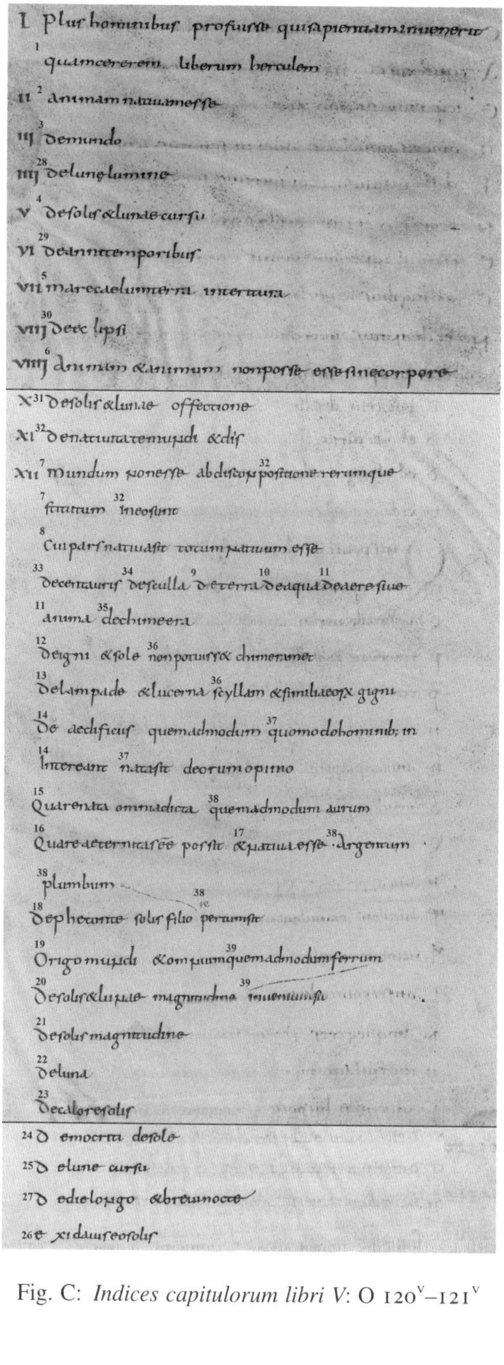

(I) The transmission of the *capitula*

Fig. C: *Indices capitulorum libri V*: O 120^v–121^v

1 I Plushominibus profuisse quisapientiam in
ueneritquae cererem liberum herculem

2 II Animam naturam esse

3 III Demundo[28] IIII Deluneluminne

4 V Desolis&lunae cursu

29 VI Deanni temporibus

5 VII Mare caelon terram interitura

30 VIII Deeclypsi

6 VIIII Anima&animum nonposse ee sinecorpore

31 X Desolis&lunae offecaione

32 XI Denaturate mundi &dis quaemeosunt[32]

7 XII mundu noneSSeabdis conStiuitu copositionereru[32]

8 XIII Cuspars naturaasir totumnatiuum esse

33 XIIII Decentauris xu descylla xui detia[34]

10 XVII deaqua XIIII deaere siueanima[11]

35 XVIIII dechimeera xx deignni &sole[12]

36 XXI nonpossechimeera&scyllasimiliaeo gigni

13 XXII delampade &lucerna

14 XXIII deaedificiis queadmodu intereai t

[15] XXIII quaritione omnia dicat t

37 XXV quomodo hominibus innatasir deo optmio

15 XXVI quarenataomme dicta queadmodu duraii[38]

16 XXVII quarea&eternitasesse possit &natiua ee[17]

38 argentum plumbum

18 XXVIII deph&ontesolisfilio[38] repaunsit

19 XXVIIII Origo mundi &omniu queadmodu ferru[39]

20 XXX desolis&lunae magnitudine inuenius sir[39]

21 XXXI Desolis magnitudine XXXII Delunie[22]

23 XXXIII Decalore solis XXXIIII Democritde sole[24]

25 XXXV Delunae cursu

27 XXXII Dedie longo &braui nocte exauiseo solis[26]

Fig. D: *Indices capitulorum libri* V: Q 42ᵛ–43ʳ

158

I **P** lus hominibus profuisse qui sapientiam in
uenerit quam   cererem   liberum   herculem
II Animam natiuam esse   III De mundo   IIII De lunae lumine
V De solis et lunae cursu   VI De anni temporibus
VII Mare caelum terrā interitura   VIII De eclipsi
VIIII Animam et animum non posse esse sine
corpore X Desolis & lunę offectione XI Denatiuitate mundi & dis
XII Mundum non esse ab dis con positione rerum quæ
    Stitutum   in eo sunt
 Cui pars natiua sit totum natiuū esse De centauris De scylla
 De terra   De aqua   De aere siue anima   De chimera
 De igni et sole   Non potuisse chimeram &
 De lampade & lucerna   scyllam et similia eorum gigni
 De aedificiis quem ad modum   quomodo hominibus in
 intereant   natasitdeorumopinio
 quare nata omnia dicta   quem ad modum aurum
 quare aeternitas esse possit & natiua esse argentum plumbum
 De phetonte solis filio   repertum sit
 Origo mundi et omnium   Quemadmodum ferrum
 De solis & lunae magnitudine   inuentum sit
 De solis magnitudine
 De luna
 De calore solis
 Democriti de sole
 De lunae cursu   De die longo et
 Ex ida uiseo solis   breui nocte

Fig. E: *Indices capitulorum libri V* (reconstructed): Ω 96ʳ

the close of the third line. Without unnecessarily departing
from the ruling of the page, he proceeded downwards, adding
parts of the *capitula* where possible. Unsurprisingly, he was
forced to write a number of these *capitula* on more than one line;
only in one instance (l. 10) did he deem it viable to add more
than one *capitulum* in these right-hand additions. The resultant
page was evidently not particularly clear and the scribe may

have taken little pains to make apparent that the right-hand column was a distinct entity.

When O came to copy the list, he saw no need to keep it on a single page (indeed he had not done so with the list at Book IV) and therefore aimed to start a new line for each *capitulum*. It seems probable that the confused *index* in the archetype had been numbered up to *mundum non esse ab dis constitutum* but by one able to count horizontally across the page; the numbering does not continue into line 9, which would evidently have caused problems.[46] O reproduced this numbering but was also misled by it when interpreting the rest of the *capitula*. Having written *Mundum non esse ab dis con*, he failed to realise that *stitutum* of the next line should be incorporated, and instead moved on to *positione rerumque* (misunderstanding *rerum quæ*). As a result, he added *stitutum* and *in eo sunt* in the next line but with a considerable space between them; since he realised that *stitutum* could not be a *capitulum* in itself, he left it uncapitalised. From this point on, serious mingling continued. Since *de centauris* and *de scylla* are already on the same line, as are *de terra, de aqua, de aere siue anima* and *de chimera*, these are understood as all being related to one another and are therefore copied as one block. From *de igni & sole* onwards, the corresponding right-hand part of the line is written after the left part, sometimes with a slightly larger gap left between the two. Since O regarded line 17 as a unit of sorts, *plumbum* is moved onto a second line for reasons of space. The final part of the *argentum* et seq. *capitulum* (i.e. *repertum sit*) was also kept on a separate line, with the *re* initially omitted. Yet Dungal realised (probably from Ω) that the 38th and 39th *capitula* were to be taken together and joined them with his somewhat rough ink lines, apparently having no desire to disambiguate the other *capitula*.

We come now to the form of the *index* in Q. ψ was evidently able to distinguish the two columns of *capitula* with slightly more success than O but it (or Q) often elected to keep them on the same

---

[46] Since the same numbering exists in O and Q, and since O does not number the *capitula* in the *indices* to Books IV or VI, it is more prudent to regard it as a one-off feature of the archetype, which is further evidence of its being carefully read.

line, separating them by numerals. The practice, however, is not consistent (for instance *IIII de lunae lumine* is on the same line as *III de mundo* but *VI de anni temporibus* is forced onto a new line) and the numbering is unreliable.[47] It is possible that the longer *capitula* were not kept on the same line by ψ for reasons of space. With regard to the problematic section at lines 8–9, since *quae in eo sunt* appears in Q on the same line as *de natiuitate mundi & dis* but not for evident reasons of space, this overspill presumably originated in ψ.[48] The scribe of ψ also incorrectly wrote *constitutum compositione*, repeating *con* with *positione* as well as *stitutum* for good measure. He also managed to reunite certain divided *capitula* (particularly those numbered XXI, XXIII and XXV), which a moment's thought would have allowed O to do.

Another error here needs to be noted, one almost certainly made in ψ and not corrected by Q, namely copying *quare nata omnia dicta* (for *dicat*, a corruption present in the archetype) twice. Returning to Figure E, it seems that once the scribe had united and transcribed *de aedificiis quemadmodum intereant* as a single *capitulum*, he unthinkingly moved vertically to the next *capitulum* rather than across (and up a line) to *quomodo*. Having copied *quare nata omnia dicta*, he then moved to *quomodo hominibus innata sit deorum opinio*, which he recognised as a unit. Once this was done, however, he returned to the correct ordering of *capitula* by moving to the left of the page and unwittingly copying *quare nata omnia dicta* for a second time. Furthermore, it seems that in the former instance of transcribing these words, *quarenata* was perhaps written as *quareneta* or a form alike in *ductus* to *quarōneta*, which was easily understood as *qua ratione* by Q (with the meaningless *ta* omitted). Also, perhaps influenced by *intereant* in the preceding *capitulum* (as transcribed), *dicta* was mistakenly written as *dicant* in the former instance. Finally, it is presumably for reasons of space alone that the *capitulum* numbered XXXVI

---

[47] Indeed, although there are forty *capitula* in the *index*, his numeration only reaches thirty-seven.

[48] It was probably at this stage, rather than in the writing of ψ, that *Cui* was misread as *Cur* (for O shows no sign of such an error). Similarly, the misreading of *potuisse* as *posse* in the *capitulum* marked as XXI presumably arose at this same stage. For the possibility that *cuius* should be read, see n. 33 above

was placed on a separate line from XXXV, although XXXVII could have sat alongside it.

The foregoing reconstruction was made independently of Lachmann, who presented his layout of the *index* in the archetype (319 *ad* V.928), and we are largely in agreement. Nonetheless, I regard five features of his analysis as flawed: (i) he had the scribe of the archetype add the eighth *capitulum* (*cui pars natiua sit totum natiuum esse*) on the same line as *stitutum* and the trio of the ninth, tenth and eleventh (*de terra, de aqua, de aere siue anima*) on the same line as the end of the eighth; therefore (ii) the scribe, when working down the right-hand side of the page, had filled in gaps between, as well as after, two *capitula* of the 'left' column; (iii) *plumbum* was artificially placed in the middle of the page and between the seventeenth and eighteenth ruled lines; (iv) the *capitula* added in the second column were unnecessarily crowded into the *capitula* of the left; (v) the central positioning of the bottommost *capitulum* of the page (*de die longo et breui nocte*) is without motivation. These infelicities my own reconstruction removes, particularly its not departing from the twenty-six ruled lines of the archetype.

We come finally to the *index* for Book VI, whose form is somewhat easier to reconstruct based upon the confused *indices* found in OQ (Figs. F and G): the reconstructed layout is given in Figure H. Once it is apprehended that the 27th and 28th *capitula* (*raras res omnis esse* and *pestilentia unde creatur*) were understood as following the nineteenth (on which see below), the twenty-six lines of the appropriate page of the archetype (= 126ʳ) can easily be reconstructed. Since O was able to place interpuncts between most instances of two *capitula* on one line, and since Q (and therefore ψ) was able to copy them with little confusion, it seems that the *index* was somewhat more clearly organised than that for Book V. The difficult question in reconstructing the page is explaining why the final three *capitula* (of which the last had already become understood as the opening *capitulum* of the book, no doubt because of its proximity to the first poetic line and the lack of a genuine initial *capitulum*) are not written alongside the ninth and tenth *capitula* in O or Q; there seems no obvious reason why the scribe of Ω could not have written *Autumno magis fulmina raras res omnis esse* and so on. We must turn to OQ for answers.

O began to copy the index in a single column, although preserving the instances where *capitula* had been added in the right-hand margin along with their left-hand counterparts. Having reached the bottom of the page with *de terrae motu*, however, and observing that his last six *capitula* had been noticeably brief and that most of the following *capitula* were also short, he decided to minimise wastage of parchment by adding *quare mare maius non fit* across from *et tonitrua fieri* with clear spacing. He was therefore able to add six *capitula* at the bottom right of the page. Interestingly, however, the last that he wrote on the page was *raras res omnis esse*, the third last of the book. It is evident, therefore, that as far as the scribe was concerned, the ordering of the last three apparent *capitula* of the *index* was (i) 749, (ii) 936, (iii) 1090; 1138 was understood, as stated above, to be the *capitulum* opening Book VI. We must therefore posit that the layout of the *index* in the archetype prompted this ordering in OQ, that is, that corruption had taken place prior to the archetype with the result that the antepenultimate and penultimate (and probably the final) *capitula* were placed in the *index* between *cornices Athenis ad aedem Mineruae non esse* and *in Syria quadripedes.*[49] How could this have happened? It is simplest to imagine a list of *capitula* that began as one column (ending with *cornices* et seq.) and then continued somewhere in the right margin but, whether as a slight miscalculation or because of scribal indifference, the final three *capitula* spilt over onto the left side of the next (fresh) page. As a result, the following scribe interpreted the three *capitula* on their own page as a continuation of the left column of the previous page, thereafter moving to its right margin. Such an error would have been more easily made if the two pages of the index were verso–recto. It is evident with the *indices* to both Book V and Book VI that in the hyperarchetype certain irregularities existed

---

[49] An antecedent version of the *capitula* is also suggested by the clear-cut division of a number of them onto two lines (*in nubis semina | ignes inesse; fulmina in crassioribus | nubibus et alte gigni; Autumno magis fulmina | et tonitrua fieri; cur aqua in puteis frigidior | sit aestate*).

Q ¹ui procurationem dis attribuit mundi sibi ipsum

D ¹ edus immoralib; sollicitudine constituere

D ² econtru

D ³ e fulgure ²⁰ in syria quadrupedis

I ⁴ innubib; eminet · ²¹ Cura qua in puteis frigidior:

I ⁴ gne rin esse · ²¹ Sit aestate

D ⁵ e fulmine · ²² De fonte adammonis

I ⁶ gnis ex ful minenatura · ²³ In aqua taedam ardere

F ⁷ ulmina mora nioribus · ²⁴ De fonte aridi mmare

N ⁷ ubibus & altegignit · ²⁵ De lapide magnete

D ⁸ econtribus & terraemotu · ²⁶ fluere ab omnib; reb;

A ⁹ in umno magis fulmina

E ⁹ tonitrua fieri   ¹⁵ Quare mare maius non sit

D ¹⁰ enubibus   ¹⁶ De aetna

F ¹¹ piracula mundi   ¹⁷ De nilo fluuio

D ¹² e imbribus   ¹⁸ De lacu auerni

D ¹³ e arquo   ¹⁹ Cornicis athenis aedem minerue ii esse

D ¹⁴ e terremotu   ²⁷ Tartares omnis esse

P ²⁸ e silentia un de creantur

²⁹ De pestilentia athenien sium.

Fig. F: *Indices capitulorum libri VI*: O 159^{r-v}

Fig. G: *Indices capitulorum libri V*: Q 56[r]

Q ui procurationem dis attribuit mundi sibi ipsum
De dis immortalibus sollicitudines constituere

De tonitru
De fulgure
In nubibus semina
Ignes inesse
De fulmine
Ignis ex fulmine natura
Fulmina in crassioribus
Nubibus & alte gigni
De tonitribus & terrae motu
Autumno magis fulmina
Et tonitrua fieri
De nubibus
Spiracula mundi
De imbibrus
De arquo
De terrae motu
Quare mare maius non fiat
De aetna
De nilo fluuio
De lacu auerni
Cornicis athenis aedem minerve non esse
Raras res omnis esse
Pestilentia unde creatur
De pestilentia Atheniensium

in syria quadripedes
Cur aqua inputeis frigidior
sit aestate
De fonte ad hammonis
In aqua taedam ardere
De fonte aradi in mare
De lapide magnete
Fluere ab omnibus rebus

Fig. H: *Indices capitulorum libri VI* (reconstructed): Ω 126^r

which could only have been inherited from a previous list, which was apparently unclear in format. It is therefore likely that the *indices* existed in two (rather than one) manuscripts prior to the archetype: it seems that a further intermediary existed between stages (ii) and (iii) listed above.

The foregoing reconstruction differs from that of Lachmann (398 *ad* VI.839), significantly on several points. I concur with the Lachmann–Goold reconstruction that 125^r of the archetype contained V.1445–57 and the two lines of subscription and *incipit*. Nonetheless, whereas I posit that the *index capitulorum* began on the next fresh recto (126^r, 125^v being left blank) and covered twenty-six lines, Lachmann (and subsequently Merrill (1913), Goold (1958)) supposes that the *capitula* to the book were crammed into the twelve remaining lines of 125^r, spread over four columns. My reconstruction allows, as elsewhere, (a) the *capitula* to begin (and occupy exclusively) a fresh page and (b) the poetry to begin on a different leaf from the preceding book. Furthermore, there are several problems with Lachmann's cramped placing of the *capitula* at the base of 125^r: (i) the use of three columns per page, not to mention four, is unparalleled in the archetype as well as descended manuscripts; (ii) Lachmann places *Autumno magis fulmina* and *raras res omnis esse* on the same line as *LIB. V. EXPLICIT. INCIPIT LIB. VI.*, which subscription would typically be centrally placed and cover most of a line; (iii) if the scribe was consciously trying to compress the *capitula* into so small a space, he would not have written his columns in the order of first, third, second, fourth; (iv) if space was at such a premium, we would expect *in Syria quadripedes* to have been placed after *de tonitru* and not *de fulgure*; (v) with the proximity of the third and fourth columns, one would expect *Autumno magis fulmina* to have been followed on the same line by *raras res omnis esse* in OQ (and similarly with the two following lines) but there is no trace of such a close pairing; (vi) it is surprising that so cramped a format was evidently interpreted with more ease by O and ψ than that of the considerably neater *index* to Book V. I believe that my reconstruction is much more in accord with the scribal practice of the archetype and more naturally explains the state of the *indices* in our extant manuscripts OQ.

From the preceding reconstructions it is clear that the *indices* necessarily existed in a manuscript prior to the archetype and, quite possibly, in two phases prior to it. This firms up the posited manuscript phases above in (B), with the suggestion of a manuscript intermediary between (ii) and (iii).

(D)   The miscopying of capitula *as the text of the poet and* uice uersa

A curious feature of the preservation of the *capitula*, evident to different degrees in OQS, and in part attributable to the archetype, is the mistaken copying of *capitula* as if the text of the poem and, conversely, the copying of verses of the poem as if *capitula*. The variant forms of these errors have already been touched upon in the summary that opens this section. I shall now provide more detailed analysis and offer suggestions about how these errors arose.

– Errors attributable to the archetype: in seven instances verses of Lucretius were written as if *capitula*: II.42–3, 710 (/706a),[50] III.672a, 759, 805, 905, 949. On the contrary, in two instances *capitula* were written as if verses of Lucretius: I.419 (although O corrected this mistake) and 705.[51]

---

[50] This instance repays scrutiny: in O, 710 appears as if a *capitulum*; in S it appears as normal in its place but is also repeated as a *capitulum* before 707 (which I call 706a); in Q, 710 also appears normal in its place and a space of two verses is left before 707. Evidently, then, 710 was presented as a *capitulum* in ψ before 707 *and* repeated as normal in its place at 710. I conclude that in the archetype 710 had accidentally been copied after 706 (presumably owing to the similarity in ending between *-entis* of 706 and *-emus* of 709). Once the error was realised by the scribe or a subsequent corrector, some mark signifying expulsion of 706a was added beside, below or above it, and the verse was then copied out in the margin alongside 710. O came to understand the signs for expulsion (and duly removed 706a) but in inserting the verse at 710 interpreted it as if a *capitulum*; ψ misinterpreted the marks about 706a as if denoting that it should be rubricated and went on to incorporate marginal 710 as a normal verse. With III.672a we can posit something similar: the scribe wrote 678 incorrectly by anticipation after 672 but noticed his error and proceeded to write 673ff. He added a mark alongside the verse to signify that it should be deleted but (as with ψ at II.706a) this was misunderstood by Oψ to mean that it should be written as a *capitulum*. (It is possible, but by no means required, that this error occurred prior to Ω.)

[51] How the final entry in the *index capitulorum* to Book VI had become understood as the initial *capitulum* of the book has been briefly discussed above in (C).

(I) The transmission of the *capitula*

- Errors specific to O: in twelve further instances O treated verses of Lucretius as *capitula*: I.11, II.94, 502, 508, 608, 809, 887, 909, 962, 1012, 1023, 1112; no further instance of the converse error occurs.[52]
- Errors specific to Q: once, at I.565, Q wrote a *capitulum* as a Lucretian verse; no further instance of the converse error occurs.[53]
- Errors specific to S: once, at II.112, S wrote a *capitulum* as a Lucretian verse; no further instance of the converse error occurs.

Let us first consider the errors in the archetype. It has already been demonstrated that the archetype contained *capitula* in rubricated capitals (perhaps uncials). It is difficult to see how a verse within the text, written in black minuscule, could have been understood as a *capitulum* unless it was somehow distinguished from the rest of the text; there is nothing inherently objectionable or irregular about the verses wrongly transmitted as *capitula*. My hypothesis is simple. I have already asserted that the *capitula* began their life as marginal notes. I now suggest that it was in the transference from a manuscript in which the *capitula* were marginal to one in which they were in the main body of the text that legitimate Lucretian verses were wrongly interpreted as *capitula*. The cause of error would have been that these verses had, either through initial omission or for another reason, likewise been added in the margin of the text. Whether it was because the marginal *capitula* were rubricated but had darkened to a black hue (and therefore could not be distinguished from marginal verses) or because a subsequent scribe could not understand, or failed to notice, a siglum distinguishing marginal *capitula* from marginal verses, this seems the easiest way to explain how a number of Lucretian verses came to be wrongly added as *capitula*.[54] That five of the seven instances occur in the latter half of Book III (but with no precise pattern of separation) suggests that the scribe in operation at this point was either particularly

---

[52] I exclude II.710, as the confusion lying behind it affected ψ also (see n. 50).

[53] For the erroneous gap of two lines left by Q at II.600 see my discussion elsewhere (2008a, 354–7).

[54] That II.42–3 is so badly corrupt supports its formerly marginal presence.

careless or dim-witted. Our extant manuscripts inherited the mistake without significant correction.[55]

What then of the inverse error in the archetype at I.419 and I.705, wherein the *capitula* have been written as if the text of the poet? A simple variant of the theory just mentioned can be offered, namely that some marginal *capitula* were not understood as *capitula* but rather as Lucretian verses to be added. It is perhaps more likely, however, that these verses were already *capitula* in the body of the text but, perhaps because they were written either (accidentally) in black, or in red lead that had since blackened, the primary scribe copied them as if Lucretian verses. The fact that one *capitulum* is six words long and the other eight words no doubt increased their similarity to hexameter verses. Perhaps there was something particularly odd about the form of I.419 in the archetype that allowed the rubricator (i.e. the scribe) of O to notice the mistake himself and correct it accordingly.

Before turning to the curious state of affairs in O, we can quickly treat the two anomalies in Q and S. Since the latter preserves I.565 as a standard *capitulum* but, somewhat bizarrely, twenty-two lines earlier (i.e. before 523), presumably ψ had neglected to leave a gap for the *capitulum* and the rubricator had had to add it at either the top or the bottom of a page, with the result that there was a slight ambiguity as to whether it should precede 565 or the new paragraph at 523. If the *capitulum* was thus added marginally, it could well have been understood simply as a Lucretian verse by Q, as it is seven words long, the first three of which (*de molli natura*) could open a Lucretian hexameter. S's miscopying of II.112 (*quae in solis radiis appareant*) was a simple error: he read and copied the *capitulum*, neglecting to realise that it should be rubricated. The same scribe (inferior to the one who copied up to 7ⁿ) copied at II.142 half of the subsequent Lucretian verse before realising his error, so that

---

[55] To explain the striking fact that no Lucretian verse in the last three books is transmitted as a *capitulum*, whereas the error is prevalent in the first three, I suggest that the presence of *indices capitulorum* for the latter half of the work provided a means by which scribes could ascertain whether a marginal note was a genuine *capitulum* or not.

the *capitulum* appears between the two halves of the following verse (spread over two lines).

Yet it is with O that things become a little mysterious. It is the only extant manuscript to write further Lucretian verses as *capitula*, and, since it does this twelve times, there must have been either something peculiar about the practice of the scribe in the earlier books or, more probably, ambiguities in Ω that O handled with considerably less skill than ψ. The possibility of a manuscript intervening between Ω and O cannot be ruled out but other explanations first merit close investigation. There has been little discussion of the problem and indeed Lachmann – in a rare moment of caution – declared (78, *ad* II.42–3) that he could not explain it. The only attempts at doing so have been made by Diels and Heyworth (Martin (*Praef.* V–VI) offers no explanation). Diels simply suggested that O, if it could not decipher the archetype, left gaps which the rubricator filled without apparently caring that he was writing in minium. Four facts stand against this thesis: (i) since the rubricator of O wrote some verses in minuscule rather than capitals/uncial (II.608, III.445, 805, 905, (949)), we would expect him to have availed himself of this licence elsewhere when he was copying what he knew to be Lucretian verses; (ii) if O could not decipher these various instances, it is remarkable that the rubricator of O, with access to the same manuscript, could transcribe them with no obvious error, as evidently could ψ later; (iii) I regard all rubrication in O as concurrent work by its scribe(s); (iv) no explanation is given for why rubricated initials are employed after III.94, 502, 508 and 710 but not for the other cases.

A different tack was taken by Stephen Heyworth at the close of an important article on poem and book division in Latin manuscripts (1996, 146–8). He observed that, taking account of *capitula*, the instances II.508, 608, 710, 809, 909, 1012 and 1112 are all 103 verses apart in the transmitted text. The number gains further significance from the fact that it is $(26 \times 4) - 1$, twenty-six being the number of lines posited for each page of the archetype (Ω). Heyworth therefore conjectured that an intermediary manuscript lay between the archetype and O, in which two columns of twenty-six lines were written on each leaf, but the first line of the left column of each recto was embellished so as to cover two lines (each leaf thus containing 103 lines). Heyworth conjectured that these ornate opening verses were mistaken as *capitula* in O. The suggestion is undoubtedly ingenious, but I have to reject it for a number of reasons. First, the error at 710 (one of Heyworth's important numbers) is evidently linked with the confusion in Q *ad loc.* (see n. 50 above). Secondly, the supposition does not explain why verses I.11, II.94, 502, 887, 962 and 1023 are also wrongly transcribed by O alone as if *capitula*: in the manuscript Heyworth posits, not one of these would be placed at the top of any column. Thirdly, it is difficult to explain why the scribe of O made the error of regarding such embellished verses as *capitula* only in the latter half of Book II (and in two random instances in Book I) if the adornment occurred on every leaf (we would rather expect the error throughout or at the beginning alone). Fourthly, reconstruction of the manuscript according to Heyworth's stipulations produces some odd results: on reconstructing earlier leaves, one finds that Book II would apparently have begun twelve lines down the second column of a verso and Book I halfway down the first column of a verso. Fifthly, it would be surprising if a manuscript copied from the archetype preserved on the one hand the number of verses per page (twenty-six) but nonetheless wrote the initial verse of each page so as to cover two lines and added a second column per page.

It cannot be pure coincidence, however, that six of these mistakes are so evenly spread: such an error can hardly be attributed to random chance or capricious interpolation. Where I think Heyworth erred was in taking the gaps between them as amounting to 103 rather than 104. I believe it possible to show (with some minor tweaks) that all of Heyworth's selected verses occupied the same place on the page in the archetype (each being one leaf apart). From my reconstruction of the archetype (Appendix IV) it will be seen that each of these verses occurred on the same place of the recto leaf, namely the third line: it could well be that there was some damage (e.g. water staining or fading) at or around the top of the opening of the recto of leaves, and that verses in this position often had to be traced over again, perhaps making them look distinct from the text and somewhat akin to

(I) The transmission of the *capitula*

capitula. There is evidence in O that the initial letters of following verses in the archetype were not enlarged or rubricated, as after *capitula* (cf. n. 56). From the 34th leaf of the archetype (opening with 506) onwards, it thus seems that the scribe of O mistook seven of the fourteen verses in this same position (line 3) as *capitula.* Presumably the damage (or possibly subsequent decoration?) began here and ended before the close of Book II (on 47ʳ) and did not affect the recto and verso of each leaf to an equal degree; curiously, the first two lines of each page were not so affected. Whatever the explanation, ψ seems not to have been misled by the state of Ω.

What of the other mistranscribed verses in Book II (94, 502, 887, 1023)? My supposition about these verses is that two (94, 502) were omitted by the scribe of the archetype and placed in the margin, from where they were mistakenly incorporated as *capitula* by O, and two were in the text (887, 1023) (presumably corrected by ψ, if not a later (early saec. IX) reader of Ω).[56]

---

[56] That most of these mistaken *capitula* (I.11, II.608, 710, 809, 887, 909, 962, 1012, 1023, 1112) do not have their following initials enlarged (as elsewhere) suggests their illegitimate origin. In two instances (II.502, 508) the Lucretian verses are presented in the same format as genuine *capitula*; this is because they apparently arose from a rewriting of an earlier form of the manuscript, and were then further regularised: the peculiar form of leaf 42 in O has rarely been mentioned and never discussed. The facts are as follows: on every page in O the scribe has ruled twenty lines (although Dungal's alterations result in the addition of further lines on 10ʳ, 15ʳ, 22ʳ, 27ʳ, 36ʳ, 40ʳ, 51ᵛ and 53ʳ, and the original scribe added an interlinear verse on 177ᵛ; in certain places ruled lines are left blank, as is all of 161ᵛ). Only on the 42nd leaf is this not the case, for here there are twenty-seven equally spaced lines on the recto and verso in the hand of a contemporary scribe. There is nothing outwardly irregular on the preceding or succeeding leaves; the only anomaly in the gathering is the fact that the leaf attached to the 43rd (with which it formed the central bifolium of the quaternio) has been cut away. Importantly, the 42nd leaf remains joined to what is therefore numbered the 44th (on which the writing of verses is not anomalous). The matter is probably to be explained by scribal error: the present state of 42 may result from O's accidentally skipping fourteen lines on what was once the 42nd leaf and therefore beginning the 43rd with 536 (rather than 522, as would be expected). If the 43rd had already been written on, and if rewriting that leaf as well was too expensive an option, the new version of the 42nd leaf would evidently have had to contain all fifty-four lines (forty plus omitted fourteen). A necessary consequence of the fact that the 43rd leaf begins with 536 is that the error was realised only after the writing of this leaf had begun. Importantly, the new version of the 42nd leaf is joined to the 44th (which continues from the 43rd as normal). This does not, however, mean that we can posit that the error was noticed during the writing of the 43rd leaf and a new sheet was supplied containing the 42nd and 44th leaves

This supposition helps to refine the reconstruction of the archetype, as demonstrated in Appendix IV.

It seems, then, that in every instance from the 34th leaf onwards, the scribe of O had no problem in treating genuine *capitula* and transcribing them as normal. Finally, what of the one remaining instance of the error, at the beginning of Book I? There is no good reason to believe that I.11 was omitted and added in the margin as a depressingly early error of the scribe. Rather, I think the verse's rubrication was a by-product of its presence on the opening leaf of the work. Two motivations are possible: O perhaps thought it would make a more striking opening if, along with the enlarged initial of the poem, a verse around the middle of the page was also rubricated; alternatively, the sense of the verse may have appealed to a religiously minded scribe (*et reserata uiget genitabilis aura Fauoni*), the language of a 'life-giving wind' that 'flourishes free' being redolent of the Holy Spirit potentially worthy of the ornament of rubrication.

before O continued to write beyond the 43rd; instead, the error could have been apprehended significantly later, with the whole of the sheet containing the 42nd and 44th leaves being replaced and rewritten. But what of the fact that the original 44th leaf, joined to the 43rd in the central bifolium, has been cut away? The theory does not, as far as I can see, present an explanation for this. Nevertheless, in two other instances in O leaves have been cut away from the central bifolium: in the seventh quaternio (the leaf which was joined to 50) and the fourteenth (the leaf which was joined to 105). As Chatelain justly observed about these instances (1908, II cols. 1–2): 'Cur eae resectae fuerint, difficile dictu, nisi fortasse membrana rarescente quaterniones non integri, id est septem schedarum, scriptoribus traditi fuerint.' The only scribal difference between the 42nd leaf and those preceding and following is an evident discrepancy in nib-thickness: the 41st and 43rd leaves are of the typical thinness but the 42nd and 44th leaves (at least the recto of the latter) present the thicker form of writing evident elsewhere in O. On returning to add the further text, the difference of the scribe's nib (and ink consistency) became evident. So, can a good suggestion be offered as to how thirteen lines were omitted (if 502 was marginal, as I believe)? A strong candidate is provided by *sapores* closing 504 and *tepores* closing 517. O began what was the 42nd leaf with 484 and ended with 504; having turned onto the verso (and duly ruled the page, etc.) he accidentally began copying again after *sapores* closing 517, and thus copied 518ff., closing the leaf with 535 (leaving the single-space gap for the *capitulum* at 522). The error was apprehended only later, perhaps by Dungal, who desired that the same scribe write out such a large portion of text. A further piece of evidence favouring this theory is the fact that nowhere else in the manuscript is there evidence of serious textual dislocation (on the scale of pages rather than lines) that was rectified by untidy marginal notation. Accordingly, if such an error was made by O, it would seem necessary, owing to his strict levels of scribal tidiness, to rewrite the leaf (and consequently the 44th) as a whole. For an interesting consequence of this theory concerning the corrupt *capitulum* at 522 (linked with 589), see section I(E).

Such, then, is my explanation of the misinterpretation of Lucretian verses as *capitula* and vice versa. At least two phases of errors have been highlighted, the latter (affecting only O) being more complicated: (all/most) omitted verses were apparently treated as *capitula* and verses in the same position on certain leaves closing Book II were wrongly thought to require this distinction from the main text body.

(E) The dislocation and loss of capitula

The final point tackled in this section is the extent to which *capitula* have been dislocated or lost entirely in the manuscript tradition. It is evident that, with the total omission of a *capitulum* in the margin or the text proper, no gap would be left in the main text, and that, without an *index capitulorum*, there would be no means for discerning its absence. The *indices capitulorum* to Books IV–VI demonstrate that the loss of *capitula* was not particularly rare. Of the ninety-nine *capitula* in these last three books, eight had been lost in the main body of the text by the time of the archetype. If the same scale of loss occurred in the first three books, some six would have been lost, and this could well have happened: there are indeed a number of passages in these first three books where a *capitulum* does not occur for a good number of lines (cf. esp. II.221–333 and 445–624) but, since large gaps can be found in the last three books with no loss attested in the *indices* (cf. esp. IV.1030–1287 (end), V.916–1161, VI.936–1090), these could be stretches of the poem genuinely never provided with *capitula*. More on this topic will be said in section II of this chapter. The loss of *capitula* was not difficult: either their marginal status was overlooked by a subsequent scribe (after they had been collected for an *index capitulorum*, if in the latter half of the work) and, whether he noticed his mistake or not, no place could be left for the *capitulum*, or the rubricator whilst working through the headings simply overlooked one (or more)[57] of the

---

57 The ratio of plural interstices left by Q for *capitula* compared with OS is as follows: I.951: Q 2: O 1: S 1; II.42 -3: Q 3: O 2: S 2; II.184: Q 2: O 2: S 1 (but forced onto 3); II.522: Q 2: O 1(?); II.730 Q 2: O 1: S 1; II.842: Q 3: O 2: S 2; II.1105: Q 2: O 1: S 1;

blank verses left for him, and such interstices were omitted in a later stage of transmission.

There are few certain instances of the misplacing of *capitula* in the archetype: II.1058 (reconstructed as ἄπειρος *mundus*), which is in itself an odd repetition of II.1048 (*omne infinitum in omnis partes*), can hardly be in the right place, since the text that follows (1058–53) does not relate to infinite worlds; similarly, II.408 would seem more appropriate before 410 and IV.387 a few lines earlier. Yet it is futile to suggest, as have numerous critics, that I.419, III.381 and V.92 should be moved one or two lines earlier to the syntactical and/or logical beginning of the appropriate section; other *capitula* provide good parallels for their immediately preceding the actual point, even mid-syntax (more on this in section (II)). More importantly, I argue further in the following section that the *capitula* arose as casual marginal jottings and in numerous cases were neither conceived nor placed with exact precision: if a five-line section dealt with subject X, then a note in the form *de X* (*uel sim.*) was added roughly alongside the section, although closer to its opening than its close. On the transfer of the *capitula* from margin to text, this heading would naturally have been inserted at the beginning of the section but this was at the mercy of the intelligence (or interest) of a later scribe, and often the *capitulum* was presumably inserted at the very place where it was written. It is therefore misguided to speak of the exact location of *capitula* in relation to Lucretian verses, there never (or rarely) having been a correct answer: moreover, as I state at the close of this chapter, it is inappropriate for any editor to place the *capitula* in the body of the text at all.

Only in three instances was a *capitulum* misplaced by individual extant manuscripts. S wrongly placed I.565 before I.522, as

II.1144: Q 2: O 1: S 2; III.445: Q 3: O 2: S 2; III.711: Q 2: O 1; III.759: Q 2: O 1; IV.132: Q 2: O 1; IV.312: Q 3: O 2; IV.836: Q 2: O 1; V.132: Q 2: O 1; V.471: Q 2: O 2; V.780: Q 2: O 1; V.916: Q 2: O 1; V.1161: Q 2: O 1; V.1241: Q 2: O 1; VI.357: Q 2: O 1; VI.749: Q 2: O 1: S 1; VI.840: Q 2: O 1: S 1; VI. 1090: Q 2: O 1: S 1. At III.370 S, unlike OQ, covered two lines; IV.1, written as poetic text, is irrelevant. Ignoring the first subscription, where ψ left a gap of ten (Q) or eleven (S) verses (perhaps reflecting the blankness of 23ᵛ in Ω: see Appendix IV), it is worth noting that for the remaining five inscriptions a more similarly sized gap was left by Q and O: II (5 : 2), III (3 : 3), IV (3 : 1), V (4 : 2), VI (4 : 4).

treated in (D) above. ψ (and thereby Q and S) misplaced II.400 before 404. In this case the scribe of the text of the archetype probably neglected, after the preceding run of *capitula* (388, 392, 398), to leave a gap for 400, with the result that the rubricator had to add the text in the margin, perhaps with little precision as to its positioning; O, the more careful scribe, placed it immediately before the verse that mentions *absinthium*; ψ transcribed it before 404 at what seemed the most obvious break in the syntax. O mistakenly placed a corrupt form of the *capitulum* II.589 in lieu of that at II.522 (about which see (B) above and n. 79). How could this have happened? Let us imagine that the scribe who was charged with rewriting the 42nd and 44th leaves (cf. n. 56) copied them out as required, necessarily ruling twenty-seven lines of either side of the 42nd leaf and twenty (as usual) on the 44th. He then added the text as instructed, leaving gaps at 502, 508, 522, 589 and 598 for where either he or someone else could duly add the *capitula*. The rubricator began with the side of the bifolium that contained 42^r and 44^v, adding as *capitula* verses 502, 508 and the true *capitulum* 598. He then turned onto the other side (containing 42^v and 44^r). Importantly, however, he made a signal error: finding *in terra semina inesse* in the archetype as the first *capitulum* preceding *de matre magna* at 598, he carelessly added it out of habit on the left-hand page (42^v) rather than the right (44^r), where it belonged. On moving to add the *capitulum* at 44^r, he realised his error, but there was nothing that could be done about the mistake on the preceding page (rewriting a whole new sheet being too costly an option). Instead, he simply added the *capitulum* also in its proper place, avoiding the careless *insemina* for *semina* but accidentally banalising *inesse* to *insunt* (perhaps as his mind dwelt on his scribal shortcomings). His error, apparently innocuous at the time, resulted in the true *capitulum* at 522 not surviving in Lucretius' transmission.

The final matter to treat in this section is the location of *capitula* in Books IV–VI which are omitted without space in the text and survive only in the *indices*, namely IV.127, 230, V.1, 575, 751, VI.50, 906, 936. All turn out to be easy to position, except the terse *capitulum* at IV.230 ([*res?*] *tactu uideri*), which probably headed the discussion in which the operation of sight is said to occur by touch (230–8),[58] IV.127 (*esse item maiora*), which cannot be given a specific location for the simple fact that it must have heralded text lost in a lacuna, and the first *capitulum* in the *index* to Book VI (*qui procurationem mundi dis attribuit, sibi ipsum de dis immortalibus sollicitudines constituere*), which could have preceded the whole book but more probably related to verses 50ff. (rather than 68ff.).

(II)   The authorship and purpose of the Lucretian *capitula*

We may now turn to the more rewarding question concerning the origin of these headings. The distribution of genuine *capitula* throughout the six books is as follows (see Table 4), with a rough indication of their frequency for every one hundred lines. *Capitula* that came to be transmitted as if Lucretian verses are included but not instances of the inverse error.

It is immediately clear that the spread of the 171 surviving genuine *capitula* is by no means even throughout each book or indeed the poem as a whole: there is a distinct decline of headings towards the close of each book,[59] and Book V contains *capitula* almost twice as frequently as III. Whether this reflects the nature of Lucretius' composition or rather highlights something about the purpose of the *capitula* will be considered in (C) below. We need only observe for now that *capitula* are generally found in all parts of the work. What of the larger figures in the table? Between V.200 and 299 we find six *capitula*; five can be found in seven other blocks of one hundred lines. Noticeably, however, these concentrated passages of *capitula* typically contain headings of a concise form with more specific reference than others: for instance, V.200–99 offer five *capitula* in the brief and simple form *de X*.

---

[58] For thorough discussion see Deufert (2010) 50–8, who argued for placing *tactu uideri* after his 216a, deleting 219–28.

[59] The comparative rarity of *capitula* in the latter half of the text can be illustrated by comparing the frequency of the *capitula* in the last 500 lines of each book (the first figure) with the frequency in the lines before that point (the second figure): Book I 83.3 (lines per *capitulum*) : 32.5; II 50 : 32.1; III 166.7 : 45.7; IV 100 : 31.5; V 166.7 : 25.6; VI 55.5 : 39.3.

(II) The authorship of the *capitula*

Table 4

Book	I	II	III	IV	V	VI
1–100	3	3	2	3	5	2
101–200	3	3	2	4	3	1
201–300	4	1	4	2	6	5
301–400	4	5	3	5	5	1
401–500	3	5	2	1	2	3
501–600	2	3	0	5	3	2
601–700	1	1	1	3	4	2
701–800	2	2	1	2	5	4
801–900	1	4	0	2	2	4
901–1000	1	0	1	2	2	3
1001–1100	1	2	0 (−1094)	1	0	1
1101–1200	0 (−1117)	2 (−1174)	–	0	1	1
1201–1300	–	–	–	0 (−1287)	2	0 (−1286)
1301–1400	–	–	–	–	0	–
1401–1500	–	–	–	–	0 (−1457)	–
Total	25	31	16	30	40	29
Lines per *capitulum*	44.6	37.9	68.4	42.9	36.4	44.3

With the figures thus laid out, we must now turn to the analysis of the *capitula* themselves. I shall address their (A) form, (B) language, (C) purpose, and (D) authorship.

(A)   The form of the capitula

The *capitula* can be divided almost entirely into a small number of categories with regard to their form or syntactic construction. Of the very few exceptions (listed under (viii) below), I will argue that some are genuine anomalies and that others require slight emendation to be brought into line with preceding categories. The forms are as follows:

(i)   *de* + noun phrase. This particular form of *capitulum*, in which one or more nouns follow *de* in the ablative, occurs seventy-six times throughout *DRN* and is thus much the most common, found often throughout all six books. Typically (i.e. in sixty-five (85.5 per cent) of seventy-six instances) only a single entity depends upon *de*, often modified by an adjective or genitival noun. Twice (V.396, VI.712) another noun appears in apposition, once (V.273) modified by *siue* + noun, once (IV.877) by *hoc est de* + noun. In eight instances a second noun phrase is added by *et* (with ellipse of *de*); in three instances, three additional nouns are added, either in asyndeton (I.311, II.447) or with *et ceteris* as the final, unspecific element (I.565).

(ii) *de* + noun phrase + indirect question. A variant is form (ii), whereby an indirect question is attached after the noun introduced by *de*. This form occurs four times, all in the latter half of the work. In three instances (IV.907, V.306, 471) *quemadmodum* introduces the question, once (IV.476) *quare*. In three cases the question is attached (without a conjunction) after *de* + a single noun, but at V.471 it follows two nouns and *et* (*de solis et lunae magnitudine et motu eorum et quemadmodum nascantur*).[60]

(iii) Accusative + infinitive. The second most common form of Lucretian *capitula* is the accusative and infinitive construction employed virtually (i.e. without a verb explicitly introducing it), which occurs fifty-three times spread regularly throughout the work. It appears that the construction understands something along the lines of *Lucretius hic dicit*. In this group are included those instances where there is a natural ellipse of *esse* (II.1048, 1105, 1144, III.241). Present infinitives are typically employed throughout.[61]

(iv) Indirect question. Alongside the indirect questions incorporated in (ii), thirteen[62] independent indirect questions occur in the work, all but one (II.112) in its latter half. Again, the questions (expressly marked as indirect by the subjunctive: see n. 60) are to be regarded as dependent upon an understood *Lucretius hic dicit* or similar. Of the interrogative particles, most common

---

[60] I restore *nascantur* for *nascuntur* since in the other three instances and in those in (iv) below, the verb is naturally subjunctive. The evidence in favour of the subjunctive is sufficiently large for this instance to be treated as a scribal, rather than an original 'authorial', error: of the twenty-seven cases in the *capitula* where the rules of classical Latin demand a subjunctive in the subordinate clause, the manuscripts present twenty-three subjunctive forms. The two counterexamples (alongside *nascantur* at V.471) occur in relative clauses (*sunt* (for *sint*) at V.780 and *attribuit* (for *attribuerit*) at VI.50), easily explicable as banalisations of subjunctives to their much commoner forms. I have excluded VI.1090 (*pestilentia unde creatur*), which in its present form can support the indicative; I argue below, however, for emendation so that it conforms with type (i) *capitula*. It is possible that my intervention is misguided pedantry, and that the circumspection shown in other traditions is perhaps prudent (e.g. by Reeve (2004) xlix n. 59).

[61] In IV.131 *de nubibus et simulacra gigni*, *et* is evidently to be understood as 'also' and *de* as *e*.

[62] II.112 (*quae*), IV.116 (*quam* +adj.), 269 (*cur*), 326 (*cur*), 633 (*quare*), 779 (*quare*), V.324 (*quare*), 351 (*quare*), 1161 (*quomodo*), 1241 (*quemadmodum*), 1281 (*quemadmodum*), VI.608 (*quare*), 840 (*cur*).

Aeneadum genetrix hominum diuumq: uoluptas·

Alma uenus caeli subter labentia signa·

Quae mare nauigerum quae terras frugiferentis·
  [gloss: uae ferat]

Concelebras· per te qm genus omne animantum·

Concipitur uisit que & oritur lumina solis·

Te dea te fugiunt uenti te nubila caeli·

Aduentumq: tuum tibi suauis dedala tellus·

Summittit flores· tibi rident aequora ponti·

Placatumq: nitet diffuso lumine caelum·
  [gloss: uer nat qualitas]

Nam simul ac species patefactast uernacies·
  [gloss: genitabilis aura fauoni]

Genitabilis aura fauoni·

Aeriae primum uolucres te diua tuumque·
  [gloss: conceptum]

Significant initum· perculsae corda tua ui·

Et rapido stranam animis· te capra lepore·

Inde ferae pecudes persultant pabula laeta·

Te sequitur cupide quo quamq: inducere pergis·

Denique per maria ac montes fluuiosq: rapacis·

Frondiferasq: domos auium camposq: uirentis·

Omnibus incutiens blandum per pectora amorem·

Iste liber phnet ad lihanious
sancti Martini
  [gloss: ecthe illagithu]

·LV·I·

y sandia sf̄t
Ano 1819

ACADLVGD

e rre immortali primordia corpore debent

D issolui quoquaeq; supremo tempore possiN

m aceries ut subpedit &reb: reparandis·

S um igitur solida primordia simplicitate

N & ratione queunt alia servata per aevum

& x infinito iam tempore nr reparare··

CONTRA ISAPIRON TEXTO MEN·

D eniq: si nullam finem natura parasset

f rangendis rebus iam corpora materiae

u sq: redacta forent aevo frangente priore

u t nihil ex illis a certo tempore posset

C onceptum summum aetatis pervadere finis

N am quiduis [quidvis] dissolui posse videmus

q uam rursus refici· quapropter longa dies

I nfinita aetas ante acti temporis omnis

Q uod fregit res adhuc disturbant dissoluensq;·

N um quam reliquo reparare tempore posset·

A t nunc nimirum frangendi reddita finis

C erta manet qm reficiam quamq; demus

(x finita simul generatim tempora rebus

S tare quibus possint aevi contingere florem

Q uam ꝑeg& esse Ignis tamenesse relinquat · ⟨igne⟩

A equa uideturenim dementiadicere utrumq;

⟨capitulū⟩ H eq: Ignem ꝁeq; aera ꝁeq: umorem principiaesse ·

Q uapropter quimateriemrerum esseputarud

I gnem atq; &:igni summamconsistere posse

& quiprincipium gignundis aerarebur

C onstituere autumorem quicumq: putantur·

F ingereres Ipsum perse terram uecreare

O mnia·&hrerum ꝑaturasuerti omnis

m agno opere auero longꝛ derasse uidentur·

A dde&iam quiconduplicant primordiarex

A enilungentesIgni terramque liquori

E tquiquatuor &rebus posseomniarentur

E xigniterra atq; anima procrescere &imbri

CONTRA   eꝳpe do cLeꝶ ·

Q uorum agraꝫanūnus cumprimisempedoclefest·
⟨sicilia lacine diꝗquaeꝗis gꝛ trinacria ꝑꝯꝗꝓꝗ nuncopia⟩

I nsula quemtriq; tris terrarum gessit inoris

Q uam fluitans circummagnis anfractib; aequor

I onium glaucis asparguatur abundis

A ngustoq: fretu rapidum mareditudit undis

Plate III: O 19ʳ: *DRN* I.703–20 (the corrections and glosses of O³ are visible)

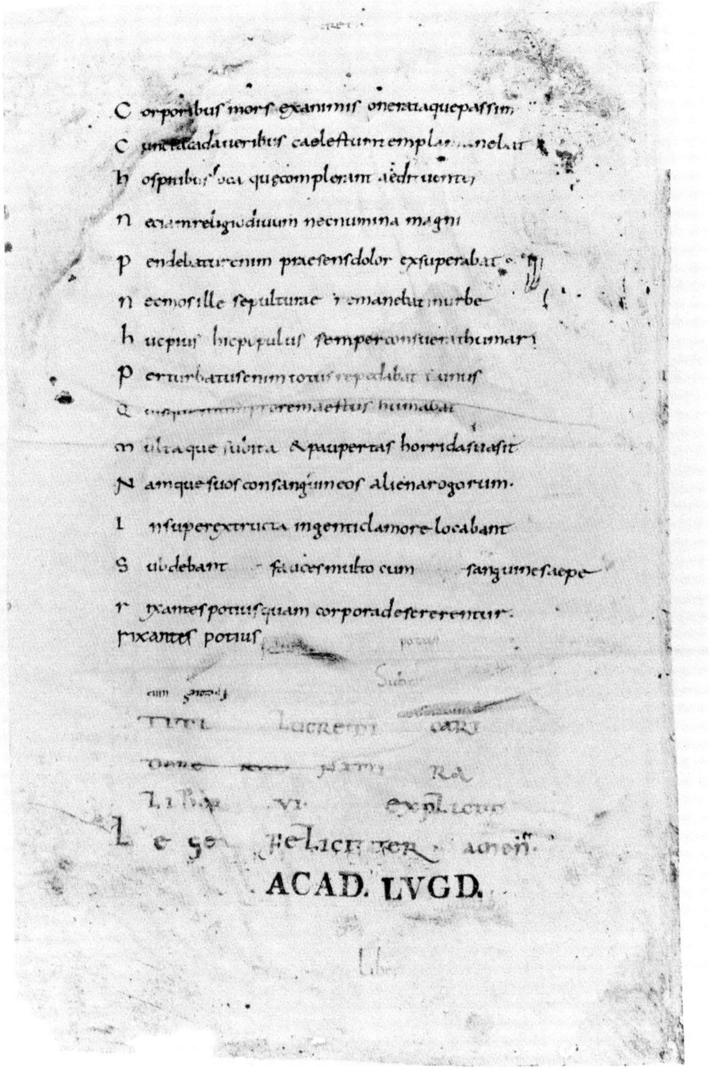

Plate IV: O 192^{v}: *DRN* VI.1273–86 (the final leaf of O)

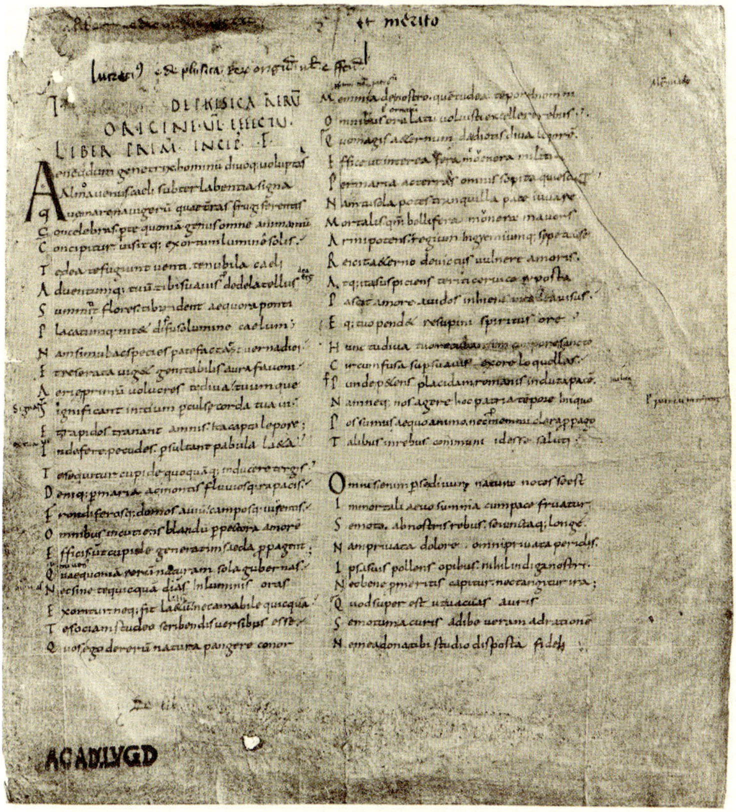

Plate V: The first leaf of the Codex Quadratus (Q): *DRN* I.1–51

DESIMVLACRIS   11

Plate VI: Q 31^r: *DRN* IV.11–65 (the rubrication at 38 is from an appreciably later hand)

f astumqd ualidi uegentes equora uentq
D immuuntq adnis quae r&exensa&herussol
f astim qd supter per terras didtur omnis
f exolatur enim uirus r&roque remanat
M atenes umoris &adcaput amnibus omnis
C onuentun desuper terras fluit agmine dulci
Q uauia ssuisdiseca semelli quido p ot&l &ūtmundas

eranunciguur dicamquicorpore toto
1 numerabiliter priuas mutatur te oras
S empernmqdcūq fluit derebus idom te
A ensinmagnū festur mare quinisicorttta
C orporaràiribuatrebus setr&eque fluentis
O mniaiamresoluta foret&inaera uersa
H audigitur cessat gigni derebus &inres
R accidere adsidue quoniā fluere omaconstat

argussum liquidi fons luminis a&herussol
1 nrigatadsidus caelum candore regenti
S uppeditantque nouoconfestim lumine lum

(marginal notes: percolat; prius; prius)

Plate VII: Q 45ᵛ: *DRN* V.266–83 (the marginal hand is that of Q¹)

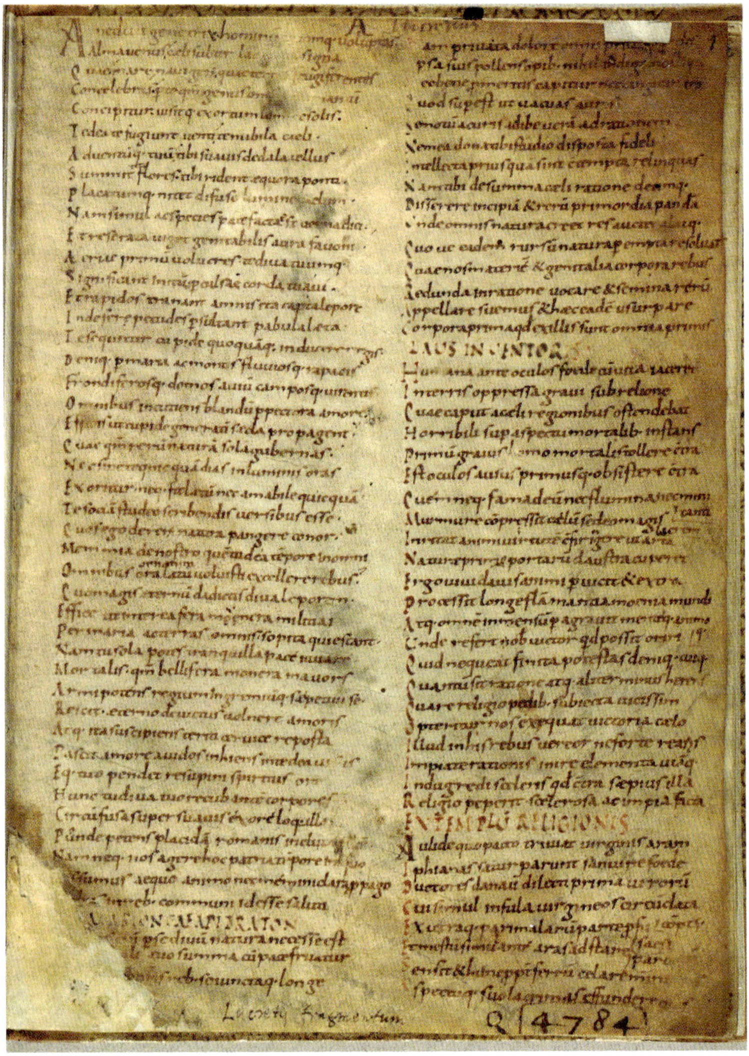

Plate VIII: The first leaf of the *Schedae Gottorpienses* (G), the opening fragment of S

is *quare* (five times), with *cur* occurring thrice, *quemadmodum* twice and *quae*, *quomodo* and *quam* + adjective once.

(v) Nominative phrase. In a small number of cases *capitula* record the subject of the following Lucretian passage in the nominative. Among the ten[63] instances stand some neuter forms and third declension masculine/feminine plurals that are better understood as nominative than accusative: *exemplum religionis* (I.84), *spiracula mundi* (VI.493) and *in Syria quadripedes* (VI.756).[64] Of these instances, eight could have been alternatively represented (if we are to imagine a consistent and methodical approach to them) by form (i), namely the *de* construction; one (ἄπειρος *mundus* II.1058) could rather have been in the form of (iii), that is, *apiron esse mundum*.[65] The remaining two, both in the first one hundred lines of the poem (62, 84), refer to the nature of Lucretius' introduction rather than its actual content (*laus inuentoris, exemplum religionis*).[66]

(vi) *contra* + noun phrase. In four instances the *capitula* record the object of Lucretius' philosophical attacks after *contra*. In three instances only the name of a Greek philosopher follows (I.635 *Heraclitum*, 716 *Empedoclen*, 830 *Anaxagoran*); once the topic is also added in the *de* form (III.370 *contra Democritum de animo et anima*).

(vii) Greek forms. This category holds little formal unity beyond its grouping *capitula* written entirely in Greek; in all cases the Greek is transliterated, except II.646, where we find (effectively accurate) Greek script. The five such *capitula* occur in the first two books alone (I.44, 951, 1052, II.14, 646). Since it is natural to expect consistency on such a point, and since the direction of scribal corruption is obvious, it is highly probable that these five

---

[63] I.62, 84, 107, III.262, V.200, 419, 663, VI.225, 493, 756.

[64] This last could hardly have *esse* in ellipse, for such a statement ('quadrupeds exist in Syria') would be banal and irrelevant: the passage 756–9 treats cattle that inexplicably fall to the ground in a certain place in Syria.

[65] It was suggested by Ernout (and perhaps tacitly accepted by Diels, who retained *mundos* and stated 'capitulum pertinet ad 1066 [= 1067] sqq.') that this *capitulum* is actually in the acc. pl. and represents ἀπείρους *mundos* (sc. *esse*), 'there exist boundless universes'. Some Italic manuscripts of the φ group took the same lead, offering *infinitos mundos*. The sense is good, but there are two problems: first, the transliteration of Greek ου is rendered in Latin of all periods as *ū*; second, the other *capitula* involving Greek words (as opposed to adapted forms), excluding direct quotations (as I.951), are in the nominative (so we would expect *apiri mundi*). I rather regard *mundos* as assimilated to the ending of the preceding *apiros*. I thus disagree with Fischer (1924, 65), Pasetto (1962–3, 41) and Sconocchia (2002, 70), who believed that *mundos* represents an original, bastardised form on the analogy of κόσμος.

[66] It is noteworthy that the first three Latin *capitula* (I.62, 84, 107) are all of this nominative form, elsewhere rare.

instances were originally written in Greek script by their author,[67] and I will discuss them in that language.

Why are these *capitula* Greek? The answer is simple: they are drawn directly from Greek philosophical texts, often Epicurean and often verbatim.[68] Before both I.44–9 and (the identical) II.646–51 occurs τὸ μακάριον καὶ ἄφθαρτον (transliterated into Latin in the former instance), '<a> blessed and immortal <being>'. As Lachmann (426) first noted, this is an Epicurean collocation evidently standardised from an early stage that opens the first of the Κύριαι δόξαι and is quoted by Plutarch, Sextus Empiricus and authors of a similar period, as well as Servius and thereby the *scholia* to Statius' *Achilleis*.[69] I.951 is a quotation from Epicurus' *Epistola ad Herodotum* (41): τὸ πᾶν ἄπειρον· τὸ γὰρ πεπερασμένον ἄκρον ἔχει. Although the manuscripts end with ACROE, we could well posit the loss of ECHI (or, not impossibly, ECI), as Lachmann did; nevertheless, the ellipse of the verb from the quotation would not be too harsh, as the absolute use of the neuter (necessarily emending to ACRON) would be intelligible and bear sufficiently similar force.[70] At I.1052 we find *is to meson ephora*, εἰς τὸ μέσον ἡ φορά, a nominative phrase denoting that the following passage treated universal movement towards the centre. Yet since Lucretius is here countering this particular point, not arguing for it, a preceding κατά or *contra* would have been apt, especially since I.551 (on which see below) is preceded by *contra*.[71] No exact verbal parallel for this phrase appears to survive in Greek but a number of authors (including Zeno,

---

[67] Why, if a scribe (presumably at an early stage) transferred the other Greek *capitula* into Latin script, was the same not done with II.646? I deal with this question in n. 75.

[68] The *capitula* differ from the rest, therefore, not only in their language of composition but in that (with the possible exception of I.1052) they are quotations and not specially composed summaries. (I regret that Herren (2012) emerged too late.)

[69] Plut. *De superstit.* 16b, *Quaest. conu.* 655d; ps.-Plut. *Plac. phil.* 881b; Gal. *Phil.hist.* XVI.25; Sext. Emp. *P.* III.219, *M.* IX.44; Diog. Laert. X.123, 139; Seru. *ad* Verg. *Aen.* VI.134; *schol.* ad Stat. *Achil.* I.480.

[70] Diels, a fanatic for supralinear abbreviations and variants in manuscripts, offered the following explanation for the extant readings: 'archetypus uidetur habuisse in extremo uersu AKPŌE'. This seems improbable, particularly since the first author of this *capitulum* would have written in the margin, and therefore was presumably not compelled to use an abbreviation. I am also confident that this and the other transliterated *capitula* were not written in Greek letters in the archetype.

[71] This hybrid *capitulum* (*contra* εἰς ἄπειρον τὴν τομήν) presents Greek that is evidently based upon Epicurus' own words (*Ep. Hdt.* 43, cf. also 56): in numerous other authors from Aristotle onwards we find mention of a τομὴ εἰς (/ἐπ') ἄπειρον or, more succinctly, an ἄπειρος τομή: Arist. *An. pr.* 59b29, *Metaph.* 994b25; Aristox. *Harm.* 60; ps.-Plut. *Plac. phil.* 883d8, Ar. Did. 26.27; Sext. Emp. *M.* X.42.2, 141, 168, III.104; Apollon. Perg. I.8, II.14; Hero, *Deff.* 135; Posidon. fr. 270.15ff.; Stob. I.8.42.35; Simp. *passim*.

(II) The authorship of the *capitula*

Aristotle and Plutarch) employed the expression with differing word order (and with πρός or ἐπί for εἰς).[72] Although it is quite possible, as was suggested by Pasetto (1962–3, 38), that the phrase occurred in Epicurean writings that have since been lost, the *capitulum* is probably the author's *ad hoc* creation using the most appropriate language available. Finally, at II.14 occurs the Epicurean formula σαρκὸς εὐσταθὲς κατάστημα, 'the healthy state of the body', a phrase common in Greek and Roman texts of varying natures.[73] The version preserved by Plutarch differs slightly, either εὐσταθὲς σαρκὸς κατάστημα or κατάστημα ... εὐσταθὲς σαρκός.[74] The phrase ἄπειρος *mundus* has already been mentioned under form (v): ἄπειρος collocated with *mundus* (the closest Latin parallel to κόσμος) is probably a casual rendering of *Ep. Hdt.* 45 (κόσμοι ἄπειροι) and/or *Ep. Pyth.* 89 (τοιοῦτοι κόσμοι εἰσὶν ἄπειροι), and should therefore be classed with I.551. Thus, it is evident, as will be reaffirmed in (C) below, that the composer of these Greek notes was well familiar with the core Epicurean works;[75] beyond this knowledge of central philosophical texts,

---

[72] Arist. *Ph.* 205b24; Zeno, *Stoic. fr.* 99; Ar. Did. fr. 23 9ff.; Simp. *In cael.* A8 p. 277 (Heiberg); Strat. I.1.20; Plut. *De fac. in orbe lunae* 924a. Simplicius mistakenly attributed this theory to Epicurus (as well as Strato).

[73] Gell. IX.5.2; Clem. Al. *Protr.* II.20.219.3, 21.131.1; Cleom.156.12, 166.2 (= Posidon. fr. 290a 395, 497), *De meteoris* II.1.91 (in the plural); Origen, *Cels.* III.80.26.

[74] Found, respectively, at Plut. *Contra Epic. beat.* 1089d and 1090a; Fischer (1924, 63) correctly regarded Plutarch's versions as incorrectly ordered, whether through Plutarch's error or his scribes'.

[75] I restrict to this footnote my treatment of the transmission of these Greek *capitula*. The most important fact, already mentioned, is that only one of the five headings (II.646, preserved in O alone) is written in Greek script; the remaining *capitula* are transliterated into Latin. The accuracy of the transliteration is consistent and typically correct: κ is rendered as *c*, αι as *ae*, ει as *i* and ευ as *eu*; the one clear instance of φ is transliterated as *ph* but that of θ as *t*. These two transliterations are perhaps evidenced in the transmission of ἄφθαρτον as *apitraton* at I.44, from which it seems easiest to conclude that the error arose from a capital Latin transliteration of the form APHTARTON, wherein the *h* was misread as an I and TART unknowingly altered to TRAT (producing a more natural sequence of letters for a Latin scribe, (-)*tart*(-) being found in no word of Latin origin). *h* is lost in initial position at I.1052 (ἡ being rendered as *e*). Dittography of *s* was natural at II.14 once *stat-* was mistakenly taken as the beginning of a new word. It is evident that the transcriber of the Greek text into Latin was sufficiently familiar with Greek letters and their proper transliterated values to carry out the transcription at a high level of accuracy. We may ask why, if the *capitula* were originally written in Greek, this form was left at II.646 alone. I suggest that the phrase's familiarity (on which see n. 69 above) rendered it readily recognisable in its native form. Once the manuscript was copied with only II.646 left in Greek, subsequent scribes simply copied as diligently as they could the forms in front of them, thereby preserving the anomaly. The same *capitulum* occurs in Latin at I.44 for the reason that it was copied there along with I.44–9 by this later hand.

these Greek annotations do not suggest great intelligence or engagement with *DRN*.

(viii)   Anomalies. Six *capitula* remain uncatalogued. Three are fusions of the above groups: at I.551 we find the aforementioned *contra* εἰς ἄπειρον τὴν τομήν, 'against the division *ad infinitum*', in which the Greek element (drawn from *Ep. Hdt.* 43) follows *contra* as employed in (vi); at II.1058 (ἄπειρος *mundus*) we likewise find a mix of Latin and Greek; although the use of the nominative is in accordance with (v), the fully Greek status of ἄπειρος[76] links this heading with the Greek *capitula* (vii); at II.62 we find the perplexing combination of forms (i) and (iii): *de motu principiorum et infinita esse*, which we must understand as 'Lucretius here speaks of atomic motion and says that they [= atoms] are infinite', thus employing (somewhat artificially) the double construction of verbs of speaking.[77]

Two of the remaining three instances are unique: at VI.1090 we find a nominative noun followed by a direct question (*pestilentia unde creatur*), which could be brought in line with (ii) if we suppose the loss of *de*[78] and read *creetur* for *creatur*; at II.589 we find our only (Latin) verb in a main clause (and thus rightly indicative): *in terra semina insunt*. With this unique form is connected the *capitulum* presented by O at II.522 (discussed in section I (B) and (E)), which is evidently a case of careless copying from the archetype of II.589, the subsequent *capitulum*. It would cohere well with our other evidence if the form found at II.589 is itself a banalisation of *in terra semina inesse*[79] and is therefore a standard accusative and infinitive (form (iii)). II.522, our final *capitulum*, is anomalous because no certainty exists about its original form; nonetheless, as I suggested earlier, its apparent length and context suggest that it was also an accusative and infinitive *capitulum* (form (iii)).

Disregarding the awkward pairing at II.62, therefore, and the Greek forms (vii), there is some uniformity evident throughout

---

[76] The closest instance is Aulus Gellius' employment of *apirocali* of those who lack culture or taste (XI.7.7, XVIII.8.1), although these too could originally have been written in Greek script.

[77] It is possible that the *capitulum* was written in two stages or is the conflation of what were once two separate jottings.

[78] The subsequent *capitulum* (VI.1090) is *de pestilentia Atheniensium*. For the loss of the initial words of *capitula* see n. 23 above.

[79] The fact that *inesse* is written at II.522 suggests that II.589 was not corrupt in the archetype but the scribe in both his first (II.522) and second (II.589) attempts at transcription committed a different error.

the *capitula*. Nevertheless, the employment in eight instances of a nominative (v) instead of the possible and pervasive *de* construction (i) is curious and too frequent to be removed by emendation. It therefore seems the most natural assumption to regard all *capitula* in constructions (i)–(vi) as arising from the same individual, with some carefree variation in the course of his work, although (v) may be connected with (vii): the Greek *capitula* (and hybrids involving Greek) may have a different origin, as is suggested by the two facts that they are almost entirely quotations rather than summaries, and that this more learned form of annotation ceases, for no obvious reason, in the second book (with II.1058).

(B)   The language of the capitula

It is evident that the phraseology of the *capitula* is generally drawn from the Lucretian passages they introduce. Indeed, in a large number of instances, the *capitula* are a mere repetition of Lucretius' words[80] (although the normalisation of word order[81] and vocabulary means that only occasionally – thirty-six instances, with the five-word *capitulum* at VI.888 being the longest – do *capitula* form a possible metrical sequence in dactylic verse). It would be a mistaken inference, however, to conclude that because much of the language of the *capitula* is Lucretian it is therefore most likely to be from Lucretius' hand. Such a flawed conclusion was reached by Sconocchia (2002), but since his case lacks positive evidence and is consequently most unpersuasive I only make passing mention of it.[82]

---

[80] Cf. Pasetto (1962–3) 35; Sconocchia (2002, 53) calculated that only twenty-three of the 676 different Latin words in the *capitula* are not found in *DRN* but too readily dismissed the significance of some of the most surprising instances among the absentees.

[81] This phenomenon is so common that observation of almost any of the longer *capitula* will confirm it. At times particularly alien features were removed (such as the anastrophe of a monosyllabic preposition: *albis ex alba* (II.730) standardised to *alba ex albis* in the *capitulum* immediately preceding).

[82] Sconocchia concluded that because *capitula* were used in the works of Valerius Soranus (according to Pliny, *HN pr.* 33), Celsus, Polybius and other writers of a similar period (occasionally with *indices*), and because most of the words in the *capitula* can be found in *DRN*, it is natural to attribute the *capitula* to Lucretius himself. He concluded (2002, 89) that 'l'*onus probandi*, cioè di dimostrare che non sono autentici, spetta a chi

Alongside the evident debt of the *capitula* to Lucretian language there are, I believe, three further factors in play: (i) the banalisation of Lucretian terminology; (ii) apparent familiarity with the Greek language; (iii) where innovation is required, scholastic Latin without good classical roots. Before I illustrate each of these, two of the more obvious differences between the *capitula* and the text of the work itself should be noted. First, because the *capitula* were not written with regard to metre, we find a large number of forms, and indeed words, that were inadmissible to Lucretius in dactylic verse.[83] I shall discuss a number of these newly introduced forms shortly. Second, as has already been suggested, the tone of the *capitula* is elliptical and somewhat informal (we may note here the use of *et* [sc. *de*] *ceteris* at I.311 and 565, and the common employment of asyndeton).

(i)   Banalisation. The author of the *capitula* evidently strove to write his headings in such a way that they were immediately intelligible from cursory reading, a feature obvious in their choice of language and content. The poeticism of Lucretius' language has been for the most part consciously replaced by more natural, prosaic expressions. This is most clearly manifested in the rejection of certain Lucretian terminology: for instance, with regard to atoms we do find the use of Lucretian *principia* (I.705, II.62) and *corpuscula* (II.184) but also the distinctly unlucretian *atomi* (II.333, 842).[84] More subtly, it is noteworthy that *et* is the only conjunctive particle employed (with the sole exception of III.94, where the repetition of *et* was

eventualmente li ritenga successivi a Lucrezio, o addirittura medioevali'. Yet, as we shall see, it is improbable that the *capitula* were composed by one person alone; nor would Lucretius wish to break up his *carmen continuum* with such, often invasive, headings; furthermore, there is evidence of an unfamiliarity with classical Latin, and their overall form and arrangement betray an uneven knowledge of, and interest in, the text. Indeed, Sconocchia's claim (88) that in the *capitula* 'nessuno di essi è con certezza postlucreziano' will prove to be false. Sconocchia at least serves to justify Fischer's *vix* in his statement of the obvious (1924, 66): 'capitula a Lucretio ipso conscripta esse vix quisquam crediderit'. Only slightly less problematic than Sconocchia's suggestion is that of Bergk (1872, I 232 n. l), who ascribed the composition of the *capitula* to Cicero, a thesis that Pasetto (1962–3, 42–5) did well to refute.

[83] For instance, *diuisio* (II.200), *necessario* (II.730), *maxime* (III.41), *coniunctio* (III.262), *uarietas* (III.788), *Veneriis* (IV.1030), *aedificium* (V.306), *aeternitas* (V.351), *magnitudo* (V.471, 564), *uisio* (V.663), *offectio* (V.774), *dispositio* (V.780), *opinio* (V.1161), *procuratio* (VI.50), *sollicitudines* (VI.50), *pestilentia* (VI.1090, 1138).

[84] *atomus* was used by Lucilius (753 M) but apparently avoided in prose by Epicurean writers such as Amafinius (cf. Cic. *Acad.* I.6), whose dates are uncertain; cf. Reinhardt (2005) 155ff.

unwanted), often rejecting Lucretius' own use *ad loc.* of *ac*, *atque* or *-que*.[85] *ex* is also rarely used,[86] typically encroached upon by *de* (cf. esp. II.865 and IV.131), as in vulgar and late Latin; only at VI.225 (*ignis ex fulmine natura*) was *ex* apparently chosen on its own merits; at II.730, IV.312 and V.663, by contrast, the preposition was directly drawn from Lucretius' text.

We find numerous instances of certain lexical items being replaced by commoner forms: *doloris* for *aerumnarum* (I.107), *gigni* for *creari* (I.155), *aresci* (*arescere* being a common verb; on the bizarre medio-passive form, see (iii) below) for the ἅπαξ *serescunt* (I.298), *celeritate* for *mobilitate* (II.142, although this noun is retained at IV.182), the unlucretian *pusilla* for *parua* (II.1144), *mortem* for *letum* (III.41).[87] The *capitulum* at V.294, *de lampade et lucerna*, could be a deliberate attempt to avoid the vague use of *lumina* and the rarity of *lychni* (both in 295); similarly, Lucretius' poetic usage of *tempestates* for 'seasons (of the year)' at V.744 is banalised in the *capitulum* at V.737 to *de temporibus anni*.[88] We also find the common *pestilentia* in the *capitula* at VI.1090 and 1138 in preference to Lucretius' (metrically tractable) coinage *pestilitas*.

It is no surprise that an archaic termination such as genitival *-ai* was simplified to *-ae* at VI.535 (*terrae* for *terrai*); although this could be the result of subsequent scribal banalisation (as *-ai* survived into O in just seven places), I am certain that *-ae* was written by the author of the *capitulum* himself throughout.[89] On the use of ablatival *mare* at VI.888, see (iii) below. In the *capitulum* at II.392 we find the typical *oleo* (<*oleum*), whereas Lucretius employed only the more archaic *oliuom* (II.392, 850, VI.1073), although anapaestic *oleum* was a perfectly acceptable alternative.

There seems evidence also of a banalisation of two mythological characters: *Pallas* (VI.750, 753) was naturalised as *Minerua* in the *capitulum* at VI.749; similarly, *Phaethon*, somewhat unnecessarily, is qualified as *Solis filius* at V.396; analogous was the gloss at VI.712 *de Nilo fluuio*. Two other qualifications in the *capitula*

---

[85] Cf. esp. *solis et lunae* for Lucretius' *solis lunaeque* (V.471). The use of *et* seems otiose by classical standards at VI.246 (*fulmina in crassioribus nubibus et alte gigni*) and is the result of reworking Lucretius' Latin too literally (and not seeing that the *-que* binds *extructis*): *fulmina gignier e crassis alteque putandumst | nubibus extructis* (246–7).

[86] *e* is never found; at IV.312 Lucretius' *e tenebris* appears as *ex tenebris* in the *capitula*.

[87] Although these replacements are evidently more natural and prosaic expressions, a number are characteristic of late rather than classical Latin (see section II B(iii)).

[88] *tempora* may also, or rather, have been used in the *capitulum* because *tempora anni* was so used by Lucretius earlier in the work (II.32–3 and V.220).

[89] I.e. here and at II.408, III.94, 624, 978, V.76, 200, 471, 629, 705, 774, VI.285, 749.

suggest the simplification of Lucretian terminology: at IV.877 in the main body of the text we find *de motu membrorum hoc est de ambulando*, where *hoc est d. a.* summarises the purport of the Lucretian periphrasis with a word that is prosaic in tone as well as intractable for dactylic poets; at V.273 *de aere siue anima* precedes a passage (V.273–80) that discusses *aer*, the element air. Lucretius did not here use *anima*, which he typically reserved to signify the soul or one's breath (at III.573ff. he explicitly denies the possibility of *animans ... aer*); nonetheless, he did occasionally employ *anima* of air (I.715 (alluding to Empedocles), V.236, 1230, VI.578, 586, 591, 693). It seems to me, however, that the rather high-flown *aer* was glossed with its commoner and more prosaic counterpart *anima*.

(ii)   Hellenising elements. The five *capitula* written in Greek, and the two instances in which Greek stands alongside Latin (I.551, II.1058), have already been discussed. In the remaining *capitula*, however, knowledge of words of Greek origin is evident, even though Lucretius typically avoided employing such vocabulary.[90] We find *atomus* used twice (as stated above) and *eclipsis* at V.751;[91] this latter transliteration of ἔκλειψις is attested elsewhere in Latin but is certainly not common.[92] We should also note that, although *Heraclitum* and *Democritum* are found in the *capitula* at I.535 and III.370, we find Greek terminations in *Empedoclen* (I.716) and *Anaxagoran* (I.830).[93] Nonetheless, in employing a form of *magnes* at VI.906, we do not find ablatival *magneti* (a Greek termination in line with Lucretius' acc. sg. *magneta* at VI.908) but *magnete*.[94] The *capitula* therefore demonstrate cognisance of the Greek elements in numerous aspects of the Latin language but, excluding those written partly or entirely in Greek, there is no evidence of close knowledge of the Greek language itself. It therefore seems that a line can be drawn between the seven 'Greek' *capitula* and the remaining, far larger, body of headings. More on this potential division will be said in (C)–(D) below.

[90]   For Lucretius' treatment of Greek words, see esp. Sedley (1999).
[91]   For my explanation of the transmitted form *mundos*, see n. 65 above.
[92]   *eclipsis* is found only in the anonymous *Rhet. ad Her.* (III.36), Varro (*Men.* 231), Pliny the Elder (I.2a.96, II.53.6), Hyg. astron. (*pr.*I.5, IV.9, IV.14), Hyg. fab. (258.1) and Servius (eight times).
[93]   The form *Empedoclen* is presented by the manuscripts of Cicero (*Luc.* 14) and Gellius (IV.11.10), *Anaxagoran* in Cicero (*Luc.* 14), Pliny the Elder (II.149.1), Valerius Maximus (VIII.7ext.6) and Servius (*ad* Verg. *Aen.* IX.625); no doubt it was Latinised by subsequent scribes in a number of other manuscript traditions.
[94]   The form *absent(h)io* at II.400, however, found elsewhere only in Columella, Varro and *Script. hist. Aug.* (*Gord.*), tells us less: *absint(h)ium* or *apsint(h)ium* is found commonly elsewhere, retaining the vowel of Greek ἀψίνθιον.

(II) The authorship of the *capitula*

The structure of some of the *capitula* containing indirect questions could be regarded as somewhat Hellenising, for those of form (ii) place the relevant indirect question after *de* and a noun (e.g. IV.476 *de uero sensu quare cognoscatur*), an order of words rare in Latin but curiously reminiscent of the Greek idiom οἶδά σε ποῦ οἰκεῖς. On reflection, I think it more likely that this unusual word order originates owing to the quick-reference purpose of the *capitula* (on which see (C) below).

(iii)   Innovations: non-Lucretian and post-classical terminology. A number of lexical items in the *capitula* deserve particular attention for their irregularity. Some illustrate that the author of the *capitula* was prepared to employ, or possibly coin, alternative parts of speech based upon Lucretius' wording. We find *stridor serrae* employed in the *capitulum* at II.408 on the basis of *serrae stridentis* at 410, although *stridor* is not found in Lucretius; the only close parallel for the collocation of the two is Cic. *Tusc.* V.116 *ne stridorem quidem serrae* [sc. *non audiunt*], *tum cum acuitur*. The noun *inferi*, rarely found in prose, is introduced at III.978 in lieu of *inferni*. More remarkably, on the basis of *offecto lumine* at V.776 (and perhaps *officimus* at IV.372 and *officiens* at V.718), *offectio* is employed in the *capitulum* at 774 (*de solis et lunae offectione*) in the sense of 'eclipse'. Yet *offectio*, literally a 'blocking', is not otherwise attested in Latin literature; its only appearance is at *CGL* II 256.41, where it appears after βαφή: *tinctura, infectus, infectio*. Grattian used *offectus* (406) but with the sense 'harmful influence'; *offector* refers to a class of dyers who renewed or restored cloth to its original colour (*CIL* IV.864, Fest. 112.6 L). By contrast, alongside the transliterated *eclipsis*, the typical Latin term for 'eclipse' is *defectio* or, particularly in dactylic poetry, *defectus*, which Lucretius himself used just before at 751.[95] It seems, then, that the author of the *capitula* was unaware of a specific Latin word for an eclipse and therefore coined the abstract *offectio* from *offecto lumine*, unaware that it had no classical basis and indeed no (extant) Latin support for this sense. Another potential irregularity is the use of *ignita* in the *capitulum* at VI.204, an adjective rarely found in Latin[96] that may point towards later authorship.[97]

---

[95] It seems improbable that the appropriate *defectione* would have been corrupted to *offectione*.

[96] It is found once in Gellius (XVII.8.10), six times in Apuleius' *Florida* and *De mundo*, once in Philumenus (II.121) and *Script. Hist. Aug.* (*Car.* 8.5)

[97] Servius alleged *ad* Verg. *Buc.* VI.33, however, that Cicero (presumably in his poetic works) employed *ignitum liquorem*.

The possibility stands that the transmitted text at II.221 (*de clinatione simulacrorum*) was what the author of the *capitulum* originally wrote, and that the humanist emendation (AF) to *de declinatione* is therefore a mistaken normalisation. If so, it is interesting to note that, on the basis of Lucretius' *clinamen* (which exhibits a suffix that had little general productivity after the first century BC, replaced as it was almost entirely by the compounded *-mentum*), he offered *clinatio* (a form exhibiting this extremely productive feminine suffix, whose reflexes pervade the Romance languages), perhaps once again unaware or uninterested that the word was apparently never employed in the classical period or elsewhere. The use of *senex* of the *mundus* at II.1144 is striking: it is true that Lucretius personifies the *tellus* as an aged and weary mother (cf. II.1150–9, V.795–836) but there is no personification of the *mundus* as a whole; further, *senex*, whether an appositional noun or adjectival, neither of which Lucretius used, was rarely employed of inanimate entities by classical writers.[98] For the collocation of *mundus* and the root *sen-*, the only surviving instances are *mundo senescente* in Gellius (III.10.11, dismissing a view attributed to Homer) and Zeno of Verona (*Tract.* II.7.5). The use of *pusillus* in the same *capitulum* likewise is suggestive of later Latin prose, as the word is mostly poetic (but non-Lucretian) or colloquial in the classical period. *uisio* at V.663 in the sense of 'view' is unknown in classical Latin, the word being limited either to the faculty of vision or, with specific reference, to a vision (visual or mental). Although the usage here is an evident extension of the latter, it betrays an unfamiliarity with classical Latin, where we would expect to find *species* or *spectaculum*.

In the *capitulum* at III.978 (*quae ad inferos dicantur ea uitae uitia esse*), *dicantur*, if from *dīco*, would require *ad* to mean, rather harshly, 'regarding': 'the things that are said regarding those in the Underworld are vices of life'. Alternatively, if it is a form of *dĭco* in the sense of 'assign', emendation of the verb, preserved by O alone, to *dicentur* would be probable; such a use of *dico* would be rare (particularly with *ad* as opposed to the dative) but would be fashioned on Lucretius' *quaecumque Acherunte profundo prodita sunt esse* (978–9): 'the things which are assigned to deep Acheron . . .'

[98] We may compare its use of a *dens* (IX.57.11), a *cadus* (IX.93.2, XI.36.6) and of wine (albeit *Bacchus*, XIII.23.1) by Martial; Cicero apologised with *ut ita dicam* when speaking of *senior . . . oratio* (*Brut.* 160); Ovid's *senioribus . . . annis* (of *senectus* at *Met.* XV.470) and *senibus . . . saeclis* (*Ciris* 41) are more minor semantic developments.

(II) The authorship of the *capitula*

Particularly striking is the appearance of two verbs in an (unattested) deponent form (it being highly improbable that they were intended to be passive): the author of the *capitulum* has summarised Lucr. I.305–6 (*denique fluctifrago suspensae in litore uestes | uuescunt: eaedem candenti in sole serescunt*) as *uestes uuesci et aresci*. *uuescere* 'become wet' is a distinctly rare verb attested only once elsewhere but in Horace (*S.* II.6.70); since it is an inchoative and intransitive verb, it must stand in the active voice. Nevertheless, for no obvious reason, the author of the *capitulum* has employed the medio-passive infinitive *uuesci* in lieu of *uuescere*.[99] *serescere* is a ἅπαξ found here alone, which perhaps led to its rejection from the *capitulum*; *arescere* 'to become dry' is certainly a common verb but apparently rare in classical Latin.[100] Being of an identical formation and semantic field to *uuescere*, it is likewise confined to the active voice. And yet we also find *aresci*. These two anomalous instances point to the confusion of voice in classical lexemes that became ever commoner in the late-antique period.[101]

Finally, the use of *ad* at VI.848 (*de fonte ad Hammonis*) is distinctly curious as the text stands. We must assume one of four things: (a) that a word was lost from the end of the *capitulum* – most likely *fanum*, since *apud Hammonis fanum* occurs in the following Lucretian verse; (b) that the author of the *capitulum* gravely misunderstood Lucretius' Latin and believed the exotic *Hammonis* to be an accusative form governed by *ad*;[102] (c) that this is a rare archaising employment of *ad* with the ellipse of its accusative and instead only the dependent genitive;[103] that (d) *ad* is an accidental

---

[99] No ancient script could easily explain the corruption (in both instances) of *-ere* to *-i*.

[100] Forms in *aresc-* are found in this period in Cato (four times), Plautus (*Rud.* 575), Varro (*R.R.* I.49, *L.L.* V.38), Cicero (*Part.* 57, *Rep.* V.8, *Inu.* I.109 (translating a sentence from Apollonius rhet.); Nonius quoted Cicero with this verb at 449M) and Ovid (*Met.* IX.657, no doubt under Lucretian influence).

[101] In classical Latin the only active transitive verbs (by extension from their intransitive use) that possess the inchoative suffix *-sco* are *compesco*, *extimesco* and *insuesco*, each of which is consequently found in the passive; both *pasco* and *uescor* are of uncertain etymology. The employment of the impersonal passive *quiesci* at Ter. *Andr.* 691 is a true anomaly.

[102] Proper nouns are comparatively uncommon in the *capitula*, limited to the names of philosophers (I.635, 716, 830, III.369, V.621), mythical creatures or gods (V.1, 397, 878, 892, 901, 916) and places (V.553, VI.639, 712, 738, 749, 756, 848, 888, 906, 1090); the nature of Book VI – providing case studies of natural phenomena – offers almost all examples of the last category. Their use is unremarkable, although VI.738 (*de lacu Auerni*) retains Lucretius' poetic genitive at 736 (*lacus … Auerni*), avoiding the apposition typical in classical Latin, which could suggest some linguistic uncertainty about the word on the author's part.

[103] This device is primarily found in early Latin, e.g. Ter. *Ad.* 530; Var. *Men.* 439; Livy XXVIII.11.

addition and the intended *capitulum* was *de fonte Hammonis* (paralleled by VI.888 *de fonte Aradi in mare*). Most probable seems to posit the loss of *fanum* (if not a commoner noun such as *templum*).

I have highlighted a number of clear features of the language of the *capitula*: simplicity of expression; apparent familiarity with words of Greek origin; a willingness to coin forms from Lucretius' Latin with either ignorance of or disregard for the fact that they are (apparently) unattested in classical Latin; use of Latin of a character more appropriate to the post-classical period. The combination of these features suggests that the Latin *capitula* are the product of the later centuries of antiquity, when Latin of a truly classical form was preserved only among the most elite of Romans and even then based only upon close reading of classical texts in manuscript form. The very fact that one needed access to such manuscripts, which (as codices) were costly items, in order to learn to write (and speak?) in this manner, was a further factor behind their exclusivity. Before saying more about the possible authorship of the *capitula*, I consider their apparent purpose.

(C)   The purpose of the capitula

As we have seen, the *capitula* usually attempt to note, as concisely as possible, the main subject of the subsequent Lucretian passage.[104] The extent of verses that they cover differs strongly and significantly; it is not the case that each *capitulum* summarises the text up until the next heading. To offer a particularly striking example, two adjacent *capitula* are V.916 (*non potuisse chimeram et Scyllam et similia eorum gigni*) and 1161 (*quomodo hominibus innata sit deorum opinio*); the former applies only to lines 916–24 with the result that 925–1160 are without any summary.

---

[104] I have found little benefit in following the distinction of Fischer (1924, 56), who divided the *capitula* into two types, those 'quae breviter perstringunt argumentum' and those 'quae pleno enuntiato exponunt quid doceatur de aliqua re in capite sequenti'; Pasetto (1962–3, 35) independently made the same bipartite distinction.

(II) The authorship of the *capitula*

The *capitula* serve more, then, to highlight sections or features of Lucretius' poem than to break its more interesting elements down systematically.[105]

A number of *capitula* are inserted between verses that are not separated by strong punctuation (I.269, II.392, IV.29, 131, 476, V.251, 774, 780, VI.493, 526).[106] This mid-sentence positioning (typically after the first sentence of a new paragraph) is curious and necessarily interrupts smooth reading. The irregularity can be explained, however, by positing a marginal origin of the *capitula*: such headings were added in the margin around the top of a new section and later came to be inserted, somewhat mechanically, between the verses to which they were nearest, even if this broke a syntactical structure (punctuation, of course, was probably not present to clarify the matter).

Some *capitula* seem not so much to introduce sections but, owing to their brevity, simply mark the appearance of a specific entity, for example *ex Ida uisio solis* (on V.663–5), *de Scylla* (on V.893 and, in part, 894), *de arquo* (on VI.526), and *in Syria quadripedes* (on VI.756–9). Yet more striking are II.1058 and VI.493. Before II.1058 we find ἄπειρος *mundus*, which has no particular bearing on 1058ff. but rather is a rough summary of 1048–53; yet preceding II.1048 is a *capitulum* of a similar force, *omne infinitum in omnis partis*. As stated above, the similarity between ἄπειρος *mundus* and the other Greek *capitula*, involving as it does the use of the nominative and a transliterated Greek noun not regularised in Latin, should lead us to attribute II.1058 to the author of the Greek *capitula*. The author of the rest of the *capitula*, who provided the more general heading for the section, nevertheless added his own note slightly higher in the margin or on an earlier page. ἄπειρος *mundus* was therefore transferred later into the main body of the text, a few lines lower than its original marginal placement.

We have seen in preceding sections that the *capitula* were written in plain language without superfluous expression. The

---

[105] The *capitula* at IV.524 and 526 and V.59 and 64 suggest that the dividing of the text occurred during a given person's perusal rather than from carefully planned division.
[106] Compare my remarks above in the first paragraph of section I(E).

word order of several likewise highlights their attempt to aid easy reference, with subjects being brought to first position, often overriding typical word order (e.g. V.621 *Democriti de sole* and 663 *ex Ida uisio solis*, where the primary foci of Democritus and Mount Ida have been brought to an emphatic but irregular initial position; cf. also I.419 and 430). Likewise, at IV.269 (*ultra speculum cur uideatur*) and in the subsequent *capitulum* at 326 (*plures imagines cur fiant*), the subject has been drawn to the front and *cur* placed by unnatural anastrophe in third position.[107] The former instance is all the more noteworthy, since the language is drawn from Lucretius IV.129, where the natural word order is presented: *cur ultra speculum uideatur imago*. At VI.225 (*ignis ex fulmine natura*) we find particularly awkward word order, since the initial *ignis* is genitival; this ambiguity probably led the first hand of O astray in writing *et* for *ex*; Dungal then made the further mistaken alteration of *fulmine* to *fulminis*.

Along with the emphasis of subjects we may notice the apparent lack of interest in padding. Conjunctions are often eliminated in favour of asyndeton (I.298, II.447, V.1241), and a few *capitula* represent rough conjunctions of two different ideas (e.g. II.62, 1144); perhaps at both IV.240 and 269 the bare passive is harshly employed. Some headings are brief to the point of possible ambiguity. At I.498 (*solidum esse*), the author must mean 'solidity exists' rather than 'it [some topic at hand] is solid'. At IV.127 (*esse item maiora*), we should presumably understand *animalia* (as *item* suggests) from the preceding discussion and *capitulum* (IV.116 *quam parua sint animalia*). The fact that the heading can only be fully understood in light of the text has two important consequences: it speaks strongly against a thoughtful editor's having applied a fixed methodology to the distribution and formation of *capitula*; it corroborates the theory that the *capitula* were marginal annotations and the *indices* later transcribed from them (for *esse item maiora* placed at the beginning of the book could scarcely be understood). At V.376 (*et natiua esse*), the force of *et* (which opens no other *capitulum*) is unclear, but the heading must

[107] I have found no prose example of *cur* later than second position but cannot assert with confidence that it is unattested.

mean 'the world is mortal'; even if *et* is a corruption of *etiam*
(*etiam natiua* occurring in 376) or of *haec* (occurring in 377,
perhaps via *ec*), the subject qualified by *natiua* can only be
supplied from the context, with *esse* taken as copulative.[108]

Another instance that repays attention is VI.493 (*spiracula
mundi*), which cannot be an acc. + inf. (form (iii)) with ellipse
of *esse* nor truly the corresponding nominative phrase (form (v)).
Rather, *spiracula mundi* is simply a quotation from VI.493 and
could only apply to verses 493–4. Further, Lucretius here merely
refers to the motion of the elements of the world *quasi per magni
circum spiracula mundi*, thus apologising for the non-literal sense
of *spiracula*. The purpose of this *capitulum*, then, is not epexe-
getic or informative, but simply to highlight an interesting phrase
employed by Lucretius.

In several places there is an evident lack of concern with the
specifics of the passage, for we read *et ceteris* after lists in I.311
and 565. The latter instance (*de molli natura aqua aere et
ceteris*)[109] provides possible evidence of inattention, for the text
ordering of *aer aqua* is reversed. Similarly, at II.447 (*de adamante
ferro silice aere*) the ordering *silices ... ferri* (449) has
been switched, and at II.842 (*atomos nec colorem nec odorem
nec sucum nec frigus nec calorem habere*) the text ordering
(*color ... tepor ... frigus ... calidus uapor ... sonitus ...
sucus ... odor*) has been significantly altered and *nec sonitum*
(if it has not been lost through a scribal *saut*) has been overlooked
by the annotator.

In light of the discussion of forms of *capitula* above, we can
offer further evidence for a shift in the methodology of the author
of the Latin *capitula*. It is striking that the first three (62, 84, 107)
are of the nominative form (v), which is otherwise rare in the
headings. Similarly, *capitula* involving indirect questions (ii, iv)
occur almost entirely in the latter half of the work (II.112 being

---

[108] Along with V.376, Fischer (1924, 58) also cited IV.633 (*quare alia aliis contraria sint*,
which applies in context only to foodstuffs) and VI.756 (*in Syria quadripedes*) as
examples of ambiguity, observing 'haec capitula non intelligimus nisi versus ipsos,
quibus attributa sunt, inspicimus.'

[109] The very fact that instances of *mollis natura* are in apposition with it shows haste of
composition.

the only exception). There is nothing in Lucretius' text to encourage such a change of approach and it is most likely to represent a casual shift in the annotator's method. All in all, more detail in annotation is provided in the *capitula* to the latter three books of the work, the half which is typically the more popular with readers, ancient and modern. I do not think it coincidental that the frequency of *capitula* is highest in Book V, perhaps Lucretius' most celebrated and intriguing book. Not only then do irregularities in the language and form of the *capitula* suggest that they were not created for public use by an editor of sorts but the unequal distribution of *capitula* and the imbalanced distribution of forms encourage that inference.

One remaining anomaly is the *capitulum* at V.324, which is curious for explicitly recording a verb of which Lucretius must be the subject: *quare natiua omnia dicat*. Owing to the subjunctive and the nature of other *capitula*, we should translate '[Lucretius here says] why he states that all things have a birth'. As it happens, Lucretius does not explain why he says it; rather, more directly, he offers as an argument of the earth's mortality the fact that history does not stretch far back, that arts and sciences are still being refined and that he is the first *in patrias qui possim uertere* [sc. *naturam rationemque rerum*] *uoces* (337). The casual slip of the verb into the *capitulum* is further evidence that there was no careful editorial hand behind the *capitula*'s creation.

A word should be said about the lengthier *capitula*. The longest precedes IV.312, and the rest that reach double-figure word counts (II.184, III.445, V.471, 780) often compound plural ideas. A series of long *capitula* are presented by those opening the last three books (IV.1, V.1, VI.50), which are eight, ten, and twelve words long respectively. Why do we not find similarly lengthy *capitula* to open the first three books? I would suggest that, respectively, the hymn to Venus (I.1–43), the praise of the simple Epicurean life (II.1–36) and the address to Epicurus (III.1–30) were so well known to the given reader that he had no need to provide personal annotations upon these passages.

The purpose of the *capitula* is therefore inherently clear: to provide quick, marginal reference for the content of the poem, highlighting major topics and lines of argument. It is therefore misguided to describe them all as 'summaries', for instances such as VI.493 (*spiracula mundi*) and VI.756 (*in Syria quadripedes*) do nothing more than pick out a particular phrase or subject. In an age when no more specific reference in literature was available than the book number, the pragmatic benefit of such *capitula* hardly needs emphasis. Yet the cursory and irregular form of these headings suggests that they were employed in passing by a reader and were never intended for use beyond his own manuscript, and perhaps even his own eyes.

The purpose of the Greek *capitula* is quite different: passages are drawn from Epicurus and other philosophical texts to provide Greek parallels of Lucretius' argument. They do not summarise the text's development but rather offer primary evidence of the Epicurean tenet in question. They show a level of textual acquaintance wholly absent from the Latin *capitula* and are confined to the first two books.

(D) The authorship of the capitula

To conclude this chapter, we can now draw from the evidence above some conclusions about the *capitula*'s authorship. Most importantly, it seems highly probable that we have more than one stratum of notations, the seven that involve Greek words (plus perhaps I.62, 84 and 107), alongside the rest.[110] But which preceded which? It has been noted by Fischer (1924, 64), and subsequently recorded as his own suggestion by Pasetto (1962–3, 37–8), that the *capitulum* at I.551 (*contra* εἰς ἄπειρον τὴν τομήν) is of primary importance for elucidating the order of composition. The argument runs that, if one were to go to the trouble of writing in Greek to illustrate this passage, it would be natural to use a Greek preposition (presumably κατά) to indicate that Lucretius is countering this particular theory. It is therefore assumed that the first author wrote εἰς ἄπειρον ἡ τομή in the nominative case, as with the

---

[110] Fischer (1924, 61, 63) first posited dual authorship; although sparing in detail, he named the author of the former 'Epicureus quidam' and that of the latter 'grammaticus ille', terms that are not particularly useful.

other Greek *capitula* (it being more likely that those in the neuter
are nominative rather than accusative); *contra* was then added by
the author of the Latin *capitula* when he adopted – and here
adapted – the Greek citations. We should here compare the
capitulum at I.1052, εἰς τὸ μέσον ἡ φορά, where we would likewise
expect a preposition, Greek or Latin, bearing the meaning 'against',
for Lucretius here explicitly counters the theory. If the writer of the
hybrid *capitulum* at I.551 was a single individual, why, we must
ask, did he not add *contra* at I.1052, a word of central importance?
Further, if *contra* was here added but subsequently fell out of the
text, it is highly improbable that the nominative case would
have been thus restored by a subsequent scribe. It also seems to
me improbable that the simple negative *non* could have stood
before the phrase prior to its loss. For the *capitulum* at I.551,
therefore, we should instead suppose that one scribe noted the
Greek as an illustration of the topic of the passage, without stating
that Lucretius' aim was to counter that thesis, and that a later reader,
owner or scribe added for clarity's sake the Latin preposition
contra, which he went on to employ in an identical sense at I.605,
716, 830 and III.370 (all preceding the names of Presocratic
philosophers). It was perhaps simply through negligence or inattention on his part that he did not add *contra* at I.1052.

If this hypothesis is accepted, we can posit two separate
annotators in the manuscript tradition and infer their chronology.
The first was apparently concerned primarily with adding
Greek phrases, largely drawn from Epicurean doctrine and
often simply nominative phrases. This author need not have been
Greek but was evidently both conversant and well-read in the
language, as was perfectly possible at Rome as well as in
Greece under the Empire. He need not even have been an
Epicurean (*pace* Fischer, as n. 110) but, whatever his philosophical interests, it is clear that the primary Epicurean texts were
well known to him.[111] The phrases are sufficiently well positioned

---

[111] I.551 and 951 are the most learned citations, but neither is truly recondite. It is not
impossible that the quotations from Epicurus' introductory *Epistulae* were ultimately
drawn from Diogenes Laertius X, as there is little evidence that Epicurus' own writings
were in active circulation in later antiquity. If so, this would mean that the author of the
Greek *capitula* was working, at the earliest, in the early/mid third century AD.

to show close engagement with the poem's content.[112] For one reason or another, however, his annotations did not advance beyond Book II.[113] The second annotator, responsible for the rest of the *capitula*, is far more prevalent but also far more simplistic in his coverage, typically limiting himself to brief Latin phrases and keywords. There are no signs of erudition. We have to assume that his knowledge of Greek was sufficient to understand transliterated forms of Greek words and to alter a nominative into an accusative having added *contra*. Whether this second annotator used the same manuscript as the first annotator, or rather a copy that included his Greek annotations, cannot be decided with certainty, but I incline to the former possibility. At any rate, these *capitula* survived in the direct line of transmission from which the Carolingian manuscripts sprang.

Minor problems with this hypothesis can easily be explained away. First, a number of the supposedly later *capitula* exhibit a familiarity with Greek that could be sufficient for their having also authored the Greek *capitula*, that is, Greek terminations at I.716 and 830 and Greek transliterations at V.294 (*lampade*) and 751 (*eclipsi*). Yet the use of *-n* as the accusative in Greek names is well paralleled in all genres of Latin literature over the centuries and both *lampas* and *eclipsis* are common enough in authors outside Lucretius. As has been said, the apparently Greek form of type (ii) *capitula* (e.g., IV.476 *de uero sensu quare cognoscatur*) can rather be explained as an attempt to bring the primary topic of the section into prominence at the beginning of the phrase.

---

[112] Bignone (1919, 426) offered in passing the theory that the *capitula* were not sought out by the intelligence of their author(s) but were rather drawn from a commentary upon *DRN*, such as that to which Jerome alluded (see Introduction, n. 12). As well as highlighting the level of learning in the Greek *capitula*, he argued that the *capitulum* opening Book IV seems to have application to the opening of Book III and was therefore probably drawn from a commentary which, at the beginning of Book IV, offered a summary of Book III. This conjecture is improbable not only because it is difficult to explain the present form of the *capitula* as the result of a single hand, whether a commentator's or reader's, but also because many headings could not conceivably have been in an ancient commentary (e.g. I.305 *uestes uuesci et aresci*, II.1144 *iam senem mundum et omnia pusilla nasci*, and presumably also those of type (i), *de X*), not least because of the inaccuracy of many *capitula*.

[113] I thus disagree with Pasetto, who believed that this annotator was a scholar with serious aims for the text (1962–3, 48).

The features listed above in section I B(ii) could therefore be attributed simply to one who was fairly cognisant of Greek linguistic features. As Fischer and Pasetto have observed, from the second century AD onwards, awareness of Greek was at a particularly high level among literate Romans. Nor need two further apparent problems delay us. To the question of why the author of the Greek *capitula* stopped his annotations we may simply answer that the task, evidently demanding time and not a little learning, was interrupted by other business and not completed (cf. Pasetto (1962–3, 42). As to why a scribe copying the manuscript containing these annotations decided to preserve these occasional Greek marginalia (beginning at I.551), three possibilities exist: (i) the commissioner of the new manuscript asked the scribe to retain these learned notes; (ii) the scribe (a learned Roman?) made it for himself and therefore chose to retain the notes; (iii) the manuscript containing the Greek annotations was that in which the author of the later *capitula* made his additions,[114] with the result that the scribe who came to copy this manuscript (or its commissioner) decided that the body of annotations as a whole deserved preservation.

I believe that the repetition of II.646 as I.44 is prime evidence for deciding between these options. If the *capitulum* was originally copied by the second author into his manuscript in Greek, then it is difficult to explain why it alone but not I.44 is preserved in Greek. Since it makes good sense to equate the transcriber of II.646–51 to after I.43 with the author of the rest of the *capitula* (one who made good use of his copy of Lucretius), then we can readily suppose that he, whose annotations are in Latin throughout, made the simple transference of the *capitulum* into Latin. If, however, the second author worked in the original manuscript and therefore only transcribed this one of the Greek *capitula* and did so in Latin (which more suited his purpose), then this opening *capitulum* would subsequently have served as an indication for the subsequent scribe that the remaining Greek headings could/should

---

[114] If so, the second author changed H TOMH (minuscule ἡ τομή being improbable) to THN TOMHN; with the addition of virgulae and a thin *tau*, this would not have been particularly difficult.

be written in transliterated form. It was the choice of the scribe therefore to retain only the very well-known phrase at II.646 in its Greek form (see n. 75). In the second author's system of annotation, Latin was evidently the only option he considered: even before the Greek *capitulum* at I.551 he had no qualms in adding *contra* rather than κατά. I therefore incline to option (iii) above.

This supposition could be logistically problematic if we posit that the author of the Greek *capitula*, with Fischer (and subsequently S. B. Smith and Pasetto), worked in the second century, which would almost certainly require that he annotated individual papyrus rolls. Such *uolumina* presumably had narrower margins and were thus not espectially suited to the sort of annotation we find from the second author. It is perhaps easier to move the author of the Greek *capitula* to a later date (perhaps around the time of Diogenes Laertius; see n. 111 above) and therefore posit that he annotated a single codex, which the second author, on acquiring it, duly annotated to a serious degree (perhaps in the following century). I therefore suggest that the first author of the *capitula* made his notes some 250–300 years after Lucretius' death, the second author during the following two centuries.[115] Although it was only by way of this annotated codex that our Lucretian tradition chanced to survive antiquity, the very existence of such marginalia as these may be representative of the annotations of other learned readers of the poem.

Conclusion

Although it has transpired that the *capitula* are not Lucretian but rather two stages of marginal accretions from several centuries after the poet's death, they have shed light on a number of intcresting points. First, we have clear evidence that the extant Lucretian tradition passed through the hands of a learned individual, accomplished in Greek and philosophical matters, perhaps in

---

[115] That *Phaethon* (V.396) and *Pallas* (VI.749) are glossed and banalised could suggest an unfamiliarity with the religion and mythology of the Greeks. If the author was Christian, we may understand why Book III is the least annotated in the work and its famous last few hundred lines have no *capitulum* beyond 977 (the sole heading after 711).

the third century AD, and likewise was closely read and worked
upon by someone in the following two centuries. Furthermore, the
capitula have demonstrated with some certainty that, at the very
least, three manuscripts intervened between Lucretius' circulated
uolumina and the archetype of the direct tradition. The following
manuscript phases can tentatively be summarised thus:

second/third century(?) AD	manuscript annotated marginally by author of Greek *capitula*; later annotated marginally by another hand with the rest of the *capitula* (part damaged)
fourth–fifth century(?) AD	manuscript in which *indices* were copied from *capitula* for Books IV–VI; the *capitula* themselves remained minuscule and probably marginal
[fifth–seventh century(?) AD	manuscript in which *capitula* were transferred into text in (rubricated?) capitals? *Indices* confused.
seventh–eighth century AD	the archetype, in which *capitula* stood in the text in rubricated capitals
ninth century AD	O and ψ

The analysis above leads me to the following recommendation for
future editors of *DRN*: the *capitula* and *indices* (for Books IV–VI),
which bear no official or editorial relation to the text of *DRN*,
should be annexed to an appendix in an edition and should only be
mentioned elsewhere if they genuinely impinge upon the reading
of the poetic text. As it happens, this only occurs twice: IV.526
(*enim <uocem>*), restored from *corpoream esse uocem*, and
VI.890 (*marist Aradi*), emended from *de fonte Aradi in mare*.

4

THE CORRECTING HANDS OF O

The *Codex Oblongus*, despite its great fame as a manuscript of a classical author, still rewards close inspection. In this chapter the results of a renewed investigation are presented, which have wide-reaching significance for the broader tradition of *DRN* as a whole. It emerges that no fewer than six distinct hands can be discerned in the manuscript that postdate the writing of its text by the initial scribes (whom I shall unite under the one siglum O).[1]

Throughout the manuscript, although the feature is absent in a number of places owing both to scribal omission and to subsequent trimming, O has added in a more casual hand *Lucreti(i)* and *Lib̄ X* at the top of each recto and verso leaf respectively, with slight variations after 161ᵛ. Of the later hands, four attempted corrections of the text, two of them very regularly. This chapter aims to assess, on the basis of my fresh assignations of corrections occurring throughout O to each of these individual hands, the manner in which they worked, their source (if any) and their relative chronology. Very little will be said about the few corrections made by the original scribe(s) of O, as they were presumably instant alterations of miscopyings from the exemplar, corrected on the basis of that same manuscript.[2]

---

[1] It is odd that, with so much discussion about O, it has not been remarked, as close inspection shows, that two (or more) scribes worked on it: note especially the change in hand at 162ʳ, in particular the alteration of page heading from *Lucretii* to *Lucreti*, and the majuscule forms of *B*, *T* and *N*. I believe only Chatelain (1908) has recorded this plurality of hands in print (repeated by Reeve (2005) 159). Nevertheless, there is nothing to suggest that the change of scribe affected the transmission of the text, and it is thus of palaeographical and codicological interest alone.

[2] Among original alterations made by O one could cite: I.289 <*qua*>, 880 *repulsumit* to *repulsumst*, 892 *praefacta* to *praefracta*; II.362 *illa* to *ulla*; III.311 *decurrit* to *decurrat*; IV.396 *iustatione* to *in statione*; V.489 *elas* to *elap*; VI.120 *Eucitur* to *Ducitur*, 1189 *uic* to *uix*. Among corrections in/with erasure, we find: I.230 *ingenuei*(?) corrected to *ingenui*; II.479 *fid//* to *fidem*; III.65 *egel//* to *egestas*, 691 *uenas neruos*, 928 *disiectus*

203

(A) The work of Dungal (D)

Soon after being written (i.e. around the year 800), O received corrections throughout from an insular hand of the early ninth century,[3] which Bernard Bischoff identified as the Irish scholar-monk Dungal (*c.* 780–*c.* 834),[4] a figure who became involved with the court of Charlemagne around the turn of the ninth century. More will be said about Dungal and this identification later in this section under (iii). Given that the scale of the alterations to the text of O made by Dungal (whom I will call 'D') is so large, his work requires careful analysis. Reference will be made throughout to the full list of the alterations of the text by D that I have compiled, which is available online.[5] No earlier attempt has been made to record in full D's corrections nor to analyse them separately in any detail.[6] Almost all of the corrections in the list can confidently be attributed to D, who wrote with a darker ink and thicker nib than the various later correctors, and with a very distinctive set of letter forms.[7] As regards the small number of corrections recalcitrant to palaeographical analysis, since many are of a similar nature to those securely attributed to D, they probably came from his hand. The apparatus of Diels, the most

---

materia, 958 *elapsast ingrata* (*elap . . . a* m. pr.); V.155 *posterius*, 614 *Oec* to *Nec*, 673 *inpu/em* to *inpubem*; VI.435 *& extendatur* (*datur* m. pr.); II.1158–9 are *in rasura*.

[3] We may cite Lindsay (1925) 17: 'The progress of palaeographic study between 1908 (when [Chatelain] wrote the introduction) and 1925 is shewn by the amazingness nowadays of the phrase "corrector Saxo vel Hibernicus". No one now would dream of calling this hand anything but Anglosaxon. And I fancy that for "corrector" should be substituted "praeceptor".' The Irishman Dungal, as Reynolds (1983b) 219 wryly remarked, may have had misgivings about 'Saxonicus'.

[4] The identification was first made by Bischoff (1965) 206 no. 365, aided by the corrections in Milan C 74 sup., explicitly in Dungal's hand. Bischoff subsequently confirmed this identification in Ferrari (1972) 38 n. 3, Bischoff (1966–81) vol. III, 64, and Bischoff (2004) 50 no. 2189. The hand can be seen in Plate II and on this book's dustjacket.

[5] See Appendix III; a fuller version is available online at www.cambridge.org/butterfield.

[6] Chatelain (1908, III col. 2) prefaced his list by stating '[p]raecipua saltem recensere hic debemus' but recorded only about a third of the instances; his final observation (V col. 1) is unhelpfully broad: '[p]raeterea syllabam vel litteram passim mutavit tum recte tum perperam, morem sui temporis secutus.' The discussion of Bitterlich-Willmann (1951, 56, 150) is brief and without new evidence.

[7] The most distinctively insular letter forms are the *r*, whose curl descends so low as to make the letter similar to *n*, the embellishments to the top left of *s* and *f*, with the generally low bar of the latter, and the flat-topped *g*, as well as the curls added to the top of ascenders and the typically more crabbed appearance of the text.

(A) The work of Dungal (D)

Table 5

Book	Number of corrections	Lines per correction
I	67	16.7
II	61	19.2
III	71	15.4
IV	82	15.7
V	143	10.2
VI	261	4.9
Total	685	10.8

detailed to date, includes at least sixty mistaken reports of the readings of O and D (both his and typographical errors)[8] and fails to associate very many corrections with Dungal, rather attributing them to the shadowy figure represented by his 'O¹'.[9]

The 685 alterations recorded in the list (Table 5 includes some compound corrections better treated as a union but disregards those that are so minor as to make attribution almost impossible) are spread throughout Lucretius' text as follows.

There is a marked increase in alterations in Book VI, averaging more than once every five lines, four times more frequent than in Book II; Book V also enjoys obviously greater interest than the four that precede. At this point it should be noted that, in terms of archetypal corruption, the final book is indeed the most corrupt of the poem;[10] however, D's critical activity is at its lowest in the second most corrupt book (II), and second highest in a book that is the third least corrupt (V): this varied distribution of corrections probably reflects the extent to which D engaged with the subject matter of the text in front of him, the content of Books V and VI being deemed particularly interesting (see further (iii) below).

If we consider as the work of D those corrections that involve no ink but erasure alone (for which see the end of n. 1 in the full

---

[8] The more significant of these are I.320, 477, 588, 739, 767; II.158, 277, 396, 486, 657, 844, 867, 943; III.287, 408; IV.570, 653, 897, 912, 1030; V.211, 403, 1004; VI.60, 555.

[9] For the imprecision of Diels' 'O¹', see Reeve (2005) 159.

[10] Using Martin's Teubner apparatus as a guide, Book VI suffers an archetypal corruption every 2.8 lines; the frequency of corruption decreases, through II, III, V then IV, to Book I, least corrupt with an archetypal error every 5.8 verses.

list of corrections online (as n. 5 above)), as seems probably correct, we see a similar state of affairs in which the spread of figures again reached a peak in the final book: I: 21; II: 20; III: 11; IV: 14; V: 13; VI: 36. If these corrections, and those made in notes 1–2 of the list, are also included (which cannot be proven palaeographically but is the least improbable assignation), the total number of alterations that I attribute to Dungal is 1,375, an average of a correction every 5.4 lines (i.e. eighteen to nineteen times every one hundred lines).

I now turn to three separate questions: (i) what sort of corrections interested D? (ii) by what method did he make them? (iii) how secure is the attribution of them to D?

(i)   The nature of D's alterations

It is clear from the full list that the scale of D's alterations ranges from single-letter corrections to the wholesale introduction of multiple verses. Close inspection of the inks of O's various annotators has led me to attribute a far larger number of corrections to Dungal than did Diels, upon whom all subsequent Lucretian editors have based their reports.[11] Although we have seen that D's corrections are most prevalent in the last two books of the work, the largest-scale alterations, that is, the introduction of many whole verses, are strangely limited to its first two.

A fair proportion of alterations (136, i.e. 20 per cent) involve the simple correction of orthographical matters, especially

---

[11] For instance, at IV.653 Diels reported that O[1] restored the missing *aliis*, a statement found in all five editions of Martin's Teubner (1934–63), Bailey's *ed. maior* and Büchner, as well as Cini (1976, 156). In reality, no hand in O offers such a correction, nor even in Q; one had to wait fifty years for Müller casually to correct this error in his pared-down appendix, stating '*aliis* rest. Itali'. Dozens of instances smaller than the false creation of a word could be given, this and other errors occurring up to the time of Flores. To give just one: it was first reported by Lachmann that *prosatur* was corrected into *profatur* by O at I.739. This assertion we find also in Munro, Brieger, Ernout, Diels, Martin, Bailey and Flores. As it happens, *profatur* (also found in Q and no doubt Ω) is the original (and unaltered) reading of O, the *f* being written in a rare, but distinctive, form of the letter with a lower bar on the right: this form occurs first only before *l* (see, e.g., I.8, 17, 73, 281, 290, 291, 374), but spreads to other letters as the manuscript develops (see, e.g., I.290 (before e), 296 (a), 308 (u), 333 (i), 401 (e), 424 (e)). See further (iii) below.

(A) The work of Dungal (D)

standardising certain features of early Latin spelling:[12] *-uos* > *-uus*, *uort-* > *uert-*, *quom* > *cum*,[13] *-cu-* > *-quu-*, *supt-* > *subt-*,[14] *ads-* > *ass-*, *quidq-* > *quicq-*,[15] *aliut* > *aliud*, *capud* > *caput*, *rutund-* > *rotund-*, *sorsum* > *sursum*, *nihil* > *nil* (*metri causa*), the interchange between *-īs* and *-ēs*, and *u* and *b* (the latter usually correcting a pronunciational error), the addition or removal of *h*, and the doubling of consonants. Five times we find the alteration of *quamquam* by erasure to *quanquam*, a form that came into vogue from the fourth/fifth centuries onwards. Rarely do we find alterations of orthography that bring about a form that is definitely incorrect: for example the alteration of *tremibunda* to *tremebunda* (I.95), mistakenly changing forms of *auere* (a verb seemingly unknown to D)[16] to (*h*)*abere*,[17] and the replacement of *mari* with ablatival (and here unmetrical) *mare* at VI.696 and 698. This concern with restoring what were thought to be the forms most representative of classical Latin was a standard hallmark of Carolingian scholarship and should not cause particular surprise. Although D's work in this field was active, it was not comprehensive: for instance, *com* remains in the text for *cum* at I.1077 and II.194, although D would hardly have welcomed it as an appropriate form; *oliuom* is found unchanged at II.392 (though corrected at VI.1073), *anticum* at II.1170 and *aeuom* at V.61, 82, 172, 427, 1089 and 1150 (though corrected eight times elsewhere in the text).[18]

---

[12] If we include in the calculation the eighteen instances correcting orthographic matters among the simple erasures, and the 404 additions of the cedilla to *e* in order to produce *ae*, then the proportion of such corrections throughout the text rises to a half.

[13] If *quum* (as Q) was indeed erased at IV.1097, and *quequumque* at VI.45, we should consider these as instances of this same standardisation.

[14] There seems some uncertainty on this point, since D's method changed as he worked through the text: although *subter* is regularly changed to *supter* in three instances (V.268, 515, VI.537), forms of *suptilis* are initially changed to *subtilis* (II.385, IV.88) but thereafter the change is reversed (IV.743, 747, 901, VI.1031). By contrast, D's regularity is evident at III.713–14, where *linquontur* (713) and *lincuntur* (714) are both altered to the standard *linquuntur*.

[15] Uncertainty is again evident, for *quicqu-* is changed to *quidqu-* at II.166, but conversely *quidqu-* to *quicqu-* at III.587, V.264, 304 and 577.

[16] The retention of *auentes* at IV.1203 should be regarded as an oversight; the correction of *auintis* to *auentis* at VI.531, the only instance of *auere* not accounted for, could be interpreted as *a uentis*, which would bring some sense to the line (*uenti* being mentioned at VI.529).

[17] II.265; III.6, 259, 957, 1082, 1083; IV.778; V.1019; cf. also II.216.

[18] II.561, 1171; III.605; IV.1235; V.1145, 1431, 1440; VI.58.

We should presumably see such anomalies as oversights on his part, and possible evidence that he did not work through the text closely more than once. We may here add that D seemingly had no knowledge of Lucretius' use of the archaic disyllabic genitival termination -*ai* for –*ae*, a fact largely lost in the direct transmission of the text,[19] as he took no opportunity to make simple metrical corrections of -*a* or -*ae* to this form.

Besides merely orthographical changes, the remaining active alterations to the text can be classed as follows: minor alterations of inflections, often correcting non-existent forms;[20] minor additions or alterations of letters to the stem of the word, often inserting missed initial letters;[21] the addition of missing words, typically in or above the line in question,[22] but four times (IV.244, VI.241, 644, 1117) in the margin; the joining together of misdivided words and the separation of some words written without word division,[23] often in tandem with minor

---

[19] Terminations in –*ai* are preserved by the original scribe(s) of O only at II.249; III.396, 670, 838; V.720, 726; and VI.693, all of which stood in the archetype; in addition, ψ preserved the termination at I.29, 112, 283, 307, 406, 415, 453, 1051; II.663, 666, 735; V.946, and Q alone at I.285, 516, 565, 997; II.544, 562, 737; III.928, all but II.544 and 562 (where S does not exist) against S. Since there is no reason to suppose that either ψ or Q made corrections in this vein as they wrote, it is probable that the archetype preserved twenty-seven cases (15.6 per cent) of this termination. The scribe of ψ managed to retain more, either through knowledge of termination or ignorance of its rarity, than O, who often rejected the form: that so few instances survive in the latter half of *DRN* could denote a change of scribal practice at some stage in the poem's transmission.
[20] I.63, 449 (*bis*), 477, 619, 684, 887, 943, 1060; II.291, 384, 478*cap.*, 577, 652, 840; III.156, 443, 829, 883, 906, 960; IV.63, 79, 363, 643, 1196, 1224; V.57, 406, 418, 511, 580, 707, 718, 721, 727, 823, 1141, 1220, 1221, 1259, 1273, 1331; VI.50*ind.*, 1, 66, 68, 95, 134, 145, 153, 160, 208, 225*cap.*, 249, 297, 344, 416, 444, 447, 481, 512, 521, 526*cap.*, 526, 558, 597, 600, 604, 609, 611, 661, 667, 726, 761, 815, 834, 969, 1017, 1136, 1139, 1153. In a number of instances a final letter is added to a word that either does not exist or is a different, incorrect word: II.342, IV.554, V.1172, VI.482, 512, 667.
[21] I.84, 465, 668, 753, 857; II.82, 613, 615, 721, 1006; III.6, 156, 293, 321, 336, 462, 578, 596, 719, 994; IV.253, 882, 886, 1053, 1058, 1083 (*bis*), 1124, 1137, 1154, 1194, 1202, 1229, 1237; V.158, 209, 226, 287, 496, 675, 714, 790, 810, 933, 995, 1008, 1085, 1145, 1162, 1234, 1255, 1322, 1324, 1331, 1370, 1429; VI.53, 60, 132, 136, 138, 162, 180, 288, 296, 306, 315, 337, 350, 356, 364, 366, 372, 393, 431, 440, 453, 454, 482, 512, 531, 652, 658, 749*cap.*, 803, 820, 868, 878 (*bis*), 931, 969, 1003, 1009, 1037 (*bis*), 1041, 1062, 1071, 1077, 1125, 1126, 1166, 1167, 1172, 1195, 1228, 1267. It so happens that the changes recorded in this and the preceding note rarely affect the separated initial opening each line (only in verses written in full and at VI.344, 715, 728 and 1228).
[22] I.699; III.3, 251; IV.244; V.630, 790, 1044, 1233; VI.241, 374, 615, 644, 814, 897, 1117.
[23] Although many words lack division from one another in O, D clearly felt a need in certain instances to make the division explicit.

corrections;[24] large-scale erasure and subsequent addition of verses.[25] In some cases the correction made by D was purely motivated by sense.[26]

We may now turn to instances that involve erasure by D. Of cases where letters have simply been erased without any further additions to the text, we generally find deletion of unwanted final letters (especially *s* and *m*), or the erasure of wrongly doubled consonants, incorrectly inserted vowels (especially *i* and *e*), accidentally repeated syllables or the correction of *m* and *l/u* into *n* and *i* respectively. In several instances where erasure has occurred, the nature and method of D's correction cannot be discerned since the erased text cannot be securely reconstructed.[27] Disregarding these, we see that a number of alterations merely involve the easy correction of a non-Latin word to its correct form,[28] sometimes correcting two misdivided words in the process.[29] In other instances the correction is of a valid Latin word to the correct one.[30] Although very many of these changes are simple, the general level of accuracy shows a close engagement with the text, and in many cases a careful reading of the passage. We should note, however, that a number of erasures produced

---

[24] I.427, 887; III.1073; IV.202, 224, 545; V.714, 985, 1416; VI.31, 109, 249, 512, 664, 700, 941; see also the use of underlining and commata alone for this purpose, as recorded in n. 1 under (d) and (e) of the online list (see n. 5 above).

[25] I.352, 357, 364–8, 549–50, 836–7, 1022–3; II.257–63, 313, 410–12, 454, 883–6, 943–4; III.588, 596; V.653.

[26] For example, in the following instances, although the transmitted word is Latin, D decided correctly or saw in his exemplar that something must stand in its stead: I.668 *amor* in *ardor*, 741 *causa* in *casu*; III.236 *multam quaeri* in *multa moueri*; IV.78 *concessum* in *consessum*; VI.35 *caelis* in *caecis*, 372 *uouitur* in *uoluitur*. To this number should be added the four alterations of forms of *flumen* to *fulmen* or *uice uersa* (I.489, 663; IV.423; V.400).

[27] I.37, 115, 182, 272, 321, 448, 648, 651, 781; II.136, 147, 181, 192, 283, 486, 543, 983, 1114; III.12, 257, 330, 479, 531, 618, 651, 660, 752, 858, 941, 996; IV.31, 124, 217, 224, 232, 344, 570, 653, 1059, 1170, 1234; V.199, 206, 314, 324*cap.*, 481, 560, 681, 702, 727, 852, 998, 1257, 1317, 1348, 1441; VI.24, 45, 81, 94, 112, 115, 122, 208, 237, 239, 254, 285, 396, 447, 485, 497, 511, 524, 533, 613, 634, 653, 695, 703, 715, 725, 728, 751, 754, 763, 782, 813, 888, 891, 908, 915, 947, 951, 993, 1033, 1035, 1062, 1075, 1147, 1170 (*bis*), 1199, 1222, 1228, 1266, 1280.

[28] I.286, 477, 610; II.1119; III.293, 437, 443, 462; IV.95, 253, 710, 1124; V.697, 790, 994, 1126, 1248; VI.35, 214, 243, 268, 288, 324, 639, 665, 787, 915, 1139, 1148, 1198, 1272.

[29] III.236; IV.202; V.985, 1416; VI.31, 109, 141, 664, 941.

[30] I.489, 561, 741, 1061; II.313, 576, 663; III.156, 644, 658, 868, 906; IV.78, 219, 423; V.400, 580, 626, 653, 852 (*bis*), 853, 1108, 1142, 1427; VI.1, 35, 134, 237, 558, 597, 621, 673, 749, 923, 967, 1150, 1251.

an incorrect reading;[31] in some instances (II.227 *plag*,[32] VI.2
didederunt, 747 *ecri*, 858 *perquoccere*) the word offered as a
correction is not Latin.

Of more interest to us are those cases where a significant
amount of text has been added *in rasura*, ranging from a few
letters (II.227, V.790, 1257, VI.1280) to one or more words
(I.352, 357, 634, II.79, 233, 384, 454, 827, III.588, V.653) or
even verses.[33] It is a curious fact that these more large-scale
additions are limited (with the exception of the addition of *aere
multo* at the close of V.653) to the first three books of *DRN*. As
Reeve (2005, 156–8) has noted, the insertion of whole verses by
D has suffered from poor reporting by various editors. I have
confirmed by autopsy that in all instances where D supplied full
verses, he had erased verses already written by the text hand of
O that accidentally omitted one or more verses: accordingly, in no
instance were gaps of blank parchment purposefully left for D to
fill at a later date.[34] In all instances where D erased whole verses,
he supplied a larger number than the gap originally allowed,
adding in total twenty-six verses[35] in the space of fourteen. It is
therefore clear that he was simply correcting the mistaken omission of verses by O. Reeve (2005, 156–8) has shown that the
majority of these omissions can be regarded as *sauts du même au
même* (through homoeoteleuton): *inanis* at I.363 and 365, *de
pauxillis atque minutis* at I.836 and 837, *quaeque sagaci mente
locarunt* at I.1022 and 1023, *uoluntas* at II.258 and 261, *anima-
ntem* at II.943 and 944; at II.411 and 412 the sequence of letters

---

[31] II.197, 227; III.597, 1034; IV.66, 103, 277, 869; V.1259, 1301; VI.2, 237, 368, 639, 718, 747, 762, 787, 823, 858, 1059, 1139, 1165, 1167.

[32] In section (ii) I will say more about this alteration.

[33] The complete list of complete added verses is: I.364–8 (10^r; 5 in three lines), 549–50 (15^r; 2 in one line), 836–7 (22^r; 2 in one line), 1022–3 (27^r; 2 in one line); II.257–63 (36^r; 7 in four lines), 410–12 (40^r; 2 + 1 word in one line), 883–6 (51^r; 4 in two lines), 943–4 (54^r; 2 in one line).

[34] Therefore Woltjer (1881b, 779), Chatelain (1908, III col. 2, IV col. 1), Diels (XIII), Leonard and Smith (89), Büchner (XIII), De Meyier (1973, 66), Cini (1976, 147), Reynolds and Wilson (1991, 102), Ganz (1996, 93 and 97), Flores (*app. crit. ad loc.*) and Munk Olsen (2009, IV 295) were incorrect to state that gaps were left by O. Cf. also Heinsius' note on the flyleaf ([2]^v) of Trinity College Cambridge Adv. d 13 3 (cf. Appendix V, n. 11): 'In A [= O] plurimae erant lacunae, quae postea manu recentiore[m] litera longobardica ante sexcentos circiter annos exarata magnam partem erant suppleta.'

[35] This figure excludes the addition of *acerbum* at the close of II.410.

elem occurs in *elementis*, which is similar to *mele* in 412. At I.549–50 and II.883–6, by contrast, the chance omission of one and two verses respectively seems the most probable explanation. We shall return briefly to these additions in the following section.

As regards the remaining large number of corrections which do not involve erasure of any sort, their range typically concerns the addition of one to three letters, although in a few instances words were added to the text *in toto*.[36] For further analysis, we must turn to consider D's *modus operandi*.

(ii) The method of D's alterations

Two questions now present themselves: to what extent did D work *ope ingeni*? And, in instances where he worked *ope codicis*, what was the nature of the manuscript used? We must first lay out the figures (see Table 6). If we disregard the 136 merely orthographical alterations, the following number of corrections were made by D, with these levels of success.

From the above figures we can see that Book VI remains the book by far the most commonly altered by D, containing more corrections than the first four combined, and over twice as many as the second most altered, Book V. There is remarkable constancy in the success

Table 6

Book	Number of alterations	Number correct (%)	Number differing from Q(S) (%)
I	53	40 (75.5%)	24 (45.3%)
II	43	35 (81.4%)	14 (32.6%)
III	56	38 (67.9%)	25 (44.6%)
IV	58	46 (79.3%)	30 (51.7%)
V	100	76 (76.0%)	46 (46.0%)
VI	239	197 (82.4%)	102 (42.7%)
Total	549	432 (78.7%)	241 (43.9%)

[36] Cf. n. 22 above; most words were supplied *in textu* but the four cases at IV.244, VI.241, 644 and 1117 were added in the margin.

rate of D's alterations, ranging in each book between 67.9 per cent (in Book III) and 82.4 per cent in Book VI; his average hit rate of almost 79 per cent is remarkably good in a text as difficult to tackle as *DRN* in its battered Carolingian dress. So what should be made of the source of D's alterations? How does he come to make, in the 549 alterations considered above, no fewer than 117 (21 per cent) mistaken corrections? Further, how do almost half (44 per cent) of his corrections differ from the reading of ψ (QS)?[37]

The answer to these questions can easily be found. First, it can be said with certainty from the instances where D provides multiple lines in his corrections, after O had accidentally skipped over one or more verses, that he had access to a manuscript that contained these verses: given that these supplied lines agree with Q(S), they cannot be of his own invention. Furthermore, the level of accuracy with which D recorded these verses makes impossible the notion that he was working by memory from previous knowledge of another manuscript of the text; clearly, then, a manuscript stood alongside him as he worked through O. Since there is no need to posit that D read carefully through O more than once (for at no point did he emend or alter his own corrections), we should work with the provisional hypothesis that, where he made an alteration to the text which is also found in Q(S), or at least one of them, that is, in 308 (56.1 per cent) of the alterations tabulated above, he drew this correction from his manuscript source, one that was clearly related closely to our extant ninth-century manuscripts. The fact that this manuscript was a near relation to these codices is proven by those instances where D altered the text transmitted in O to an (often manifestly) incorrect reading, which is likewise transmitted by Q(S); the chance of a coincidentally wrong emendation being made is most unlikely. I collect the more striking instances in the list below, with an

---

[37] The work of D was treated very briefly, and without verbal analysis, by Bitterlich-Willmann (1951, Chapter H, 53–5), where he asserted (54) that D made use of the archetype. He also reported that 89 per cent of D's corrections agree with P [= π], only 57 per cent with Q; my figures for the coincidence of significant errors with Q(S), based on many more instances, is 55.9 per cent. Bitterlich-Willmann therefore conceded (55) that the high level of agreement between the work of D and the readings of P could imply that P is derived from O, before rejecting this possibility on trivial grounds.

asterisk marking the few cases where the mistaken correction could possibly have been made independently:

I.120 *praeterea* in *praetereat* (QS) mut. (pro *praeterea* O)

I.634 aliquot uerbis erasis add. *quas* (QS) *res quaeq: geruntur* (pro *quae* Marulli)

II.79 maiore uersus parte erasa add. *cursores uita* (QS) *lampada tradunt* (pro *uitai* Italorum)

*II.216 *abemus* in *habemus* (QS) mut. (pro *auemus* Q²)

II.313 maiore uersus parte erasa add. *natura iacet quapropter ubi ipsum* (QS; pro *ipsa* Gifani)

*II.613 *r* super *obes* (i.e. *orbes* Q) perperam sscr. (pro *orbem* Pontani)

III.289 *feruescat* in *feruescit* (QS) mut. (pro *feruescit* BFC)

III.596 poster. uersus dimid. eraso add. *cadere omnia membra* (QS; uoce ultima deficiente, forte *colore* Winckelmann)

III.941 *offens///* in *offensost* (Q) mut. (pro *offensast* Italorum aut *offensust* Lachmann)

III.960 *dicere* in *discere* (Q) mut. (pro *discedere* L)

III.1073 *aeternitatem corporis* in *aeterni temporis* (Q) mut. (pro *temporis aeterni* Italorum quorumdam)

IV.545 *nectitortis* in *nete tortis* (Q) mut. (locus nondum sanatus)

IV.1124 *uicillans* in *uigillans* (Q) mut. (pro *uacillans* Marulli)

*IV.1200 *sallentem* in *fallentem* mut. (pro *salientum* Marulli)

V.533 *pedetem* in *pedetemti* (Q) mut. (pro *pedetemptim* L)

*V.723 *donique* in *denique* (Q) mut. (pro *donique* O)[38]

V.1141 *recidit* in *recidat* (Q) mut. (pro *redibat* F)

*V.1253 *altis* in *altas* (Q) mut. (pro *altis* O^a.c.)

*V.1259 *capite* in *capiti* (Q) mut. (pro *capti* F)

V.1429 *itque* in *idque* (Q) mut. (post *plebe lata mens*, pro *plebeia tamen sit quae* F)

*VI.290 *concussas* in *concussus* (Q) mut. (pro *concussu* Q²)

VI.524 *in/e* (*ime* a.c.?) in *inte* (Q) mut. (pro *inter* L)[39]

VI.604 *subdit* in *subdita* (Q) mut. (pro *subdit* ^a.c.)

VI.747 *egri* in *ecri* mut. (QS) (pro *acri* Salmasi)

VI.1165 *iotius* in *totius* (Q : *iocius* S) mut. (pro *potius* Marulli)

The foregoing twenty-five coincidences with the incorrect readings of Q(S) show conclusively that D depended upon a manuscript closely related to them. The most economical explanation of this fact, given that he worked prior to the creation of QS

---

[38] The transmitted *donique* is unchanged at II.1116.

[39] *inte* (for *intus*) is unchanged at II.716.

(and perhaps even before ψ) is simply that D had access to the very exemplar of O, the archetype of the tradition (Ω), which allowed him to make corrections to the considerable extent he did. It is important to note, however, that D restores only verses omitted by O but attested in QS, that is, D could not restore any verses that were missing in the archetype. There is thus no good reason to suppose that D ever had access to any manuscript other than the archetype, and, given that he necessarily worked soon after the production of O, it is probable that he worked in the same place as the archetype's home, where O was presumably copied.[40] From the uneven nature of the work, it also seems an obvious inference that D was not beholden to work through O so as to implement all correct readings of the archetype, with the result that Q(S) still often transmits correct readings against O; had he done his work fully, ψ (i.e. QS) would practically have no stemmatic import.[41] The list above, therefore, can also be read in reverse as a selection of the more notable errors made by the original scribe(s) of O: at III.1073, for instance, we must assume that O's eye saw the run of letters *aeternitem* as the legitimate form *aeternitatem* but nevertheless came to write *temporis* in full after this word. To return to D's use of the archetype, brief consideration of the more bizarre of these corrections – the meaningless *praetereat* (I.120), the nonsensical and unmetrical *discere* at III.960, the non-existent *uigillans* (IV.1124), *pedetemti* (V.533) and *ecri* (VI.747) – underlines the extent to which D was prepared to follow the *ipsissima uerba* of Ω, even perhaps against his better judgment. At II.79, III.596, 960, 1073,

---

[40] If there was a second manuscript alongside D as well as the archetype, it would presumably have been an apograph of Ω and thus without value (unless Ω was not in view and Oψ differed in their reading); that D had access to a second, unrelated Lucretian manuscript is extremely improbable for such a rare text.

[41] Further support for positing the archetype Ω as D's source is provided by the fact that he was able neither to complete the unfinished lines at I.1068–75 (alongside which he may have added the single marginal points himself) nor to supply the omitted verses I.1094–1101; if his source was not the archetype or a descendant of this manuscript, it would certainly have had these lines and D would have delighted in adding them. As it was, the archetype was the very manuscript that suffered damage and the loss of most of these lines, and D seemingly felt no greater confidence than O in attempting to transcribe what was illegible. See Appendix IV for the claim (after Goold (1958) 25) that this corruption was on facing pages.

VI.524 and 1165 the resultant verse is metrically deficient, a matter hardly beyond the ken of D.

Beyond these twenty-five instances, however, D is also wrong in another ninety-two cases. The nature of these mistaken alterations, however, more naturally suggests his working *ope ingeni* than from any given codex; since they often differ markedly from the reading of ψ, as reconstructed from Q(S), the archetype is an improbable source for his work. D made at least five alterations that show a misunderstanding of the syntax,[42] sixteen that are unmetrical,[43] and six that involve the mistaken replacing of forms of *aueo* (sometimes corrupted to *abeo*) with those of *habeo*;[44] in two cases a rare word was substituted for a commoner alternative;[45] the remaining changes were understandable alterations of words or terminations,[46] save for the substitution of *opturet* for the inappropriate *obduret* at IV.869, *infandum* for *infantum* at V.810, and the three cases which merit further consideration: I.486, II.227 and VI.526*cap*. To take the last of this trio first, we find *de arquo* altered to *de arci*, presumably by a confusion of *arcus* and *arx* in correcting *-qu-* to *-c-* according to classical orthography, with the result that *arci* (evidently considered a valid ablative form by D based upon his corrections elsewhere in the work) appeared in lieu of *arcu* or *arco*. The alteration by D of *arqui* to *arci* in the following line could be conceived as a possessive dative rather than a genitive. As regards the change of *stinguere* to the non-existent *stringuere* at I.486, it is true that the former is attested only in Cicero[47] outside Lucretius, but the three other instances where the latter employed this verb are left unchanged (I.666, II.828, IV.1098 (transmitted as *tinguere*)); even if *stringuere* was

[42] II.233, IV.1170, V.727, VI.225*cap*., 1195.
[43] I.857, 1061; IV.882; V.406, 418, 609, 995, 1008, 1145; VI.296, 324, 492, 694, 718, 721, 858.
[44] II.216, 265; III.6, 957, 1082, 1083.
[45] *adsuetis* for the Lucretian ἅπαξ *adsuctis* at IV.1194, and *frugiferos* for *frugiparos* at VI.1, attested in Lucretius and Avienus alone. At VI.237, the incorrect *tellens* (probably in lieu of *pollens*, conjectured by Lambinus) was replaced by the closest Latin word *tollens*, regardless of its making no sense.
[46] The *prima facie* strange alteration of the correct *hirundo* to *herundo* at III.6 reflects the spelling as attested in late-antique and early mediaeval Latin works, such as those of Agroecius, Gregory the Great and Rather of Verona.
[47] *Arat.* 133, inc. fr. 1.

thought to be a bye-form of *stringere*, the resultant sense would be inappropriate. Finally, at II.227, we must consider the bizarre reading *ita plag* (*a plag* in ras.). The most natural explanation for this state of affairs, given that *plaga* occurs forty-nine times elsewhere in *DRN* and has its termination altered only once, is that the transmitted *plagis* (reconstructed on the basis of its appearance in QS) was correctly deemed to be corrupt, and D erased the word, perhaps accidentally removing the *a* of *ita* in the process, and restored *plag* (and the *a* of *ita*) before checking his exemplar for the correct reading. On seeing that it (presumably) also offered *ita plagis*, he restored the letters *ita plag* but refrained from entering what he deemed to be the correct reading until he had given further thought to the correction. It seems that, whether he pondered the problem at length or not, an opportunity never came for him to complete the correction.

As regards the 160 (29.1 per cent) correct alterations that are not attested in Q(S), and therefore quite probably not in Ω, their distribution is as follows: I: 16; II: 10; III: 14; IV: 20; V: 30; VI: 70.[48] Once more the final book reaps by far the greatest rewards from D's mind: this particular interest in Book VI probably springs from Dungal's evident specialism in meteorological matters (cf. (iii) below). The great majority of these corrections should be considered the independent work of D rather than readings drawn from Ω but corrupted by ψ (or Q/S). For the most part, however, these corrections are very simple applications of a reader's intelligence and would rarely have required external aid. We have seen that D was often (i.e. 117 times) incorrect in his work, however, and could not be guaranteed to restore correct metre or sense. In only ten instances do the corrections of D show real ingenuity on his part;[49] most noteworthy among these are the following three corrections: I.352 *radicibus imis* for *radicimus* (QS), 357 *fieri* for the erased *ualerent* (QS), VI.512 *urget et e supero premit* for *urgite super oprimit* (Q). The first may have

---

[48] The figures for a correct emendation *ope ingeni* per lines for each book are: I: 69.8; II: 117.4; III: 78.1; IV: 64.4; V: 48.6; VI: 18.4. These figures do not include mere orthographical changes.
[49] I.321, 352, 357, 668; II.827; III.236; V.1416; VI.122, 512, 1119.

been encouraged by the recurrence of *radicibus ... ab imis* at VI.141, or could rather be a genuinely intelligent correction of the unmetrical and unmeaning *radicimus*. The correction of the text at VI.512, transmitted identically by Q, shows an impressive ability to redivide words, restore Lucretian idiom (for *e(x) supero* is only attested in three instances elsewhere – all Lucretian – in classical Latin) and repair the metre. Most impressive, however, is the correction made at I.357–8:

> quod nisi inania sint, qua possent corpora quaeque
> transire, haud ulla fieri ratione uideres
> (fieri ratione uideres *in ras*. D : ualerent r. u. QS)

There seems little doubt that D's correction of *fieri* for the impossible *ualerent* is correct. Given that no trace of *fieri* appears to have stood in ψ, and therefore probably did not stand in the text of Ω, we may suppose that the emendation is solely the work of D. Close reading of *DRN* would suggest the insertion of *fieri* (cf. I.214, II.701, 710, III.182, IV.751, 773). We should assume, I think, that D noticed that *ualerent* was impossible in both syntax and metre, and that he was sufficiently confident that *fieri* was the desired word to replace it. Almost all editors have believed D to be right, although there have been varied opinions as to the origin of *ualerent*. Since there is no convincing evidence of authorial variants in the tradition (from which D could have found *fieri* as a marginal variant in the archetype), the most natural explanation is that one branch of the Lucretian tradition came to close 357 with *ualeret* in the stead of *uideres*; this came to be written as a supralinear variant and, perhaps under the influence of *possent* in the preceding verse, a plural form was inserted into 357, duly ousting the correct *fieri*.

To close the discussion of D's corrections, we may consider briefly a number of cases where we find the probable combination of the use of both Ω and his own intelligence. At I.668, the incorrect *amor* has been corrected, on the basis of the nonsensical *arbor* (ψ), to the appropriate *ardor*; it is alternatively possible that the archetype correctly read *ardor*, and that this was corrupted to the more common noun by ψ. At IV.202, the unmetrical and unmeaning *diffunderes esse* was corrected to *diffundere sese*, perhaps on the basis of *defundere sese* (Q and possibly Ω?). At VI.241, O had missed the word transmitted as *igna* in the archetype, which was duly copied by Q from ψ; D noticed this omission but simultaneously corrected the word to one appropriate in sense: although his *ligna* is Lucretian and restores sense, the collocation *tigna trabesque*, also attested at II.192 and 196, suggests that *tigna* (Lambinus) is much more probable. Finally, at VI.344, *regionem* in O is corrected to *e regione*, perhaps on the basis of the archetype's *e regionem*, as found in Q. It may well therefore be the case that in several other instances where D's corrections differ from the reading of Q(S), they were prompted by the reading of the archetype, which was more apposite than the transmitted reading in O, but duly improved with a view to sense, metre and Lucretian style.

(iii)   The identification of D

The first discussion of these frequent and intelligent corrections in O came with Lachmann (5), who attributed them to a *corrector Saxo* (or sometimes *Hibernicus*), a name regularly repeated by editors until 1965, when Bischoff reported his view that the Irish scholar Dungal,[50] successor to Alcuin as the head of the so-called 'Palace School' of Charlemagne, lay behind them (see n. 4 above). Bischoff's attribution, on the basis of comparison with books annotated and donated by Dungal to the library at Bobbio, has not been seriously challenged and no other plausible candidate has been suggested to date.[51] Although Dungal need not have been in the very highest echelons of the Carolingian court, he must have been of sufficient standing to be the first to correct, often in a most invasive fashion, a new and most lavishly produced manuscript of an especially rare text.[52] The corrections *ex ope ingeni* reveal an

---

[50] As many as four different Dungals have been posited as figures active in the mediaeval period: one of St Denis, one of Bobbio and Pavia, one linked with Sedulius Scottus (all of the early ninth century), and a Dungal of Bobbio flourishing in the eleventh century; I follow the *communis opinio*, espoused by, e.g., Bischoff (*passim*), Collura (1965), Ferrari (1972) and Vezin (1982), that all these Dungals were one and the same man.

[51] Savage (1958, 228–31) suggested that John Scottus Eriugena (*c.* 815–77) made these annotations, but this identification was based upon tentative reasons that evaporate on closer inspection.

[52] In correcting O, as seems highly probable, from Ω itself, we have seen that Dungal worked with varying degrees of care and thoroughness: he may well have been in a

accomplished Latinist with the ability to understand rare Latin words and forms (note, for instance, the restoration of a passive infinitive in *-ier* at III.443). Ferrari (1972, 38 with tav. III), in an admirable survey of the life and work of Dungal, did not unearth any specific problem of location or chronology with Bischoff's assertion that he worked on the manuscript. From the late eighth century, Dungal, the nature and place of whose own education are unknown, was operating in northern France, and in the early ninth century (if not earlier) he worked as a *reclusus* at St Denis near Paris. He was transferred to serve as a teacher at the monastery in Pavia in 825 before his death around 834 at Bobbio, to where he retired later and to whose monastery he donated books he had conveyed from France. We need only posit, therefore, that somewhere in the court of Charlemagne, probably St Denis or perhaps Metz, D was given the chance in the first quarter of the ninth century to correct O, with simultaneous access to its exemplar (Ω). That D had access to the exemplar implies, but need not mean, that he worked very soon after the copying of O, which would explain why so few corrections in the hand(s) of O (see n. 2 above) occur throughout the text.[53]

It is interesting to observe that D wrote to Charlemagne in 811 an erudite 'letter' on the double solar eclipse of 810,[54] which, although it does not mention or cite Lucretius explicitly, would certainly have profited from reading him (V.751–79). It is clear from this letter that D had remarkable expertise in cosmology and meteorology, a fact which would help to explain his especial interest in reading and correcting Book VI of *DRN*, and to a lesser extent Book V (see Tables 5 and 6 above). With all of this favourable context, and given the striking similarity of hands unearthed by Bischoff, it seems highly probable that D was the first major corrector in O. Accordingly, some appropriately personal siglum can be used by future Lucretian editors instead of O^s or O^1; if O, or $O^{a.c.}$, is to be used of the uncorrected text hand, 'O^D' (if not the full name of Dungal) should

position where his intellectual standing meant that his work was not submitted to or inspected by a higher authority.

[53] Since, however, Dungal's hand differs so clearly from Carolingian minuscule, I think it safer to suppose that Dungal did not himself supervise the creation of O: if the scribe(s) were at his side, why not have them restore omitted verses?

[54] *MGH Ep.* IV *Kar. Aevi* II, 570–8.

signify his emendations, that is, changes apparently not in Ω; in cases where D has merely restored the reading of Ω, an apparatus need not record the *lectio singularis* of O's error, although a truly full apparatus could record something like 'Ω (O^Dψ)'.[55]

(B) The marginal punctuation in O: the work of the Annotator

Often throughout the text of O an early hand has added in the margin either three dots in the form of an upright triangle (which I shall call a 'triangular point') or two dots akin to a colon.[56] This section will analyse the distribution and function of these instances in full and offer a suggestion as to the circumstances of their origin. There has been almost no discussion of these marks to date,[57] which is unfortunate, as they provide interesting evidence of an early critical reading of the whole text.

In total, there are 177 instances of marginal marks in O, the majority being triangular points,[58] but cola also occur (particularly in the final two books)[59] and on one occasion (IV.537) a single dot

---

[55] I am confident that the great majority of citations I have ascribed to D have been made by his hand. A set of corrections involving a *v*-shaped *u* being added above the text (I.29, 87, 119, 393, 404, 450 (gloss.), 467, 567, 583, 615, 643, 818) have been ascribed previously to Dungal but they are rather the work of the Glossator, O³ (on whom see section D below): at I.651 D corrected the text to *langidior*, as found in Ω, the necessary *u* being added later by O³. The alteration at V.743 of *aeuom* to *aeuam* of the archetype (for *Euan*) was made by the original scribe; the corrections at V.172 and 884 are the work of Dungal.

[56] Throughout this section I shall refer to the author of these marks as the 'Annotator' and the use of three dots as a 'triangular point'; given that this figure does not aim to correct the text, the assignation of ordinal numbers to 'O' should not include him.

[57] Chatelain (1908, III col. l) recorded: 'non raro tria puncta in formam trianguli apposuit in margine corrector quidam quoties metrica vel sensu claudicante versum non intellegebat. Idem est quod alii signo q̄ (quaerendum) vel ⏑ (quod in Floriacensibus occurrit) notare solebant. Tria puncta vide fol. 133 (ante versum 1, 476) ... [then thirty-three further instances given]. Aliquando etiam duo puncta (:) eundem sensum habere videntur. Cf. fol. 127ʳ 5.211 [then twenty-two further instances given].' Over one hundred instances were overlooked by Chatelain. Bitterlich-Willmann (1951, 57) briefly stated that the marks occur 167 times (a figure not further explained) but attempted no analysis. The marks were also mentioned but not studied by Ganz (1996, 95–6), whose attribution of them to D cannot be correct, as will be seen. Instances of the marks can be seen in both Plates II and III.

[58] The occasional employment of points after *capitula* (and lines wrongly treated as *capitula*) in the hand of O (e.g. at II.94) is a distinct flourish that has no bearing on the current investigation.

[59] The two pairs of adjacent dots marking the transposition of *uiscera* and *per uenas* at III.691 could also belong to the same hand, if not Dungal.

(B) The marginal punctuation in O

Table 7

Book	Instances	Lines per instance
I	18	62.1[*]
II	38	30.9
III	17	64.4
IV	19	67.7
V	27	54.0
VI	58	22.2
Total	177	41.9

[*] This figure is reduced to 35.6 if calculated from I.476, where these marks begin.

(see Table 7).[60] With only three exceptions (II.646*cap.*, III.310, V.619), these marks always appear in the right-hand margin on both recto and verso; in the three anomalous instances the triangular point is placed in the left-hand margin. Although they do not begin to appear in the margin until 13[r] (alongside I.476),[61] the distribution between books is thereafter relatively even.

The only remarkable point from these figures is the sheer predominance of the notations in Book VI, which contains a third of the total; this is doubtless linked with the fact that the book is the poem's most corrupt (see n. 10 above): we may also note their comparative regularity in Book II, the second most corrupt book but that least altered by Dungal.

We now turn to the full list of instances, from which it is clear that the primary reason for correction was faulty metre. Indeed, of the 177 cases, only sixteen (9 per cent) stand alongside lines that scan. One other reason appears to have motivated the Annotator's marginal marks: words of doubtful Latinity (such as ἅπαξ εἰρημένα) or false Latinity (through genuine corruption or the Annotator's ignorance). Only in three cases did the actual

---

[60] Ninety triangles in Books I–IV except II.167 (colon) and IV.357 (single dot); twenty-seven cola in Book V; eighteen triangles in Book VI (VI.83–385 and VI.701), otherwise forty cola (VI.10 and VI.401ff.)

[61] For the likelihood of the same hand adding analogous annotations earlier in the work in the text block itself, see the close of this section.

sense of the line seemingly prompt annotation. Of course, more than one of these faults often coexist in the same line; I have tended in such instances to regard the metrical defect as the primary motivation for the mark. For a full list of these annotations, see Appendix III.[62]

We may first note that the rather distinct distribution of triangular points and cola (see n. 60) nevertheless suggests that they come from the hand of a single annotator: although the colon comes to be used predominantly in Books V–VI (and is the only symbol employed in V), it was already used anomalously at II.167; likewise, during the spate of cola in V–VI, a run of triangular points occurs between VI.83 and 385 and in a single instance at VI.701. It is much more economical to posit a single annotator who occasionally changed his practice in different phases of his reading without conscious purpose than a pair of annotators who sometimes did a few lines' work (whence the anomalies at II.167 between 166 and 184, and VI.701 between 500 and 710). If we equate the significance of the triangular points and cola (and the unique single dot at IV.537),[63] we may note that the marks appear to have no more specific force than 'this verse is problematic and presumably corrupt'. The use of the triangular point and colon is found in other Carolingian manuscripts to serve a role analogous to the commoner *R(equire(ndum))* or *Q(uaere(ndum))* (see n. 57 above).[64] In a text as difficult as *DRN*, transmitted neither with fidelity nor with surviving commentaries and/or *scholia* to protect the text, it was easiest for a Carolingian scholar to spot metrical errors, followed in difficulty by locating apparently non-Latinate words; to find actual errors in the syntax (or logic) would have required a very close and accomplished reader.

---

[62] A more detailed version of this list appears online at www.cambridge.org/butterfield.

[63] I disregard III.855, where three horizontal dots appear after *materia* (for *materiai*) and a single dot occurs slightly into the margin but is too far left to be classed as a purposeful mark.

[64] Lindsay and Lehmann (1925, 36) recorded that the colon as well as the triangular point was used in CLM 8105 (Aug. *De Genesi ad litteram*, saec. X); CLM 8104 (Greg. *Moralia*, saec. X) and 8111 (Hrab. *In Iud. et Ruth*, saec. IX) contain the marginal triangular point alone. That the mark is found in other Mainz manuscripts suggests that O could have moved there in the ninth century (cf. Chapter 1, pp. 7–8).

(B) The marginal punctuation in O

Evidently the Annotator was a relatively competent metrician. Although a very large number of unmetrical lines were left unmarked (e.g. in the first one hundred lines of Book II, some fourteen verses that do not scan are unmarked), he had a keen eye for noticing metrical defects, and in the great majority of instances he correctly recorded a genuine fault in a line. However, as well as not being comprehensive in his coverage, he was also prone to error, for in some instances he was unaware of the correct prosody of rare words, such as the trochaic *indu* (II.1096), *noenu* (III.199, IV.712) and *endo* (VI.890); no doubt he was working with a prosodic rule that, excluding certain common pyrrhic words, all instances of final *-o* and *-u* should be long. Occasionally the mistaken division of words seems to have led the Annotator wrongly to suspect a metrical fault: *animensum* (I.957), *uaporis* (II.150), *inclam &* (III.953) and *dexteraea* (IV.313 (337)).[65]

In other instances the Annotator appears to have been vexed by words of dubious Latinity, often correctly: *omnus* (I.966), *plag* (II.227), *pletate* (II.1170), *acortalibus* (or *a cortalibus*) (VI.10), *perueneret* (VI.87), *ungipiti* (VI.226), *renouara* (VI.1076), *cultaetris* (VI.1205), *apiscit* (VI.1235). Elsewhere, however, it appears that the sheer rarity of a word employed by Lucretius wrongly induced him to suspect corruption: *illim* (III.881),[66] the ἅπαξ *unorsum* (IV.262),[67] *crepitacillis* (V.229),[68] the ἅπαξ *austra* (V.516).[69] With *superadereddere* (VI.855) and *perproque* (VI.1264), Lucretius' loose postposition and tmesis of prepositions instead left him baffled. In one instance the abbreviation for *esse* appears to have foxed him (VI.770), but not at III.41 (which he may have missed, the first annotation in Book III being at 151); at I.562 $\overline{qm}$ for *quoniam* could have prompted the

---

[65] Perhaps also *resigniscribant* at V.953, discussed below.

[66] *illim* is found primarily in the scenic poets but also eight times in Cicero and once in Gellius.

[67] The uncontracted *uniuorsum* occurs elsewhere only twice in Terence.

[68] The noun *crepitacillum*, 'rattle', is found elsewhere only in the *titulus* of Mart. XIV.54; *crepitaculum* is found at Quint. IX.4.67 and Apul. *Met.* XI.4.8.

[69] It is unclear whether at IV.1028 the sigmatic ecthlipsis of *corporis fundunt* (a prosodic feature not marked as problematic elsewhere) or the comparative rarity of *saccatus* (once in Scribonius Largus, Manilius, Seneca the Younger and Serenus, thrice in Pliny the Elder) prompted the annotation.

annotation. On two occasions he failed to understand words of Greek origin: <a>egocerotis (= αἰγοκέρωτος) at V.615 and Scaptensula (= Σκαπτὴ Ὕλη) at VI.810. As regards the remarkable writing of the capitulum at II.646 in Greek (ΤΟΜΔΚΔΡΙΟΝ ΚΑΙΑ ΦΘΑΡΤΟΝ),[70] a slight variant of the triangular point (apparently bearing a dot within it)[71] occurs in the left-hand margin. Its anomalous placing in this margin appears to indicate more worry or surprise at the state of the heading than the bold assertion of error; perhaps it is akin to Graecum est: legi non potest. Given that the Annotator almost certainly lacked any knowledge of Greek, this rather tentative response is not surprising.

Consideration should at this point be given to the two other instances of annotation in the left margins (III.310 and V.619), both triangular points. With III.310 it is quite possible that the line was perceived to possess no verbal or metrical error (and there is no sign of erasure or correction); in the latter case there likewise seems no obvious reason for the mark. Without any obvious solution, I suggest that the use of the left-margin annotation was variable but avoided asserting that the line was in error: at II.646cap. it served to flag the anomalous appearance of Greek in the manuscript; at III.310 it may highlight the interest of the verse in question (nec radicitus euelli mala posse putandumst), the idea that evil traits in some people's characters cannot be erased being of some interest to the mind of a Christian monk (radicitus does not seem a sufficiently rare word to merit concern);[72] at V.619 (annua sol in quo consumit tempora cursu), the verse could have been highlighted because it seemed to be similar to, but was different in transmission from, V.692 (ann<u>a sol in q<u>o contudit tempora serpens). Accordingly,

---

[70] See Chapter 3, n. 75.

[71] It is possible that a single dot was initially placed in the left-hand margin and then subsequently expanded by the usual triangular point around it, a mark attested elsewhere in O.

[72] I may here mention the unique annotation that occurs in the margin alongside I.483, namely the NT ligature, which serves no corrective purpose but rather stands for imperatival nota. This siglum, not recorded by scholars previously, is of some interest, since it is associated with Carolingian scholars (particularly Lupus of Ferrières and Heiric of Auxerre). It here signals the beginning of the argument about the solidity and indestructibility of atoms.

the extraordinary marking of a verse in the left margin served various purposes less definitive than flagging up textual error.

Finally, it is exceptionally rare for a verse to have been highlighted apparently on the ground of dubious sense alone.[73] There seem to be only two instances where the sense of the verse was the primary reason for the Annotator's worry, both in the same part of the work:

> V.953: the sense of *scribant* for *scibant* (if not metre / Latinity of *resigniscribant* wrongly divided *rĕsigni(*s*) ...)?
> V.980: the sense of *nedifidere* for *nec diffidere*?

That these two instances occur close together may suggest a spell of particular interest on the Annotator's part, the account of primitive man (V.925ff.) perhaps appealing to him sufficiently to notice dubious matters of sense (although obvious instances such as V.947, 970, 976 and 977 remain unmarked). This may tie in with the fact that Books V–VI appear to have been long-standing favourites in the late-antique and early mediaeval periods, particularly to those with an interest in astronomical affairs (cf. the uneven spread of D's corrections above). For the majority of the text, however, the Annotator appears to have been unconcerned about seeking out errors in logic, grammar or sense, or indeed the discovery of lacunae.

Therefore only one of the 174 right-margin annotations recorded above frustrates this taxonomy, namely the appearance of the mark alongside V.320, a verse transmitted faithfully and without linguistic or prosodic irregularity. Chatelain's facsimile may suggest that erasure has occurred around the close of *memorant*, but no editor has recorded any such detail, and having twice inspected this passage in O by autopsy I can state confidently that no change to the text has occurred. There is, however, a supralinear trace of an *a*, and what seems an *a* (or *o*) with a circumflex above it, above the ending of *memorant*; it may well be that a matter of sense was here highlighted, the Annotator being

---

[73] Chatelain's statement (n. 57 above) is therefore misleading in implying that errors of sense are recorded as commonly as those of metre.

confused about the change of number in the collocation *memorant recipitque*, taking the preceding *quidam* as singular.

We must now examine the relationship of these marginal annotations to the corrections made in the text by D and O^2. The matter is at first sight difficult to resolve, for there are no means of discerning in palaeographical or codicological terms when such minute triangular points or cola would have been added (beyond the observation that similar marks occur in other ninth- and tenth-century manuscripts: see n. 64 above). However, careful examination of their deployment can shed some light on their origin. Of prime importance are the following two facts: (i) both D and O^2 make corrections to the text in places where no marginal note exists; (ii) many marginal annotations stand alongside faulty verses that did not enjoy any attempt at correction, even when the required correction was remarkably obvious to anyone with knowledge of metre and Latin. Such a fact appears to make these annotations distinct from the work of both D and O^2, or at least their spells of inserting explicit corrections.

The primary clue to the problem is given at II.227 (treated above), where the original verse presumably ended with the metrical and Latinate (but ungrammatical) *plagis*. According to the principles of the Annotator elsewhere, this grammatical anomaly would not have been a sufficiently obvious reason for him to mark an error in the verse. Furthermore, there is no other cause elsewhere in the line for metrical or lexical concern. Rather, the fact that D completely erased *plagis* at the close of the line and replaced it – most puzzlingly – with the unlatinate and unmetrical *plag* seems instead to have served as the basis for the Annotator's marking a problem. Such an instance therefore demonstrates that the marginal annotations occurred after D's work; this fact is corroborated by my own assignation of corrections in O, as I find no instance in which the mark of the Annotator concerns the text in its state before correction by D. In the four other instances where D corrected a verse by which the Annotator's mark stands (II.197, VI.153, 226, 803), a signal fault remains in the line which presumably prompted the subsequent mark. Accordingly, there is no evidence that D worked after the Annotator but firm evidence that he preceded him.[74]

In four instances (IV.244, VI.241, 644, 1117) D made a correction to the verse by writing marginally the word(s) to be supplied. To mark these corrections, he placed a similar triangular point (though slightly smaller than that of the Annotator) alongside the addition and in the verse at the point where it should be added. These marks are evidently in D's hand and therefore do not form part of my discussion in this section; they may even, by contrast, have served as inspiration for the Annotator's own use of the symbol. It is also possible that the odd use of the symbol at I.544, where D had already corrected *nihil* to *nil*, is in the hand of D rather than the Annotator. These annotations are not from D at a later stage than his corrections, for in so many cases we would expect him rather to have implemented the most simple emendation (obvious even without access to the archetype, e.g. I.690 *ignem* for *iq:nem*, 843 *idem* for *iden*, 966 *omnis* for *omnus*) than leave future readers puzzled.

As it has been established that these annotations follow the work of D, it can be clearly demonstrated that they antedate the corrective work of O^2 (to which I will come presently): in seven instances the only possible problem with the verse has been removed by the work of O^2 (I.758, II.318, III.839, V.581, VI.366, 523, 820) and the Annotator could have had no other legitimate cause to signal error.[75] We are therefore left with the necessary conclusion that the Annotator's marks stand temporally between the corrections of D and O^2, not to mention O^3 (as evidenced by I.476 (*ut uid.*), 562, 759, 827) and O^4 (as evidenced by I.382).

To conclude this section I offer some more general observations about the work of the Annotator. First, it is somewhat cursory, for a great number of obvious errors in the manuscript are missed and, for no obvious reason, they only begin to appear on the recto of the thirteenth leaf (*ad* 476), nearly halfway into Book I. Nevertheless, it is possible that a few earlier marks show the

---

[74] We must therefore regard *durateus* as the source of the mark at I.476 not *trolianis*, which was presumably already corrected to *troianis* by D.

[75] It is therefore unproblematic that in eight other instances (I.984, II.291, IV.66, VI.481, 511, 524, 887, 890) the work of O^2 left uncorrected elements of the verse that could still have caused the Annotator concern.

Annotator's activity already in force: at I.50, a verse signally defective in metre, three horizontal dots stand in the line beneath *ut*, marking the deletion of this conjunction; at I.384 three similar dots stand beneath the unmetrical *initium* for *initum* (later corrected by O^3).[76] More noticeably, at I.177 a small triangular point stands above the nonsense *orcatu* (corrected to *creatur* by O^3) at the close of the verse, and at I.263 above the non-existent *allo* (altered to *alto* by O^3) for *alio*, presumably to mark both words as corrupt. Given that the first two triangular points recorded in the list above (I.476 and 544) are closer to the end of the verses than later in the manuscript, it may well be that the Annotator's practice slowly formalised as he read through O, with his mark of suspicion being placed more firmly and distinctly in the right-hand margin from the third instance (I.562) onwards, his confidence growing as he progressed. The apparently insignificant alternation of the symbol employed (triangular points and cola), combined with the failure to specify the nature of the fault or seek out a correction, also strengthens this impression. The Annotator may have been, for instance, a senior monk who was at sufficient leisure to work through the text in private although under no obligation to be consistent in his personal annotations or thorough in his work, and not at liberty to obtain and/or insert corrections from another source.[77] His working after D gives us a rough *terminus post quem* of 810–25; the following section, treating the work of O^2, will provide us with a similar *terminus ante quem*.

(C) The work of O^2

After Dungal, the most prolific figure in altering the text of Lucretius is one whose corrections are written in a Carolingian hand typical of the mid ninth century. This hand, however,

[76] The two pairs of dots that stand above *uacuum* and *inane* at I.509 probably originate from a reader (D?) who wished to mark the use of these two synonymous words in conjunction.

[77] Incidentally, I know of no reason that would rule out Hrabanus Maurus, Bishop of Mainz in 847–56, as the author of these marks: although he cited Lucretius at second hand in his *De universo* and *Excerpta* from Priscian (cf. Chapter 2, p. 91 with n. 110), his knowledge of Lucretian sigmatic ecthlipsis may stem from direct contact with the work: cf. Chapter 1, n. 15.

(C) The work of O^2

Table 8

Book	Number of alterations	Lines per alteration
I	60	18.6
II	26	45.2
III	42	26.0
IV	37	34.8
V	45	32.4
VI	63	20.4
Total	273	27.2

differs clearly from that of the initial scribe in ink and ductus, and can certainly be distinguished from D; its similarity to the Glossator (O^3) is occasionally problematic, but close inspection leaves few truly ambiguous corrections to the text, and these only in Book I. These corrections, like those of D, involve the variable employment of corrections in the text (erasure, additions, occasional sub- and superpuncts and underlinings) but are rarely as neat as the work of D. (The hand can be seen in Plate II, adding *que* at the close of I.552.) Reference will be made throughout this section to the full list of the corrections I attribute to O^2.[78]

In total, O^2 made 273 alterations to the text, distributed as shown in Table 8.

As with D, we find a somewhat uneven spread of alterations throughout the work; whereas D showed a marked increase in his activity in the final two books, and particularly in the sixth, the main scope for work by O^2 was in Books I and VI, where he averages a correction within every twenty lines. It is remarkable that O^2 was most active in the poem's least corrupt book (I) but least active in its second most corrupt book, which immediately followed (II). We may imagine that the initially close and careful attention paid to the poem by O^2 had to decrease in order for him to progress through the whole manuscript at a reasonable pace, and beyond Book I the subject matter affected his levels of

[78] A summary of this list can be found in Appendix III; a fuller version is available online at www.cambridge.org/butterfield.

interest, Book II being understandably overshadowed by books as engaging as III and VI.

As with the work of D, O²'s attempted corrections range from simple changes of letters through to the full-scale correction of words and phrases. However, the insertion of omitted verses is not a feature. An interest in mere orthographical matters is also almost non-existent, and markedly rarer than in D, for against the 25 per cent of written corrections in this genre by the latter, O² made only seven (i.e. 2.6 per cent) alterations of this type.[79] Evidently, in D's wake, O² preferred to correct errors that he deemed to be of greater import. For the most part his intervention was small-scale:[80] nonsense words were corrected to genuine words of similar letters,[81] incorrect terminations were altered,[82] and genuine Latin words were modified to others;[83] in six cases new words were added, but these are almost always of minor semantic force.[84] Although the corrector does not show any signs of great genius, he deserves credit in a number of areas. Unlike D, O² apparently had clear knowledge of the use of disyllabic -ai as a legitimate form of the archaic feminine genitive singular, as he restored the inflection on nineteen

[79] I.427, II.938, IV.586, V.351, 510, 1308, VI.905.
[80] The majority of corrections were made either by in-text alterations or the supralinear addition of letters. As with D, the alteration of initial letters of verses is particularly rare, occurring only at VI.323. Although O² shared with D a willingness to erase the original text and place corrections in its stead, rather than supralinearly or in the margin, he appears to have acted with particular care and neatness: we may note as one example of his scrupulousness that at IV.237 it was probably he who chose to correct *quia* to *qua* by erasure, even though D had already cancelled out the *i* by a subpunct.
[81] I.27, 30, 168, 264, 271, 414, 455, 528, 682, 779; II.54, 68, 657, 804, 826, 975, 977, 1116; III.73, 136, 192, 399, 430, 495, 546; IV.21, 315, 595*cap.*, 673, 696, 743, 834, 879 (*bis*), 1229, 1262; V.295, 317, 326, 381, 482, 492, 551, 554, 692 (*bis*), 742, 780*cap.*, 802, 851, 934, 935, 1001, 1072; VI.48, 88, 92, 144, 221, 260, 436, 546, 589, 673, 707, 713, 756*cap.*, 779, 811, 821, 913, 928, 929, 943, 954, 972, 976, 991, 1008, 1021, 1091, 1134.
[82] I.24, 29, 41, 84, 212, 249, 251, 283, 285, 307, 406, 415, 427, 475, 565, 586, 588, 606, 725, 758, 764, 777, 875, 877, 944, 1036, 1044; II.115, 337, 452, 466, 595, 694, 839, 840, 920, 965, 982, 1116; III.23, 97, 132, 233, 311, 357, 382, 408, 486, 564, 656, 665, 713, 730, 785, 790, 982; IV.393, 502, 844, 1055; V.26, 293, 428, 713, 765, 784, 930, 937, 946, 1055, 1150, 1244, 1336, 1392, 1456; VI.608*ind.*, 386, 411, 453, 531, 552, 679, 742, 820, 847, 913, 946, 1000, 1127, 1132, 1215.
[83] I.16, 33, 43, 99, 191, 296, 358, 384, 429, 459, 587, 777; II.318, 953, 1153; III.132, 232, 317, 375, 403, 581, 733, 764, 771, 807, 982, 985, 1056; IV.51, 53, 109, 153, 237, 486, 548, 609, 730, 935, 947, 1021, 1038; V.375, 684, 799, 930, 1393; VI.109, 220, 323, 450, 522, 536, 547, 662, 860, 874, 890, 943, 960.
[84] I.36 (*te*), II.475 (*in*), III.654 (*-que*), IV.473 (*id*), V.5 (*-que*), 136 (*in*).

(C) The work of O²

Table 9

Book	Number of alterations	Number correct (%)	Number differing from Q(S) (%)
I	59	50 (84.7%)	32 (54.2%)
II	25	19 (76.0%)	9 (36.0%)
III	42	30 (76.9%)	16 (38.1%)
IV	36	27 (75.0%)	16 (44.4%)
V	42	35 (83.3%)	24 (57.1%)
VI	62	52 (83.9%)	27 (43.5%)
Total	266	213 (80.1%)	124 (46.6%)

occasions.[85] The following alterations also show intelligence: the insertion of *te* before the mention of the addressee *dea* (= *Venus*) at I.36, *tanta* for *tam* at III.1056, the correction of *obsidit quia* to *obsiditque uias* (aided by the collocation *uias oculorum* at IV.319), the insertion of *id* between *ad* and *ipsum* to restore metre at IV.473 (perhaps aided by the fact that *id ipsum* closes I.433, IV.780, 1082), the correction of *lerneque* to *lerneaque* at V.26 (modifying *pestis Hydra*), perhaps on the basis of wider reading of classical literature,[86] and the correction of *lyclini* to the rare *lychni* at V.295 (attested in Cicero, Virgil (and thus Servius), Seneca the Younger and Statius).[87] These are, however, his most impressive corrections.

We may now turn to analyse this corrector's general success rate. Of his 273 alterations, the percentage that are correct can be tabulated as in Table 9. As with D, I disregard the seven merely orthographical changes (see n. 79).

The success rate of O² is therefore very similar to D, averaging 80 per cent against D's 79 per cent, ranging between 75 per cent

[85] I.29, 41, 84, 85, 112, 212, 249, 251, 283, 285, 307, 406, 415, 565, 586, 725; III.713; V.713, 946; at I.552, by contrast, the easy option of correcting *materiae* to *materiai* was missed, and an inappropriate second subject introduced in *materiaeque*.

[86] The adjective *Lernaeus* was used by Virgil, Propertius, Ovid and Seneca the Younger, and it modifies *Hydra* in Varro, Propertius, Silius, Hyginus and Nonius.

[87] The credit for two *prima facie* impressive emendations is greatly reduced once their context is inspected: the correction of *demine* to *de semine* at IV.1229 was prompted by the pairing *de semine* in both IV.1225 and 1227; at VI.88 the correction of *patio* (after *quo*) to *pacto* would have been helped not only by the occurrence of *quo pacto* eighteen times elsewhere in *DRN* but also by VI.384 (identical to VI.88)

(Book IV) and 84.7 per cent (Book I). The independence from Q(S) of 47 per cent is also surprisingly similar to D's 44 per cent. The question therefore arises whether we are dealing with a similar state of affairs, whether O^2 had access to a manuscript related to Q(S) or Ω itself, as had D. To tackle this question, we must again consider instances where O^2 altered the text incorrectly to a reading that is also attested in Q(S). However, here the difference with D emerges, since these cases are very rare. Of 274 alterations, only seven (2.6 per cent) are relevant:

II.694 *constet* in *constent* (S : *constant* Q) mut. (pro *constant* Q)
III.656 *animi* in *anima* (Q) mut. (pro *animai* Q^2)
III.807 *respuereictus* in *respuereiectus* (Q) mut. (pro *ictus* $O^{a.c.}$)
IV.334 *retrorursum* in *retrorsum* (Q) mut. (pro *retro rursum* $O^{a.c.}$)
IV.736 *queflunt* in *quae fluunt* (Q) mut. (pro *quae fiunt* Marulli)
IV.1021 *qui* in *quasi* (Q) mut. (pro *qui* $O^{a.c.}$)
VI.589 *dossum* in *possum* (QS) mut. (pro *pessum* Q^2)

It should first be observed that all of these corrections could have been made by O^2 alone *ex ope ingeni*, coinciding only by chance with the readings of other manuscripts related to Ω: at II.694, *constet* was naturally corrected to the plural as in V, the mistaken subjunctive (also transmitted in the identical II.724) being retained; at III.656 *anima* is the more natural noun, as this section of the work focuses upon it rather than the *animus*; at III.807 it seems that O^2, like Q, misdivided the collocation *respuereictus*, as either *respue* or *res puer* followed by *(r)eictus*, which required expansion to the participial *(r)eiectus*; at IV.334 (310) *retrorsum* is an obvious suggestion, given that adverb's appearance a little before at IV.295; at IV.736 *fluunt* is the closest Latin verb to the non-existent *flunt*; at IV.1021 *quasi* was thought to introduce the hypothetical clause more naturally than the harsh *qui* (and *ut quasi* also opens IV.1035); at VI.589 *possum* is the closest Latin verb to the non-sensical *dossum*. There is thus no compelling evidence that O^2 made any use of any manuscript when reading and correcting O. Furthermore, given the small-scale nature of his corrections, and the fact that he was still incorrect in fifty-three cases (20 per cent) (disregarding orthographical matters), we can confidently assert that all of the work of O^2 proceeded solely *ex ope ingeni*.

I here differ from several earlier commentators, in particular Lachmann (5) and Diels (XIII–XIV), who asserted that their 'corrector alter' (Lachmann) or 'O^{1}' (Diels) used another manuscript. That both editors assigned numerous corrections of D to the mass of those by O^2 and the Glossator (O^3, on whom see section D below) could have suggested some external source for his corrections, but the close inspection of corrections reveals that the facts stand otherwise. Lachmann supported his assertion by stating that many of these corrections 'aut intellectum non habent aut eodem modo in exemplari quadrato ... scripta extant' (5) but gave no instance to defend either claim; Diels (XIII–XIV) followed the same argument, offering only two examples of corrections that suggest an exemplar (which he thought was related to Q), and one of a correction too foolish to be conjectured. Yet the bases for this paltry argument were flawed: of the two examples of corrections allegedly drawn from a manuscript, at V.533 the correction *pede-temtim* was in fact made by D, and that at V.743 (*aeuom* altered to *aeuam* (for *Euan*)) should be attributed to an original scribe O (see n. 55 above). Finally, the evidence adduced by Diels that a manuscript must here lie behind the most foolish corrections was the gloss on I.411, where *ptano* was bizarrely explained as *proprium nomen* (perhaps thought to be Greek?); yet this note was by the Glossator (O^3), a product of that figure's limited intellect. And here Lachmann and Diels run out of steam. I hope to have shown above not only that the corrections of O^2 are relatively simple and unambitious (although rarely foolish), which explains their comparatively high success rate, but also that his incorrect conjectures very seldom coincide with Q(S), and then only through minor coincidences in seven cases. There is thus no compelling evidence that O^2 used any resource other than his brain to alter O. For the sake of convenience, the date at which O^2 operated will be discussed in the introduction to the following section.

(D)   The work of the Glossator (O^3)

Independently of the work of the four figures mentioned already – the scribe(s) of O themselves, Dungal, the marginal Annotator and O^2 – two separate, later strata of corrections can still be identified.

Unfortunately, the current state of evidence in this area is poor, since no Lucretian editor has troubled to distinguish these later hands from those of O^2, save for Diels, who occasionally attributed some corrections to his 'O^2', a designation that seemingly covered plural correctors from the sixteenth century onwards (Diels (XIV)) and was very rarely employed in his apparatus, and the incomplete reports of Müller. Even beyond the scope of editors, there have been very few scholars who have attempted to separate any corrections in O that are distinct from Dungal's characteristic hand.

The truly diverse state of affairs regarding the correctors in O was first touched upon by Chatelain (1908, II col. 2), although his comments do not suggest that he had a clear picture of the exact state of play. Having stated that '[c]orrectorum plurium operam agnoscere licet', he referred to at least four different correctors and could be taken to distinguish as many as seven hands: one who used subpuncts, one superpuncts, one both marks simultaneously, the Annotator of triangular points, who may or may not be the same as the individual who used cola, the writer of glosses and certain corrections, and the 'corrector Saxo' (i.e. Dungal). The corrections that, fifteen years later, Diels was certainly right to attribute to a corrector distinct from the Anglo-Saxon hand (his O^1) were presumably not distinguished by Chatelain, and instead encapsulated by his statement about (Dungal) (V, col. 1) that '[p]raeterea syllabam vel litteram passim mutavit tum recte tum perperam, morem sui temporis secutus'. Despite his profound expertise, Chatelain did not record anything more precise on these various correctors in the introduction to his facsimile. Regrettably, no further progress beyond Diels' division was made by Martin, who ignored such corrections, Bailey, who had no interest in matters of this kind, or Büchner, who merely recorded that 'O^2 est minoris pretii et recentioris aetatis' (viii). Most recently, Flores (vol. 1 (39)) used the siglum 'O^3' of corrections 'post saec. XV' but did not discuss this hand further and very rarely cited its readings in his own apparatus.

Konrad Müller is the only editor to have made concrete assertions in this difficult field. He observed (1975 edn, 313) that 'duae fere correctorum manus uersatae esse uideantur' in Books II–VI, one 'ab ipsius librarii manu non multum differ[ens]', the other being the Anglo-Saxon hand, which Müller only mentioned as possibly being Dungal in his addenda (357–8). The phrase 'non multum differt' is frustratingly vague, as it is not clear whether Müller regarded the hand of O² as originating from the approximate time in which O was written, or rather from a later hand that could emulate the script well. Further, the fact that he mentioned the hand of O² prior to Dungal's suggests that he may have regarded it as the earlier of the two correcting hands, which I have shown above to be the reverse of true chronology. As regards the first book, however, Müller wrote, again with lamentable inspecificity, that alongside these two hands 'aliae quaedam comparent aliquanto recentiores' (313). He confessed that he was not always able to distinguish these hands from one another but could separate them with confidence from the species of 'antiquae' corrections, which 'litteris fere minutioribus et nitide pictis usi sunt' in contrast to the 'grandior[es] et minus elegant[es] (interdum etiam deform[es])' letters of the later correctors that 'ipsa specie recentiorem aetatem indic[ant]' (313–14). These plural later correcting hands he proceeded to assign to the late tenth or early eleventh centuries (sometimes (315, 317) referring simply to 'circa annum millesimum'), and to one such corrector he attributed the various supralinear glosses that occur in the first book (on which see below). Although Müller never stated whether he believed there to be two or yet more later correctors, he did assert that these corrections do not progress beyond I.827, and on this point my opinion tallies with his: of the ten places in his discussion (314–16) where he explicitly attributed a correction to such a later hand, I agree in all instances but the difficult case of I.651, where I regard *disque* as an addition by the scribe. Although Müller stated that '[e]iusdem generis alia exempla sciens praetermitto', I hesitate as to whether he would have attributed, as I advocate, 110 further corrections in Book I to correctors postdating O². At the close of this section we shall return to an important theory proposed by Müller about the relationship of these corrections to the transcription of O from which the Italian tradition descends.

The later discussions of palaeographical experts have done little to advance knowledge in this field. De Meyier, in his survey of the manuscript (1973, 65–8), merely recorded that '[t]extus correctus est aliquot manibus', a comment followed by brief mention of the 'corrector Saxonicus' and an '[a]lius corrector saec. XI ut videtur'. The various tangential mentions of O by Bischoff have not tackled Müller's assertion, and his last comment on the correcting hands (2004, 50) was merely that, beyond the hand of Dungal, there are '[w]eitere Korr[ekturen] u[nd] Glossen ca. s. X², von mehr als 1 Hd. bis 22r'; this information is not particularly helpful, again referring to a plurality of hands without precision, but it implies that they stopped at 22^r (i.e. I.827). Nothing specific is said of the corrections of O² that occur throughout the manuscript. Cini, writing in the wake of Müller's article but not drawing upon the slightly revised version of the work in his 1975 edition, was not clear about the issue of later corrections: he wrote that '[a]lcune correzioni, anche sbagliate, del I libro ... sono state in realtà eseguite da alcune *manus recentiores* intervenute nell'*Oblongus* fino al v. 827 di tale libro' (1976, 150 n. 110), a statement clearly based upon Müller. Given that Cini assigned corrections not on autopsy but strictly upon the apparatus of Büchner, who did not attribute any reading whatever to his 'O²' in Book I, he was implicitly happy to regard most of the non-Dungalian corrections in that book as from one and the same hand.[88] He did observe, however, what Müller had chosen not to mention (perhaps because the reading coincided with that found in π from an early date), that the correction at I.177 seems to be of a later date (163 n. 146), although he did not offer his own dating; this correction I attribute to the Glossator, whom I will discuss presently. Cini also objected

---

[88] At 154–5 n. 117 he argued for the attribution of I.453 not to a later corrector but to his O¹ (= my O²) owing to the form of the long *i* used. Further inspection shows this conclusion to be problematic: rather, *i longa* was typically the form of the letter used by the Glossator O³ when correcting *e* (I.71, 256, 412, 438, 527, 550, 562, 613, 680). The five other cases of *i longa* in corrections throughout the manuscript are rather different: at I.725 and III.546 it is far shorter, with a sharp turn at its base; at III.311, IV.344 (which Cini chose as his sole *comparandum*) and V.930 it has a marked curl at its base, and its bar at IV.344 and V.930 runs to the right of the descender (thus looking like a modern 'J'), these last two correcting *o*. These five anomalous corrections are most probably the work of O².

(D) The work of the Glossator (O^3)

(163–4) that Müller's date for the later corrections (*c.* 1000) is apparently anterior to what he took to be the typical date assigned to his O^1, namely the eleventh century; but this is to impose a dating not accepted by Müller himself, who rather regarded these earlier corrections as being of a similar nature (and presumably period) to those of the scribe himself. Cini also complained that it is generally difficult to distinguish a later hand from the corrections of his O^1, which is occasionally true but nevertheless a hurdle that must be surmounted by the enquirer.

Finally, we may note the further important contributions to the discussion made by Reeve. In his earlier article on the Italian tradition of Lucretius (1980) no separation of correcting hands in O was attempted, nor an explicit preference for Müller's or Cini's arguments recorded (41 with n. 3). In his second article (2005), however, Reeve treated the correctors of O (157–61), offering several new observations. He first recorded (157) that O 'has corrections by at least three hands'. Having clarified the state of play regarding Dungal, he fairly stated that '[a]bout the other correctors no agreement has been reached, though editors behave as though it had' (159). He rightly objected that Diels used 'O^1' of corrections which were made 'sive a librario sive ab aequalibus correctoribus' (XLIV), and perhaps also by Otloh (on whom see below). Moving to Cini's arguments against Müller's position on the matter, Reeve stated that it is difficult to decide one way or the other about the attribution of cases such as I.453, 711 and 759, each of which Cini had briefly called into question.[89] Reeve did agree (160) with Cini that Müller's examples of corrections definitively later than O^2 are 'molto poche' but disagrees that they are 'quasi tutte di scarso rilievo'. I shall demonstrate in this section that there are very many corrections later than O^2, many of which are significant. At the close of this section we shall return to an important question posed by Reeve.

I come now to treat the glosses made in Book I and the corrections I attribute to this hand (a link explicitly recorded *en passant* by Chatelain alone). Assignation of glosses has been easy (cf. Plates I–III); that of corrections has been aided by certain

---

[89] These three corrections I attribute to O^3.

idiosyncrasies of the hand.[90] Diels was the first to record the glosses (albeit with a few omissions) in his textual appendix but offered no analysis; fifty years later Müller produced in his own edition (314) a very partial list.[91] For a complete list see Appendix III, p. 298.[92]

It will be easiest for us to consider the glosses from this hand first. There are seventy glosses, running from verse 4 (1ʳ) to 782 (21ʳ) of Book I (i.e. once every eleven verses), not to appear even once again thereafter. In all but one instance (I.722ff. *topografia* (i.e. 'here follows a topographical account')) the glosses serve to explain a given element of Lucretius' text. For the most part, these supralinear glosses explicate words deemed by the Glossator to be unusual; less often, they explain the grammar of a given passage[93] or morphological oddity,[94] or offer a more general remark on the meaning of a phrase. It is interesting that the Glossator detected that 705*cap*. was a chapter heading, duly recording '*capitulum*' in the left margin, perhaps since he lacked any means of marking the rubrication of the line with red ink.

We find a slight inconsistency between certain glosses, for in four instances (I.11, 326, 386, 660) *pro* is followed by the appropriate case if the glossed word were standing in the text; in two instances (I.383, 657), however, it is followed by the ablative, inappropriate in context; at I.206, 499 and 665 the words are indeclinable, which suggests the former type of citation. In all but one instance (if we take *ductus* as accusative plural at I.659) *i.e.* is followed by a gloss in the appropriately inflected

---

[90] These include: the use of underlining for deletion (see I.70, 119, 177, 233, 237, 372, 395, 620, 640 (repeating the deletion of *de* in *quamde*), 680, 818), not found in D or O² (who both used suprascript lines for deletion), or occasionally the strikethrough (see I.296, 769), the long descender of the *r* (*passim*), the use of the *v*-shaped *u* in smaller corrections (cf. n. 55 above), the regular use of straight-backed *d* (with only very occasional employment of the uncial form: I.403 and 711), the rising bar (from left to right) in *e*, the flick to the final leg of the *m*; *i longa* is more complicated, as it was used by two correctors (see n. 88). The ink of a gloss is very often evidently the same as that used in nearby corrections (e.g. at I.386).
[91] K. Müller (1973) 173–4 = (1975 edn) 313–14.
[92] A more detailed version of the list is available online at www.cambridge.org/butterfield.
[93] I.57 *quoue eadem*] *in quam partem*; 216 *si nulla*] scilicet *semina*; 269 *ne qua*] scilicet *ratione*; 292 *ante ruuntque*] scilicet *se*; 378 *quo*] *ad quem locum*; 509 *ea*] scilicet *natura*.
[94] I.300 *tuimur*] *a tuor uenit*; 403 *tute*] *adiectio sillabica*.

form: at I.551*cap.* (to which I will come) the foreign nature of the
word perhaps led to his anomalous use of the nominative. Such
irregularities need not worry us, for the impression given is that
these glosses were made in a relatively haphazard fashion; we may
note the uncorrected error of *pertuitate* for *perpetuitate* at 460 and
the odd use of three distinct glosses above three adjacent words at
I.747 rather than a single explanation of the phrase as a whole.

This figure's Latinity does not seem especially advanced. We may
note, for example, the glosses of simple adverbs (I.57 *quo*, 378 *quo*,
383 *unde*, 484 *qua*) and common forms: I.185 *nilo* = *nihilo*; 300
tuimur explicitly associated with *tuor*; 326 *mare* as the ablative for
mari; 499 *ades* as an alternative to *adesto*; 400 *tute*, the emphatic
form of *tu*, is explained as *adiectio sillabica* [= *syll-*], a phrase
common enough in grammarians, and used in conjunction with *tute*
by Sedulius Scottus (*In Don.* p. 34 (Löfstedt); cf. also Alcuin's use of
adiectio syllabae of the same word at *Gramm.* 871). The glosses do
not typically exhibit any wider learning or the use of other texts: the
sole exception is the gloss upon *triquetris* at I.717, which suggests
knowledge of Isidore (*Etym.* XIV.6.32 *prius autem* [sc. *Sicilia*]
Trinacria dicta propter tria ἄκρα, *id est promontoria … Trinacria
enim Graecum est, quod Latine triquetra dicitur*). We find the
correct glossing of *Tyndaridem* as *Helenam* at I.464 but the truly
bizarre explanation of *deptano* or *de ptano* (for *de plano*) at I.411 as
'*proprium nomen*'. In several other places the Glossator was wrong-
footed: at I.103 *desciscere* was oddly glossed as *nescire*, leaving *a
nobis* of 102 without sense; at 267 *qua* was incorrectly explained as
understanding *ratione*, whereas it agrees with the following *forte*; at
422 *dedicat*, 'declares', was strangely glossed as *nouit* ('knows'?),
presumably since this was thought a more appropriate verb with
sensus as its subject; at 509 *ea* (= *ibi*) was wrongly taken as
understanding *natura*; finally, at 580 *ciueant* was not understood as
a mistake for the rare *clueant*, and instead glossed as *coeant*, which
could make little sense in context.

Two final oddities remain to be noted. First, at I.551*cap.* an
attempt was made to understand part of the Greek *capitulum*
(*contra eis apeiron ten tomen*): an interpunct was added before
tomen to mark it as distinct and the gloss *i.e. elocutio* added above.
It seems that the word was understood correctly as the accusative of

τομή, regardless of context, in its Latin grammatical sense, which Terentianus Maurus used of caesurae (310, 1674) or parts of a verse divided by caesurae (1734, 1748). If the Glossator thus understood the word as signifying something akin to rhetorical *membra*, it is perhaps on this basis that he guessed that the *capitulum* referred to elocution; the use of the nominative may reflect uncertainty about the exact meaning and syntax of the heading.[95]

Second, in three instances the Glossator wrote '*al*' as if introducing a textual variant: I.71 *cupiret* (corrected by the same hand from *cuperet*)] *al uideret*; 288 *et*] *al ac*; 306 *serescunt*] *al rigescunt*. Although the symbol *al* [= *alius* [*codex*] / *alibi* / *aliter*] naturally suggests that variant readings were here being offered, I regard that as most improbable. For we shall see that not only does this hand make many alterations that are of such a low standard that they could not come from another manuscript's text, but also their frequency is too small to imply that the Glossator had any such manuscript to hand. A better explanation was first hinted at by Chatelain, who observed simply that such instances 'potius ad glossarum genus referendae sunt' (III col. 1): they serve to resolve difficulties of the text rather than record variants found elsewhere. I believe that *al* should therefore be taken as *aliter*, that is, *aliter legi/-ere possit/-s*: the three alterations seem to be tentative emendations of three potentially difficult elements of Lucretius' Latin. At I.71 *cupiret*, as corrected by the Glossator from the metrically impossible *cuperet*, is glossed as *uideret*, a suggestion that may have sprung from the fact that *-eret* stood in the text, and the infinitive of I.70 was probably not taken with this part of the text: Epicurus was the first, we are told, to see the bonds of nature. At I.288 the rare use of *et* as if *ac* or *quam* in a comparative clause was explained away by conjecturing *ac*. Finally, above the ἅπαξ *serescunt*[96] at I.306 the Glossator tentatively suggested replacing it with *rigescunt*, which may spring from a reminiscence of *sole*

[95] It seems merely a coincidence that, in discussion of atoms, Isidore (*Etym.* XIII.2) glossed τομήν '*id est sectionem*', which could hardly have inspired the Glossator's *elocutio*.
[96] The verb is attested only here in Lucretius and in Nonius' citation of this passage (175,4 M).

rigescunt at Ou. *Met.* II.364 or, given the context of Lucretius'
sentence, of *uestesque rigescunt* at Verg. *Geo.* III.363. The Glossator evidently thought that these tentative suggestions would
better be offered as supralinear alternatives rather than explicit
corrections.

In order to build a fuller picture of the work of O³, we must turn
now to look at his attempted corrections. As one would expect, the
range of these alterations in the manuscript is similar to the
glosses, since they stop abruptly on 22ʳ at I.827, and no further
activity of the hand seems to exist in the manuscript.[97] We find, on
the basis of my own assignment of hands, seventy-six corrections,
to which can be added at least two corrections by virgulae or sub-
and superpuncts (I.74, 383). Although these alterations amount to
a decent number, they do not reflect a concerted effort to improve
the text methodically.[98] Twenty-two correct simple matters of
orthography or resolve ligatures so as to facilitate the immediate
reading of the text, the restitution of the *e* of prodelided *est* being a
particular favourite.[99] To turn to the remaining fifty-four alterations of greater significance, we may note that twenty-seven
(i.e. 50 per cent of this batch) are incorrect; of the correct
twenty-seven, a dozen are very simple emendations (and surprisingly not made by D or O²)[100] and one was certainly aided by
Lucretian passages repeated elsewhere (I.77 = 1.596/V.90/VI.66).
In two instances (I.315, 334) the Glossator erased a verse of O and
inserted another himself: closer inspection of traces of the erased
verses suggests that he was simply rewriting more legibly lines
that had become obscured in the vellum, both being the eighth

---

[97] There is a small possibility that the correction at I.944 of *tracta* to *tractata* is in this
hand, but it seems much more probably the work of O² (and see below for possible
evidence that the Glossator did not read even up to I.909).

[98] They give the impression of a single read-through and seem generally to antedate the
glosses (as one would expect): clear evidence of this typical ordering of the two can be
seen from the fact that the correction at I.639 is glossed in its corrected form (*propter*
equating to *ob*) and the gloss on I.659 only makes sense if based upon the correction
uera uiai. It is also worth noting that the alteration of *reparare* to *reparari* antedated
the gloss on I.551*cap.*, since the ink of the latter runs over the former.

[99] I.29, *88, *96, 119, *203, *205, 237, *269, *377, *381, *382, *465, *504, 567, 583, 586,
*607, 620, 643, *684, 739, 796 (those marked with an asterisk expand prodelided *est*).

[100] I.87, 138, 256, 296, 438, 467, 562, 651, 654, 736, [769], 827.

down on the ninth leaf.[101] To turn to the remaining corrections, nine show some ingenuity on the Glossator's part:

I.177 *patefit quodcumque orcatu* (*oracantu* QS) was intelligently corrected to *patefit quodcumque creatur*. The Glossator correctly detected the passive ending -*atur* in the incomplete *atu*, and duly found the verbal stem of a first conjugation verb opening with a consonant and a short syllable; although *c* and *r* were supplied by the jumble of letters, the emendation is still a good piece of work.

I.395 *condenserier* was corrected to *denserier* to save the metre, the spurious *con* probably arising from *condenseat* in 392; the correction is simple, but removing this rogue prepositional compound did not occur to preceding correctors.

I.400 *commemorandi*, a genitive that cannot make sense, was corrected to ablatival *commemorando*; it is probable that the erasure of the *t* of *contradere* to *conradere* was made by O³ in the same instant.

I.520 The unmetrical and ungrammatical *si nihil est* was corrected to *si nil essed* (= *esset*) by a simple contraction and expansion (a present counterfactual conditional is desired). The fact that *essed* was so written, either through ignorance or an easy lapse, suggests (as many of the incorrect alterations do) that the Glossator's Latinity was not especially polished.

I.639 The metre was intelligently corrected by interpreting *ob* of *obscuram* as the preposition, and inserting *o* thereafter to make *oscuram* [= *obscuram*], a form again reflecting an imperfect knowledge of Latin orthography. This particular correction (probably made independently of Festus 314,2–3 L) shows the link between the glosses and the correcting hand, for the gloss on this verse is

---

[101] Traces of the *g* of the original *uolgi*, and perhaps the *p* of *pedibus*, can still be seen at I.315. Most editors have been silent on these verses, but I disagree with Diels in attributing the writing of I.334 to the original scribe (presented as if this were the only alternative if not D or O²), as inspection of the hand (and its freer use of ligatures) makes obvious. Given that the Glossator was merely rewriting verses he could read, he need not have had access to an external source, even if he knew of Isidore's citing I.315 at *Etym.* XV.16.6. Finally, given that QS present the better form *uolgi* at I.315, it is probable that the Glossator, subconsciously or otherwise, banalised this form to *uulgi* in his rewriting of the verse.

based upon *ob o<b>scuram linguam*, as shown by its beginning *i.e. propter falsitatem locutionis.*

I.659 The unmetrical and unintelligible *uer aula* was well corrected to *uera uiai* by uniting *uer* and *a*, cancelling the tail of *l* to make an *i* and adding a final *i*. The emendation was perhaps helped by the mention of *uestigia certa uiai* at I.406,[102] and the presence of the neuter plural substantive *ardua* earlier in the line.

I.680 Here we see the Glossator using common sense: *descendere* scans but makes no sense of atomic movement from a compound object. Accordingly, *discedere* was very aptly conjectured to signify atoms' separation from the compound; Lambinus' *decedere*, favoured by many editors, weakly precedes the effectively synonymous *abire*.

I.711 The hiatus caused by *longi errasse* was removed by the insertion of *d*, so as to produce a verb that would have been understood as *deerrasse*. We need not suppose that the Glossator was aware of the rarity of the resultant synizesis, even though Lucretius here did employ that licence here with the verb (as the reading of ψ attests), nor that he had encountered the similar usage of *derrarunt* at III.860.

I.767 The impossible *aternis* (or *a ternis*) was corrected by a single stroke to the adverbial form *alternis*, already encountered by the Glossator at I.524.

Although these are the most impressive corrections made by the Glossator,[103] none is sufficiently insightful to suggest that he had access to any other manuscript or used anything beyond his own (limited) nous. Although in ten instances (I.87, 138, 256, 400, 453, 467, 711, 736, 825, 827) his corrections restore a correct reading also found in Q(S), all of these corrections (save I.711, discussed above) are of the most elementary nature. More tellingly, only once (I.708 *putantur* for *putant*) is an incorrect reading shared with the ψ branch, the correction being simply the easiest way to restore metre.

---

[102] This correction, along with I.453, shows that (perhaps from reading in the wake of O^2) the Glossator, unlike D, understood the termination *-ai*.

[103] For discussion of the text at I.613, see Butterfield (2012c).

There seems to be evidence that some corrections were added on a second read-through at a later date, as their hand is somewhat freer and larger (I.138, 177, 233, 372, 680); it may have been on this perusal, rather than as an immediate correction, that he corrected *fortuita* (an error by mistaken anticipation of the following *uenientia*) to *fortuitu* in the gloss at I.450, using his characteristic *v*-shaped *u*.[104] The confidence of many corrections, given their prominent size and strong hand, is interesting, although the Glossator typically avoided making corrections within the line itself (as opposed to supralinearly). At any rate, there is no evidence that he read beyond I.827 in the manuscript, and he perhaps ended his reading neatly enough at the break for the *capitulum* before I.830, never to return to the book again.

Despite these occasional virtues, however, there is much that is perverse among his incorrect alterations. Although some mistaken changes are understandable,[105] a good number are

---

[104] If this hand is thought to differ too much from that of O³, which I would dispute, it can nevertheless be proven from what follows that it postdated O² (and O³).

[105] I.70 *confringere* simplified to *frangere* in order to restore metre; 223 *consumpse* was not recognised and the synizesis of *ante acta* was not understood metrically; 263 the rare form *alid* was altered to a Latin word close in form (*ali*) and *ex alto* in lieu of *ex allo* restored a common Latin prepositional phrase (and one used by Lucretius at IV.73, 92, 200, 694, 863); 269 the hyperbaton of *quae* and *corpora* was misunderstood, so *quod* was entered to introduce a noun clause; 383 *concurso* restored the original reading of the text for O²'s *concusso*; 404 *ferarum* restored the metre and sense but ignored *montiuagae* (not to be taken with *canes*); 407 the rare form *alid* was altered to the metrical (and intelligible) plural *alia*; 476 *durateus*, a transliteration of Greek δουράτεος not attested elsewhere in Latin and apparently unknown to the Glossator, was altered to *duraceus*, a form equally unknown but at least bearing the legitimate Latin suffix *-aceus* (cf. *gallinaceus, herbaceus, rosaceus, uinaceus*) in lieu of the unattested *-ateus*; 527 the nonsense *poena* was emended to the metrical, and not nonsensical, *poenitus* [= *penitus*, for which orthography cf. *extoenta* in the gloss at I.324], perhaps prompted by the adverb's appearance two lines below; 550 the alteration of *reparare* to the passive infinitive *reparari* could make sense, save for the presence of *seruata* (cf. *reparari* at 560); 560 the choriambic scansion (and form) of *relicuo* was not understood and replaced by *de reliquo*; 640 because the rare *quamde* was unknown, its *de* was deleted (as D already had marked) and *est* added in the hope of restoring metre (and not impairing the sense), without apprehending the iambic scansion of *grauis*; 665 *minus* was the closest Latin word the Glossator divined to restore a genuine metrical word in place of *mia*; 708 despite the presence of *putarunt* in 705, *putantur* was perhaps thought the easiest metrical correction of *putant*; 721 *haeliae* was corrected with ingenuity to the metrical and Latinate *haeoliae* [= *Aeoliae*], a word that would have been familiar from Virgil, Ovid, Statius and Martial; 759 the metre was completed by a sensible plural formed from the base *uene-*, namely *uenena*, which is not necessarily an incorrect conjecture.

perplexing. At I.282 the perfectly intelligible *auget* was confidently altered to *urget*, perhaps because it seemed odd to the
Glossator for a *decursus aquai* to increase the *mollis natura
aquae*. At I.372 *alunt*, already corrected to *aiunt* by D or (much
less probably) O², was altered to *aluei*: the earlier correction
was therefore rejected, perhaps because an uncommon poetic
verbal form,[106] and instead the *l* was retained, and *aluei* 'of a
riverbed' conjectured, which is intelligible in context, if 372–4
is thought to be in virtual *oratio obliqua*, supplying *fingunt*
from 371.[107] At I.386 a more elaborate alteration occurred:
accepting D's emendation, *flat*, but not recognising the form
of the rare verb *possidat*, O³ found that the verse did not scan;
to correct these problems, he therefore inserted a passive form
of the usual second conjugation verb *possidere*, namely *possi-
deatur*. Consequently, as his gloss shows, *inane* (the previous
subject of *possidat*) must be understood as an instrumental
ablative, with *aer* being the new subject of the verb, a change
that inverted the sense of the passage. At I.412 the nonsensical
magnes was altered to *amnis* by the Glossator, which was
presumably intended as a genitive singular dependent upon
the immediately preceding *fontibus*; perhaps he noticed the
impossibility of the word but had not apprehended
that sigmatic ecthlipsis was employed by Lucretius, which
precluded his correcting to *magnis*. In making this correction,
he employed a bar above his added *m*, if not to mark it as the
correcting letter (for which I have found no parallel), then
perhaps through recollection of the abbreviation for the
similar-sounding *omnis*, i.e. $\overline{om}$ + termination;[108] I therefore
believe the similarity to *amnes* of QS to be entirely coincidental, and not so improbable in the context of water. At I.479 *uti*,
a form already seen five times in the book, was altered to
(rather than glossed as) *ueluti*, which could only scan if the
preceding *ita*, which much aids the construction, were deleted,

[106] Given that the Glossator used a subpunct similarly at I.659 to cancel *l* into *i*, it is
improbable that he either did not notice or failed to understand this use of the subpunct
at I.372.
[107] The synizesis is common in dactylic Latin poetry.
[108] I am grateful to Michael Reeve for suggesting this possibility to me.

but there is no sign that this was the Glossator's intention. At
I.703 *ignem* was wrongly inserted before *tamen* to complete the
defective metre, although the passage actually requires any
other word to be supplied than fire itself.[109] Finally, at I.818
we find the perfectly intelligible *contineantur* ('are held
together') altered to *continuentur* ('are placed together'); *con-
tinuare* is not used by Lucretius and the resultant sense is less
appealing. Given that the Glossator did not add corrections
beyond I.827, and that this change is left in this form in the
text, it is probable that he did not reach I.909 in his reading
(let alone II.761 and 1008) where the same verse recurs, con-
firming the veracity of the transmitted *contineantur*.

To summarise the Glossator's activity, he was seemingly
at leisure to work through the text of *DRN* rather carefully,
which may have taken some time, and clearly felt free to treat
the manuscript as his own text: glosses are frequent, and there
was no attempt to make corrections particularly neat or place
them separately in the margin; however, the few apparent
conjectures were suggested supralinearly rather than in the text
itself. For whatever reason, his work did not progress beyond
the recto of the 22nd leaf, and he apparently did not read
beyond that point. We have seen that there is no need to posit
that he used any resource beyond his own intellect, which
was not of the highest order, but he could scan verses correctly
(with due concentration) and recognise non-Latinate forms. We
may now turn to offer a tentative date (and possibly location)
for this hand.

One of the most experienced Latin palaeographers of the
twentieth century, Bernhard Bischoff, judged that this hand was
of the late tenth century; other scholars have agreed, or placed it in
the early eleventh. The hand was first attributed to Otloh of
St Emmeram, a monk active in Fulda around 1062–6, by Michael
Tangl, an assertion seemingly made in private to Diels (XII–XIV)
but not in print.[110] This attribution was rightly rejected by Martin
(1934, IV), on the testimony (again given privately) of Anton

[109] I have discussed this problem at Butterfield (2008f) 18–19.
[110] Diels referred to Tangl (1916) 693–713 but the latter makes no mention of Lucretius or O.

Chroust. Nevertheless, Büchner (VIII, XLV) and Flores (vol. 1 (39)) supported the attribution to Otloh after Diels without argument, and De Meyier (1973, 66) reported it without further discussion. The association has since been again rejected by Ganz (1996, 94 n. 16) and Reeve (2005, 161, citing further confirmation from Ganz in n. 134). There is very little similarity between the hands to judge from published facsimiles,[111] and I too am sure that the identification is wrong. Indeed, to turn back to the most expert of judges, Bischoff wrote: 'Die Annahme, dass Otloh in Fulda Lucrez korrigiert habe ... ist ebenso haltlos wie grotesk.'[112] No plausible figure has been suggested in his place, and I do not offer one here. Rather, on the basis of the pedestrian and pedagogical nature of the glosses, and the poor success rate of the corrections, I see no compulsion to assign these notes to a figure of sufficiently scholarly credentials for his name to be known: their calibre is entirely in line with an unknown monk.

As regards the dating of the hand by logic, rather than palaeography, it can swiftly be shown that he postdated D, the Annotator and O². He must follow the Annotator because at I.263 the Annotator has put a triangular point within the line to mark the non-Latin form *allo*, which was altered to a Latin word *alto* only later by the Glossator, who was perhaps drawn to the error by the mark: we have seen that the Annotator did not (save for two possibly anomalous instances in Book V) leave his mark alongside passages of questionable sense. He must also follow D, not only because the Annotator does, but also because he altered D's *reparare* to *reparari* at I.550.[113] Finally, the Glossator must follow O² because at I.384 he changed the alteration by O² of *concurso* to *concusso* back to *concurso*. There is a more striking reason, however, to believe that the Glossator followed O². For this we must turn to the matter of the Codex Poggianus (π), discussed in Chapter 1 and touched upon at the beginning of this section.

---

[111] For images of Otloh's hand see those cited by Tangl (1916, 706 n. 3) and, more recently, Bischoff (1981) pl. 25.

[112] Bischoff (2004) 50 no. 2189.

[113] This correction, first noted by Lachmann (5), has typically been attributed to O² but it is more of the form of the long *i* written by the Glossator (cf. n. 88 above).

247

The descent of the Poggianus from O

Scholars who have regarded the Poggianus (π) correctly as a descendant of O typically have taken the manuscript to be a direct apograph of O itself. Without close attention paid to the correcting hands in the manuscript, there is no obvious objection to this application of Occam's razor: O was based in Mainz in the late fifteenth century,[114] and it therefore seems entirely possible, on the basis of Diels' assertion that the Poggianus was a direct copy of O, that Mainz was the *locus satis longinquus* where Poggio found a Lucretian manuscript in 1417. This opinion was left unchallenged by those astute enough to accept it until, in 1973, Konrad Müller made an important further observation. He argued that close observation of the corrections in Book I of O suggests strongly that an intermediary existed between it and π. The crux of his argument was simply that, in this early section of the manuscript, one or more mediaeval correcting hands appear to have made alterations to the text which, for whatever reason, the scribe of the Poggianus did not adopt.

Müller recorded (1975 edn, 314–16) ten instances in which a correction in O that would either have been accepted by the scribe of the Poggianus or influenced his action somehow appears not to have had any effect. As stated above, I accept the attribution of nine of these alterations (I.453, 467, 520, 560, 659, 680, 711, 759, 827) to O^3. In these cases it is true that the Poggianus, as reconstructed from its primary witnesses,[115] either followed the original text of O or emended independently of the correction. In some of these cases (I.467, 520, 680, 711, 759, 827) it is truly remarkable that these corrections were not accepted, not only because of their plausibility but also because many stand in the main text and differ little from the hand of O, so could scarcely have been avoided in a typical transcription. On the basis of my own assignation of hands, where previous editors have been inaccurate or silent, we may also regard as bizarre the failure to adopt several more correct or plausible annotations of O^3: I.29, 70, 77, 87, 395,

---

[114] See my remarks in Chapter 1, pp. 7–8.
[115] See Chapter 1, n. 68.

404, 412, 550, 639, 640 and 736, many of which were made neatly *in textu*.[116] There is also no trace in the Italian manuscripts of any material from the many glosses added by this hand. So inexplicable is the reproduction of the earlier text of O that it seems necessary to posit instead that an intermediary manuscript was copied from O before these corrections were added (although after it had already been corrected by D and O², as the readings of π show). Whereas Müller chose capital Π as his siglum for this lost exemplar of π, which suggests a misleading similarity in the nature of these two manuscripts some four centuries apart, I propose χ as a clearer alternative.

Without explicitly committing himself to either view about whether the Poggianus was a direct or indirect copy of O,[117] Reeve closed his discussion by posing an important question: 'Did any of the corrections in O obliterate, whether by erasure or by heavy overwriting, an original reading found in the Poggianus?' (2005, 161). Although it happens that no written correction of O³ completely obliterated the original text, Reeve drew attention to what seems to be the sole instance where an erasure of the text was made by O³ or someone of a yet later date: at I.401 *contradere* of the original text has been altered to *conradere* by erasure, yet the Italian manuscripts demonstrate that π read the incorrect, and non-classical, *contradere*. This is difficult to explain if O is the direct ancestor of π, as there would have been no need to preserve the (scarcely legible) initial reading: it would be extremely difficult to suppose that the *t* was erased after the early fifteenth century, for the nature of corrections made after this date, apparently in one brief period alone (see section E below), did not involve erasures. To regard *contradere* as an accidental corruption or purposeful change made early on in π, coincidentally restoring the incorrect reading, would be special pleading. It is much more probable to regard the erasure of the unwanted *t* as having

---

[116] We cannot suppose that π was indeed copied from O but that Poggio ordered the scribe to ignore any corrections and variant readings, for many of the alterations of O² are supralinear and easily distinguishable from the main text but were nevertheless regularly adopted in π. The same applies to the occasional words supplied in the margin by D that are still found in π.

[117] His expression (2005, 161) suggests a preference for Müller, however.

occurred after the time of the transcription of χ, that is, to ascribe it to the work of O^3.

The obstacles to accepting the existence of χ between O and π are very few, especially in the wake of my fresh assignation of hands; by contrast, its existence explains away many difficulties regarding not only the readings of π but also the diffusion of the readings of O and this mediaeval intermediary. In order to accept the theory, one need only explain (a) why in a few instances a correction already existing in O when it was copied (between the work of O^2 and O^3, i.e. in the early–mid tenth century) apparently did not enter into π and (b) how some readings which were added in O after the transcription was made also occur in the main Italian tradition (and are therefore attributable to π). I take these two matters separately:

(a)   *Instances of good readings of Dungal (O^D) or O^2 apparently not accepted by the Poggianus*

I.85 *Iphianassa* in *Iphianassai* corr. O^2 : *Iphianasseo* π. The presence of the adjectival form in π (modifying *sanguine*) simply suggests that the adjective was conjectured (by Poggio?) as a more probable emendation of the text than the supralinear addition of an *i* above the line by O^2. It remains possible that *Iphianassai* was the original reading of π.

I.384 *concurso* in *concusso* (*concurso* rest. O^3) mut. O^2 : *concurso* π. The scribe of χ, faced with the reading of the text *concurso* (which stood unchanged in the verse itself) and its supralinear alteration *concusso*, chose to follow the initial text; there is no reason to suppose that the restoration of *concurso* (also supralinear) by O^3 was visible to him.[118]

I.427 *haustus quam* in *haut* (postea in *haud* O^2) *usquam* corr. O^D : *haud quaquam* π. Whether we assume that π contained *haud quaquam* as a conscious emendation of the incorrect *haustus quam* or as a corruption influenced by *quoquam* in the same position in line 428 below, the evidence of readings in φ and S. Onofrio 85[119] suggests strongly that χ still retained the original

---

[118] It would be a further complication to suppose that the scribe of χ preserved the two alternative readings and that it was the scribe of π who elected to follow *concurso*.

[119] Cf. Chapter I, n. 107.

reading of O *haustus quam*. We must therefore assume that, faced with the confusing concatenation of errors in I.427 – interpunct and comma after *haust*, underlining between *us* and *quam*, subpunct beneath *s* of *haustus* and a *t*, later corrected to a *d*, above that same letter – the scribe of χ elected to follow the Latin (and metrical) words of the original text rather than reconstruct the correction from evidently later hands.

I.651 *disiectisque supatis* O in *disiectis disque supatis* corr. O ipse (ut uid.) : *disiectisque supatis* π (*dis* ante *que* suppl. $L^2φ$). The supralinear *disque* (with *que* of *disiectisque* cancelled beneath), added by O, was presumably rejected on the ground that it was not understood as Latin, whether -*que* was taken as the enclitic particle or *disque* was thought to be one word. As a result, the scribe of χ copied the text as it stood;[120] faced with the impossible *supatis*, an intelligent annotator of φ hit upon the correct emendation by positing Lucretian tmesis, which correction may have occurred to L^2 (Niccoli) independently.

III.1061 *per quem* in *quem* corr. O^D (ut uid.) : *per quem* π. The three subpuncts deleting *per* do not appear to be of a late date, and I would not wish to attribute them to O^3 or a subsequent hand; for whatever reason, however, these rather untidy marks of deletion were overlooked or disregarded by the scribe of χ, as could easily be done, perhaps because *per* appeared to make some sense before *quem*.

V.1085 *grecis* to *greges* corr. O^D : *greces* π. The method of correcting the *c* to *g* is here not clear – the mere addition of a stroke – and it is perfectly possible that in this instance the correction was not noticed by the scribe of χ, with the result that only half of O^D's alteration could be transmitted into the Poggianus.

V.1150 *colore* in *colere* corr. O^2 : *colore* π. The *o* of the original text is still very much apparent, and may well have been taken as the more probable reading on palaeographical grounds by the scribe of χ.

V.1393 *proptereaque* in *propter aquae* corr. O^2 : *proptereaquae* π. The superpunct above the *e* was not quite centrally placed

---

[120] The correction therefore does not appear among those in S. Onofrio 85: cf. Chapter 1, p. 36.

and is not particularly obvious, nor was any word divider employed, with the result that the text of O passed unaltered into χ and π.

VI.141 *arbusta*(?) *uoluens* in *arbusta euoluens* corr. O^D : *arbusta uoluens* π. The failure to include the prepositional compound *e-*, added by Dungal and essential for the metre, was presumably a simple error of transcription made by either χ or π; it is clear from the presence of *arbusta* in π that the first part of Dungal's correction (made *in ras.*) was transmitted as expected.

VI.887 *non tam uita* in *non ita muita* mut. O^2 : *non tam uita* π. This incorrect alteration was passed over probably because the added *i* was so small, no word division was recorded and the correction of *i* to *l* was not made; thus the original *non tam uita* still found its way into π.

VI.915 *uinclaque* corr. O^{D}φ : *uintiaque* O$^{a.c.}$: *uinciaque* ψ : *tundaque* L : *cundaque* o : om. AB. Dungal's correction of the nonsense *uintiaque* was made such that *cl* appears as a large *d*: as a result, *cundaque* could easily have been misread by χ, have stood in π, and been subsequently misread as *tundaque* by the time of L's transcription in the mid-1430s.

VI.1167 *ui* in *ut* corr. O^2 : *ui* π (*ui* L : *in* μ). The bar with which O^2 sought to convert the *i* to a *t* is so high that it looks more like the virgula to mark a nasal; if the scribe of χ paid heed to the correction, he presumably disregarded it as nonsensical.

It is thus not particularly difficult to explain the only twelve anomalous cases (in a work of over 7,400 verses) where we find the scribe of the Poggianus overlooking or actively rejecting a genuine correction implemented by O^D or O^2: we will do well to recall that it was not the great Poggio himself, but an unknown figure, who was entrusted with transcribing this difficult text of χ, and the intellectual merits of both of these mediaeval scribes are unknowable. Typically, the scribe of χ appears to have followed corrected readings, often when close consideration would have revealed them to be less attractive than the original text. Ancient and mediaeval scribes were, of course, under no obligation to follow either the base text or suggested corrections, and inconsistency in their practice is entirely unsurprising.

(D) The work of the Glossator (O³)

(b)   Instances of corrections made by O³ also occurring in the Italian tradition

More potent for those wishing to reject the hypothesis of Müller are those instances where corrections by the Glossator (O³), which I have shown to have been made independently of any manuscript, coincide with the reconstructed readings of π. In order for Müller's hypothesis to stand, it must be argued that these alterations coincide purely by chance. The relevant coincidences are as follows:

I.87 *comptus* O³π : *comptos* O^a.c.
I.177 *creatur* O³π : *orcatu* O^a.c.
I.256 *undique* O³π : *undeque* O^a.c.
I.438 *transire* O³π : *transere* O^a.c.
I.562 *refici rem* O³π : *reficerem* O^a.c.

None of these five instances should be regarded as particularly troubling to Müller's hypothesis: four corrections (I.87, 256, 438, 562) are of such a simple nature as to be without any significance. We are thus left with only I.177, which has already been lauded as an intelligent correction, restoring a passive verb from the nonsense *orcatu*; nevertheless, a corrector who knew metre, was following the sense of the passage and was able to salvage *-atur* from *-atu* could hit upon the correction without too much trouble. Other coincidences in the tradition are the result of fifteenth-century conjecture,[121] and π itself clearly preserved the pre-O³ reading.[122]

The objections to positing the existence of χ are therefore too weak to pass muster. If we look at the problem from the other angle, we can see how difficult it is to explain how certain corrections of O³ could have been ignored:

---

[121]   For the discussion of a separate class of readings in small pockets of the Italian tradition and unconnected with the Poggianus, see the close of Chapter 1, pp. 32–41.

[122]   The primary instances (using Flores' sigla) are: I.29 *moenera* O : *munera* O³φxr¹ : *monera* π; 138 *uersibus* O³L¹ : *uerbis* L² Itali cett. (the reading of L shows that *uersibus* still stood in π but was soon emended); 395 *condenserier* O : *condensarier* L² : *condensier* x : *denserier* corr. O³AF¹ : *densaerier* e : *densarier* Lμ (the evidence of x strongly suggests that the unmetrical longer form *condenserier* stood as a primitive reading in π but was soon emended, x choosing to employ it in a metrical form); 736 *inuenientes* O³A²r²φ : *inueniente* O Itali plerique (a most simple correction).

253

I.263 *alit ex allo* in *ali ex alto* mut. O^3 : *alit* (L^{1}d : *alid* L^2 Itali plerique) *ex alio* π. The alteration, although not correct, would have been actively disregarded, since it stands in the text proper, and the *i*, which had clearly been corrected to *t*, restored.

I.613 *tam* in *iam* corr. O^3 : *tam* π. This clear alteration would have been ignored and the impossible *tam* restored from beneath it.

I.659 *ueraula* in *uera uiai* corr. O^3 : *uer aula* (*uera ulla* P) π. This fine correction of O^3, made intelligible to any reader by its accompanying gloss '*i.e. ductus itineris*', would have been ignored and the meaningless and unmetrical text of O restored in silence.

I.759 *uene* in *uenena* mut. O^3 : *uene* π. The perfectly intelligible and attractive conjecture *uenena*, whose *na* is hardly distinguishable *prima facie* from the preceding letters of the word, would have been spotted and rejected for the unmetrical and unmeaning *uene* (which could only be Latin if taken as *uenae*).

I.767 *aternis* in *alternis* corr. O^3 : *aternis* (*aeternis* P) π. This obvious correction of the meaningless *aternis* to the correct and Lucretian adverb *alternis* would have been disregarded and nonsense instead followed.

All of these corrections, and many others provided in the full list (see n. 92), were made in a clear hand by O^3 and could only have been rejected purposefully. It seems impossible that they were present in O if the Poggianus was copied from it (which chronology would demand they would have been); to suppose that they were present in O and were added as variants in the Poggianus but were not transmitted any further than that manuscript (despite its many copies) is merely to postpone the problem, if not to increase it given the standing of humanistic learning: if that manuscript oddly chose to have, for example, the nonsense *aternis* in the text, with *alternis* written above, why would not a single later copier of that manuscript either adopt this eminently correct variant, or at least mention it?

We may close this digression by clarifying the level of conjectural activity in χ and π. It does not seem that χ was written by a scribe who emended as he worked nor that the codex was much annotated, or at any rate corrected, between being written and being rediscovered in 1417. By contrast, we should note that the scribe of the Poggianus and/or Poggio and other early readers, were apparently happy to emend the text: the scale of the corrections implemented by/in π can be seen in K. Müller's edition (309–12), where many emendations accepted from the Italian tradition in Books I and III are listed.[123] Although Poggio claimed in correspondence to Niccoli that he had not yet been able to work through the text of Lucretius closely (see Harth (1984–7) vol. 1, 89), it is very probable that he added various emendations to the manuscript when it was returned to him in Konstanz.

Having found its way to Niccoli, perhaps in 1418 when Poggio's work finished at the Council, it no doubt obtained further emendations and annotations, partially from Niccoli's hand, and possibly from others in his circle; when Niccoli came to transcribe L directly from π (for there is no obvious reason to posit an intermediary) in the mid-1430s, his base text already contained a good number of conjectures that must have been added in his exemplar. After π was returned to Poggio, presumably in the mid-1430s, and after the transcription of L, it seems most improbable that the great scholar did not further annotate and correct the text, with the result that later copies of the manuscript (such as Vat. Pat. 312 and Ces. S. 20.4), which could well be direct copies, often show further strata of emendations beyond L and μ. The Cesena manuscript is particularly interesting, since among a number of emendations it records some very primitive readings of π which represent the original text of the manuscript before Italian correction. Given that this codex was copied in 1458–65, it is attractive to assume that it was made on the result of Poggio's own paper manuscript circulating more widely after his death in 1459.[124]

We have seen, then, that the seemingly innocuous corrections made by O³, not yet analysed fully by any editor of Lucretius,

---

[123] A cursory glance at an apparatus for the other books confirms that this was the case throughout *DRN*.

[124] Cf. Chapter 1, n. 47.

can serve as a potent key to unlock an important phase of the mediaeval transmission of Lucretius and can solve a problem that has either baffled or misled the very great majority of Lucretian editors to date. Müller was correct to posit an intermediary manuscript between O and the Poggianus; my own assignation of hands has aimed to clarify and bolster the argument further.

To return to the work of the Glossator, it seems possible to say that, around the mid/late tenth century, some figure, perhaps in southern Germany, and perhaps at Mainz (see Chapter 1, pp. 7–8), had access to the Oblongus at his leisure and began to read through the poem closely, annotating it – presumably for his own benefit and what he perhaps perceived to be that of others – until, around I.829, he ceased reading (or at any rate marking) the text. Before this point in time, but after the work of O^2 (of the mid/late ninth century), a full copy of O was made; it was very probably this apograph, rather than a further descendant, that Poggio found in 1417.[125]

(E)   The corrections of O^4

We come at last to a corrector who postdated the aforementioned figures by many centuries. It is therefore somewhat unsurprising that no scholar has sought to record a full list of these corrections and annotations, let alone discuss them. Diels very occasionally made mention of his 'O^2', which covered 'correctores recentissimi' (XLIV) or 'manus recentiorum uirorum doctorum, qui raro notas uel signa omissionis adsperserunt' (XIV–XV); subsequent editors have either followed the lead of Diels or simply ignored these corrections. They are proven to be late not only by the modern form of many letters[126] but also by the use of arabic numerals at II.277, III.305 and 332,[127] as well as the method of cancellation (by vertically striking out a letter) at I.539

---

[125] For discussion of the appearance of Lucretius in various mediaeval catalogues, see Chapter 1, pp. 29–30 with nn. 90–5.

[126] Compare the dotted *i* at I.539, III.321 and V.28, and the shape of the *s* at III.719.

[127] The only two other instances of transposition among corrections, by D at III.691 and O^2 at IV.1097, are instead marked by pairs of two dots above the adjacent words.

and IV.429. For a list of these corrections, see Appendix III, p. 298.[128]

Of these forty-four marks and corrections few can be said to bear much scholarly weight. Twenty-two merely note the loss of something from the text (whether letter, syllable or word), without explicitly recording what the missing element is; syllabic or word omission can be detected easily from the verse's faulty scansion, and often the defect can occur in only one specific place. Three (I.518, 708, VI.221) are merely changes of orthography, three (III.304, 894, IV.792) of word division, two (III.305, 332) transposition of adjacent words. All but two of the remaining fourteen corrections merely affect a single letter (whether by alteration, addition or cancellation), two such occurring adjacently in III.319. Of the final two corrections, which involve greater intervention, neither is particularly striking: at I.539 *docui* of *docuissent* was separated as the desired verb of the *uti* clause, and *ssent* corrected without difficulty to *sint* to provide the *necessest* clause of the apodosis with a dependent subjunctive; at II.277 *extrema* was corrected to *extera* (as in QS).

It is difficult to assign the hand with any confidence to a particular period, since its alterations are so minor, but a clue can be given by the fact that a few corrections seem to draw upon printed editions: at III.289, *acrius* (which reading may be right) is marked as lacking a letter after the *i*, which could only signify alteration to *acribus*, a suggestion first made by Avancius in 1500 (though commonly attributed to Lambinus). Similarly, the corrections at III.304, 305 and 523 first appeared in Avancius' Aldine (save for a small number of manuscript sources in the case of III.304 (φ) and 523 (EaI^m.r.)). The correction of *uideo* to *uideor* at III.319 could well have been made after 1662, when mention of it was first made by Faber in his edition, since, although he stated '[q]uarundam editionum lectionem revocavi', no preceding edition printed it.[129] By contrast, the simple addition of a virgula to the final letter of *uapore* at III.432, a perfectly natural correction,

---

[128] For a more detailed list, see the online version at www.cambridge.org/butterfield.
[129] Cf., however, Deufert (1998) 376.

was not made until 1725, when Haverkamp published Preiger's suggestion (although editors misattribute the correction to Lachmann). Of course it is possible that these textual innovations were emendations on the part of O^4 himself, but, given the rather pedestrian nature of his other corrections, this seems rather improbable. The hand of the corrector is not that of the Vossii, in whose hands O was between 1635/1649 and 1689, nor Heinsius'; furthermore, the collations of O made by Heinsius (probably in the 1650s) and Isaac Vossius (c. 1650–80) show no knowledge of these later readings.[130] I therefore suppose that the small-scale corrections of O^4 were entered into O in Leiden itself, perhaps by Haverkamp, or Preiger, or an early librarian at the Leidse Universiteitsbibliotheek; at any rate, by the time of Lachmann's collation (1846), these readings were present in O,[131] although he often ignored them since he fully understood that they were of no textual significance.

If this surprisingly late dating is correct, it seems that, around the turn of the eighteenth century, an individual was casually working through the manuscript with one or more printed texts of Lucretius to hand (perhaps Faber or Creech, if not – through patriotism or egotism – Haverkamp); given that all O^4 corrections can be found in earlier witnesses or editions, the hand bears no authority and should not be cited by an editor. The fact that the written alterations of O^4, when they do occur, are either very slight (with small letters, or thin cancellations) or merely mark the loss of text, suggests that the reader was aware that he did not have the licence to mark the manuscript regularly and in so invasive a fashion.

(F) Remaining jottings

There is one final hand to be mentioned in this chapter, namely that which wrote the *ex libris* at the foot of 1^r, a note already

---

[130] See Appendix V, pp. 306–8.

[131] See his notes *ad* II.553, III.917 and IV.429; no further information regarding these readings issued from Munro's collation (1849) and it was not until Diels (1923) that an almost complete record of these readings was given. The information provided by Haverkamp is too insufficient to record whether the readings of O^4 had entered the manuscript or not, but I assume that they had.

mentioned in Chapter I (see Plate I).[132] This hand wrote 'Iste liber pertinet ad librariam Sancti Martini ecclesie Maguntine. M. Sindicus subscripsit anno 1479': 'this book belongs to the Library of the Church of St Martin in Mainz; M[acarius von Busek] the Syndic wrote [this] in the year 1479'.[133] Von Busek, Canon and Syndic of the cathedral chapter of St Martin's in Mainz from the mid 1460s until his death in 1482, regularly entered this inscription at the beginning of manuscripts under his charge, typically at the foot of the first leaf.[134]

It is difficult to tell whether it was the hand of von Busek or a predecessor that added the two catalogue marks at the top and bottom of I^r ('O II XI' and '·LV· I·': see Plate I); at any rate, the second of these notes clearly antedated the catalogue inscription, as the positioning of the latter shows. It also seems probable that von Busek, or a similar hand of that period, made two marginal notes in Book I of O: we find a northern European hand of the fifteenth century[135] on 9^v alongside I.334cap., where *de inani* is written in the left margin alongside the somewhat faded or erased heading *De inani*; the purpose of the note is probably to clarify the reading of the *capitulum* without venturing to affect the rubricated ink of the text proper. On 23^r, in the right margin alongside I.875, we find in a similar hand the note *Anaxagoras dixit omnia esse in omnibus*.[136] Given that (a) there are only two such annotations, (b) only one aims to be exegetical, and (c) the hands seem similar to that of von Busek's *ex libris*, I think it simplest to attribute these notes to him: perhaps on a cursory read through Book I he merely sought to make clear the reading of the *capitulum* at I.334, and to offer what amounted to his own basic *capitulum* at I.875.[137]

---

[132] It is characteristic of Bailey (1947, vol. III, 38) that he recorded that this is the 'subscription at the end of the MS'

[133] For discussion of the general context of this note, see Falk (1897) 24–5, and Lindsay and Lehmann (1925) 16–17.

[134] It is also found, with very little variation, in, e.g., Vat. Pal. Lat. 575, 578, 579, 580, 582, 1447.

[135] I thank Michael Reeve for offering his own dating of the hand.

[136] It seems that the rather hurried virgulae marking the abbreviations for *omnia* and *omnibus* are similar to those used in the (more careful) *ex libris* on the front of the first leaf.

[137] The scribbles that occur on the last page of the manuscript (192^v) are rather varied in content but have little significance (see Plate IV). The opening of the work's last line

Conclusion

Clearly a far more varied range of hands worked on O than has been recognised previously: taking the original scribe(s) as one, we can identify seven hands in the manuscript, and perhaps as many as ten. Only the corrections assigned to D can be treated as having any textual authority: all the corrections of O^2 and the Glossator (O^3) must be deemed mere conjectures. Even if they have enjoyed travelling for some one thousand years in the most august vehicle of Lucretius' transmission, the celebrated *Codex Oblongus*, such alterations should be weighed in identical fashion to emendations published in modern scholarly journals. Nevertheless, care must still be taken with the readings attributed to D, for there are no sure means of determining whether a given correction from his hand is made on the basis of Ω or his own intellect, both of which were employed in his sporadic work. In cases where D's reading is inherently plausible but differs from that of ψ (or Q alone), future editors will do well to consider whether it is probable that the reading of ψ could have issued from D's correction if originally the reading of Ω; if not, we may rather be faced with the conjectural work of D, which must therefore be assigned to him alone and critiqued like any other emendation.

(VI.1286), *Rixantes potius*, has been repeated, *potius* twice, as also has *subdebant* of the penultimate line. The form of this line in the text does not seem to be linked with these jottings; rather the scribe probably wrote *subdebantque fauces multo cum saepe sanguine*, which was duly corrected by erasure of *saepe*. In another mediaeval note, after *cum*, *species* has been written upside down. Another scribble merely reads *liber*. It is possible that over *CARI* of the rubricated subscription *c(h)arismatum* was written: whether this was just the musing of a monk upon a religious word that shares a similar beginning or something of greater significance, it seems impossible to tell. 'ACAD. LVGD.', the uncompromising Leiden UB stamp also found twice on 1^r, seems to have been stamped over an erasure, and some letters remain visible under the end of it and to the right. The last of those under 'LVGD.' appear to be $d\overline{no}$, i.e. *domino*, which suggests that it was simply another religious scribble, possibly *laus domino*, a prudent outcry from a monk who had just worked through a highly impious work of pagan literature.

5

THE MARGINAL ANNOTATIONS OF Q[1]

The *Codex Quadratus* (Q) suffered from comparative neglect after it was written:[1] we have already seen the haphazard state of its sparse rubrication (cf. Chapter 3, n. 9). The later hand that dominates the manuscript in its present form is of an Italian humanist of the mid fifteenth century (Q[2]).[2] Close analysis of its corrections shows that they are the result of conjecture alone, and a number of scholars have been wrong therefore to suppose that he made use of some other manuscript, whether ancient or Italian.[3] Q[2] was also responsible for the great majority of ghost letters added where rubricated initials should stand,[4] along with the catchwords at the end of gatherings, and the numbering of the last five leaves.

---

[1] Chatelain (1913) III col. 1: 'codex omnis quasi neglectus non ad unguem absolutus est.'

[2] See the citation of A. C. de la Mare's opinion at Reeve (1980) 27 n. 3.

[3] This conclusion, reached by Cini (1976, 139–45), has rightly been accepted by Reeve (2005, 135); of the significant coincidences (I.893, II.543, IV.460 (FAB), VI.376, VI.962 (FAB)) only II.543 (*non sit in orbe* Q[2]π : *sit orbi* O : *orbi* Q) and IV.460 (*noctis* Q[2], which also appears in the margin of several fifteenth-century Lucretian manuscripts : *montis* OQ) are striking. The corrections of Q[2], which bear no textual authority and can easily be distinguished from the original text, are not treated in this book. For a relatively comprehensive list of these corrections, see Chatelain (1913) VII col. 1–XI col. 2. The comparative positioning of the marginal jottings of Q[1], and the few corrections of Q[2] placed in the margin, is typically regular: those of Q[1] appear spaced only slightly into the right margin whereas, if space allows, those of Q[2] are moved as far as possible from the text (see esp. 14[r]). The only instances of Q[2] marginalia that are centrally placed in the margin are I.263 (when perhaps the policy of spacing had not yet been fully established) and I.1071, probably positioned with more freedom in the wake of the preceding note.

[4] Such catchletters begin with the first absent enlarged initial, I.1052 (on 10[r]), and appear in all such gaps thereafter until IV.526 (inclusive), save at III.624 and 806 (both opening with *praeterea*) and those instances in Book IV where enlarged initials already existed. From IV.615 (opening *hoc*) until the end, catchletters do not generally appear (the anomalies are IV.633, 907, 962, V.780, VI.160, 712, 848, 869, and – at the end – II.801, 806). The only errors are at III.1, where *a* has been supplied for the archetype's *o*, and V.928ff. (at the end), where *n* (creating the nonsense *nundatum*) appears instead of *f*. Initial *N* at II.184 is the work of Q[2]. The black capital *N* at III.678 and the similar *H* at II.44 and *C* at III.378 are additions postdating Q[2]'s minuscule catchletters but are probably the work of the same reader at a later stage. The catchletters added at V.780 and VI.451, by contrast, may be the work of Q[1].

Leaving this later reader aside, however, a Carolingian hand distinct from the scribes of the poetic text has annotated the manuscript in almost thirty places (cf. Plate VII). Since this is the first correcting hand distinct from the scribes of Q (made clear by its script, positioning and lighter ink), I call it Q^1. These marginal annotations have not been discussed beyond the minimalist statement of Chatelain (1913, III col. 1: 'Correctiones fere nullae temporibus Carolinis insertae') and a brief paragraph by Ganz (1996) 102.[5] These annotations have three purposes: to highlight a word of difficult and/or interesting prosody, to flag up rare Latin words, and to correct the manuscript.

To begin with the prosodic annotations, we find sixteen instances in which Q^1 recorded words of interesting scansion, repeating the word in the same form[6] in the middle margin (should space allow, even sometimes dividing the word over plural lines) or the outer margin. These notes are distributed rather unevenly throughout the work: none in Book I, three in II, none in III, one in IV, four in V and six in VI; if we count in this tally the two instances in the parts of the text annexed after the end of VI, the totals for I and V rise to one and five respectively. Furthermore, it will be seen that those occurring before Book V may have been externally rather than internally motivated annotations. There appear to be five distinct marks employed: a suprascript virgula (ˉ), a diagonal slash (/), a suprascript tilde (˜), the original form of the circumflex (^) and a cryphia (ϲ).[7] The list of instances is as follows, with a record of the relevant notation.

II.128 *clandestinos*] tilde above *i*.
II.447 *adamantina*] diagonal slash above *nt*.
II.557 *infidum* (*infidi* in text)] tilde above first *i*.[8]
IV.9 *musseo* (*museo* in text.)] tilde above *e* (as in text).[9]
V.53 *suerit*] tilde above *e*.

---

[5] Ganz did not record the instances at I.82, V.809, 977, 997, VI.424, 651, 1247, 1279 and introduced five errors in his transcription.
[6] In five instances this is not the case: I.779, II.557, V.269, 778, VI.91.
[7] For an earlier established use of this symbol, cf. Isid. *Etym.* I.20.10 *cryphia, circuli pars inferior cum puncto, ponitur in his locis, ubi quaestio dura et obscura aperiri uel solui non potuit.*
[8] Diels wrongly referred this reading to his Q^2 (saec. XVI).
[9] The same hand also added a suprascript *s* above *museo* in IV.22.

V.269 *percolat* (*percolatur* in text)] tilde above *o*.[10]
V.778 *coniuent* (*conibent* in text)] circumflex above *iu*.
V.1362 *bacae*] tilde above first *a*.
VI.91 *fieri* (*fier* in text)] tilde above first *i*.
VI.127 *fiat*] virgula above *i*.
VI.175 *ibidem*] tilde above second *i*.
VI.413 *fierent*] cryphia above *i*.
VI.607 *fiat*] virgula above *i*.
VI.1279 *consuerat*] tilde above *e*.
V.977 *consuerant*] tilde above *e*.
I.779 *clandestinam* (*glandestinam* in text)] tilde above *i*.[11]

We may first observe that the sigla are not used with complete consistency: the tilde typically signifies long syllables but also short at VI.91. It is possible that the circumflex above *iu* of *coniuent* at V.778 is a poorly written tilde; if so, this symbol is removed from the list of sigla and we have another instance of a tilde denoting a long syllable. There remains, however, no obvious reason to explain the preference for the definitely straight virgula to mark the long *i* of *fiat* at VI.127 and 607 in lieu of the tilde. Finally, the strange mark (/) above *nt* of *adamantina* seems misplaced: the point of interest is the short quantity of *-i-*; perhaps the mark merely draws attention to the word, and scanning the line reveals the important quantity. The cryphiae alongside V.977 and VI.413 (to which I will come) are curious, the former marking a rare word, the latter apparently denoting a short syllable. The same symbol occurs three times at the beginning of Book IV (but nowhere else in Q), where its purpose seems more analogous to Isidore's definition (for which see n. 7).[12]

These sixteen instances can be divided into a number of categories: the retention of long individual vowels in prevocalic position (e.g. *fiat*, *muséo*), the variable length of an *i* in the termination *-tinus* (*clandestīnus* I.779, II.128, *adamantīna* II.447), unexpected long vowels (*percōlatur* V.269, *conīuent* V.778, *bācae* V.1362) as well

---

[10] The omission of *-ur* is no doubt a scribal error rather than a conscious attempt at correcting the paradosis.

[11] Diels wrongly assigned the annotations at IV.9, V.778 and VI.413 to Q[1], and at II.557 to Q[2].

[12] It is found alongside IV.52 (perhaps owing to *sp[er]eciem* for *speciem*?), 88 (*uolitani-suttili* a.c.) and 104 (*&nuest* for *et tenues*) and seems to indicate that the transmitted verses were unintelligible, which was certainly the case before the Renaissance corrections of Q[2]. Perhaps this form of correction began in earnest at the opening of Book IV but was soon abandoned owing to the extent of labour it required.

as instances of surprising prosody (*fĭĕrent* VI.413, *ibīdem* VI.175 (as at III.1080), disyllabic *sue-* (<*suesco*) for monosyllabic: *suĕrit* V.53 versus the molossi *consuerant* V.977 and *consuerat* VI.1279). We may first observe that the annotator has not consistently chosen the first or all instances of each point of interest that appears in the poem: for the syllabic division of *-sue-* in forms of (*con*)*suesco*, earlier examples are found at I.60, 301, II.903, IV.327, 369 (thereafter V.912 and VI.953); for *musaeo*, earlier instances are found at I.934, 947 and II.412; 55 instances of *fĭĕri* occur before VI.91, four of *fĭĕrent* before VI.413 and two of *ibīdem* at verse-end before VI.175 (as well as three after); *percolatur* is also used by Lucretius at II.475 and VI.635. This suggests that the text was being read on its own merit, with points of prosodic interest only noted casually.

A number of the words highlighted are of relevance for scholars of Latin metrics in the Carolingian period. Three of the principal *gradus* in circulation, the *Florilegium Sangallense*, the *Exempla diuersorum auctorum* and Mico's *Opus prosodiacum* (for whose citations see Chapter 2, section J), not only contained many of the words that Q¹ highlighted but also recorded a number of the Lucretian verses in question: II.128 was cited in all three collections to illustrate the prosody of *clandestinus* (*Flor. Sang.* p. 11,8; *Ex. diu. auct.* 198; Mico, *Op. pr.* 63); II.447 was cited for *adamantinus* (*Flor. Sang.* p. 11,19; Mico, *Op. pr.* 9;); IV.9 was cited in the *Florilegium Sangallense* to illustrate *musaeon/-um* (p. 12,2); I.779 was cited by the same work also to illustrate *clandestinus* (p. 11,2). This extent of overlap, four of the five instances outside Books V–VI, suggests that the writer was influenced by some metrical florilegium related to these (if not one of them) for instruction in prosody, and when he passed Lucretian verses cited in this treatise, he took the trouble to record relevant words in the verses brought to his attention. In the instance at II.557, it is possible that the long *i* of *infidus* was elucidated in some lost prosodic florilegium, but it could be an annotation of Q¹'s own choosing. We may also note that the words *infidus* and *ibidem* appeared in Mico's *Opus prosodiacum*: 202 *ibidem* (illustrated by *Carm. de sodoma* 72) and 206 *infida* (illustrated by Ou. *Ars* III.578). Outside the context of prosodic florilegia, II.557 was cited at *Breu. expos. ad* Verg. *Geo.* I.254 (246,8–9 H).

In Books V–VI, by contrast, the annotations are markedly more common (though still very occasional) and have no obvious connection with extant metrical florilegia from the period. This may well reflect the greater attention that these two books apparently received from scholars of the late-antique and early mediaeval periods (as seen with O in Chapter 4).

We may now turn to the second type of annotation, although almost identical in its appearance in the manuscript to the first, namely the highlighting of rare words.[13] I class nine instances in this group:

> I.82 *indugredi* (citation marked by a tilde of sorts above word in text
>   and margin)
> II.459 *indupedita*
> V.151 *tactile*
> V.876 *indupeditas*[14]
> V.997 *uermina* (with cryphia alongside it)[15]
> V.1036 *scimni* (*symni* in text)[16]
> VI.424 *quid sit prestera* (*presteras* in text)[17]
> VI.908 *quare magnes* (*quae magneta* in text)
> II.292 *clinamen* (in the section closing the manuscript)

It is immediately clear that *indu*, the archaic form of *in*, was of interest to this annotator;[18] nevertheless, many instances go unrecorded, both individual *indu* (II.1096, V.102) and compounds of it (*indupeditus* I.240, II.102, VI.453, 1010, *indupediri* IV.70, *indugredi* IV.342, 367, *induperator* IV.967, V.1227). Also of interest to Q^1 were rare words: the adjective *tactilis* is attested in Latin literature only at Lucr. V.151, and the annotator did well to draw attention to it (although the equally unparalleled *intactile* at I.437 was not highlighted); *scymni*, the transliteration of σκύμνοι, is also

---

[13] Thus the assertion of Ganz (1996, 102) was misleading: 'None of Lucretius's distinctive uses of archaic Latin seem to have attracted the attention of the compilers of metrical florilegia or of the annotator of the Quadratus '

[14] Diels wrongly referred this to his Q^1 (saec. XV).

[15] This cryphia is carelessly formed, with the dot protracted into a short line and slightly above the bowl. Although it is unclear from the facsimile, autopsy reveals that the *u* of *uermina* has been obscured by a fold in the middle of the leaf.

[16] Diels incorrectly assigned this to his Q^1, wrongly stating that -*que* of *scymnique* was repeated.

[17] The two glosses in the left margin of the first column of 1$^\Pi$ on I.13 – *signant* for *significant* and *ex tua ui* for *tua ui* – may also be from the hand of Q^1.

[18] I.82 was also cited in *Flor. Sang.* (p. 10,10) and ps.-Prob. *De ult. syll. GLK* IV 263,1; V.1036 (*scymnique leonum*) was cited at Non. 457,15 M and Isid. *Etym.* XII.2.6.

attested in classical Latin only at Lucr. V.1036; that the *y* is transcribed as an *i* is an orthographical error (or misguided correction) that need not trouble us; the three occurrences of *uermen* in classical Latin literature are Lucr. V.997, Arnob. I.50 and Fest. 514,18 (Paul. 515,6 L). The annotations at VI.424 and VI.908 are remarkable in introducing additional words of comment almost analogous to a *capitulum*: 'quid sit *prestera*', 'what a *praester* is',[19] and 'quare *magnes*', 'how a magnet (works)'. Finally, the noun *clinamen* is a ἅπαξ of Latin literature and deserving of emphasis.

We come at last to instances in which Q^1 seems to have corrected only the transmitted text. These three instances are as follows:[20]

> V.809 *petessens*[21] (*petersens* in text a.c. perhaps corrected by Q^2 on the basis of this marginal correction; a small triangle of dots stands above the word in the margin and text)[22]
>
> VI.651 *multesima* (*multaesima* in text; *l* and triangular point stand above the word in the margin and before that in the text)[23]
>
> VI.1247 *sepelire* (*saepelire* [nisi *faepelire*] in text)

Only the first of these corrections required any ingenuity, but it is not so difficult as to suggest access to another manuscript: the verb *petessere* is also used by Lucretius at III.648 and thrice in Cicero.[24] We may remark that it is odd that the annotator limited himself to so small a number of corrections when many very simple emendations could have been made throughout the work. As before, these three instances are concentrated in Books V–VI and could suggest that his reading of the text was more diligent here than elsewhere.

---

[19] This note reveals that the annotator mistook Lucretius' *presteras* as a feminine accusative plural, rather than a transliteration of πρηστήρ (a word probably unknown to him). The addition of a verb is perhaps meant to demonstrate the nominative form of the word, even if he was mistaken on this point.

[20] I here disregard the silent corrections of the Latin text made by the annotator at V.778 (*coniuent* for *conibent*), VI.91 (*fieri* for *fier*) and I.779 (*clandestinam* for *glandestinam*) because metrical sigla stand above the words in the margin. At VI.1107, the untidy crossing out of the repeated *prolapsa* in the text and the marginal recording of *coniuncta* are, in spite of the apparent similarity of script, the work of the original scribe.

[21] Diels wrongly referred this to his Q^1.

[22] For the use of such triangular points, see the corrections of Dungal and the marginal notes of the Annotator in O (Chapter 4, sections A and B).

[23] This well-established symbol for a variant lection was also used by Q^2 but in a slightly different form, with a second shaft rising diagonally from the stroke of the *l*, rather than a bar cutting horizontally through its middle.

[24] *Tusc.* II.62 and twice in *De cons. suo* (*FLP* 10.2, 22 Courtney).

To close this chapter, I turn to the one remaining note, which I cannot explain. Alongside V.274 (*innumerabiliter priuas muta-tur in oras*), transmitted without scribal error, Q¹ has added the opaque marginal note *priu; priua* (see Plate VII).²⁵ Is the former word *priuus*? Is *priua*, bizarrely, intended as a correction? Is the adjective *priuus* recorded owing to its comparative rarity (though used by Lucretius at III.389, 723, IV.261, 566 and V.733), or does he merely record the masculine and feminine nominative singulars? Answers are not forthcoming.

These few annotations provide useful evidence of the perusal of Q in the early Carolingian period²⁶ by a reader (in Corbie or St Bertin?) who, though apparently not linked with a scriptorium or entrusted with any official task concerning the manuscript, was a diligent Latinist who saw value in noting interesting instances of prosody or vocabulary for his private use, as well as adding the occasional correction. Q was not to fall again into such interested hands until the mid fifteenth century with Q².²⁷

²⁵ Diels wrongly referred this to his Q¹.

²⁶ Since the cryphia is apparently introduced at the beginning of Book IV to highlight unintelligible verses, and it is this book which received later rubrication, it is not impossible that Q¹ and this later rubricator were one and the same individual.

²⁷ We may pass over other later hands evident in Q: the hand on 7ᵛ (numbering I.733 and 786), 13ʳ (numbering II.252 and 305), 17ʳ (marking the lacuna of II.757–806) and 51ᵛ (marking the lacuna of V.928–79) is of the seventeenth/eighteenth centuries at the earliest (Chatelain (1913) X col. 2 assigned it to the seventeenth), and also inserted the initial letter at II.755, not already added by Q². This same hand, which may be identical to O⁴ (see Chapter 4), was probably responsible for the numbering of initial and final lines of certain leaves in the early part of Book V (43, 44, 45 and 46ʳ). The hand at the top right of 37ʳ is the same as the author of the second title on 1ʳ. One slight anomaly is the pencil annotations on 64ʳ and thereabouts: *Laus deo* has been added in a large free hand in the bottom margin at 64ʳ, and the same hand has added the initials to VI.840, 848, 887 (all on the open spread of 63ᵛ–64ʳ) and probably to VI.1090 on 66ʳ; he has also added *equor* (= *aequor*) incorrectly to close VI.891. This hand is not that of Q¹ or Q²; rather, it postdates both (as the presence of Q²'s catchletter to the left of its *E* at VI.848 indicates) and I call it Q³. The random marginal note alongside VI.29–30 (on 56ᵛ): *O iuvenis audi bonum consilium* and just below, alongside VI.40: *nunc igitur*, dates from the tenth or eleventh centuries; whereas the latter copies the poetic text as if to highlight an important conclusion, the former is in language reminiscent of expositions of Christian texts (e.g. Aug. *Serm.* 86.14.17 *ipsum audi, accipe bonum consilium*). The strange markings that appear above the two instances of the rare *protelo* (II.531 (15ʳ) and IV.190 (32ᵛ)) were probably added by Q². Finally, yet another hand (saec. XIII?) has added *nequeat* (to clarify *neq; at* of the text) in the margin at I.76, and *De rerum natura* or at least (*rum natur*) at the top of 2ʳ.

CONCLUSION

This book has surveyed the available evidence for the fate of Lucretius' *DRN* from its being written in Rome in the 50s BC to its rediscovery in 1417. Focus has moved through the direct tradition, from marginal jottings entered around the second/third century AD, through their subsequent adoption as seemingly authoritative *capitula*, up to the creation of OQS in the ninth century. The fate of these manuscripts – whether heavily corrected (O), lightly annotated (Q) or largely left alone once written (S) – has been outlined up to their finding a permanent home in Europe's academic libraries.[1] Alongside this direct line of transmission, we have seen that the value of the manifold citations of and appropriations from Lucretius' poem in the indirect tradition is not particularly high for reconstructing his text: although *DRN* seems to have been generally available in Rome and even North Africa until the turn of the fifth century, it soon faded from the public domain thereafter, a text being accessible to Isidore in Seville at the turn of the seventh century, and another manuscript (Ω) somehow becoming available at the dawn of the Carolingian era. After the flurry of intense interest the age of Charlemagne fostered, *DRN* apparently disappeared once more from general circulation until Poggio Bracciolini successfully turned up χ (saec. X?) in or around southern Germany, perhaps at Murbach, perhaps not.

Before closing with some general prescriptions for future editions of *DRN*, a little more should be said about the nature of Ω and its ancestors. Lachmann (3) mistakenly regarded the archetype as a capital manuscript of the fourth/fifth century, similar to the oldest Virgilian codices.[2] It was shown, however, by Duvau

---

[1] For greater detail with regard to the sixteenth and seventeenth centuries, see Appendix V.

[2] Purmann (1846, 14) had already conjectured that Ω was written in *scriptura Langobardica*.

(1888, 32–5) that various errors in the tradition point instead to a minuscule hyperarchetype, and that, given the palaeographical context, the direct or indirect successor of such a manuscript, namely Ω, was very probably also in minuscule.[3] Lachmann thus mistook as the 'archetype' a hyperarchetype at least twice removed from Ω. Although Duvau (34) merely argued that the Lucretian archetype was 'en écriture minuscule', he tentatively suggested that one of the intermediaries between Lachmann's capital manuscript and the Lucretian archetype was 'en écriture anglo-saxonne', nevertheless conceding that 'céla n'est qu'une hypothèse accessoire' (1888, 37). Subsequent scholars who discussed this problem – Diels (VII, X), Martin (VIII), Leonard–Smith (88–9) – were open to the romantic idea of an insular intermediary (possibly involving Alcuin at York) until the idea was torpedoed by Virginia Brown (1968): there is no convincing evidence for either scribal errors suggesting insular script or the presence of a Lucretius in Britain until the mid fifteenth century (c. 1460), when John Tiptoft (1427–70) acquired X (Oxford Bodl. Auct. F I 13).[4] Thereafter, almost no scholar has tackled the question of the nature of Ω and its predecessors; the sole exceptions are a rigorous appendix by Timpanaro (1963, 100–11 = 2005, 145–56) and an article of Fiesoli (2004), whose improbable conclusions were dismissed in Chapter 1 (p. 31).

The analysis of scripts of the archetype and hyperarchetypes is complicated by a number of factors, and one must be careful to disregard the evidence presented by cases that could rather be explained as phonetic or psychological errors, or as attempted corrections (conscious or unconscious); instances that are attested only in O or ψ (or Q, where S is lacking) can potentially provide

---

[3] n for u (V.891), iu for ui (III.581, IV.1150), u for a (V.551, VI.811), e for c (VI.498), c for e (III.456, V.698), t for c (III.403, IV.787), c for t (III.1085), d for cl (I.1080, IV.417, 460, 1123), n for r (I.884, VI.805), r for n (I.664, IV.141, 157, VI.466), f for s (II.497), s for f (I.739, II.683–4, IV.840, V.359). It should also be noted that, since O and Q(S) share errors of word division (e.g. I.85 Iphianas satur OQ, 305 flucti frago OQ), the script of the archetype must have been already misdivided, which means a post-capital script.

[4] Cf. Kennedy (1943) 141, Ogilvy (1967) 196 and Lapidge (2006) 101–5; despite the arguments of the last, I believe that Aldhelm cited Lucr. II.661 from Nonius or a lost grammatical work. The 'parallels' between Lucretius and Aldhelm alleged by Orchard (1994, 130–1 n. 19) are unconvincing.

information about the archetype's script, although there is a danger that the other of these branches corrected an obviously incorrect reading, in which case the script suggested by the error is more probably an error that occurred on the basis of that of a hyperarchetype. If we accept these caveats, it can be established on the basis of scribal errors that Lucretius' transmission had a capital phase (as one would naturally expect) and a later minuscule phase (also predictable, given that our earliest witnesses are of the ninth century).[5] The most natural conclusion is that the archetype and its hyperarchetype were written in minuscule, and that the work passed through an earlier capital phase, which itself followed a manuscript (presumably in six rolls) of older Roman cursive. The researches of Brunhölzl (1962; 1971), along with Bischoff (1990, 61–3), have demonstrated that many works of Latin literature passed through a pre-capital phase of cursive (that Brunhölzl termed *Majuskelkursive*), and textual corruptions evince that *DRN* is no exception.[6] Indeed, if Lucretius' work was left in an informal and unarranged state on his death, as is typically supposed,[7] the poem probably began its transmission in some form of cursive (rather than a polished book-hand).[8]

It is clear from a further stratum of errors that ψ was written in pre-Carolingian or early Carolingian minuscule.[9] There is no need, despite the observations of Timpanaro (1963, 105–8 = 2005, 150–3), to posit that either O or ψ had an immediate exemplar in capitals.[10] The unnecessarily complicated stemma

---

[5] The remarks offered here are necessarily cursory. The comprehensive *thesaurus emendationum* that I am currently preparing will contain as an appendix a full collection of scribal errors in the Lucretian tradition (correcting the myriad errors and omissions of Merrill (1913), which drew much evidence from the *Itali* alone), so as to provide a complete repertory of evidence for firming up the existence of given scripts in Lucretius' transmission.

[6] Cf. the confusions of *b* and *d* (V.1003, VI.71), *r* and *a* (I.919, VI.716), *p* and *t* (I.16, II.43), *ar* and *al* (II.54, 414, VI.1177).

[7] For a discussion of the poem's incompletion, and its relationship to the question of interpolation, see Butterfield (2013).

[8] For previous discussions of scripts of the Lucretian archetype and hyperarchetypes, of varying degrees of rigour and accuracy, see Diels (VII, XIII), Ernout (XVI–XVII), Leonard–Smith (107, 115), Büchner (1956, 201 = 1964, 121) and Brunhölzl (1962, 98).

[9] Cf., e.g., *r* and *s* (I.424, V.1147, VI.1175, 1268), *u* and *a* (I.282, 413, 506, II.206, VI.1106), *f* and *s* (II.891, V.374, 482).

[10] The confusions of *i* and *t* in O (II.1088, V.902) could all arise from a minuscule manuscript, in which *i* with a flick to its top and bottom did not differ markedly from *t*.

Conclusion

he tentatively suggested (1963, 107 = 2005, 152) need not be credited; as Timpanaro conceded himself (1963, 108 = 2005, 153), it is more probable that the evidence can be explained away and that Ω was in minuscule.

The variations in script cannot establish with security the reconstruction of how many manuscript stages stand between Lucretius' autograph and our earliest extant manuscripts. Nevertheless, from my researches it seems that we can posit at least seven phases of transmission in the direct tradition:

(i) Lucretius' manuscript original (papyrus rolls and leaves; older Roman cursive?).

(ii) A 'fair copy' made, presumably by someone close to Lucretius, after his death, who gathered and arranged as appropriate the materials that were available (papyrus rolls; older Roman cursive? capitalis?).

(iii) A manuscript, perhaps a codex, in which the first marginal annotator, and subsequently the second, made their notes (capitalis?).

(iv) A manuscript in which the *capitula* were copied into *indices* for the last three books and the *capitula* were copied in minuscule (either in the margin or the main body) (uncial/capitalis?).

(v) A manuscript in which the *indices* were corrupted somewhat, the *capitula* perhaps standing rubricated (and capitalised?) in the text body (early minuscule).

(vi) The archetype (Ω), in which the *capitula* stood in the text, rubricated and capitalised (pre-Carolingian minuscule).

(vii) O and ψ (Carolingian minuscule), the latter producing Q and S (both Carolingian minuscule).

One or more intermediaries could stand between (ii) (50s BC) and (iii) (saec. III?). (vi) (= Ω) was clearly in a sorry state by the time O was transcribed (and more so by the time of ψ), so it is possible that this archetype was already of some age when it found its way into the Carolingian court; more probable is that it had been keenly read and had perhaps been written in the eighth century, possibly in the later

The confusions of *e* and *f* in ψ (I.233, III.90) and Q (IV.733, V.1337) probably do reflect capital errors, but those at I.233, IV.733 and V.1337 were corrected with ease by O; likewise, the error of *homofomerian* for *homoeomerian* at I.830, highlighted by Lachmann *ad loc.*, could easily have been corrected on the basis of I.834 by ψ and thus rather reflect a capitalis error earlier in transmission (such as I.27 *ornatum* for *oralatum*).

Lombard Kingdom (†774). At any rate, greater certainty can be obtained in the reconstruction of the foliation of the archetype. Since my researches in Chapter 3 have thrown up slight variations on the detailed reconstruction of Ω (Goold (1958)), I offer my own revised tabulation in Appendix IV.

The stemma defended in this thesis (Chapter 1, p. 32), combined with the arguments about the methodology of O's various correctors (see Chapter 4), renders the editing of *DRN* a very simple process in stemmatic terms. If QS agree, that reading (= ψ) is to be weighed against O; if both agree, they present the reading of the archetype Ω; if QS disagree, that which agrees with O preserves the reading of Ω; if Oψ, or OQS, disagree with one another, the editor must weigh the readings against one another and attempt to reconstruct Ω from the evidence presented. Of course, even if Ω can be perfectly reconstructed, it was a manifestly corrupt codex that still requires a good dose of conjecture and, where appropriate, support from the indirect tradition. Any attractive readings of O^2, O^3, O^4, S^2, Q^2 and those found only in the Italian tradition have no textual authority and must be handled like any modern emendation; an alteration made only by Dungal, by contrast, could have been drawn from Ω, if it is plausible that the reading of ψ (or Q) has been corrupted from it, otherwise it likewise needs to be treated as mere conjecture.

In constructing the *apparatus criticus* for future editions, therefore, one need not cite the readings of π or any later corrections in OQS save those of Dungal; only appealing emendations from these sources deserve record. A comprehensive edition could list the full corrections from these hands in an appendix, to which the non-Lucretian *capitula* and *indices* should likewise be relegated. *DRN* lacks an opening title, preserves no sure evidence for authorial divisions (paragraphs, episodes, etc.) and retains no clear evidence of authorial variants or glosses. A number of cases of transposition are necessary to heal the transmitted text, but this is limited primarily to individual verses from scribal error.[11] Since

---

[11] For discussion of this and other assertions made in this paragraph, see Butterfield (2013).

Lucretius' poem was manifestly unfinished, distinguishing between whether he produced the poem's final ordering and whether the initial compiler or 'editor' confused that order can be achieved in theory but scarcely in practice: the Lucretian editor should certainly not improve the ordering of the poem for him by rearranging paragraphs and arguments, regardless of what Lucretius might have intended, unless the transposition could be correcting a genuine error of transmission. Various lacunae occur throughout *DRN* and in such cases the loss should be marked (perhaps by asterisks), the apparatus merely containing a short indication of the possible amount of text lost and, if discernible, its probable subject matter.

The scope for emending the text of *DRN* remains significant: future editors will do well to avoid uncritical conservatism,[12] to weigh all plausible conjectures (from the ninth century to the present) with open minds, and to cite the most probable emendations and their originators in the apparatus. If a modern conjecture is preceded by a codex (whether a later corrector of OQS or one of the *Itali*), that manuscript should precede the relevant scholar's name; in cases where Q^2 restored the text but that emendation also occurred independently in the *Itali*, the latter should be cited first for chronological reasons if found in π or a pre-1450 source. This book has aimed ultimately to provide firmer foundations for the difficult task of editing *DRN*, and that undertaking has largely proved, in a manner redolent of the poem itself, to be a series of simplifications of apparently diverse phenomena.

---

[12] One of the most difficult aspects of Lucretian textual criticism is the frequent ambiguity as to whether an error or infelicity springs from corruption in transmission or the poem's incomplete state.

APPENDICES

APPENDIX I

CAPITULA LUCRETIANA[1]

Liber I

44 τὸ μακάριον καὶ ἄφθαρτον
TOMA CARION CAE APITRATON O : *om. sp. rel.* Q : [TOM]ACARION CAE
APITRATON S

62 laus inuentoris
sic OS : *om. sp. rel.* Q

84 exemplum religionis
sic O : entemplum religionis S : *om. sp. rel.* Q

107 finis doloris
sic OS : *om. sp. rel.* Q

112 de anima
sic OS : *om. sp. rel.* Q

150 nihil de nihilo gigni
nihil de nihil gigni OS : *om. sp. rel.* Q nihilo *corr. Itali*

215 nihil ad nihilum interire
sic OS : *om. sp. rel.* Q

269 corpora quae non uideantur
sic O : corporaque non uideantur S : *om. sp. rel.* Q

277 de uento
sic OS : *om. sp. rel.* Q

298 de odore, calore, frigore, uoce
sic OS : *om. sp. rel.* Q

---

[1] This list does not include the cases where Lucretian verses have wrongly been transmitted in the form of *capitula* (on which see Chapter 3, section I(D)): I.11 (O), 411 (O),
II.42–3 (Ω), 94 (O), 502 (O), 508 (O; om. Q), 608 (O), 710 (O; *ante* 707 S; *sp. duorum
uu. rel. ante* 707 Q), 809 (O), 887 (O), 909 (O), 962 (O), 1012 (O), 1023 (O), 1112 (O),
III.672a (Ω), 759 (Ω), 805 (Ω), 905 (Ω), 949 (Ω).

274

305 uestes uuesci et aresci
sic O : uestes uuesci et artesci S : *om. sp. rel.* Q

311 de anulo in digito et ceteris
sic OS : *om. sp. rel.* Q

334 de inani
sic OS (de inani *iterum add. in marg.* O *man. s. XV*)[2]: *om. sp. rel.* Q

370 de piscibus in aqua
sic OS : *om. sp. rel.* Q

419 corpus et inane esse naturam rerum
sic OS *ante* 419 (O *in ras.*; *et* om. S add. S[1]) : *sine sp. om.* Q *ante* 418 *pos. plur. edd.*

430 tertiam naturam nullam esse rerum
sic OS : *om. sp. rel.* Q

498 solidum esse
sic OS : *om. sp. rel.* Q

551 contra εἰς ἄπειρον τὴν τομήν
CONTRA ISAPIRONTEN·TO MEN O (.i. elocutio *sscr.* O[3]) : CONTRAISAPIRONTEN
TOMEN S : *om. sp. rel.* Q

565 de molli natura, aqua, aere et ceteris
sic OS (*sine punct.*; *ante* 523 S) : *ut text. poetae* Q

635 contra Heraclitum
sic OS (Eraclitum S) : *om. sp. rel.* Q

705 neque ignem neque aera neque umorem principia esse
ut text. poetae OS (*sed* capitulum *add. in marg.* O[3]) : *ut text. poetae* Q *sed uncis exclusit* Q[2]

716 contra Empedoclen
sic OS : *om. sp. rel.* Q

830 contra Anaxagoran
sic OS (<c>ontra S) : *om. sp. rel.* Q

951 τὸ πᾶν ἄπειρον· τὸ γὰρ πεπερασμένον ἄκρον ἔχει
TOPANAPIRONTO GARPEPIRAS MENONACROE O : TOPANAPIRONTO GARPE-
PERASMENONACROE S : *om. sp. duorum uu. rel.* Q ACRON *recte Lachmann, qui*
ECHI (= ἔχει) *post* ACRON *suppl., coll.* Epic. *Ep. ad Hdt.* 41

1052 εἰς τὸ μέσον ἡ φορά
isto meson ephora OS : *om. sp. rel.* Q

---

[2] This is probably the hand of M. von Busek: see Chapter 4, section F. Alongside I.875–6 a
fifteenth-century hand, perhaps likewise that of von Busek, added: *Anaxagoras dixit
omnia esse in omnibus.*

Appendix I

Liber II

14 σαρκὸς εὐσταθὲς κατάστημα
SARCO SEVS STATES CATASTEMA O : SARCOSEUS STATE SCATA STEMA S :
sp. rel. om. Q

62 de motu principiorum et infinita esse
sic OS : *om. sp. rel.* Q

89 imum nihil esse
sic OS : *om. sp. rel.* Q

112 quae in solis radiis appareant
sic O : *ut text. poetae* S : *om. sp. rel.* Q

142 de celeritate motus
sic O *post priorem partem u.* 142 (*cuius pars altera subter seq.*) S : *om. sp. rel.* Q

184 nihil sursum ferri corpusculorum sed pressa a radicibus exurgere corpora
sic (corpusculorum $S^{a.c.}$) O *minusc. rubr.* S : *om. sp. duorum uu. rel.* Q

221 de <de>clinatione motus
sic OS : *om. sp. rel.* Q *de suppl.* AF

333 de figura atomorum
sic OS : *om. sp. rel.* Q

388 de lumine
sic OS : *om. sp. rel.* Q

392 de oleo
sic OS : *om. sp. rel.* Q

398 de melle
sic OS : *om. sp. rel.* Q

400 de absenthio
sic ante 401 O : de absentio *ante* 404 S : *om. sp. ante* 404 *rel.* Q

408 de serrae stridore
de serre (serrae *corr.* O^D) stridore OS : *om. sp. rel.* Q

447 de adamante, ferro, silice, aere
sic sine punct. (scilice S) OS : *om. sp. rel.* Q

464 de sudore salso
sic O : *om. sp. rel.* Q

471 de aqua marina
sic O : *sp. rel. om.* Q

478 figuras esse multas
figuras (O^D: figura $O^{a.c.}$) esse multas O: *om. sp. rel.* Q figuras O : finitas *tempt. Diels*

522 in terra †insemina† inesse
sic (ex 589cap.) O : *om. sp. duorum uu. rel.* Q inter se similia infinita esse *Lachmann*

589 in terra semina insunt
sic O : *om. sp. rel.* Q inesse *corr. Fischer*

598 de matre magna[3]
sic O : *om. sp. rel.* Q

646 τὸ μακάριον καὶ ἄφθαρτον
TOMΔKΔPION KAIA ΦΘAPTON *litt. Graecis* O : TO MΔKΔPION KΛIΛ ΦΘAPTON *litt. Graecis* S : *om. sp. rel.* Q

730 non necessario alba ex albis principiis fieri
sic OS : *om. sp. duorum uu. rel.* Q

755 colores non esse
sic OS : *om. sp. rel.* Q

801 de colore columbarum
sic OS (*partim maiusc. partim minusc.* S) : *om. sp. rel.* Q

806 de cauda pauonis
sic OS (*partim maiusc. partim minusc.* S) : *om. sp. rel.* Q

842 atomos nec colorem nec odorem nec sucum nec frigus nec calorem habere
sic (atmos S[a.c.]) OS : *om. sp. trium uu. rel.* Q

865 de insensili sensile gigni
sic OS : *om. sp. rel.* Q

1048 omne infinitum in omnis partes
sic (partis O) OS : *om. sp. rel.* Q

1058 apiros mundus
sic OS : *om. sp. rel.* Q mundos OS : mundus *scripsi*

1105 mundum natum et multos similis
e OS : *corr. Ed. Iunt.* mulio S *om. sp. duorum uu. rel.* Q : mundum natum et multa semina addi *Fischer* : mundum natum e multis seminibus *olim conieci*

1144 iam senem mundum et omnia pusilla nasci
sic OS : *om. sp. duorum uu. rel.* Q

Liber III

41 homines mortem maxime timere
sic (axime S) OS : *om. sp. rel.* Q

94 de animi et animae natura sensuque
sic (et anime S) OS : *om. sp. rel.* Q

---

[3] For dismissal of the supposed *capitulum* at II.600, see Butterfield (2008h) 354–7.

136 animum et animam coniuncta esse
sic OS : *om. sp. rel.* Q

182 de mobilitate animi
sic OS : *om. sp. rel.* Q

228 tertiam animam esse mentem
sic OS : *om. sp. rel.* Q

241 quartam sine nomine animam
sic (quarta S) OS : *om. sp. rel.* Q

262 coniunctio animi et animarum
sic OS : *om. sp. rel.* Q

288 de uarietate animi
sic OS : *om. sp. rel.* Q

350 de sensu corporis et animi
sic OS : *om. sp. rel.* Q

370 contra Democritum de animo et anima
sic OS : *om. sp. rel.* Q

379 corpus non sentire per se sine animi motu
sic (motus $O^{a.c.}$S : *corr.* O^2) OS : *om. sp. rel.* Q

417 animam natiuam et mortalem esse
sic OS : *om. sp. rel.* Q

445 animum et corpus simul nasci et crescere et simul interire
sic OS (*minusc. sed rubr.* O) : *om. sp. trium uu. rel.* Q

624 de sensibus animae et animi
sic O : *om. sp. rel.* Q

711 de natali animam non esse priuatam
sic (paratam O : *corr. Lachmann*) O : *om. sp. duorum uu. rel.* Q

978 quae ad inferos dicantur ea uitae uitia esse
sic O : *om. sp. rel.* Q *fort.* dicentur

Liber IV

An *index capitulorum* precedes the poetic text of OQ. It is in this book alone that Q contains some rubricated *capitula* (saec. X/XI); since these headings are drawn, with errors, from the preceding index, they are not recorded here. With the appearance of a second witness in the form of the *indices capitulorum* I now use the further designation *ind.* (= *in indice*) and *text.* (= *ad loc. in textu poematis*) alongside the manuscript sigla.

Capitula Lucretiana

1 sibi iucundissimum esse quod claram lucem mortalibus ostendat
sic (quo O^{a.c.} : *corr.* O^{D}) *ut uerba poetae text.* O *text.* Q : *sic ind.* O *ind.* Q

29 de simulacris
sic text. O *ind.* O *ind.* Q : *om. sp. rel. text.* Q

98 de imaginibus
sic text. O *ind.* O *ind.* Q : *om. sp. rel. text.* Q

116 quam parua sint animalia
sic text. O *ind.* O *ind.* Q : *om. sp. rel. text.* Q

127(?) esse item maiora
sic ind. O *ind.* Q : *om. sine sp. text.* O *text.* Q minora *Bernays* animalia *post* maiora *suppl. Mussehl*

131 de nubibus et simulacra gigni
sic text. O : de nubibus *ind.* O *ind.* Q : *om. sp. rel. text.* Q

176 de celeritate simulacrorum
sic text. O : de celeritate *ind.* O *ind.* Q : *om. sp. rel. text.* Q

230 <omnia> tactu uideri
sic ind. O *ind.* Q : *om. sine sp. text.* O *text.* Q res *ante* tactu *tempt. Fischer* : omnia *suppleui*

269 ultra speculum cur uideatur
sic ind. O *ind.* Q : ultimum saeculum cur uideatur *text.* O

312 ex tenebris in luce quae sint uideri et rusum ex luce quae sint in tenebris uideri non posse
sic (que (quae *corr.* O^{D}) sunt in O : quae sint in *Itali*; uidere O : *corr. Itali*) *text.* O : ex tenebris in luce (lucem *ind.* Q) quae sint uideri *ind.* O *ind.* Q : *om. sp. trium uu. rel. text.* Q

326 plures imagines cur fiant
sic text. O *ind.* O *ind.* Q: *om. sp. rel. text.* Q

353 de turribus
sic text. O : de turbis *ind.* O *ind.* Q

364 de umbra hominis
sic text. O *lnd.* O *ind.* Q

387 de uisu
sic text. O *ind.* O *ind.* Q : *om. sp. rel. text.* Q

476 de uero sensu quare cognoscatur
sic (quae *ind.* O *ind.* Q) *text.* O *ind.* O *ind.* Q

513 de falso sensu
sic text. O *ind.* O *ind.* Q: *om. sp. rel. text.* Q

524 dc auditis
sic text. O *ind.* O *ind.* Q : *om. sp. rel. text.* Q

Appendix I

526 corpoream esse uocem
sic ind. O *ind.* Q: corpoream esse uocemus *text.* O : *om. sp. rel. text.* Q

572 de uocis imaginibus
sic text O *ind.* O *ind.* Q

595 qua uisus non tranet uocem tranare
sic (quo *ind.* Q; trnet *text.* O$^{a.c.}$: *corr. text.* O^2) *text.* O *ind.* O *ind.* Q

615 de sapore
sic text. O *ind.* O *ind.* Q : *om. sp. rel. text.* Q

633 quare alia aliis contraria sint
sic text. O *ind.* O *ind.* Q : *om. sp. rel. text.* Q

673 de odore
sic text. O *ind.* O *ind.* Q : *om. sp. rel. text.* Q

722 de animi motu
sic text. O *ind.* O *ind.* Q

779 quare quod libuerit statim cogitemus
sic text. O *ind.* O *ind.* Q : *om. sp. rel. text.* Q

836 prius oculos linguam auris esse nata quam eorum usum
sic (auris *ind.* O : aures *ind.* Q *text.* O; natam *ind.* O) *text.* O *ind.* O *ind.* Q

877 de motu membrorum hoc est de ambulando
sic text. O : de ambulando *ind.* O *ind.* Q : *om. sp. rel. text.* Q

907 de somno quem ad modum fiat
sic text. O : de somno *ind.* O *ind.* Q : *om. sp. rel. text.* Q

962 de somniis
sic (somnis *ind.* O) *text.* O *ind.* O *ind.* Q

1030 de rebus Veneriis
sic (Veneris *ind.* O) *text.* O *ind.* O *ind.* Q : *om. sp. rel. text.* Q

Liber V

An *index capitulorum* is present in OQ. Since in O the task of rubrication has not been wholly completed, the *capitula* to 892, 901, 916 and 1161 do not appear.

1 plus hominibus profuisse qui sapientiam inuenerit quam Cererem Liberum Herculem
sic ind. O *ind.* Q : *om. sine sp. text.* OQ

59 animam natiuam esse
sic text. O *ind.* O *ind.* Q: *om. sp. rel. text.* Q

64 mundum et natum et mortalem esse
sic text. O : de mundo *ind.* O *ind.* Q : *om. sp. rel. text.* Q

76 de solis et lunae cursu
sic text. O *ind.* O *ind.* Q: *om. sp. rel. text.* Q

92 mare caelum terram interitura
sic (terra *ind.* O; celum *text.* O) *text.* O *ind.* O *ind.* Q: *om. sp. rel. text.* Q

132 animum et animam non posse sine corpore esse
sic text. O : animam et animum non posse esse sine corpore *ind.* O *ind.* Q : *om. sp. duorum uu. rel. text.* Q

146 mundum non esse ab dis constitutum
sic text. O *ind.* Q: mundum non esse ab dis[conpositione rerumque] | stitutum [ineosunt] *ind.* O : *om. sp. rel. text.* Q

200 diuisio terrae uel uitium
sic (terre) *text.* O : *om. sp. rel. text.* Q : *om. sine sp. ind.* O *ind.* Q

240 cui pars natiua sit totum natiuum esse
sic (cui *ind.* O : cur *ind.* Q : quo *text.* O : quoi *Lachmann* : cuius *conieci*) *text.* O *ind.* O *ind.* Q : *om. sp. rel. text.* Q

251 de terra
sic text. O *ind.* O *ind.* Q : *om. sp. rel. text.* Q

261 de aqua
sic text. O *ind.* O *ind.* Q : *om. sp. rel. text.* Q

273 de aere siue anima
sic text. O *ind.* O *ind.* Q : *om. sp. rel. text.* Q

281 de igni et sole
sic text. O *ind.* O *ind.* Q : *om. sp. rel. text.* Q

294 de lampade et lucerna
sic text. O *ind.* O *ind.* Q : *om. sp. rel. text.* Q

306 de aedificiis quemadmodum intereant
sic text. O *ind.* O *ind.* Q : *om. sp. rel. text.* Q

324 quare natiua omnia dicat
sic (natia O[a.c.]: *corr.* O[2]) *text.* O : quare nata omnia dicta *ind.* O *ind.* Q : *om. sp. rel. text.* Q

351 quare aeternitas esse possit
sic text. O *ind.* O *ind.* Q : *om. sp. rel. text.* Q

376 et natiua esse cum sint mortalia
sic (natiuet O[a.c.] : *corr.* O[2]; sit O : *corr. Itali*) *text.* O : et natiua esse *ind.* O *ind.* Q : *om. sp. rel. text.* Q

396 de Phaethonte solis filio
sic (Phetonte *omnes*) *text.* O *ind.* O *ind.* Q : *om. sp. rel. text.* Q

Appendix I

419 origo mundi et omnium

sic text. O *ind.* O *ind.* Q : *om. sp. rel. text.* Q

471 de solis et lunae magnitudine et motu eorum et quemadmodum nascantur

sic (nascuntur O : nascantur *correxi*) *text.* O : de solis et lunae magnitudine *ind.* O *ind.* Q : *om. sp. duorum uu. rel. text.* Q

564 de solis magnitudine

sic text. O *ind.* O *ind.* Q : *om. sp. rel. text.* Q

575 de luna

sic ind. O *ind.* Q : *om. sine sp. text.* O *text.* Q

590 de calore solis

sic text. O *ind.* O *ind.* Q : *om. sp. rel. text.* Q

621 Democriti de sole

sic text. O *ind.* O *ind.* Q : *om. sp. rel. text.* Q

629 de lunae cursu

sic (lune *ind.* O : *corr.* O^D) *text.* O *ind.* O *ind.* Q : *om. sp. rel. text.* Q

663 ex Ida uisio solis

sic (uiseo *ind.* O) *text.* O *ind.* O : ex ia uiseo solis *ind.* Q : *om. sp. rel. text.* Q

680 de die longo et nocte breui

sic text. O : de die longo et breui nocte *ind.* O *ind.* Q : *om. sp. rel. text.* Q

705 de lunae lumine

sic (lune *ind.* O^{a.c} *ind.* Q^{a.c.} : *corr.* O^D Q²) *text.* O *ind.* O *ind.* Q : *om. sp. rel. text.* Q

737 de anni temporibus

sic text. O *ind.* O *ind.* Q : *om. sp. rel. text.* Q

751 de eclipsi

sic ind. O : de eclypsi *ind.* Q : *om. sine sp. text.* O *text.* Q

774 de solis et lunae offectione

sic text. O *ind.* O *ind.* Q : *om. sp. rel. text.* Q

780 de nouitate mundi et dispositione rerum quae in eo sunt

de nouitate rerum mundi et dispositione quae (O² : uuae O^{a.c.}) in eo sunt *text.* O : de natiuitate mundi et dis | [con]positione rerum que | ineosunt *ind.* O : de natiuitate mundi et dis | [constitutum com]positione rerum | quae in eo sunt *ind.* Q : *om. sp. duorum uu. text.* Q

878 de Centauris

sic text. O *ind.* O *ind.* Q : *om. sp. rel. text.* Q

892 de Scylla

sic ind. Q : de sculla *ind.* O : *om. sp. rel. text.* O *text.* Q

901 de Chimera

de chimeera *ind.* O *ind.* Q : *corr. Itali* : *om. sp. rel. text.* O *text.* Q

282

916 non potuisse Chimeram et Scyllam et similia eorum gigni
sic (potuisset *ind.* O : posse *ind.* Q : *corr. Itali*; et² *om. ind.* Q) *ind.* O *ind.* Q : *om. sp. rel. text.* O : *om. sp. duorum uu. rel. text.* Q

1161 quomodo hominibus innata sit deorum opinio
sic ind. O *ind.* Q : *om. sp. rel. text.* O : *om. sp. duorum uu. rel. text.* Q

1241 quemadmodum aurum, argentum, plumbum repertum sit
sic sine punct. text. O *ind.* O *ind.* Q : *om. sp. duorum uu. rel. text.* Q

1281 quemadmodum ferrum inuentum sit
sic (inuenium *ind.* O) *text.* O *ind.* O *ind.* Q : *om. sp. rel. text.* Q

Liber VI

An *index capitulorum* is present in OQ, although in a confused form.

50(?) qui procurationem mundi dis attribuit, sibi ipsum de dis immortalibus sollicitudines constituere
sic (qui *ind.* O : ui *ind.* Q; dis attribuit mundi *ind.* O *ind.* Q : mundi dis attribuit *restitui*; de diis *ind.* O; sollicitudine Oᵃ·ᶜ· : *corr.* Oᴰ) *ind.* O *ind.* Q : *om. sine sp. text.* O *text.* Q

96 de tonitru
sic text. O *ind.* Q *ind.* O : *om. sp. rel. text.* Q

160 de fulgure
sic (fulgore *ind.* Q) *text.* O *ind.* O *ind.* Q : *om. sp. rel. text.* Q

204 in nubibus semina ignita inesse
sic text. O : in nubibus seminet (eminet *ind.* Q) | ignes inesse *ind.* O *ind.* Q : *om. sp. rel. text.* Q

219 de fulmine
sic text. O *ind.* O *ind.* Q : *om. sp. rel. text.* Q

225 ignis ex fulmine natura
sic ind. O *ind.* Q : ignis et fulminis (fulmine Oᵃ·ᶜ· : *corr.* Oᴰ) natura *text.* O : *om. sp. rel. text.* Q

246 fulmina in crassioribus nubibus et alte gigni
sic (fumina *text.* Oᵃ·ᶜ· : *corr.* Oᴰ) *text.* O *ind.* O *ind.* Q : *om. sp. rel. text.* Q

285 de tonitribus et terrae motu
sic (terre *text.* O *ind.* Q; tronitribus Oᵃ·ᶜ·: *corr.* O *ipse*) *text.* O *ind.* O *ind.* Q : *om. sp. rel. text.* Q

357 autumno magis fulmina et tonitrua fieri
sic text. O *ind.* O *ind.* Q : *om. sp. duorum uu. rel. text.* Q

451 de nubibus
sic text. O *ind.* O *ind.* Q : *om. sp. rel. text.* Q

Appendix I

493 spiracula mundi
sic text. O *ind.* O *ind.* Q : *om. sp. rel. text.* Q

495 de imbribus
sic text. O *ind.* O *ind.* Q : *om. sp. rel. text.* Q

526 de arquo
sic ind. O *ind.* Q : de arci (O^D : arquo(?) O$^{a.c.}$) *text.* O : *om. sp. rel. text.* Q *ante* 524 *pos. Gifanius*

535 de terrae motu
sic (terre *text.* O$^{a.c.}$ *ind.* O *ind.* Q : *corr.* O^D) *text.* O *ind.* O *ind.* Q : *om. sp. rel. text.* Q

608 quare mare maius non fiat
sic (fit O$^{a.c.}$: *corr.* O^2) *text* O *ind.* O *ind.* Q : *om. sp. rel. text.* Q

639 de Aetna
sic (Aethna *ind.* O) *text.* O *ind.* O *ind.*Q : *om. sp. rel. text.* Q

712 de Nilo fluuio
sic text. O *ind.* O *ind.* Q : *om. sp. rel. text.* Q

738 de lacu Auerni
sic text. O *ind.* O *ind.* Q : *om. sp. rel. text.* Q

749 cornices Athenis ad aedem Mineruae non esse
sic (cornicis *ind.* O; at *text.* O$^{a.c.}$: *corr.* O^D : om. *ind.* O *ind.* Q; Minerue *ind.* O *ind.* Q *text.* S) *text.* O *text.* S *ind.* O *ind.* Q: *om. sp. duorum uu. rel. text.* Q

756 in Syria quadripedes
sic text. O *text.* S: in Syria quadripedis *ind.* O *ind.* Q : *om. sp. rel. text.* Q

840 cur aqua in puteis aestate frigidior sit
sic (cor *text.* S : frigidio *text.* O *text.* S : *corr. Itali*) *text.* O *text.* S : cur aqua in puteis frigidior | sit aestate *ind.* O *ind.* Q : *om. sp. duorum uu. rel. text.* Q

848 de fonte ad Hammonis <fanum>
sic (ammonis *ind.* O : haminonis *text.* S) *text.* O *text.* S *ind.* O *ind.* Q : *om. sp. rel. text.* Q fanum *in fine suppleui*

879 in aqua taedam ardere
sic ind. O *ind.* Q : in aqua (aquam *text.* O$^{a.c.}$: *corr.* O^D) taedam ardere (ardore *text.* O$^{a.c.}$ *text.* S : *corr.* O^D) *text.* O *text.* S : *om. sp. rel. text.* Q

888 de fonte Aradi in mare
sic (Aradia *text.* S) *text.* O *text.* S *ind.* O *ind.* Q : *om. sp. rel. text.* Q *ante* 890 *pos. Diels*

906 de lapide Magnete
sic ind. O *ind.* Q : *om. sine sp. text.* O *text.* Q *text.* S

921 <corpora> fluere ab omnibus rebus
sic (ab omnibus *ind.* O *ind.* Q : omnibus *text.* O : abminibus *text.* S) *text.* O *text.* S *ind.* O *ind.* Q : *om. sp. rel. text.* Q corpora *suppl. Fischer*

284

936 raras res omnis esse
sic ind. O *ind.* Q : *om. sine sp. text.* O *text.* Q *text.* S

1090 <de> pestilentia unde creetur
pestilentia unde creatur *text.* O *maiusc. sed atr. text.* S *ind.* O : *om. sine sp. ind.* Q : *om. sp.*
duorum uu. rel. text. Q : de pestilentia unde creetur *restitui*

1138 de pestilentia Atheniensium
sic (Athenienium *text.* O *text.* S) *text.* O *text.* S *maiusc. rubr. ut. capit. ind.* O : *sp. rel.*
duorum uu. om. ind. Q : *om. sp. rel. text.* Q

APPARATUS FONTIUM LUCRETI (ANTE A.D. MILLESIMUM)[1]

Liber I[2]

1: Prisc. *Inst. GLK* II 292,18–19; 1–2: cf. Ou. *Tr.* II.261–2, Auson. XIII.36.1–2, XIV.3.7; 2: *Donat. *ad* Ter. *Eun.* 325; 3: cf. **Frag. Bob. de nom. et pronom.*

[1] This date is sufficient to cover all authors influenced by Lucretius by the tail end of the Carolingian period (the death of Louis V in 987). It should be noted that *DRN* was cited very rarely between the mid ninth century and the rediscovery of Lucretius by Poggio in 1417, and there is no extant evidence that any such author had direct access to a text of *DRN*. William of Hirschau (1026–91), Honorius of Autun (*fl.* early twelfth century), William of Conches (*c.* 1080–*c.* 1154), Daniel of Morely (*c.* 1140–*c.* 1210) and Gerald of Wales (*c.* 1146–1222, misattributing the verse to Plautus) cite II.888, although their corrupt texts demonstrate that they all drew the quotation from Priscian, directly or indirectly: cf. Jessen (1860). A florilegium within an eleventh-century Venetian manuscript (Marc. Z. L. 497, ff. 19ʳ col. 1–58ᵛ col. 2) cites Lucr. I.155 at f. 45ʳ col. 1 (which could be drawn from Ermenrich of Ellwangen); at f. 49ᵛ col. 1 Drac. *Orest.* 661 is wrongly attributed to Lucretius, an error inherited from the florilegium tradition. Bérenger of Tours (*c.* 1000–88), Baldrecius of Bourgueil (1046–1130), the author of the *Gesta Sancti Servatii* (early twelfth century) and the compiler of the florilegium Bonn, Universiteitsbibliothek S. 218 (saec. XI, f. 60ᵛ) cited V.905 (although the first – or his scribes – wrongly transposed *leo* and *draco*), a verse the trio drew from Hyginus, Jerome, Isidore or Hincmar. Alain of Lille (*c.* 1125–*c.* 1203) wrongly attributes (*Summa de arte praedic.* 1 (*PL* CCX 114C)) to Lucretius the fragment of Apollonius Molon *lacrima nihil citius arescit* (cited in antiquity at Cic. *Inu.* I.109). Gervase of Tilbury (*c.* 1150–*c.* 1228) cites VI.740–1 at *Otia imperialia dec. III. Tit.* 19, although it is probable that this quotation of the couplet is drawn from Nonius. Basic knowledge of Lucretian doctrine can be seen in the third Vatican mythology (twelfth century), albeit drawn in its entirety from Servius: regarding *superstitio* (III.5.2, s.u. *Neptunus*), the non-existence of the Underworld (III.6.1, s.u. *Pluto*), the sufferings of the Underworld occurring in humans' span of life (III.6.5, s.u. *Tityus*), the rivers of the Underworld (III.6.7, s.u. *Lethaeum*), Lucretius' being a poet with a philosophical commitment (III.9.9, s.u. *Mercurius*), and the tripartite constitution of humans (III.9.10, s.u. *Mercurius*). In the *Glossarium Osberni* (mid twelfth century) we find citation of Lucretius II.662 (s.u. *bos*, with *buceriasque* for *buceriaeque* and *pauit* for *caeli*; see Mai (1836) vol. VIII 70), V.516 (s.u. *haurio*, with *in fluuio* for *ut fluuios*, attributed to Lucan; (1836) vol. VIII, 271) and II.888 (s.u. *sentio*, with *insensibili* for *insensilibus* and *nasci* for *gigni*; (1836) vol. VIII, 515); the nature of these corruptions strongly suggests that their sources are, respectively, Mico (with contamination at verse-end by Ou. *Met.* VI.395), Isidore and Priscian. It is presumably on the basis of Ou. *Tr.* II.425–6 that Conrad of Mure (*c.* 1210–*c.* 1281) wrote in his *Fabularius* (f. k9ᵛ, Basel, 1470) *Lucretius est proprium nomen cuiusdam poete qui multa scripsit de natura fulminis*. The anonymous composer of the pseudo-Boethian *De disciplina scholarium* (early thirteenth century) states *si etiam aliud quam tortuosa volumina Lucretii in partibus suis inuenissent, consilio nostro non tantum prodiissent* (II.5) and *contumelioso coitus appetitu sanguineum Lucretii filium, Zenonis discipulum, omnis Roma fleuit inuiscatum* (II.8), neither of which could prove direct access to *DRN*. I disregard the curious and frequent repetition of IV.1232, which

GLK II 555,3; 3–4: Non. 274,32–4; 7: *Macr. Sat.* VI.4.20, *Fest. Paul. 59,27 (cf. etiam II.228); 12: *Schol. Bern. ad* Verg. *Geo.* I.375; 18: *Seru. ad* Verg. *Geo.* II.372; 27: Prisc. *Inst. GLK* II 444,24–445,1, 527,7; 29: Prisc. *Inst. GLK* II 285,8; 31–4: Lact. Plac. in Stat. *Theb.* III.296; [44–9 uid. II.646–51]; 50: cf. *Schol. Veron. ad* Verg. *Geo.* III.3 (408,12–13 H) (cf. etiam IV.912); 54–7: Sen.

comes to be attributed to 'Statius', by Aimeric of Gastinaux (whose *Ars lectoria* dates to 1086), Siguin (whose work of the same title dates to the late eleventh century), Alexander Neckam (1157–1217), Beda of Florence (died *c.* 1240) and Giovanni Balbi (whose *Catholicon* dates to 1286); see Sivo (1988). Similarly without significance is the gloss upon a verse (575) of Sigebert of Gembloux's *De passione sanctorum Thebeorum*, where *Lucretius: naturam clandestinam* is no doubt drawn from a prosodic florilegium (such as the *Florilegium Sangallense*). Nothing can be concluded from the appearance of *genus omne animantum* in Reiner of Liège (*c.* 1120–*c.* 1182), since the phrase also occurs in Claudius Marius Victorius' *Alethia*, the *Laudes Domini* (*c.* fourth century) and Walahfrid Strabo (808/9–49); likewise Strabo's *indugredi* (*Vita Sancti Galli conf.* 910) is presumably drawn from the citation of I.82 by both the author of *De ultimis syllabis* and the *Florilegium Sangallense* (or a similar source). Finally, *uitigenum* in the *Vita Sancti Blandini* (235) of Fulcoius of Beauvais (*fl.* eleventh century), as well as the works of Thomas Aquinas (1225–74) and William of Ockham (*c.* 1285–1349), could echo its appearance in the translation by Hilduin of St Denis (*c.* 755–855) of the pseudo-Dionysian *De diuinis nominibus* (p. 378), and Robert Grosseteste's (*c.* 1170–1253) use of the rare noun *formamentum* could be drawn from Arnobius (III.16) rather than Lucretius, if not a coincidential coinage. The three supposed imitations in the *Encomium Emmae Reginae* (mid eleventh century), for which see Campbell (1949) cxiv, are far too tenuous to allow any excitement about its author's geographical proximity to St Bertin (as exhibited by Hunt (1971) 51–2, and Reynolds (1983b) 220 n. 10): although *membris abradunt* at II.11 is similar to *abradere membris* of Lucr. IV.1103, *sagaci ratione* (III.7), reversed at Lucr. I.130 and 368, also occurs in Claudian and the *Gesta Berengarii*, and *inviolabile viget* (III.14) need not reflect *inuiolabilia . . . uigere* of Lucr. V.305. No convincing instance of Dante's imitating Lucretius has been proposed. Petrarch's knowledge of Lucretius is drawn directly from Macrobius: see Bignone (1913) 254–7, Gasparotto (1967–8; 1972; 1972–3; 1991), D. Canfora (1994–5). It is improbable, as argued by Cook (1907) esp. at 44, Bloomfield (1952), Getto (1958), Hemmerdinger (1968), Gasparotto (1968–9), that Boccaccio had direct contact with *DRN*; Giuseppe Billanovich was right to dismiss in passing the idea that either Boccacio or Petrarch knew Lucretius directly (1971, 62–3). Earlier, Guido Billanovich (1958, 164–8 and 182–90) had alleged imitations in Eugenius Vulgarius (*fl.* early tenth century), the *Liber pontificalis* of Ravenna (*c.* 900), Lovato Lovati (*c.* 1241–1309) and Albertino Mussato (*c.* 1261–1329) but few have accepted the validity of any of these associations. For sound scepticism regarding Lovato's knowledge of Lucretius see Reeve (1980) 42 n. 8. As regards Mussato, Billanovich does not provide complete information, and phrases that he claims to be solely Lucretian prove not to be: the collocation of *feruidus* and *ardor* is also found in Accius (cited by Apuleius and Priscian), Bernard of Clairvaux and Christan of Lilienfeld, and *cecinere poetae/prophetae* in Paulinus of Nola, Arator, Juvencus, pseudo-Tertullian, the *Laudes Domini* and Hrabanus Maurus; *fructus dulcedinis* is found in the prose not only of Niceta but also of Arnobius, Alexander of Ashby, Gozechinus of Liège, Rupert of Deutz and Sigebert of Gembloux; if Mussato could not have known Lucretius' *semper florentis Homeri* (I.124) from its citation by Donatus *ad* Ter. *Andr.* 175, his *semper uiuentis Homeri* could be inspired by a line from a Senecan epigram (26.10: *carminibus uiues semper, Homere, tuis*), or a slight development of a clausula such as *semper florentis Hymetti* (Ou. *Met.* VII.700) and the pervasive Christian collocation *semper uiuens*. Finally, in his treatment of Eugenius Vulgarius and the *Liber pontificalis*, it is wrongly stated that *uariare figuras* and *lucida tela* are attested

Appendix II

Epp. 95.11; 62–3: Non. 314,30–3, *327,1–3, 379,10–12; 64: Lact. *Inst.* III.27.10; 66–7: *Non. 411,2–4; 70–1: *Non. 506,37–507,1, *Prisc. *Inst. GLK* II 499,8–10 (cf. Dicuil, *De prim. syll.* p. 146,28–147,1 (= f. 20$^{a\text{-}b}$)); 75–6: *Non. 381,30–1; 82: ps.-Prob. *De ult. syll. GLK* IV 262,34–263,1, *Flor. Sang.* p. 10,10; 83: Lact. *Inst.* I.21.14 (*cit. post* I.101); 84: *Consent. *Ars GLK* V 389,15–16; 84–5: Prisc. *Inst. GLK* II 285,10–11; 92: *Schol. Veron. ad* Verg. *Aen.* XII.718.

101: Lact. *Inst.* I.21.14 (*cit. ante* 83); 102: Seru. Dan. *ad* Verg. *Aen.* IV.606, Prisc. *Inst. GLK* II 591,10–11; 107: Non. 205,8–9; 111: Seru. *ad* Verg. *Aen.* XI.230; 119: *Flor. Sang.* p. 10,11; 123: Macr. *Sat.* VI.1.49, *Schol. Bern. ad* Verg. *Geo.* I.477; 124: *Donat. *ad* Ter. *Andr.* 175; 134–5: Macr. *Sat.* VI.1.48; 147: Max. Vict. *De rat. metr. GLK* VI 221,10–12, Cruindm. *De arte metr.* p. 44 (cf. etiam II.60, III.92, VI.40); 150–6: Ermenric. *Ep. ad Grim.* 17 (*MGH* V.3 p. 554,7–13); 152–8 (sine 155) *Exc. cod. Vat. Reg. Lat.* 598; 156: *Flor. Sang.* p. 6,8; 159–60: Lact. *De ira* 10.16; 186: ps.-Prob. *De ult. syll. GLK* IV 263,13–14, *Donat. *Ars gram.* 392,14, Max. Vict. *De rat. metr. GLK* VI 216,9–11, *Diom. *Inst. GLK* I 430,2, *Mar. Plot. *Gramm. GLK* VI 448,9, Pomp. *Comm. GLK* V 109,18, Dicuil, *De prim. syll.* p. 176,16–17 (= f. 34^b), Cruindm. *De arte metr.* p. 14, *Flor. Sang.* p. 10,12; 191: Non. 115,7–8.

205–7: Lact. *De ira* 10.16; 210: *Flor. Sang.* p. 10,13; 212: *Prisc. *Inst. GLK* II 476,24–477,1; 227: *Charis. *Inst.* 77,18 B (*GLK* I 62,13–14), 150,19 B (*GLK* I 117,18–19); 228: Macr. *Sat.* VI.4.20, Fest. Paul. 59,27 (cf. etiam I.7); 257: *Seru. Dan. *ad* Verg. *Geo.* III.124; 259–61: *Ter. Scaur. *Orth. GLK* VII 25,4–7; 269: Prisc. *Inst. GLK* II 591,7–9; 275: Mico, *Op. pr.* 278; 281–6: *Exc. cod. Vat. Reg. Lat.* 598; 292–3: *Lact. Plac. *ad* Stat. *Theb.* VII.585.

304: Sen. *Ep.* 106.8, Gell. V.15.4, Tert. *De anima* 5.6, *Adu. Marc.* IV.8.3, Non. 408,25–26; 305–6: Non. 175,5–7, *Flor. Sang.* p. 10,14–15; 313: *Sen. *Quaest. nat.* IVb.3.4; 313–14: *Isid. *Etym.* XX.14.1 (cf. Hraban. *De uniu.* 22,14 (*PL* CXI 610D)); 314: *Seru. *ad* Verg. *Geo.* I.46, *Schol. Bern. ad* Verg. *Geo.* I.46, *Breu. expos. ad* Verg. *Geo.* I.46 (214,11 H), [Anon.] *De dub. nom.* 867 (= *GLK* V 593,9–10); 315: Isid. *Etym.* XV.16.6; 326: *Seru. *ad* Verg. *Geo.* III.175, *Donat. *ad* Ter. *Phorm.* 180, Fest. Paul. 506,10–12 (cf. Gell. XVI.5.7); 396: Mico, *Op. pr.* 267, *Flor. Sang.* p. 10,16.

only in Lucretius: the collocations occur respectively in Manilius and Prudentius, and in the Lucretian citation of Max. Vict. *De rat. metr. GLK* VI 221,10–12 (repeated by Cruindmelus). Lastly in this survey, we may observe that it is presumably from Lactantius (*Inst.* III.17.28) that John of Montreuil (1354–1418; *Ep.* 70 (*c.* 1417)) cited a fusion of III.1044 (rather than V.215, 267, 281 and 389) and VI.24: *de quo disertissimus poeta Lucretius ait: aetherius sol | ueridicis hominum purgauit pectora dictis.* Sound discussion of the knowledge of Lucretius among Renaissance authors was offered by Lehnerdt (1904).

2 References to Festus follow Lindsay's pagination; those to Nonius, Mercer's; grammarians are cited largely with reference to Keil's *Grammatici Latini* (but Barwick for Charisius); Hagen's page numbers are provided for non-Servian Virgilian commentators. Those instances marked with an asterisk do not preserve the complete line(s) for which they are cited.

448–9: *Flor. Sang.* p. 10,18–19; 449–50: Non. 203,33–204,2; 470: Non. 204,3–4.

525: cf. Charis. *Inst.* 268,5 B (*GLK* I 207,3); 571: Non. 225,21–2, *Donat. *Gramm. GLK* IV 393,31, *Pomp. *Comm. GLK* V 291,15 (cf. Seru. *ad* Verg. *Aen.* VIII.233, Iul. Tolet. *Ars* XV.12) (cf. etiam II.449, V.313); 580: *Flor. Sang.* p. 11,1; 587: *Diom. *Inst. GLK* I 371,20–1, Prisc. *Inst. GLK* II 542,19–20.

639–40: Fest. 314,2–4; 653: Non. 184,8–9; 671: Seru. *ad* Verg. *Geo.* IV.226 (cf. etiam I.793, II.754, III.520).

715: Seru. *ad* Verg. *Aen.* I.123, *Buc.* VI.31, Boeth. *Inst. arith.* II.1, Isid. *Etym.* XIII.10.4; 717: cf. *CGL* V 251,13, *VII 368 col. 1,8; 720: Prisc. *Inst. GLK* II 27,2–3; 733: Cens. *De die nat.* 4.7; 771: *Isid. *Etym.* XIII.11.17 (cf. Hraban. Maur. *De uniu.* IX.26 (*PL* CXI 282D) (cf. etiam V.501); 779: *Flor. Sang.* p. 11,2; 793: Seru. *ad* Verg. *Geo.* IV.226 (cf. etiam I.671, II.754, III.520).

806: Prisc. *Inst. GLK* II 349,22–3, cit. ap. 'membraneum codicem' a C. Barth, *Adv.* 37.XIII (Frankfurt, 1624) 1691; 830: Seru. *ad* Verg. *Aen.* IV.625; 832: cf. Plin. *Epp.* IV.18.1; 837: Non. 184,12–13, 224,13, Charis. *Inst.* 114,20 B (*GLK* I 90,21–2), Seru. *ad* Verg. *Aen.* I.211, *Geo.* I.139, *ps.-Prob. *Cath. GLK* IV 9,21–2, *Mar. Plot. *Gramm. GLK* VI 474,21–2 (cf. etiam I.853 and 860); 853: *ps.-Prob. *Cath. GLK* IV 9,21–2, *Mar. Plot. *Gramm. GLK* VI 474,22 (cf. etiam I.837 and 860); *ps.-Prob. *Cath. GLK* IV 9,21–2, *Mar. Plot. *Gramm. GLK* VI 474,22 (cf. etiam I.837 and 853).

922–7: *Macr. *Sat.* VI.2.3; 925–6: cf. Front. *De eloq.* 3.2; 926: *Quint. VIII.6.44, [Censorin.] *Metr. GLK* VI 612,1 (cf. etiam IV.1); 932: Lact. *Inst.* I.16.3, cf. IV.28.13 (cf. etiam IV.7); 936–8: Quint. III.1.4, Hier. *Ep.* 132(b).3 (cf. etiam IV.11–13); 941: Mar. Plot. *Gramm. GLK* VI 504,28.

1063: *Mar. Plot. *Gramm. GLK* VI 450,20–1.

Liber II

1: *Seru. *ad* Verg. *Aen.* V.628; 1–2: *Schol. Horat. ad Ep.* I.11,9; 2: Non. 402,13–14, Mar. Vict. *Gramm. GLK* VI 31,28; 14–16: *Lact. *Inst.* I.21.48; 16: *Non. 278,17, *Donat. *ad* Ter. *Phorm.* 232; 24–33: Macr. *Sat.* VI.2.5; 25; Max. Vict. *De rat. metr. GLK* VI 220,11–12, Hraban. Maur. *Exc. de arte Prisc. PL* CXI 644C; 28: Macr. *Sat.* VI.4.21, *CGL* V 215,21; 30: Donat. *ad* Ter. *Ad.* 576 (cf. etiam V.1393); 41: Non. 503,24–5; 55–6: Sen. *Ep.* 110.6 (cf. etiam III.87–8, VI.35–6); 60: Max. Vict. *De rat. metr. GLK* VI 221,10–12, Cruindm. *De arte metr.* p. 44 (*non radii solis neque lucida tela diei*) (cf. I.147, III.92, VI.40); 76: *Schol. Bern. ad* Verg. *Geo.* I.301.

120: Non. 6,5–6; 124: *Schol. Lucan. ad* IX.563; 128: Mico, *Op. pr.* 63, *Ex. diu. auct.* 198, *Flor. Sang.* p. 11,8; 144: Macr. *Sat.* VI.1.25 (cf. Seru. Dan. *ad* Verg. *Aen.* IX.457); 152: Isid. *Etym.* XIII.20.3; 155–6: Prisc. *Inst. GLK* II 401,12–14.

Appendix II

201: *Flor. Sang.* p. 10,17; 207: Macr. *Sat.* VI.1.26; 214: Macr. *Sat.* VI.1.27; 245: *Flor. Sang.* p. 11,3; 265: Non. 517,24–5, *Max. Vict. *GLK* VI 202,19, *Aud. *Excerpta GLK* VII 348,29 (cf. *Schol. Lucan. ad* IV.265) (cf. etiam III.643). 324: Macr. *Sat.* VI.1.28; 329–30: Macr. *Sat.* VI.4.9; 342–3: *Non. 158,38–40; 351: *Flor. Sang.* p. 11,7; 352–3: Macr. *Sat.* VI.5.7; 361–3: Macr. *Sat.* VI.2.6; 365: Mico, *Op. pr.* 121; 367–8: Macr. *Sat.* VI.5.3; 368: Fest. 226,7–8; 376: Non. 503,45–6; 388: Mico, *Op. pr.* 398.

401: *Macr. *Sat.* VI.1.47; 429: *Flor. Sang.* p. 11,6; 447: Mico, *Op. pr.* 9, *Flor. Sang.* p. 11,19; 449: *Donat. *Gramm. GLK* IV 393,31, *Pomp. *Comm. GLK* V 291,15–16 (cf. Iul. Tolet. *Ars* XV.12, Seru. *ad* Verg. *Aen.* VIII.233) (cf. etiam I.571, V.313); 476: *Mart. Cap. III.305, *Donat. *Gramm. GLK* IV 432,27–8, *Seru. *ad* Verg. *Geo.* I.129, Prisc. *Inst. GLK* II 275,3–5, *Part. *GLK* III 493,15, *Cassiod. *De art. ac disc. PL* LXX 1154B; 498: Non. 136,8–9.

500–1: *Schol. Veron. ad* Verg. *Aen.* V.251; 525: *Flor. Sang.* p. 11,5; 531: Donat. *ad* Ter. *Phorm.* 213; 551: *Flor. Sang.* p. 11.4; 557: *Breu. expos. ad* Verg. *Geo.* I.254 (246,8–9 H); 559: Seru. Dan. *ad* Verg. *Geo.* IV.442; 576: Fest. 514,3–4, Non. 184,20–1; 586: *ps.-Prob. *Cath. GLK* IV 19,22–4, 31,1 (cf. etiam III.265); 586–7: *Prisc. *Inst. GLK* II 249,10–12.

618: Non. 181,22–3; 637: *Charis. *Inst.* 119,6 B (*GLK* I 93,21–3), 154,29 B (*GLK* I 120,33–4); 646–51: Lact. *De ira* 8,1, Lact. Plac. *ad* Stat. *Theb.* III.659 (*sine* 649–50); 650: Seru. *ad* Verg. *Aen.* XII.794; 651 Non. 252,38–9, 408,24, Seru. *ad* Verg. *Aen.* VI.376, *Buc.* VIII.17, Acro *ad* Hor. *S.* I.5.101; 661: Aldhelm, *De dactilo* p. 165,10 (Ehwald); 661–2: *Non. 80,27–9, 208,24–5; 662: *Charis. *Inst.* 118,2 B (*GLK* I 92,30–1), *Seru. *ad* Verg. *Geo.* III.287, Mico, *Op. pr.* 158.

754: Seru. *ad* Verg. *Geo.* IV.226 (cf. etiam I.671, 793, III.520).

815: Non. 482,5–6; 840: Fest. 426,9–11; 848: Fest. 160,20–1; 853: Non. 188,7–8, Prisc. *Inst. GLK* II 275,6–7; 888 Prisc. *Inst. GLK* II 132,21–2, *Ex. diu. auct.* 111.

927–8: *Mar. Plot. *Gramm. GLK* VI 445,19–21; 966: Mico, *Op. pr.* 315; 975: Non. 511,16–17; 991–2: *Lact. *Inst.* VI.10.7, *De opif.* 19.3; 992: cf. Lact. *Inst.* V.6.12, 14.17; 999–1001: Lact. *Inst.* VII.12.5.

1038: Non. 172,17–18; 1086: Non. 131,5–6; 1097: *Donat. *Gramm. GLK* IV 431,33, *Mar. Plot. *Gramm. GLK* VI 450,12, *Pomp. *Comm. GLK* V 162,32–163,1; 1097–8: Non. 197,2–4.

1101–4: Lact. *Inst.* III.17.10; 1116–17: Non. 160,13–15; 1122: *Frag. Bob. de nom. GLK* V 650,29; 1130: Non. 248,3–4; 1142: Fest. 480,32–3, Fest. Paul. 481,8–9; 1153–4: Gell. XIII.21.21; 1154: *Non. 205,21–2; 1160: Non. 115,5–6; 1170: Non. 255,18–19.

Liber III

1: cf. Lact. *Inst.* VI.2.6; 7–8: Non. 306,8–10, 420,37–9; 17: *Non. 446,4–5; 52: Non. 341,29–30; 70–2: Macr. *Sat.* VI.2.15; 87–8: Sen. *Ep.* 110.6 (cf. etiam II.55–6, VI.35–6); 92: Max. Vict. *De rat. metr. GLK* VI 221,10–12; Cruindm. *De arte metr.* p. 44 (cf. etiam I.147, II.60, VI.40); 94: Charis. *Inst.* 272,7–8 B (*GLK* I 210,5–6).

106: *Frag. Bob. de nom. GLK* V 650,33–4; 156: Non. 505,4–5, *Prisc. *Inst. GLK* II 445,9–10, 474,6–7, Dicuil, *De prim. syll.* p. 146,13–14; 159–60: Non. 124,9–11; 160: *Prisc. *Inst. GLK* II 510,3; 188: Fest. Paul. 123,17–18.

207: *Flor. Sang.* p. 11,12; 260: cf. Plin. *Epp.* IV.18.1 (cf. etiam I.832); 265: *ps.-Prob. *Cath. GLK* IV 19,22–4, 31,1 (cf. etiam II.586).

318: Non. 184,10–11; 381: Non. 73,4–5; 385–6: *Donat. *ad* Ter. *Eun.* 688; 386: *CGL* V 525,26, 574,52, Fest. Paul. 246,6–7.

471: Non. 199,3–4.

520: Seru. *ad* Verg. *Geo.* IV.226 (cf. etiam I.671, 793, II.754); 545: Non. 77,26–7.

612–14: Lact. *Inst.* VII.12.26; 643: *Aud. *Excerpta GLK* VII 348,29, cf. *Schol. Lucan. ad* IV.265 (cf. etiam II.265); 676: Non. 515,16–17, Charis. 265,11 (*GLK* I 204,14).

721: Non. 103,6–7; 722–4: *Non. 159,32–5; 732: *Non. 72,13–14; 765: Non. 181,3–4, Diom. *Ars GLK* I 343,8–10; 796–7: Prisc. *Inst. GLK* II 528,28–529,2.

872: *Gloss. Plac. CGL* V 78,23.

906: Non. 94,2–3; 978: Prisc. *Inst. GLK* II 27,4–5; 984: Prisc. *Inst. GLK* II 27,6–7; 987: Macr. *Sat.* VI.4.15.

1003–4: Non. 424,28–30; 1004: Non. 298,8–9; 1010: Pomp. *Comm. GLK* V 297,1–2; 1015: *Flor. Sang.* p. 12,1.

1034: *Sen. *Epp.* 86.5, Macr. *Sat.* VI.1.46 (cf. Sil. XV.340); 1035: *Mar. Vict. *Gramm. GLK* VI 56,9–10; 1037–8: *Non. 481,25–7; 1041: Lact. *Inst.* III.18.6; 1043–4: Lact. *Inst.* III.17.28; 1068: *Sen. *Tranq. an.* 2.14; 1093: Mar. Plot. *Gramm. GLK* VI 503,5–6.

Liber IV

1: *Quint. VIII.6.44, [Censorin.] *Metr. GLK* VI 612,1 (cf. etiam I.926); 1–2: cf. Front. *De eloq.* 3.2 (cf. etiam I.926–7); 2–3: *Non. 319,12–14; 3: *Non. 252,9–10; 7: Lact. *Inst.* I.16.3 (cf. IV.28.13) (cf. etiam I.932); 9: *Flor. Sang.* p. 12,2; 11–12: *Non. 190,25–7, 413,17–19; 11–13: Quint. III.1.4, Hier. *Epp.* 132(b).3 (cf. etiam

Appendix II

I.936–8); 15–16: *Non. 241,32–4; 16: Mar. Plot. *Gramm. GLK* VI 504,28 (cf. etiam I.941); 28: *CGL* V 471,56.

34–5: *Macr. *Sat.* VI.1.29; 40: Fest. Paul. 238,3–4; 51: Non. 199,35–200,1; 61–2: *Non. 231,17–19, 458,13–15; 62: Seru. Dan. *ad* Verg. *Geo.* III.444.

118: Non. 209,15–16; 132: *ps.-Prob. *ad* Verg. *Buc.* VI.31 (338 H), *Seru. *ad* Verg. *Aen.* I.58, *V.18, *X.899, *Geo.* I.51, *Seru. Dan. *ad* Verg. *Aen.* IX.20, *Isid. *Etym.* XIII.4.3.

219–20: *Non. 247,12–14, *311,1–2; 223–4: *Gell. I.21.6; 224: *Seru. *ad* Verg. *Geo.* II.241 (cf. etiam VI.934 (930)).

368–9: cf. Seru. *ad* Verg. *Aen.* IV.654.

409: *Fest. Paul. 514,22; 450: Porph. *ad* Hor. *S.* II.1.25.

516: Fest. 210,15–17; 528–9: Gell. X.26.9, Non. 453,7–9; 561: Non. 173,11–12.

636: Non. 95,28–9; 641: *Flor. Sang.* p. 11,18; 647: *CGL* V 67,26.

907–8: *Macr. *Sat.* VI.1.44; 912: cf. *Schol. Veron. ad* Verg. *Geo.* III.3 (408,12–13 H) (cf. etiam I.50); 952: Non. 218,25–6.

1009–10: Non. 192,26–8.

1129: *Isid. *Etym.* IX.5.3 (cf. Hraban. Maur. *De uniu.* VII.2 (*PL* CXI 185D)); 1161: *Gell. II.26.19; 1168: cf. Arnob. III.10.

1207: Mar. Vict. *Gramm. GLK* VI 28,6; 1212–13: Non. 230,12–14; 1232: Fest. 402,22–3, Fest. Paul. 403,6–7, Mico, *Op. pr.* 242; 1242: Non. 73,6–7; 1252–3: *Non. 158,19–21.

Liber V

6: Mico, *Op. pr.* 266, *Ex. diu. auct.* 33; 6–8: Lact. *Inst.* III.14.2; 33: Macr. *Sat.* VI.1.30; 50–1: *Lact. *Inst.* III.14.4; 71–2: Non. 415,31–3; 92–4: ps.-Prob. *ad* Verg. *Buc.* VI.31 (343 H); 94: Non. 227,21–2; 96: ps.-Prob. *De ult. syll. GLK* IV 225,29–31.

156–7: *Lact. *Inst.* VII.3.13; 165–7: Lact. *Inst.* VII.3.13.

205: Non. 487,2–3; 211: *Prisc. *Inst. GLK* II 476,24–477,1 (cf. etiam I.212); 213–17: Macr. *Sat.* VI.2.29; 227: Lact. *De opif.* 3.2; 236: Non. 234,2–3; 255–6: *Non. 203,26–8; 281: cf. Lact. *Inst.* VI.2.6; 294–5: *Macr. *Sat.* VI.4.18.

313: Non. 225,23–4, cf. Seru. *ad* Verg. *Aen.* VIII.233 (cf. etiam I.571, II.449); 335–7: Lact. *Inst.* III.16.14.

432–9: Macr. *Sat.* VI.2.23; 437–8: Macr. *Sat.* VI.4.11; 446–8: Macr. *Sat.* VI.2.24; 455: Macr. *Sat.* VI.2.24.

501: *Isid. *Etym.* XIII.11.17 (cf. Hraban. Maur. *De uniuers.* IX.26 (*PL* CXI 282D)) (cf. etiam I.771); 516: Non. 13,4–5, Isid. *Etym.* XX.15.1 (cf. Hraban. Maur. *De uniu.* 22.15 (*PL* CXI 612B)); 559: *Flor. Sang.* p. 12,3; 576: cf. Apul. *De deo Socr.* 1.7; 598: Eutych. *Ars GLK* V 484,7–8, Mico, *Op. pr.* 381.

745: Isid. *Etym.* XIII.11.5.

808: Lact. *Inst.* II.11.1; 818–19: *Breu. expos. ad* Verg. *Geo.* II.338; 818–20: *Schol. Bern. ad* Verg. *Geo.* II.336; 865: Non. 13,7–8; 889: cf. Heiric. *Vita S. Germani* I.96; 890: Non. 13,9–10.

905: Hygin. *Fab.* 57.3, 151.1, Hier. *Epp.* 125.18, Isid. *Etym.* I.40.4, Hincmar, *PL* CXXV 114A, CXXVI 118A, *Schol. in codd. Par. Horat. ad* Hor. *C.* I.27.24; 910: Non. 103,22–3; 913–15: Lact. Plac. *ad* Stat. *Theb.* VII.585; 937–8: Macr. *Sat.* VI.1.65; 945: Macr. *Sat.* VI.1.64; 950: Non. 504,8–9; 952: *Flor. Sang.* p. 12,4.

1004: *Schol. Veron. ad* Verg. *Aen.* II.90 (419,5–6 H); 1036: Non. 457,14–15, *Isid. *Etym.* XII.2.6; 1039–40: *Non. 74,16–18; 1064: Non. 221,21–2; 1070: *Non. 17,7–8, *450,7–8; 1071: Non. 80,30–1; 1094–5: Non. 506,15–17.

1192: cf. Isid. *Etym.* I.36.13 (cf. Iul. Tolet. *De uitiis et fig.* V.32, *Ars* XVIII.29); 1198–1202: Lact. *Inst.* II.3.11.

1221: Mico, *Op. pr.* 72; 1249: cf. Heiric. *Vita S. Germani* VI.456; 1273–4: cf. Isid. *Etym.* XVI.20.1; 1275–7: Isid. *Etym.* XVI.20.1; 1293–4: Macr. *Sat.* VI.1.63; 1296: Non. 13,13–14.

1318: Non. 134,7–8; 1393: Donat. *ad* Ter. *Ad.* 576 (cf. etiam II.30).

1442: cf. Seru. *ad* Verg. *Aen.* VII.804.

Liber VI

6: ps.-Prob. *De ult. syll. GLK* IV 255,10–11; 24–8: Lact. *inst.* VII.27.6; 35–6: Sen. *Epp.* 110.6 (cf. etiam II.55–6, III.87–8); 40: Max. Vict. *De rat. metr. GLK* VI 221,10–12, Cruindm. *De arte metr.* p. 44 (cf. etiam I.147, II.60, III.92); 52–3: *Lact. *Inst.* II.3.10, *Epit.* 20.4; 96–8: Apul. *De deo Socr.* 10.7; 97: *Acro *ad* Hor. *C.* II.12.14.

119: *Non. 245,7–8; 154–5: Macr. *Sat.* VI.4.5; 156: Non. 487,4–5; 160: Non. 506,11–12; 165–6: cf. Isid. *Etym.* XIII.8.2; 179: *Prisc. *Inst. GLK* II 281,18, 319,11–12 (cf. etiam VI.307).

204–5: Macr. *Sat.* VI.5.4; 205: Seru. Dan. *ad* Verg. *Buc.* VI.33; 214: Non. 506,13–14; 233: *Mart. Cap. III.295; 290: Prisc. *Inst. GLK* II 152,13–15; 297–8: cf. *Schol. Veron. ad* Verg. *Aen.* II.649.

307: cf. Prisc. *Inst. GLK* II 281,18, 319,11–12 (cf. etiam VI.179); 339: Non. 482,23–4; 364: Non. 205,25–6.

Appendix II

405: *Macr. *Sat.* VI.1.45.

526: Non. 425,4–5; 538: cf. Isid. *De nat. rer.* 41,1.

630: cf. Seru. *ad* Verg. *Aen.* X.807; 633–8: *Comm. Bern. Lucan.* X.247; 642: Non. 495,15–16; 651: Non. 136,10–12; 685: Isid. *De nat. rer.* 36.1.

725: *Flor. Sang.* p. 12,6; 736: *Charis. *Inst.* 116,8 B (*GLK* I 91,25), Seru. *ad* Verg. *Aen.* IV.250; 740–1: Non. 14,5–8; 752: Mico, *Op. pr.* 76; 781–2: Non. 394,18–20.

810: *Fest. 442,24–5, Fest. Paul. 443,14–15; 836: Fest. 182,32–3; 868: Beda, *De arte metr.* I.16.18 (*GLK* VII 253,18–19), Aud. *Excerpta GLK* VII 329,2–3; 874–5: Macr. *Sat.* VI.4.7; 876–8: *Prisc. *Inst. GLK* II 211,20–3; 877–8: *Ars anon. Bernensis GLK* VIII 127,27 8; 896: *Flor. Sang.* p. 12,5.

929–30 (934): *Prisc. *Inst. GLK* II 444,14–16 (cf. etiam IV.223–4); 930 (934): *Seru. *ad* Verg. *Geo.* II.241 (cf. etiam IV.224); 952: Non. 487,7–8; 976–7: Non. 394,21–3; 990: Non. 227,23–4.

1098: Non. 158,1–2.

1106: Serg. *De syll.* f. 19^v, p. 42; 1128–30: cf. Isid. *De nat. rer.* 39.2; 1135: Serg. *De syll.* f. 19^v, p. 42; 1138–40: Macr. *Sat.* VI.2.7; 1145–50: Macr. *Sat.* VI.2.9; 1149: cf. Lact. *Inst.* VI.18.6, *De opif.* 10,13; 1177–8 (79): Macr. *Sat.* VI.2.13; 1182–9: Macr. *Sat.* VI.2.11; 1195: Non. 181,24–5.

1219–22: *Macr. *Sat.* VI.2.14; 1222: Acro *ad* Hor. *C.* I.1.27, *Porph. *ad* Hor. *C.* I.1.27, *Schol. in codd. Par. Horat. ad* Hor. *C.* I.1.27; 1226–9: Macr. *Sat.* VI.2.12; 1275: cf. Gell. XII.10.8.

The name of Lucretius is mentioned without citation of the work by:
Cic. *Ad Q. Fr.* II.10.3; Var. *L.L.* V.17 (= fr. **XII**), VII.4 (= fr. **XIII**); Nep. *Att.* 12.4; Ou. *Am.* I.15.23–4, *Tr.* II.425–6; Vitr. IX.*pr.*17; Vell. Pat. II.36; Plin. *HN* I *ind.*; Sen. *Epp.* 58.12; Stat. *Silu.* II.7.76; Quint. I.4.4, X.1 87, XII.11.27; Tac. *Dial.* 23.2; Fronto, *Epp. ad M. Caes.* IV.3.2, *ad Anton.* II.1, *ad Verum Imp.* I.I.2, *De eloq.* 3.2, *De fer. Als.* 3; Fest. 212,10–11 L (s.u. *Oufentinae tribus* = fr. **XIV**); Seren. 606; Lact. *Inst.* II.12.4, VII.12.1; *Opif. Dei* 6.1, 8.12; Non. 229,1–2 (= fr. **V**), 503,24–5 (= fr. **XVI**); ps.-Prob. *ad* Verg. *Buc.* VI.31 (343 H) (= fr. **IX**); ps.-Prob. *Cath. GLK* IV 10,31–2 (= fr. **VIII**); *De nom. exc. GLK* IV 212,10–11 (= fr. **X**); Donat. *Vita Verg.* 2; *ad* Ter. *Eun.* 424; *ad* Ter. *Eun.* 515; Dosith. *Ars gramm. GLK* VII, 428,11; Mar. Vict. *in* Cic. *De inu.* I.6, 26; Aug. *De util. cred.* 4.10 (*bis*); Hier. *Apol. adu. libr. Ruf.* I.16, *libr. Ruf.* III.29; Iun. Philarg. *Expl. in buc.* 3,col.1,8 H, 4,col.2,14 H; Charis. *Inst.* 73,10 B (*GLK* I 58,23–5) (= fr. **III**); 268,5 B (*GLK* I 207,3) (= fr. **VI**); Diom. *Ars gram. GLK* I 482,22, 483,2; Mart. Cap. III.266; Seru. *ad* Verg. *Aen.* III.138, 587, IV.486, V.81, 527, VI.11, 127, 239, 596 (*bis*), 625 (= fr. **I**), VII.37, VIII.187, X.467, XII.87, 419 (= fr. **VII**); *Buc.* VI.31; *Geo.* I.*pr.*, II.42 (= fr. **I**), 151, 329, 479,

III.135, [Seru. Dan.] 136 (= fr. **IV**), 293, 478, 481, IV.51, 219; Macr. *Sat.*
VI.1.43 (= fr. **XI**); *Breu. expos. ad* Verg. *Geo. pr.* 195,3 H; Lact. Plac. *ad* Stat.
Theb. I.206, III.98, VI.363–4; Mar. Plot. *Gramm. GLK* VI 448,9 (= fr. **II**);
Sidon. *Carm.* 9.265; Isid. *Etym.* VIII.3, XIV.1, XXX.4, *Chron.* 222.1; Beda, *De
arte metr.* I.25.14 (*GLK* VII 259,25); *Fr. Paris. de notis GLK* VII 534,6; *Gloss.
Monac.* (cod. Lat. 14229) f. 225ᵛ; *Schol. Bern. ad* Verg. *Geo.* IV.51; Dicuil, *De
prim. syll.* p. 140,14; Hrab. Maur. *Epp.* 2a (*MGH* 5.3, 383,31); Cruindm. *De arte
metr.* p. 45.

THE CORRECTIONS AND ANNOTATIONS OF O

O^D (Dungal)[1]

Book I: 17, 37, 45, 59, 63, 84, 95, 115, 120, 182, 209, 222, 272, 286, 321, 352, 357, 364–8, 386, 427, 448, 449 (*bis*), 458, 465, 469 (*bis*), 477 (*bis*), 486, 489, 544, 549–50, 558, 561, 590, 610, 619, 634, 648, 651, 668, 673, 680, 684, 699, 729, 741, 743, 744, 753, 764, 781, 797, 836–7, 857, 887, 892, 914, 938, 943, 977, 1022–3, 1038, 1060, 1061, 1106.

Book II: 11, 79, 82, 136, 147, 166, 181, 192, 197, 216, 227, 231, 233, 257–63, 265, 267, 283, 286, 291, 313, 342, 384, 385, 410–12, 417, 451, 454, 458, 478*cap.*, 486, 493, 536, 543, 561, 576, 577, 613, 615, 624, 646, 652, 663, 664, 684, 690, 710, 721, 725, 745, 789, 827, 840, 883–6, 943–4, 983, 1004, 1006, 1114, 1119, 1135, 1171.

Book III: 3, 6 (*bis*), 12, 104, 138, 156 (*bis*), 186, 195, 205, 236, 251, 257, 259, 289, 293, 321, 330 (*bis*), 336, 385, 437, 443, 449, 462, 479, 513, 514, 531, 542, 578, 588, 596, 597, 605, 612, 618 (*bis*), 644, 651, 656, 658, 660, 713, 714, 719, 752, 784, 787, 829, 858, 868 (*bis*), 883, 902, 906, 941, 957, 960, 966, 982, 983, 992, 994, 996, 1001, 1034, 1073, 1082, 1083.

Book IV: 31, 58, 63, 66, 78, 79, 88, 95, 103, 124, 193, 202, 217, 219, 224, 232, 244, 248, 253, 276, 277, 304, 333, 344, 354, 362, 363, 368, 391, 411, 420, 423, 425, 545, 554, 570, 572, 590, 643, 653, 654, 673, 710, 743, 747, 767, 778, 843, 869, 882, 886, 901, 976, 992, 1001, 1008, 1033, 1053, 1058, 1059, 1068, 1083, 1097, 1124, 1137, 1154, 1167, 1170, 1194 (*bis*), 1196, 1200, 1202, 1204, 1208, 1224, 1229, 1234, 1235, 1237, 1239.

Book V: 146*ind.*, 1241*ind.*, 57, 158 (*bis*), 172, 199, 206, 209, 216, 220, 221, 226 (*bis*), 241, 252, 253, 264, 268, 280, 282, 287, 298, 304, 314, 324*cap.*, 341, 353, 400, 406, 418, 455, 459, 463, 481, 496, 511, 515, 527, 533, 545, 560, 577, 580, 581, 588, 609, 626, 630, 649, 653 (*bis*), 657, 675, 681, 697, 702, 707, 708, 714, 718 (*bis*), 721, 723, 727 (*bis*), 744, 749, 756, 765, 790 (*bis*), 804, 810, 823, 832, 833, 852 (*bis*), 853, 884, 886, 933, 941, 965, 985, 994, 995, 998, 1008, 1019, 1023, 1044, 1082, 1085, 1108, 1126, 1137, 1141, 1142, 1145 (*bis*), 1156, 1162, 1169, 1172, 1220, 1221, 1224, 1229, 1233, 1234 (*bis*), 1245, 1247, 1248, 1253 (*bis*), 1255, 1257, 1259*cap.*,

---

[1] Excluded from this list are the several hundred cases where seemingly Dungal has added a *cauda* to *e* to signify *ae*, as well as the markedly fewer cases where apparently a virgula has been added to signal *m* or *n*, *o* has been added before *e* to signify the diphthong *oe*, or deletion has occurred either by erasure or by sub- or supralinear points.

The corrections and annotations of O

1273, 1278, 1289, 1290, 1301, 1317, 1322, 1324, 1331, 1348, 1366, 1370, 1393, 1413, 1416, 1422, 1427, 1429, 1431, 1440, 1441.
Book VI: 50*ind.*, 1 (*bis*), 2, 24, 31, 33, 35, 45, 52, 53, 58, 60, 66, 68, 81, 94, 95, 102, 109, 112, 115, 122, 132, 134, 136, 138, 141, 145, 146, 153, 160, 162, 180, 206, 208 (*ter*), 214, 225*cap.*, 237 (*ter*), 238, 239, 241, 243, 246*cap.*, 246, 249, 254, 258, 262, 268, 285 (*bis*), 288, 290, 291, 296, 297, 299, 305, 306, 315, 324, 337, 344, 346, 350, 356, 364, 366, 368, 372, 374, 382, 390, 393, 396, 399, 416, 431, 440, 444, 447 (*bis*), 453, 454, 461, 481, 482, 485, 492, 497, 511, 512, 517, 521, 523, 524, 526*cap.*, 526 (*bis*), 531, 533, 537, 552, 554, 558, 597, 600, 604 (*bis*), 609, 611, 613, 615, 621, 634, 638, 639 (*bis*), 644, 652, 653, 658, 661, 664, 665, 667 (*bis*), 671, 673, 694, 695, 696, 698, 700, 703 (*ter*), 715, 718, 721, 723, 725, 726, 728, 747 (*bis*), 749*cap.*, 749, 751, 754, 761, 762, 763 (*bis*), 775, 782, 787, 803, 806, 813, 814, 815, 820, 823, 834, 848, 858, 868, 878, 888, 891, 897, 900, 908, 915 (*bis*), 923, 931, 941, 947, 951, 952, 955, 962, 967, 969, 974, 982, 986, 987, 993, 995, 1003, 1009, 1016, 1017, 1027, 1031, 1033, 1035, 1037 (*bis*), 1041, 1046, 1049, 1058, 1059, 1062 (*bis*), 1071, 1073, 1075, 1077, 1092, 1097 (*bis*), 1117, 1119, 1125, 1126, 1136, 1139 (*bis*), 1147, 1148, 1150, 1153, 1159, 1161, 1165, 1166, 1167 (*ter*), 1169, 1170 (*bis*), 1172, 1189, 1195 (*bis*), 1198 (*bis*), 1199, 1200, 1215, 1222, 1228 (*bis*), 1251, 1266, 1267, 1271, 1272, 1276, 1280.

O$^{Ann.}$

Book I: 476, 544, 562, 651, 690, 710, 724, 752, 758, 759, 827, 843, 861, 953, 957, 966, 984, 1016.
Book II: 43, 52, 105, 150, 158, 166, 167, 184, 187, 192, 227, 279, 281, 291, 301, 302, 315, 318, 331, 359, 382, 403, 429, 430, 468, 476, 478, 521, 646*cap.*, 686, 788, 814, 934, 966, 1079, 1096, 1122, 1170.
Book III: 151, 199, 249, 255, 310, 421, 809, 839, 881, 894, 906, 940, 953, 956, 1035, 1038, 1063.
Book IV: 53, 66, 72, 77, 166, 262, 313, 357, 537, 577, 712, 847, 877, 897, 899, 983, 995, 1028, 1145.
Book V: 142, 208, 211, 229, 272, 320, 516, 581, 586, 614, 615, 619, 651, 679, 776, 833, 838, 849, 953, 977, 980, 1003, 1071, 1102, 1110, 1124, 1302.
Book VI: 10, 83, 87, 103, 153, 168, 226, 229, 272, 281, 307, 318, 320, 335, 366, 375, 376, 383, 385, 401, 465, 466, 468, 474, 481, 498, 511, 523, 524, 537, 539, 541, 550, 701, 710, 770, 788, 800, 801, 803, 804, 810, 818, 820, 855, 857, 862, 887, 890, 916, 972, 1076, 1192, 1205, 1235, 1241, 1264, 1281.

O²

Book I: 16, 24, 27, 29, 30, 33, 36, 41, 43, 84, 85, 94, 99, 112, 168, 191, 212, 249, 251, 264, 271, 283, 284, 285, 296, 305, 307, 358, 384, 406, 414, 415, 427, 429, 455, 459, 475, 520, 528, 552, 565, 586, 587, 588, 606, 618, 646, 682, 716, 725, 758, 764, 777, 779, 875, 877, 944, 984, 1036, 1044.

297

Appendix III

Book II: 54, 68, 115, 318, 326, 337, 452, 466, 475, 595, 657, 694, 804, 826, 832, 839, 840, 920, 938, 953, 965, 975, 977, 982, 1116, 1153.

Book III: 23, 73, 97, 132 (*bis*), 136, 172, 192, 232, 233, 239, 285, 311, 317, 357, 375, 382, 399, 403, 408, 430, 486, 495, 546, 564, 581, 654, 656, 665, 713, 730, 733, 764, 771, 785, 790, 807, 839, 982, 985, 1056, 1061.

Book IV: 1*ind.*, 21, 51, 53, 109, 153, 237, 315, 334, 344, 393, 473, 486, 502, 548, 586, 595*cap.*, 609, 628, 673, 696, 730, 736, 743, 803, 834, 844, 879 (*bis*), 907, 935, 947, 1021, 1038, 1055, 1229, 1262.

Book V: 5, 26, 136, 293, 295, 317, 326, 351, 375, 381, 428, 482, 492, 502, 510, 551, 554, 684, 692 (*bis*), 713, 742, 765, 780*cap.*, 784, 789, 799, 802, 851, 930, 934, 935, 937, 946, 1001, 1055, 1072, 1097, 1150, 1244, 1308, 1336, 1392, 1393, 1456.

Book VI: 608*ind.*, 48, 88, 92, 109, 128, 144, 220, 221, 260, 295, 323, 386, 411, 436, 450, 453, 522, 531, 536, 546, 547, 552, 589, 662, 673, 679, 707, 713, 742, 756*cap.*, 779, 811, 820, 821, 847, 860, 874, 890, 905, 913 (*bis*), 928, 929, 943, 946, 954, 960, 972, 976, 991, 1000, 1008, 1021, 1088, 1091, 1126, 1127, 1132, 1134, 1215, 1243, 1248.

O³

Book I: 29, 70, 71, 77, 87, 88, 96, 119, 138, 177, 203, 205, 233, 237, 256, 263, 269 (*bis*), 282, 296, 315, 334, 372, 377, 381, 382, 384, 386, 395, 400, 404, 407, 412, 438, 453, 465, 467, 476 (*bis*), 479, 504, 520, 527, 542, 550, 560, 562, 567, 583, 586, 607, 613, 620, 639, 640, 643, 648, 651, 654, 659, 665, 680, 684, 703, 708, 711, 721, 736, 739, 759, 767, 769, 796, 818, 825, 827.

Glosses on **Book I**: 4, 10, 11, 13, 41, 57, 60, 62, 71, 79, 103 (*bis*), 185, 191, 197, 206, 212, 213, 222, 267, 277, 288, 292, 296, 300, 306, 324, 326 (*bis*), 330, 343, 378, 383 (*bis*), 386, 403, 411, 413, 422, 434, 450, 458, 460 (*bis*), 464, 482, 484, 499, 509, 542, 551*cap.*, 564, 575, 580, 629, 639, 642, 657, 659, 660, 665, 692, 705*cap.*, 717, 722, 733, 747 (*ter*), 782.

O⁴

Book I: 473, 518, 539, 708.
Book II: 85, 155, 249, 277, 305, 382, 437, 554, 590, 645, 932.
Book III: 52, 58, 145, 176, 203, 289, 304, 305, 319, 332, 432, 453, 470, 523, 719, 853, 887, 894, 917, 1001, 1008.
Book IV: 351, 429, 792, 1225, 1247.
Book V: 28, 706.
Book VI: 1221.

THE FOLIATION OF THE LUCRETIAN ARCHETYPE

A few details of Lachmann's famous reconstruction of the Lucretian archetype (Ω) were questioned in a number of articles over the subsequent fifty years, but few brought any permanent value.[1] Chatelain (1908, *Praef.* VI^r–VII^r) was the first to provide a tabulation of the contents of each leaf, but his details were significantly wrong in many respects and too brief to be of use. Soon after, Merrill (1913) provided a more thorough account on the basis of Lachmann but marred his work by recurrent error. The most important and definitive contribution was made by Goold (1958), who not only provided more accurate details for each page of the archetype but refined and discussed contentious features of the reconstruction as he progressed. There has been no further discussion of the matter since, it generally being assumed that Goold's polishing of Lachmann's reconstruction was flawless.

I accept the Lachmann–Goold model in its major details. However, my own reconstruction attempts to take some account of the rubricated verses found in O (and to a lesser extent ψ), which were treated in Chapter 3. It seems that on the first page of the manuscript (1^v)[2] the first of the twenty-six ruled lines was taken up by a title of sorts, rubricated or otherwise, or perhaps left blank (as in O), with the result that the first leaf closed with I.25 not I.26. My numeration therefore differs from Lachmann–Goold until 9^v, where I believe that both I.411 and the *capitulum* I.419 were marginal, hence O's wrongly taking 411 to be a *capitulum* and ψ not appreciating that 419*cap.* should be entered as such. My numeration then tallies with theirs until 19^v, which contained twenty-six typical verses, with 20^r having the *capitulum* I.951 over two lines (as Goold (1958, 24) tentatively suggested). My reconstruction of the foliation of Book II differs in a number of slight details in order to explain the strangely mistaken rubrication of O (see Chapter 3, pp. 171–4). Only two further points of difference remain. First, as stated in Chapter 3 (p. 167), I do not accept Lachmann's theory that the *capitula* for Book VI were placed in a space at the bottom of 125^r; rather, I conclude that a new leaf was begun, with the *tituli* written on 126^r and the text of Book VI beginning on the verso. Secondly, as argued in Chapter 2 (pp. 122–7), I do not accept a lacuna, let alone the loss of a leaf, after

---

[1] Cf. esp. Woltjer (1881b) and Brieger (1883).

[2] Although it is possible that Lucretius' *DRN* was written immediately after another work (ending on 1^r), it is more likely that the initial recto was left without text for decoration or protection of this rare work.

VI.839 in the archetype; given, however, my differing placement of the *index* to Book VI, the total number of leaves that I reconstruct is the same as that of Lachmann–Goold: 151.

I therefore reconstruct the Lucretian archetype in Table 10. Leaves preceded by an asterisk differ in their numeration of verses from those reconstructed by Goold (1958).

Table 10

Folio	Recto	capitula / [omitted or marginal] verses			Verso	capitula / [omitted or marginal] verses	
*1		*uacua*		*cap.*			25
*2	26	44	50	51		62	75
*3	76	84	100	101		107, 112	124
*4	125	150	150c	150			175
*5	176		201	202		215	226
*6	227		252	253		269	277c
*7	277	298	301	302		305, 311	325
*8	326	334	350	351		370	375
*9	376		401	402		v. 411, 419c marg.	428
10	429	430	453	454			479
11	480	498	504	505			530
12	531	551	555	556		565	580
13	581		606	607			632
14	633	635	657	658			683
15	684	705	708	709		716	733
16	734		759	760			785
17	786		811	812		830	836
18	837		862	863			888
*19	889		914	915			940
*20	941	951 (2)	964	965			990
21	991		1016	1017			1042
22	1043	1051	1067	1068			1093
23	1094	*sscr* (2)	1117			*uacua*	
24	II.1	14	25	26			51
*25	52	62	76	77		89, v. 94	102
*26	103	112	127	128		142	152
*27	153		178	179		184 (3)	201

The foliation of the Lucretian archetype

Table 10 (*cont.*)

	Recto				Verso	
Folio		*capitula* / [omitted or marginal] verses			*capitula* / [omitted or marginal] verses	
28	202	221	226	227		252
29	253		278	279		304
30	305		330	331	333	355
*31	356		381	382	388, 392, [398c? & 400c marg.]	405
*32	406	408	430	431	447	455
*33	456	464, 471, 478	478	479	v. 502	505
*34	506	522 (2)	529	530		555
*35	556		581	582	589, 598	605
*36	606		631	632	646	656
*37	657		682	683	710 anticipated	707
*38	708	730 (2)	731	732	755	756
39	757		782	783	801, 806	806
*40	807		832	833	842 (3)	855
*41	856	865	880	881	v. 887 ut capit.	906
*42	907		932	933		958
*43	959	v. 962 (2) ut capit.	983	984		1009
*44	1010	v. 1023 ut capit.	1035	1036	1048, 1058	1059
*45	1060		1085	1086	1105 (2)	1109
*46	1110		1135	1136	1144 (2)	1159
*47	1160	*sscr* (2 +9 uac.)	1174		*uacua*	
48	**III.**1		26	27	41	51
49	52		77	78	94	102
50	103		128	129	136	153
51	154		179	180	182	204
52	205	228	229	230	241	254
53	255	262	279	280	288	304
54	305		330	331	350	355
55	356	370, 379	379	380		405
56	406	417	430	431	445 (2)	454
57	455		480	481		506
58	507		532	533		558
59	559		584	585		610
60	611	624	635	636		661

Table 10 (*cont.*)

Folio	Recto capitula / [omitted or marginal] verses				Verso capitula / [omitted or marginal] verses	
61	662	v. 678a	686	687	711	711
62	712		737	738		763
63	764		789	790		815
64	816		841	842		867
65	868		893	894		919
66	920		945	946		971
67	972	978	996	997		1022
68	1023		1048	1049		1074
69	1075	*sscr* (2 +4 uac.)	1094		*tituli of Book* **IV**	
70	1c	1	25	26	29	50
71	51		76	77	98	101
72	102	116	126	127	132	151
73	152	176	176	177		202
74	203		228	222	[222–8 iterati]	247
75	248	269	272	273		298
76	323	326	347	299	312 (2)	322
77	348	353, 364	371	372	387	396
78	397		422	423		448
79	449		474	475	476	499
80	500	513, 524	524c	524	526	548
81	549	572	573	574	595	598
82	599	615	623	624	633	648
83	649	673	673	674		699
84	700	722	724	725		750
85	751		776	777	779	801
86	802		827	828	836	852
87	853	877	877	878		903
88	904	907	928	929		954
89	955	962	979	980		1005
90	1006	1030	1030	1031		1056
91	1057		1082	1083		1108
92	1109		1134	1135		1160
93	1161		1186	1187		1212
94	1213		1238	1239		1264
95	1265	*sscr* (+1)	1287		*uacua*	
96		*tituli of Book* **V**		1		26

The foliation of the Lucretian archetype

Table 10 (cont.)

Folio	Recto				Verso	
	capitula / [omitted or marginal] verses				capitula / [omitted or marginal] verses	
97	27		52	53	59, 64, 76	76c
98	76	92	100	101		126
99	127	132, 146	150	151		176
100	177	200	201	202		227
101	228	240, 251	251	252	261, 273	275
102	276	281, 294	299	300	306, 324	324c
103	324		349	350	351	374
104	375	376, 397	398	399	419	423
105	424		449	450	471 (2)	473
106	474		499	500		525
107	526		551	552	564	576
108	577	590	601	602	621	626
109	627	629	651	652	663	676
110	677	680	701	702	705	726
111	727	737	751	752	774	776
112	777	780	801	802		827
113	828		853	854	878	878
114	879	892, 901	902	903	916	927
115	928		953	954		979
116	980		1005	1006		1031
117	1032		1057	1058		1083
118	1084		1109	1110		1135
119	1136	1161	1161c	1161		1186
120	1187		1212	1213		1238
121	1239	1241	1263	1264	1281	1288
122	1289		1314	1315		1340
123	1341		1366	1367		1392
124	1393		1418	1419		1444
*125	1445	sscr (+11)	1457		uacua	
*126		tituli of Book **VI**		1		26
*127	27		52	53		78
*128	79	96	103	104		129
*129	130		155	156	160	180
*130	181	204	205	206	219, 225	229
*131	230	246	254	255		280
*132	281	285	305	306		331

Table 10 (*cont.*)

	Recto			Verso		
Folio		*capitula* / [omitted or marginal] verses			*capitula* / [omitted or marginal] verses	
*133	332	357	357c	357		382
*134	383		408	409		434
*135	435	451	459	460		485
*136	486	493, 495	509	510	526	534
*137	535c	535	559	560		585
*138	586	608	610	611		636
*139	637	639	661	662		687
*140	688	712	712	713	737	737
*141	738	749, 756	761	762		787
*142	788		813	814		839
143	840c	840, 848	863	864	879, 888	888c
144	888		913	914	921	938
145	939		964	965		990
146	991		1016	1017		1042
147	1043		1068	1069	1090	1093
148	1094		1119	1120	1138	1144
149	1145		1170	1171		1196
150	1197		1222	1223		1248
151	1249		1274	1275	*sscr* (+9 uac.)	1286
152		*fort. uacua*				*fort. uacua*

c = *capitulum*
sscr = *subscripta*

THE FATE OF OQS IN THE EARLY MODERN PERIOD

The Oblongus (O)

The history of O until the fifteenth century has been traced in Chapters 1 (pp. 6–8) and 4 (*passim*), so far as evidence has allowed; information thereafter about its movements from Mainz until the late seventeenth century is more plentiful. When the Cathedral of St Martin was sacked in 1552, it is possible that the soldiers of the Markgraf Albrecht Alcibiades of Brandenburg-Kulmbach (1522–57) removed O from the monastery to Heidelberg, as they did other prized literary codices which thereafter spread about Europe.[1] The only piece of evidence standing against this reasonable conjecture is a note of Obertus Gifanius (Hubert van Giffen, 1533–1604) inscribed in a copy of his first edition (now Oxford Bodl. Bywater P 6 14) written between 1573 and his death in 1604, quite possibly during the last five years of his life.[2] Among a list of Lucretian manuscripts known to him, Gifanius stated '[e]st et unum in bibliotheca aliqua Magontiacensi'.[3] Not only is the note curiously unspecific, which suggests that he knew of the manuscript only by indirect report, but there is no evidence, from either Gifanius' prefaces (1565, 1595[2]) or marginal notes, that he ever obtained

---

[1] See Falk (1897) 26–7 (576–7), 57–61 (607–61). It has been argued at the close of Chapter 1 (pp. 39–40) that a collation, if not an apograph, was made of O during the mid fifteenth century by at least one Italian, but there is no reason to suppose that O itself ever descended into Italy.

[2] Reeve (2006, 177) noted that Gifanius first wrote '1599' as the date for collating two Venetian manuscripts, then altered it to '1593'/'1598', before cancelling and writing '1569'. Close inspection reveals that he wrote 1596, which was crossed out (after an attempt to change the final '6' to '9') and replaced by '1569' in the same hand; Reeve (1980, 37 n. 1) reports the view of Carlotta Dionisotti that this trip must actually have occurred between January and October 1570. Such a strange error could indicate that the note was written in the 1590s, with a year such as 1596 being on Gifanius' mind, and perhaps after that year, when the mistaken date was temporally possible. We know that Gifanius had an interest in the whereabouts of Lucretian manuscripts in his final years, as two statements in letters from 1599–1604 demonstrate: one concerning Q is discussed below; the other, cited by Reeve (2006, 178), asked Theodore Canter (1545–1617) in 1602 about the location of two Lucretian manuscripts that Canter had told him the van Cuycks (Cucii) owned in 1578, in the hope of collating one. It is a reasonable assumption that the manuscript in St Martin's during Nannius' lifetime (see n. 4 below) entered the library of the van Cuycks (Johannes and Antonius), who were then based in Utrecht, a fact that, if true, Gifanius did not know.

[3] For the corrected transcription of this note, see Reeve (2006) 178.

any readings from O.[4] More probable is that he had merely heard, perhaps at some remove, that there was a Lucretius in the Mainz area, a rumour that could have originated a few decades before the sack of the library or could be a perversion of the fact that a Lucretius was then abducted. We therefore need not suppose that O remained in Mainz after Albrecht Alcibiades' pillaging, although that must be a possibility.

By the mid seventeenth century, O was in the possession of Isaac Vossius (1618–89), who had inherited it from his father Gerardus Johannes Vossius (1577–1649), as with Q (see below);[5] given that no such manuscript occurs in his private catalogue (maintained until 1622),[6] and that Claudius Salmasius (Claude de Saumaise, 1588–1653) and Johannes Gronovius (Johann Gronow, 1611–71), who both borrowed Q from Gerardus (see below), made no mention of any other Lucretian codex in their correspondence on Q in 1634–5, we may suppose that it was bought by Gerardus between 1635 and 1649. It is an interesting coincidence that he was born in a suburb of Heidelberg, and could have had close contacts with the book trade of that city, if O did eventually enter the second-hand market there.[7] The book more probably came to his attention in Amsterdam[8] through his son, who from the early 1640s was active in expanding the *Bibliotheca Vossiana*, before serving Queen Kristina of Sweden (1626–89) in a similar role from 1649 until 1654.[9]

---

[4] Gifanius stated (*Praef.* **[v]) that he evaluated the 'scripturas ... veterum librorum plusquam octo', the truth of which cannot be established from his editions, as he rarely troubled to cite the source of a given manuscript reading. Von Barth (1664, *ad Theb.* XII.238) may be correct in alleging that Gifanius did not consult any of the 'veteres libr[i]' he cited, knowledge of them being at second or greater remove. Gifanius thanked Cornelius Valerius (1512–78), successor of Petrus Nannius (1500–57) as Professor of Latin at the Collegium Trilingue in Louvain, for sending him a transcription of the latter's collation of a manuscript (probably saec. XV) in St Martin's, Utrecht. Gifanius referred to it on the flyleaf cited above (see Reeve (2006) 177–8): '[e]st aliud Traiecti ad Rhenum in biblioth[eca] summi templi'. There is no factual basis for Fleischmann's statement (1971, 351–2) that '[t]here is a chance that Obertus Gifanius ... made use of [O]', a suggestion also made (perhaps independently) by Pizzani (1986) 308.

[5] No one, to my knowledge, has explicitly argued for Gerardus' ownership of O: Smith in Leonard–Smith (96 n. 7) and Bailey (vol. I, 38) asserted that Isaac inherited O from his father, the former probably misleading the latter through misunderstanding Sandys (1915) 243; De Meyier (1973, 67) appended a question mark to the attribution of provenance, clearly drawing on Falk (see n. 7).

[6] Amsterdam UB RK III D11[a]. This catalogue records only ten codices.

[7] This connection was tentatively suggested by Falk (1897) 59 (609) n. 1.

[8] Vossius was in Leiden in 1595–1600 as a student and in 1615–30 as Director of the Collegium Theologicum (1615–18) and Professor of Eloquence and Chronology (1618–30); in 1600–15 he taught at Dordrecht and from 1632 until his death held the Professorship of History at the University of Amsterdam.

[9] Most of Gerardus' library was sold by Isaac to Queen Kristina in 1650; nevertheless, the Stockholm catalogue made by Isaac when in post contains no Lucretian codex, and there is no evidence that Vossius encountered one throughout his services there: no trace of Lucretius is turned up by the survey of Callmer (1977). It is known that he kept a private library of particular treasures at the family home, and it is highly probable that both O and Q remained there during his time abroad.

The fate of OQS in the early modern period

Gerardus evidently had access to O and Q before his death, as he collated them on his copy of Gifanius' first edition (now Leiden 757 G 25).[10] Nikolaas Heinsius (1620–81) is also known to have collated OQ *apud Vossium* by 1662, in which year

---

[10] See Reeve (2006) 180–3. This volume bears the annotation 'Gerardi Vossii, olim Fr. Nansii, cuius manu annotata quae ad oram libri cernere est'. It passed to Vossius from Janus Rutgersius (Johan Rutgers, 1589–1625), brother-in-law of Daniel Heinsius (1580–1655). The book contains various annotations, probably in the hand of Franciscus Nansius (*c.* 1520–95), which bring Gifanius' notes in line with those of his second edition (1595). Many of the marginalia appear in various books spread around Europe. A direct transcription of 757 G 25 was made in Leiden by Frans van Oudendorp (1696–1761) into his copy of Gifanius' second edition (now Leiden 757 G 28). I have identified the hand annotating a copy of Gifanius' second edition in Cambridge University Library Hhh 1085 as Isaac Vossius'; we can therefore conclude that the book's owner, Pierre de Cardonnel (1614–67), who bought the volume in 1645, lent it to his friend Isaac, who perhaps had offered to transcribe the various notes from his father's copy (757 G 25). If de Cardonnel received the book back, Vossius must have annotated it in Amsterdam between 1662 (for Faber is referred to *ad* II.344 (p. 46)) and 1667 (de Cardonnel's death). Isaac also copied significant material from 757 G 25 into his copy of Faber (now Trinity College Cambridge Adv. b 13 3), and added his own collations of OQ, and a transcription of G from his copy of Heinsius' collation (see following note). Issac mistakenly added a collation of a 'ms v.' from Leiden 757 G 25 (= O) alongside his own collations of OQ ('ms' and 'ms al(t).' respectively), suggesting that the collation of O had been made privately in 757 G 25 by Gerardus. Very many notes of Vossius in TCC Adv. b 13 3 and of Nansius in 757 G 25, along with some of Isaac's unpublished notes for a Lucretian commentary (now lost: cf. n. 13 below) and certain emendations added to his copy of Gifanius' second edition (Leiden 757 G 26), were transcribed by his executor Adrian Beverland (1650–1716) into another copy of Faber's edition (now Oxford Bodl. d'Orville 324), either when Beverland catalogued Vossius' library in the 1680s, or after the latter's death in 1689 (Beverland's *ex libris* is dated 1682). Several notes in Beverland's hand must postdate the Tonson edition of 1712, which published several readings that were otherwise unknown. Beverland catalogued Vossius' manuscripts in 1684 (now NLS MS 6134 ff. 3^v–38^v, an improved copy of BL Sloane MS 1783, ff. 17–53) after he came as an exile to England in 1679. For further information on this catalogue, which records both O and Q, see Cunningham (1983); the 'T. Fabri cum emendationibus et notis Isaaci Vossi' recorded is probably, *contra* Cunningham (22 n. 28), now TCC Adv. b 13 3. Beverland evidently wished to put the Vossian marginalia into circulation, for at least three copies of his apograph exist. One, another copy of Faber (now Leiden 759 D 21) that was sent to his friend in Utrecht, Jacob de Goyer, came to auction on 3 May 1706, after de Goyer's death. Syvert Haverkamp (1683–1742) learnt of the volume through his former teacher Jacobus Gronovius (Jakob Gronow, 1645–1716); cf. Haverkamp (vol. 1, *Praef.* *3^v, with Preiger, *apud* 3*4^v), who was seemingly unaware of the existence of 757 G 25. A transcription of Beverland's copy by Beverland himself (if Gordon (1985, 90) was correct) exists in a copy of the first English edition (Cambridge, 1675), also at Leiden (757 G 29). Finally, a copy of Beverland's marginalia in Bodl. d'Orville 324 made by an anonymous hand exists in Copenhagen Kong. Bibl. Fabr. 96 4° (8). Some of this Vossian material found its way to Thomas Creech for his Oxford edition of 1695, although he only occasionally cited its readings, and rarely acknowledged his source, and to Robert Cannon (see below).

Appendix V

he told his friend Johannes Scheffer (1621–79) that 'Lucretii tria exemplaria, ante annum DCCC exarata, mihi contigit pervolvere'.[11] Isaac Vossius' famous library[12] was brought to Britain in 1670 and, after twenty years in Windsor,[13] was eventually

[11] See Burman (1725–7) vol. V, 21; the letter was sent from Stockholm in Feb. 1662, to which city Heinsius had returned temporarily (1661–2) in the employ of the Dutch Ambassador. These three manuscripts are certainly OQ and S (G), collations of which Heinsius recorded in his copy of Gifanius' second edition (now TCC Adv. d 13 3, on which see Munro, vol. I, 24–5): O is collated fully, S for the full fragment (G) and Q up to Book IV; Heinsius also added a collation of Franciscus Modius' manuscript (= Q: see below), drawn from Modius' copy of Lambinus' pocket edition (Paris, 1565), and the marginalia he tentatively attributed to Nansius, taken from either the same Lambinian edition or another copy; whether the readings are Nansius' or not, they betray no knowledge of Q and could all be conjectural. Heinsius' annotated edition was bought by Hugh Munro in 1852; for further information, see Reeve (2006) 179–80. The collations in it were transcribed by Pieter Burman the Younger (1713–78) into his copy of Lambinus' third edition (now Leiden 759 D 20). Heinsius cited OQ in his *Adversaria* (1742) at various points, although one cannot date these notes: on IV.289 (p. 90) he mentioned 'duo pervetusti codices Vossiani' (cf. his note on [2]^v of TCC Adv. d 13 3: 'Contuli Lucretium cum duobus vetustissimis codicibus Vossianae bibliothecae'); if (as is probable) the 'duo veterrimi' referred to on V.605 (p. 310) presented *percipitat* not *perpitat* (a typographical error?) for *percipiat*, we may regard OQ as Heinsius' sources; the other readings here attributed to these two manuscripts on the same page are found in OQ, although *conciat* (for *concutiat*) at II.1001 is found only in Q; the 'scripti codices' at V.1001 (p. 118), which offer *lidebant* for *laedebant*, could well be O$^{a.c.}$Q. Heinsius' slight inaccuracies are probably due to the cursory nature of his notes, never intended for publication, and/or Burman's inaccuracy. Three manuscripts are referred to at IV.681 (p. 374) and II.1168–9 (p. 455, 'membranis trinis egregie antiquis'), two of which could certainly be OQ, the third probably being Modius' collation (which Heinsius possessed), now known also to be Q (see below). Finally, Heinsius recorded that he found *cratem* at VI.1091 (p. 400) 'in veterrimo Vossiano codice'; given that this reading occurs only in the hand of O^2 among the ninth-century manuscripts, he must have used this manuscript but failed to regard or record it as a later correction. Heinsius' knowledge of OQ can be pushed back slightly further than 1662, for in the second volume of his Ovid (1661) *ad Met.* II.275, he referred to 'optimi duo Vossiani codices'; in the preface to this work, presumably written by 1658, he had recorded Lucretius among the authors upon whom he wanted to publish emendations. We can therefore suppose that Heinsius collated OQ during the 1650s at Amsterdam in the Vossian home, after 1654 and perhaps when he was secretary there in 1656–8. Finally, Tonson's edition (London, 1712) published among its *Variae Lectiones* a transcription of collations made in the margin of a copy of Gryphius' first pocket edition (Lyon, 1540), owned by John Moore (1646–1714), Bishop of Ely, but now seemingly lost: inspection of these readings ('H1' and 'H2') shows that Moore or Tonson mistakenly took them to be the collation of two manuscripts, for they are in reality a collation of Laur. 35.25 (or a close relative), with some emendations interspersed among them: further investigation would therefore not offer any major insight into the Lucretian ms tradition.

[12] Isaac had 'the best private library, as it was then supposed, in the whole world' (Wood (1691–2) vol. II, 856), which boasted 762 manuscripts.

[13] Isaac left for England in 1670, where he was made a Prebendary of Windsor (Canon from 1673). He apparently contemplated editing Lucretius himself, for in his Catullus (1684, 249 *ad* 64.383, where he cited Lucr. V.1353) he explained '[s]ic enim legendum esse locum, ad Lucretium docemus'. A note in Graevius' edition of Callimachus (1697,

308

purchased following Isaac's death (21 February 1689) by Leiden University,[14] who bettered the University of Oxford and their offer of £3,000, as well as the Universities of Cambridge and Amsterdam, who made no formal bids. O has thus resided in Leiden University Library from 1690 until the present day.[15]

The Quadratus (Q)

As with O, we have tracked in Chapter 1 (pp. 8–9) and Chapter 5 (*passim*) the possible fate of Q until the sixteenth century, a period that was to bring the manuscript into scholarly hands. Lambinus stated (1563, $\overline{11}^v$) that Q, which he termed the 'Bertinianus', was sent to Petrus Gallandus (Pierre Galland, 1510–59) in Paris by the monks of St Bertin in St Omer, who made it available to his friend Adrianus Turnebus (Adrien de Tournebou, 1512–65).[16] It seems that Galland and Turnebus purchased Q from St Bertin when, around late 1544, they took a tour throughout northern France and Flanders in search of interesting classical manuscripts. Since they succeeded in purchasing a manuscript of the *Agrimensores* from the monks of St Bertin,[17] they could well then have secured Q too, which was perhaps transferred to Paris with the other manuscripts shortly thereafter. Although Lambinus himself never inspected the manuscript he termed the Bertinianus (= Q) and instead used Turnebus' collations, which the latter also employed in his own *Adversaria* (vol. I 1564; II 1565; III 1573),[18] he did manage to use Q by other means. Once Galland obtained the Bertinianus, it seemingly never returned to

---

vol. I, 174 *ad Hymn.* VI.137) also recorded that Vossius produced unpublished notes on Lucretius: if they existed outside the margins of printed books, they appear not to have survived.

[14] Owing to his suspicion of British bids, and perhaps institutional piety, Vossius approached Hieronymus van Beveringh, Curator at Leiden University, who eventually won with a bid of 33,000 guilders. The books were secretly brought to the house of the Dutch Ambassador, Arnout van Citters, until William III gave them safeguard and exemption from export tax. For further information on the negotiations and transference of the library in 1690, see Tydeman (1825).

[15] The corrections of O^4, treated in Chapter 4, section E, could have been added in the first few years in which O resided at Leiden.

[16] See Lehmann (1908) 112; the Bertinianus was rightly identified as Q by Bernays (1847) 544–8.

[17] See the prefatory epistle to Galland's edition of the *Agrimensores* (1554). It is noteworthy that Galland's metaphor when he stated that 'in singulis monasteriis libris veteres, veluti canes sagaces ... diligenter conquireremus' was famously used by Lucretius (I.404–9), perhaps hinting at the successful acquisition of *DRN*.

[18] It seems that no serious investigation has been made into Turnebus' use of an ancient Lucretian manuscript. As it happens, there is not abundant evidence sprinkled throughout his *Adversaria*: references to an old codex which can safely be identified as Q occur (citing the page references of the 1580 Basel edition) at 216,11, 519,34, 652–4 (multiple passages), 698,32–3, 787–8 (multiple passages), 973,20 and 1016,41. Reeve (2006, 176–7) tentatively suggested that the collation of a manuscript probably to be identified with Q in a copy of a Gryphian edition (Lyon, 1540; now Paris Bibl. Nat. Rés. p Yc 5026) is in Turnebus' hand.

Appendix V

St Bertin but was retained until his death in 1559, apparently passing thereafter to Erricus Memmius (Henri de Mesmes, 1532–96). Lambinus thanked this nobleman in his dedicatory epistle to Book I (1563, ē4^r) for lending an 'exemplar pervetustum' (which he duly termed the 'Memmianus') to him for his Lucretian researches, presumably in the early 1560s. Frère (1909) tentatively identified the Memmianus with the Bertinianus (= Q),[19] an opinion since bolstered by Reeve (2006, 175–7) and certainly correct, despite the few minor discrepancies.[20] We must therefore assume that Lambinus was unaware of this connection, for he mistakenly took the 'Memmianus' as distinct from his 'Bertinianus'.

Moving beyond Lambinus, we know that, some two decades before de Mesmes' death (in 1596), Q came into the possession of Nansius (on whom see n. 10 above), who had studied under Turnebus at Paris in 1548–51, was based in Leiden in the 1570s and 80s and moved to teach at the Latin School at Dordrecht in his final years. That Nansius possessed Q can be established by Gifanius' testimony: in a letter to Franciscus Junius (1545–1602) of 1599–1602, he stated that Nansius used to own in Leiden the manuscript that was once in St Bertin.[21] We also know that in 1579 Q was collated in Cologne by the young Franciscus Modius (1556–97).[22] It is probable that Modius merely borrowed the

---

[19] Purmann (1846, 16) and Bernays (1847, 546, 550–1) noted the similarity between the Memmianus and Q but stopped short of identifying them.

[20] This conclusion is supported by Paris Bibl. Nat. Rés. p Yc 1849 (Basel, 1531, briefly discussed by Reeve (2006) 176), which belonged to Lambinus and contains, presumably in his hand, a collation of Q, perhaps as an initial trial run (for Reeve reported that 'long stretches of Books 4–6 are untouched'). The few disagreements between Lambinus' citations of readings from the Memmianus and Q can be explained by the combined inaccuracy of Turnebus' collation and Lambinus' haphazard citation of manuscripts.

[21] 'Omiseram fere de Lucretio, cuius antiquissimum codicem ex bibliotheca monasterii Bertiniani in Flandria Leidae habuit Nansius. Codex an et ubi sit salvus magnopere scire velim.' (Leiden, UB Hs. Pap. 2).

[22] See Munro (vol. 1, 24) for a transcription of Modius' note by Heinsius in TCC Adv. d 13 3. The date given for the collation is 26 June 1579, and Modius referred to the manuscript as 'me[us]'. Bernays (1847, 548–51) showed that the 'codex Modii' was Q, but he wrongly thought that Modius had found the manuscript in St Bertin, where he visited; see also Lehmann (1908) 111–12. In the following year, Janus Meller Palmerius (Palmier, *fl.* 1580) used a manuscript 'v.c. docti adolescentis, mihique amici Francisci Modii' when citing Lucr. IV.601–2 and VI.348–9 in his *Spicilegium* (Frankfurt, 1580; see Palmerius in Gruter (1602–34) vol. IV, 614–15) whose readings duly coincide with Q. Heinsius once cited Modius' manuscript in his *Adversaria* (1742, [4]04) *ad* Lucr. VI.854, namely *udum* for *nudum*, a reading not found in Q or anywhere else that probably arose from an error in transcription or memory. Heinsius was therefore wrong to conclude privately ([2]^v Adv. d 13 3) that 'Codex Modii non est idem cum B. Vossiano nam pag. 8 ubi ex Modiano notatum *ad lumina* Vossianus in', as this difference was probably based on Modius' mistake or Heinsius' misinterpreting a conjecture of Modius as a collated reading. The copy of Gifanius' second edition into which Modius made a collation of Q came into Nansius' possession (if Heinsius did not misdate the ownership of these two related figures); thereafter it passed through the hands of Jan Gruter (1560–1627), then Justus Liraeus (1578–1646), who lent it to Heinsius. Heinsius must therefore have added the collations of Modius', and probably Nansius', marginalia before 1646; it is clear from

manuscript from his uncle Nansius, even if on a long-term loan that allowed its transference from Leiden to Cologne: no mention of a Lucretian manuscript occurs in Modius' library catalogue of 1588. We have already mentioned the copy of the first Gifanius edition (Leiden 757 G 25) that contains the hands of Nansius and the two Vossii, although Nansius' notes do not draw directly upon Q.[23]

The fate of Q between Nansius' death (if he kept it that long) in 1595 and its entering Gerardus' library by 1634, when he lent it to Salmasius, is unclear.[24] Although many of Nansius' manuscripts and books entered Leiden University Library on his death through the agency of the librarian Paulus Merula, many were sold at auction in Dordrecht,[25] which could have included (albeit rather surprisingly) Q. If the manuscript was sold at Dordrecht, it is not known into whose hands it fell thereafter. A copy of Lambinus' third edition (1570) in Vienna (now ÖNB *35 C 62) contains a marginal collation of a manuscript up to I.852 that is almost certainly Q; its siglum 'V' more probably means 'vetustus/veterrimus [codex]' than 'Vossianus'.[26] The earliest recorded owner, Janus Bylerius, about whom I have found no information,[27] stated that he bought the book in Amsterdam in 1604. It may be that, after 1595, the owner of this volume before 1604, or Bylerius himself, had access to Q and managed to collate some of its readings in Book I, before running out of time and/or interest.[28] Between 1622 and 1634, Q was at last obtained

the stratification of the collations of OQS that they were added later, first O, then Q and the fragment of S (G) perhaps simultaneously (no doubt from an intermediary transcript). The volume presumably later entered the hands of Johann Graevius (1632–1703) when in Utrecht (from 1662), who wrote to Heinsius in late 1668 that he had seen his Lucretius (Burman (1725–7) vol. IV, 77), a book that proved Modius collated a Lucretian manuscript.

[23] It was observed by Pol (1975, 98 no. 47) and Reeve (2006, 182–3) that the 'T. Lucretius Carus, collatus ab Fr. Nansio cum Antiquissimo Exemplari' attested in his posthumous library catalogue has not been traced. Yet, if Nansius' marginalia used by Heinsius occurred in a different volume from Modius' collation (see n. 11 above), this book could be 757 G 25 (see n. 10 above).

[24] For the discussion of Q by Salmasius and Gronovius see Burman (1725–7) vol. I, *Epp.* 277–82, 284, 288, and Salmasius (1656) *Epp.* 48, 50–2, 58–9, 79, 81 (cf. Reeve (2006) 182 n. 67). *Ep.* 50 reveals that Salmasius lent Q to the young Gronovius in early 1635 without Vossius' express permission. A copy of Gifanius' second edition survives in Leiden (757 G 27) with manuscript notes and a partial collation of Q by Gronovius and his son Jakob.

[25] See Pol (1975) 417. Given that Nansius served as a proof-reader to the press of Franciscus Raphelengius in Leiden, it is probable that he was able to add, before his death in July 1595, notes based upon those in Gifanius' second edition published by that press that year. If the chronology could be proven impossible, the northern hand in 757 G 25 could be that of his nephew Modius, which was easily mistaken by Gerardus Vossius as Nansius', given the book's provenance.

[26] These readings were published as 'cod. (caes.) CXXVIII' in Alter's edition (1787, 260–71, 300–13).

[27] His surname could well be Swedish in origin; he could have been related to Arnoldus Bylerius, a figure who assisted the Jesuits' *Missio Hollandica* in Alkmaar (20 miles north of Amsterdam) in 1608 (cf. van Lommel (1876) 429).

[28] The second recorded owner of the book, Petrus Lambecius of Hamburg (1628–80), evidently could not have collated Q before it came into Gerardus' ownership, nor is he known to have been in contact with either Vossius.

by Gerardus; he may have already known of its existence, if it was owned in Dordrecht after Nansius' death, from his time as the Rector at that city's Latin School (1600–15).[29] On his death on 19 March 1649, Q evidently passed to his son Isaac, through whom it eventually entered Leiden University Library in the same manner as O.

Although they had reached the safe haven of an academic library, OQ did not instantly enjoy the veneration they deserved. Public notice of their contents seems not to have been given until Syvert Haverkamp's edition of 1725, although the transcription of collations owned by Robert Cannon (1663–1722), then a Prebendary of Ely Cathedral, was published among the *Variae Lectiones* of Tonson's edition (1712); these collations were ultimately copied from Isaac Vossius' collations in TCC Adv. b 13 3, probably through a transcription of Beverland.[30] Haverkamp (1684–1742), Professor of Rhetoric at Leiden, claimed in his infamous two-volume *variorum* edition of 1725 to make further use of these two ancient manuscripts on his doorstep:

> Primarium quidem auxilium in emendando Lucretio attulerunt nobis praestantissimi Codices duo MSS … uterque Membranaceus & vetustissimus; alter quidem majori forma, in folio, ut vulgo vocant, alter in quarto, sed majore, & quidem per columnas, ita scriptus, ut antiquissima quidem scriptura nonnunquam immutata fuerit, sed superscripta modo recentiore, imo vel ipsae literae, quae viderentur superfluae vel vitiosae esse in antiquiore (unde & hic expressus erat) libro, non sublatae, sed punctulo notatae essent; ut ita permagni sit aestimandus & fidum ejusdem nobis fuerit ministerium. (Vol. 1, *Praef.* *4^r)[31]

---

[29] Vossius was taught Greek by Franciscus Nansius at the Latin School in Dordrecht in 1592–5, and his notes record his influence with affection (cf. Rademaker (1981) 18–20).

[30] Tonson thanked Cannon for providing collations of the 'frag. Gottorp. [= G] tresque codices MStos'. Inspection of these readings shows that some confusion has occurred: the numbers 1, 2, 3 represent Vossius' collations of OQS respectively, but 'V' often appears alongside them to mean 'emendation/note of Vossius', even though this must simply be his collation, and S (G) is often also cited separately as 'G'; further, the readings of '3' (= S) persist after II.456 (where the fragment G ends) until the end of Book II and tend to provide the reading of O/Q. No knowledge is shown of the other extant fragments of S (VU). A copy of Cannon's 'collations', now survive as Copenhagen Kong. Bibl. Fabr. 49 4° (8), ff. 1–20; it is followed by a transcription of Vossius' own manuscript notes in the same copy of Faber's edition (see n. 10 above) (21^r–25^v). Moore also made available for Tonson two annotated Lucretian editions, one mentioned at the close of n. 11 above, the other (now lost) reputed to contain the emendations of Jacob Susius (de Suys, 1520–92) and Theodor Muncker (1640–81). Although Tonson assigned all the material to Susius, close inspection shows that the great majority of readings are drawn from the published writings and correspondence of Salmasius and Gronovius, and from Faber's edition, presumably transcribed by Muncker to bolster his text; the few attractive readings not attested elsewhere, by contrast, can tentatively be regarded as Susius' conjectures.

[31] In his list of sigla (vol. 1, *Praef.* o^{1v}), Haverkamp designated OQ as YZ, terming them 'pulcherrim[us] … atque vetustissim[us]' and 'longe vetustissim[us]' respectively.

The fate of OQS in the early modern period

Haverkamp added that the collations of the 'Londinensis Editor' were 'manca[e] valde & passim ab auctographis, quos diligenter consuluimus, discrepantes'. Despite this claim to improve upon his predecessors, Haverkamp's work was woefully inaccurate and incomplete, and often he can be shown to have followed Cannon's mistaken testimony over the very manuscripts he claimed to have consulted.[32] The major opportunity was thus missed, and OQ were not to be collated again for 120 years.

The *Schedae* (S)

In Chapter 1 (pp. 10–13) it was observed that the fate of S after its production is almost impossible to reconstruct until the seventeenth century. Around 1650 Nikolaas Heinsius collated part of the manuscript at the Castle of Holstein-Gottorp in Schleswig;[33] since he did not progress beyond II.456 (i.e. beyond the end of G), it seems that this gathering had been separated from those in Vienna, which fragments neither Heinsius, nor Isaac Vossius[34] nor Marquard Gude (1635–89), to whom his collation was passed,[35] knew. We can therefore date the dislocation of the first Lucretian quaternio to the late sixteenth or early seventeenth centuries and suppose also that VU have not left Vienna, or indeed the shelves of the Bibliothecia Regia (> Hof-Bibliothek > ÖNB), since that incident. It is possible that this first Lucretian gathering of S reached Gottorp by way of Friedrich Lindebruch (Lindenbrogius, 1573–1648), a well-travelled lawyer and philologist who is known to have removed a number of manuscripts (in part or in total) from various European libraries, many of which ended up in Gottorp Castle, where his brother Heinrich (1570–1642) was a librarian from 1610 until his death: given that Heinrich recorded the presence of Lucretius in his

---

[32] Cf. Munro (vol. 1, 18).

[33] Heinsius is known to have collated S (G) by 1662 (see the letter cited in n. 11) and, since he visited Gottorp in late March 1650, he presumably then made his collation, which survives in his copy of Gifanius' second edition (see n. 10).

[34] The collation occurs in Voss. Gr. O. 15 (ff. 8–15), probably in Isaac Vossius' hand (as argued by De Meyier (1955) 215); it records that the 'Fragmentum Gottorpianum 800 vel 900 annorum' was transcribed from a collation in Gifanius' second edition, presumably Heinsius' copy (on which see previous note and n. 11): Bernays (1847, 537) cited a letter (Burman (1725–7) vol. III, 585) in which Vossius thanked Heinsius for a catalogue of Gottorpian manuscripts, confessing that when he visited he saw 'magnam corum partem, sed propter festinationem ipsa etiam nomina exciderant', which precludes his collating S (G) himself. Since Vossius was based in England when Gude was in Gottorp, I do not believe that he ever saw Gude's collation, also made on a copy of Gifanius' second edition (see following note). Vossius copied his transcription of this collation into his father's copy of the first Gifanius edition, which already contained collations of OQ, and the flyleaves of his own copy of Faber (see n. 11).

[35] Gude presumably collated the fragment between 1671 and 1678, when he was librarian for Duke Christian Albert at Holstein-Gottorp. It is now preserved in Wolfenbüttel (HAB Gud. 251), and was first used by Orelli (1833, 8), to whom it was lent by Jan Sillig.

313

Appendix V

catalogue (c. 1640), the fragment clearly entered during his lifetime. If this suggestion is correct, it seems more probable that, in the early seventeenth century, the removal of just one gathering of a manuscript from the Bibliotheca Regia would have been carried out by underhand means rather than through open sale.[36] G, under the radar for much of the eighteenth century,[37] was transferred to the Kongelige Bibliotek of Copenhagen, along with the rest of the manuscript collection of Gottorp, in 1735;[38] it has resided there since.

[36] Kaspar von Barth (Barthius, 1587–1658) made a number of references to Lucretian manuscripts in his posthumous edition of Statius (1664), but I do not associate them (if genuine) with OQS: *ad Theb.* V.12 he found *clangor* for *clamor* at IV.182 'secundum membranas primum veteres, vel fragmentum' (later, *ad Theb.* XII.518, he reported this same reading 'ex membranis priscis'); *ad Theb.* V.116 he claimed to have found *quodam* for *quoniam* at I.4 'in membranis, quas Wittebergae aliquando contulimus'; *ad Theb.* IV.663 he found *canere* 'in membrana vetere' for *sonere* at III.156; *ad Theb.* X.875 he found the gloss *dissipata* on *diss<a>epta* at VI.951 'in Optimo Codice'; I have not found any of these readings in extant Lucretian manuscripts of any age. Barth, whose veracity has often been questioned, is probably too unreliable a source to make the very tentative suggestion that the 'fragmentum' referred to at IV.182 could have been part of S (corrupting *clamor* of ψ), this fragment also having been removed by Lindenbruch from Vienna. For a discussion of Barth's general lack of credibility, and an attempt to defend the veracity of his citations from Statian manuscripts, see Hall, Ritchie and Edwards (2007–8) vol. III, 65–8.
[37] See Chapter 1, n. 39.
[38] The library was founded by King Frederik III in 1648; G was evidently in the library before the notorious biblioklept Daniel Gotthilf Moldenhawer (1753–1823) entered post as Chief Librarian in 1786.

BIBLIOGRAPHY

Manuscripts

O: É. Chatelain (ed.), *T. Lucretius Carus Codex Vossianus Oblongus phototypice editus* (Leiden, 1908); autopsy (April 2008, September 2009)
Q: É. Chatelain (ed.), *T. Lucretius Carus Codex Vossianus Quadratus phototypice editus* (Leiden, 1913); autopsy (April 2008, September 2009)
G: *Codices Haunienses* (www.kb.dk/en/nb/materialer/haandskrifter/HA/e-mss/clh.html); autopsy (December 2008)
VU: microfilm provided by ÖNB; autopsy (December 2007)
Flor. Sang. (Sankt Gallen *Stifstbibl.* 870: www.e-codices.unifr.ch/en/csg/0870/); autopsy (August 2008)

Editions of *DRN*

The list is limited to the more significant editions; an asterisk indicates the presence of a commentary.
1473: T. Ferrando (*editio princeps*) (Brescia)
1486: P. Fridenperger (Verona)
1495: C. Lycinius (Venice)
1496: B. Misinta (Brescia) [for this edition, of which no copy can currently be traced, see Smith and Butterfield (2011)]
1500: H. Avancius (*ed. Aldina prima*) (Venice)
1511: *G. B. Pius (Bologna; Paris, 1515)
1512: P. Candidus (M. Marullus) (*ed. Iuntina*) (Florence)
1515: A. Naugerius (*ed. Aldina altera*) (Venice)
1563/4: *D. Lambinus (Paris; 1565 (pocket); 1570; Frankfurt, 1583)
1565/6: O. Gifanius (Antwerp; Leiden, 1595)
1631: D. Paraeus (Frankfurt)
1647: *G. Nardi (Florence)
1662: *T. Faber (Saumur)
1680: *M. du Fay (Paris)
1695: *T. Creech (Oxford)
1712: J. Tonson (London)
1725: *S. Haverkamp (Leiden; 2 vols.)
1782: Anon. (*ed. Bipont. prim.*) (Zweibrücken)

315

Bibliography

1787: F. K. Alter (Vienna)

1796–7: *G. Wakefield (London; Glasgow, 1813 (with *variae lectiones*))

1801: *K. Eichstädt (Leipzig (vol. 1 only))

1808: Anon. (*ed. Bipont. alt.*) (Strasburg)

1828: *A. Forbiger (Leipzig)

1838: *P. A. Lemaire (Paris; 2 vols.)

1850: *K. Lachmann (Berlin)

1852: J. Bernays (ed. *Teubner prim.*) (Leipzig)

1864: *H. A. J. Munro (Cambridge; 1866; 1873; 1886; 2 vols.)

1873–4: *F. Bockemüller (Stade; 2 vols.)

1894: A. Brieger (ed. *Teubner sec.*) (Leipzig; 1899)

1896–8: *C. Giussani (Turin; 4 vols.)

1900: C. Bailey (OCT) (Oxford; 1922)

1907: *W. A. Merrill (New York)

1917: W. A. Merrill (Berkeley, CA)

1920: A. Ernout (Budé) (Paris)

1923: J. Balcells (Barcelona; 1932; 2 vols.)

1923–4: H. Diels (Berlin; 2 vols.; all citations are from vol. 1)

1924: W. H. D. Rouse (Loeb) (London)

1925–8: *A. Ernout and L. Robin (Paris; 3 vols.)

1934: J. Martin (ed. *Teubner tert.*) (Leipzig; 1953; 1957; 1959; 1963)

1942: *W. E. Leonard and S. B. Smith (Madison)

1944: A. Cinquini (Rome)

1947: C. Bailey (Oxford; 1950; 3 vols.)

1961: E. Orth (Salamanca)

1961: E. Valentí (Barcelona; 2 vols.)

1966: K. Büchner (Wiesbaden)

1975: K. Müller (Zurich)

1975: M. Ferguson Smith (rev. Rouse, Loeb) (London; 1985; 1992)

1997: A. García Calvo (Zamora)

2002–9: E. Flores (Naples; 3 vols.)

Partial commentaries

1885: J. Bernays (I: up to I.689) (Berlin; written 1852/3, before OUP contract terminated)

1889: J. D. Duff (V) (Cambridge)

1897: R. Heinze (III) (Leipzig)

1903: J. D. Duff (III) (Cambridge)

1921: A. Krokiewicz (III) (Lublin)

1922: J. D. Duff (I) (Cambridge)

1946: A. Barigazzi (VI) (Turin)

1971: E. J. Kenney (III) (Cambridge)

1984: P. M. Brown (I) (Bristol)

Bibliography

1985: C. D. N. Costa (V) (Oxford)
1986: J. Godwin (IV) (Warminster)
1987: R. D. Brown, *Lucretius on Love and Sex* (IV.1030–1287) (Leiden)
1991: J. Godwin (VI) (Warminster)
1997: P. M. Brown (III) (Warminster)
2002: D. P. Fowler, *Lucretius on Atomic Motion* (II.1–332) (Oxford)
2004: E. M. Woolerton (II.333–729) (Diss., Cambridge)
2003: G. Campbell, *Lucretius on Creation and Evolution* (V.772–1104) (Oxford)
2005: L. Piazzi, *Lucrezio e i Presocratici* (I.635–920) (Pisa)
2009: M. R. Gale (V) (Warminster)
2009: C. Salemme, *Le possibilità del reale* (VI.96–534) (Naples)
2010: C. Salemme, *Lucrezio e la formazione del mondo* (V.416–508) (Naples)
2011: C. Salemme, *Infinito Lucreziano* (I.951–1117) (Naples)
2011: L. Piazzi, *Lucrezio: Le Leggi dell'Universo* (I) (Venice)

Secondary literature

Abbreviations of journal titles conform to those in l'Année Philologique.

Abry, J.-H. (1999) 'Présence de Lucrèce: les *Astronomiques* de Manilius', in Poignault (1999a), 111–28.

Adams, J. and R. G. Mayer (1999) *Aspects of the Language of Latin Poetry* (*Proc. Brit. Acad.* 93). London.

Alberti, G. B. (1979) *Problemi di critica testuale*. Florence.

Albrecht, M. von (1997) *A History of Roman Literature* (tr. G. Schmeling) (2 vols.). Leiden.

Alfieri, V. E. (1984) 'Lucrezio tra l'antico e il moderno', *A&R* 29: 113–28.

Alfonsi, L. (1978) 'L'avventura di Lucrezio nel mondo antico ... e oltre', in Gigon (1978), 271–315.

Algra, K. A., J. Barnes, J. Mansfeld and M. Schofield (eds.) (1999) *The Cambridge History of Hellenistic Philosophy*. Cambridge.

Algra, K. A., M. H. Koenen and P. H. Schrijvers (eds.) (1997) *Lucretius and his Intellectual Background*. Amsterdam.

Althoff, J. (1997) 'Zur Epikurrezeption bei Laktanz', in Fuhrer and Ehler (1997), 33–53.

(2005) 'Senecas "Naturales quaestiones", Buch 2, und Lukrez', in Baier, Manuwald and Zimmermann (2005), 9–34.

André, J.-M. (1974) 'Cicéron et Lucrèce', in *Mélanges P. Boyancé*. Rome: 21–38.

Anziger, L. (1896) *Studia in Aetnam collata*. Erlangen.

Arrighetti, G. (1973) *Epicuro. Opere*, 2nd edn. Turin.

Autenrieth, J. and F. Brunhölzl (eds.) (1971) *Festschrift Bernard Bischoff zu seinem 65. Geburtstag*. Stuttgart.

Bibliography

Auvray-Assayas, C. (1999) 'Lucrèce dans le *De natura deorum* de Cicéron: une réflexion sur les implications de la poétique atomiste', in Poignault (1999a), 101–10.

Baehrens, E. (ed.) (1886) *Fragmenta Poetarum Romanorum*. Leipzig.

Baier, T., G. Manuwald and B. Zimmermann (eds.) (2005) *Seneca: Philosophus et Magister*. Freiburg.

Bailey, C. (1926) *Epicurus. The Extant Remains*. Oxford.

(1931) 'Virgil and Lucretius', *PCA* 28: 21–39.

Bains, D. (1936) *A Supplement to Notae Latinae (Abbreviations in Latin MSS of 850 to 1050 AD)*. Cambridge.

Bajoni, M. G. (1994) 'Aspetti linguistici e letterari del "De Mundo" di Apuleio', *ANRW* II.34.2: 1785–1832.

Barra, G. (1960–1) 'Il valore e il significato del "De deo Socratis" di Apuleio', *AFLN* 9: 67–119.

Barth, K. von (1624) *Adversariorum Commentariorum Libri LX*. Frankfurt.

(1664) *P. Papinii Statii Opera*. Zwickau.

Bassi, D. (1926) 'I papiri Ercolanesi Latini', *Aegyptus* 7: 203–14.

Becker, G. (1885) *Catalogi Bibliothecarum Antiqui*. Bonn.

Becker, J. (1847) 'Beiträge zur kritik des Lucretius', *Philologus*. 2: 34–56.

Beer, B. (2009) 'Lukrez in Herculaneum? – Beitrag zu einer Edition von PHerc. 395', *ZPE* 119: 71–9.

Bergk, T. G. (1850) *Commentatio de Plauti Trinummo* (Progr.). Marburg.

(1872) *Griechische Literatur Geschichte* (2 vols.). Berlin.

(1884) *Kleine philologische Schriften* (2 vols.). Halle.

Bernays, J. (1847) 'De emendatione Lucreti', *RhM* 5: 533–87.

(1848) 'Ennianum non Lucretianum', *RhM* 6: 480.

(1885) *Gesammelte Abhandlungen* (2 vols.). Berlin.

Bertelli, S. (1961) 'Noterelle machiavelliane. Un codice di Lucrezio e di Terenzio', *RSI* 73: 544–53.

(1964) 'Noterelle machiavelliane. Ancora su Lucrezio e Machiavelli', *RSI* 76: 774–90.

(1965a) 'Un codice lucreziano dall'officina di Pomponio Leto', *PP* 20: 28–38.

(1965b) 'La conoscenza e la diffusione di Lucrezio nei codici umanistici italiani', *Rass. degli Archivi di Stato* 25: 271–88.

Berthod, A. (1788) 'Notice du cartulaire de Simon, Manuscrit de la Bibliothèque de St. Bertin', *Nouveaux Mémoires de l'Académie de Bruxelles* 1: 227–31.

Bignone, E. (1909) 'Lucrezio ed Erodoto', *Bollettino di Filologia Classica* 16: 57–60.

(1912) 'Il Petrarca e la Vita borgiana di Lucrezio', *Bollettino di Filologia Classica* 19: 160–1.

(1913) 'Per la fortuna di Lucrezio e dell'epicureismo nel Medioevo', *RFIC* 41: 230–63.

(1919) 'Nuove ricerche sul proemio del poema di Lucrezio', *RFIC* 47: 423–33.

Billanovich, Gius. (1971) 'I primi umanisti e l'antichità classica', in R. R. Bolgar (ed.), *Classical Influences on European Culture AD 500–1500*. Cambridge: 57–66.

Bibliography

Billanovich, Guid. (1958) 'Veterum vestigia vatum nei carmi dei preumanisti Padovani', *Italia Medioevale e Umanistica* I: 155–243.

Biondi, G. G. (2003) 'Lucrezio e Catullo', *Paideia* 58: 207–34.

Birt, T. (1913) *Kritik und Hermeneutik, nebst Abriss des antiken Buchwesens.* Munich.

(1919) 'Lucrez-Lesungen und der Lucrez-Archetyp', *Berliner Philologische Wochenschrift* 30: 708–20.

(1882) *Das antike Buchwesen in seinem Verhältniss zur Litteratur.* Berlin.

Bischoff, B. (1965) 'Die karolingische Minuskel', in Braunfels (1965), 207–10.

(1966–81) *Mittelalterliche Studien* (3 vols.). Stuttgart.

(1974) *Lorsch im Spiegel seiner Handschriften.* Munich.

(1981) *Kalligraphie in Bayern achtes bis zwölftes Jahrhundert.* Wiesbaden.

(1990) *Latin Palaeography: Antiquity and the Middle Ages* (trans. D. Ó Cróinín and D. Ganz). Cambridge.

(1994) *Manuscripts and Libraries in the Age of Charlemagne* (trans. M. M. Gorman). Cambridge.

(1998) *Katalog der festländischen Handschriften des neunten Jahrhunderts*, vol. I: *Aachen-Lambach.* Wiesbaden.

(2004) *Katalog der festländischen Handschriften des neunten Jahrhunderts*, vol. II: *Laon-Paderborn.* Wiesbaden.

Bitterlich-Willmann, H. (1951) *Die Hauptvertreter der Italienischen Lukrezüberlieferung* (Diss.). Freiburg.

Bloch, H. (1901) 'Ein karolingischer Bibliothekskatalog aus Kloster Murbach', in Varii (1901), 257–85.

Bloomfield, M. W. (1952) 'The sources of Boccaccio's Filostrato III, 74–79 and its bearing on the MS tradition of Lucretius', *CPh* 47: 162–5.

Bo, D. (1991) 'Una *vexatissima quaestio*: Lucilio, Lucrezio e Persio I 1–2', in Varii (1991), 1095–1105.

Bodelon García, S. (1987) *Revisión y actualización de la crítica textual lucreciana* (Diss.). Oviedo.

(1988) 'Tradición indirecta en Lucrecio', *Epos* 4: 39–52.

Boeck, U. (1958) 'Zu den Fragmenten des Lukrez', *Hermes* 86: 243–6.

Bolgar, R. R. (1963) *The Classical Heritage and its Beneficiaries.* Cambridge.

Bollack, M. (1976) 'Deux notes lucrétiennes', in M. Bollack and A. Laks (eds.), *Études sur l'épicurisme antique* (Cahiers de Philologie I). Lille: 261–78.

(1978) *La raison de Lucrèce.* Paris.

(1996) 'Jacob Bernays ou l'abandon du commentaire', in J. Glucker and A. Laks (eds.), *Jacob Bernays: un philologue juif.* Villeneuve: 31–44.

Bonner, S. F. (1960) 'The "Anecdotum Parisinum"', *Hermes* 88: 354–60.

Borleffs, J. W. (1932) 'Tertullian und Lukrez', *Philologische Wochenschrift*: 350–2.

Boyancé, P. (1963) *Lucrèce et L'Épicurisme.* Paris.

Boyle, L. E. (1985) *Medieval Latin Palaeography: a Bibliographical Introduction.* Toronto.

Bibliography

Brakman, C. (1920) 'Quae ratio intercedat inter Lucretium et Prudentium', *Mnemosyne* 48: 434–48.

(1921) 'Horatiana', *Mnemosyne* 49: 214–22.

(1922) 'Maniliana', *Mnemosyne* 50: 74–83.

Brandt, S. (1891a) 'Lactantius und Lucretius', *Jahrbücher für Klassische Philologie* 143: 225–59.

(1891b) 'Über die Quellen von Laktanz' Schrift *De opificio Dei*', *WS* 13: 255–92.

Braunfels, W. (ed.) (1965) *Karl der Grosse, Werk und Wirkung*. Aachen.

Brieger, A. (1883) 'Ein vermeintlicher Archetypus des Lucretius', *Jahrbücher für Klassische Philologie* 127: 553–9.

Broughton, A. L. (1939) 'Notes on Lucretius', *AJPh* 60: 238–42.

Brown, A. (2010) *The Return of Lucretius to Renaissance Florence.* Cambridge, MA.

Brown, V. (1968) 'The "insular intermediary" in the tradition of Lucretius', *HSPh* 72: 301–8.

Brunhölzl, F. (1962) 'Zur Überlieferung des Lukrez', *Hermes* 90: 97–104.

(1971) 'Zu den sogenannten codices archetypi der römischen Literatur', in Autenrith and Brunhölzl (1971), 16–31.

Büchner, K. (1956) 'Präludien zu einer Lukrezausgabe', *Hermes* 84: 198–233.

(1964) *Studien zur römischen Literatur*, vol. 1. Wiesbaden.

Bufano, A. (1951) 'Lucrezio in Lattanzio', *GIF* 4: 335–49.

Burman, P. (ed.) (1725–7), *Sylloge Epistolarum a Viris Illustribus Scriptarum* (5 vols.). Leiden.

Butterfield, D. J. (2006–7a) 'Emendations on the sixth book of Lucretius', *Eranos* 104: 83–92.

(2006–7b) 'N. H. Romanes and the text of Lucretius', *ICS* 31–2: 75–115.

(2008a) '*Lucretiana quaedam*', *Philologus* 152: 111–27.

(2008b) '*Nonnulla Lucretiana*', *ExClass* 8: 3–23.

(2008c) 'The poetic treatment of *atque* from Catullus to Juvenal', *Mnemosyne* 61: 368–413.

(2008d) 'Sigmatic ecthlipsis in Lucretius', *Hermes* 150: 188–205.

(2008e) 'Six Lucretian emendations', *Hyperboreus* 14: 117–23.

(2008f) '*Supplementa Lucretiana*', *Arctos* 42: 17–30.

(2008g) 'Ten Lucretian emendations', *Latomus* 67: 634–42.

(2008h) 'Three Lucretian emendations', *AAntHung* 48: 351–64.

(2009a) 'Emendations on the fifth book of Lucretius', *MD* 60: 177–89.

(2009b) 'Nine unidentified verses in the *exempla diuersorum auctorum*', *C&M* 60: 327–34.

(2009c) 'Three unidentified verses in the *Florilegium Sangallense*', *Maia* 61: 348–52.

(2009d) 'Two Lucretian Emendations', *Prometheus* 35: 81–9.

(2009e) 'Unidentified and misattributed verses in the *Opus prosodiacum Miconis*', *MH* 66: 155–62.

Bibliography

(2011) Review of Flores (2009 edition) vol. III, *Gnomon* 83: 597–608.

(2012a) '*Contempta relinquas*: anxiety and expurgation in the publication of Lucretius' *De rerum natura*', in S. J. Harrison and C. A. Stray (eds.), *Expurgating the Classics: Editing Out in Greek and Latin*. London: 95–114.

(2012b) 'Emendations on the second book of Lucretius', *Faventia* 32–3: 87–91.

(2012c) 'A Lucretian emendation (I.613)', *Athenaeum* 100: 475–8.

(2013) '*Lucretius auctus?* The question of interpolation in *De rerum natura*', in J. Martínez (ed.), *Ergo decipiatur*. Madrid.

Callmer, C. (1977) *Königin Christina, ihre Biliothekare und ihre Handschriften*. Stockholm.

Cameron, A. (1966) 'The date of Macrobius', *JRS* 56: 25–38.

Campanelli, M. (1993) 'Una *praelectio* lucreziana di Pomponio Leto', *Roma nel Rinascimento*: 17–24.

Campbell, A. (ed.) (1949) *Encomium Emmae Reginae*. London.

Canfora, D. (1998) *Poggio Bracciolini: De infelicitate principum*. Rome.

(1994–5) 'Una presenza lucreziana in Petrarca', *AFLB* 37–8: 319–29.

Canfora, L. (1993) *La vita di Lucrezio*. Palermo.

(2003) 'La première réception de Lucrèce à Rome', in Monet (2003), 43–50.

Capasso, M. (2003) 'Filodemo e Lucrezio: due intellettuali nel *patriai tempus iniquum*', in Monet (2003), 77–107.

Castelli, G. (1966) 'Echi lucreziani nelle ecloghe virgiliane', *Rivista di Studi Classici* 14: 313–42.

(1967) 'Echi lucreziani nelle ecloghe virgiliane', *Rivista di Studi Classici* 15: 14–39, 176–216.

Castiglioni, L. (1937) Review of Martin (1934 edition), *Gnomon* 13: 558–65.

Cavallo, G. (1975) *Libri, editori e pubblico nel mondo antico*. Bari.

Chambert, R. (1999) 'Hercule lucrétien et Hercule stoïcien', in Poignault (1999a), 149–64.

Chatelain, É. (1883) 'Un "Gradus ad Parnassum" de l'extrême décadence', *RPh* 7: 65–77.

(1884–92) *Paléographie des classiques latins* (2 vols.). Paris.

(ed.) (1908) *T. Lucretius Carus Codex Vossianus Oblongus phototypice editus*. Leiden.

(ed.) (1913) *T. Lucretius Carus Codex Vossianus Quadratus phototypice editus*. Leiden.

Chavannes-Mazel, C. A. and M. Smith (eds.) (1995) *Medieval Manuscripts of the Latin Classics: Production and Use*. London.

Chiari, A. (1924) 'A proposito d'una nuova edizione di Lucrezio', *RFIC* 52: 233–46.

(1963) *Indagini e letture. Terza serie*. Florence.

Chiesa, P. (ed.) (2000) *Paolo Diacono: uno scrittore fra tradizione Longobarda e rinnovamento carolingio*. Udine.

Bibliography

Chiesa, P. and L. Castali (2004) *La trasmissione dei testi latini del Medioevo* (2 vols.). Florence.

Christ, W. (1855) *Quaestiones Lucretianae*. Munich.

Cini, G. F. (1976) 'La posizione degli "Italici" nello stemma lucreziano', *AATC* 41: 116–69.

Clark, A. C. (1899) 'The literary discoveries of Poggio', *CR* 13: 119–30.
   (1918) *The Descent of Manuscripts*. Oxford.

Clay, D. (1983) *Lucretius and Epicurus*. Ithaca.

Cleary, V. J. (1970) 'The poetic influence of the *De rerum natura* on the *Aeneid*', *CB* 47: 17–21.

Collura, P. (1965) *La Precarolina e la Carolina a Bobbio*, 2nd edn. Milan.

Cook, A. S. (1907) 'Chaucer, *Troilus and Criseyde* 3.1–38', *Archiv für das Studium der Neueren Sprachen und Literaturen* 119: 40–54.

Courcelle, P. (1955) 'Histoire du cliché Virgilien des cent bouches', *REL* 33: 231–40.

Courtney, E. (1993) *The Fragmentary Latin Poets*. Oxford.

Coyecque, E. (1893) *Catalogue général des manuscrits des bibliothèques publiques de France. Départements, XIX: Amiens*. Paris.

Cramer, A. W. (1823) *In D. Junii Juvenalis Satiras Commentarii Vetusti*. Hamburg.

Cunningham, I. C. (1983) 'Beverland's catalogue of manuscripts in England', *Edinburgh Bibliographical Society Transactions* 5.3: 17–22.

Dain, A. (1975) *Les manuscrits*, 3rd edn. Paris.

Daintree, D. and M. Geymonat (1988) 'Scholia', *Enciclopedia Virgiliana 4*. Rome: 706–20.

Dale, F. R. (1958) 'Caesar and Lucretius', *PCA* 55: 20–1.

Dal Pane, F. (1905–6) 'Se Arnobio sia stato un Epicureo, Lucrezio e gli apologeti cristiani Minucio Felice, Tertulliano, Cipriano, Lattanzio I', *RSA* 10: 403–35.
   (1906–7) 'Se Arnobio sia stato un Epicureo. Lucrezio e gli apologeti cristiani Minucio Felice, Tertulliano, Cipriano, Lattanzio II', *RSA* 11: 222–36.

D'Anna, G. (2002) 'Una nuova proposta sulla cronologia di Lucrezio', in Isola, Menestò and di Pilla (2002), 19–50.

De la Mare, A. C. (1973) *The Handwriting of Italian Humanists*, vol. 1.i. Oxford.

Delattre, D. (2003) 'Présence ou absence d'une copie du *De rerum natura* à Herculaneum?', in Monet (2003), 109–16.

De Meyier, K. A (1955) *Codices manuscripti Bibliothecae Leidensis*, vol. VI: *Codices Vossiani Graeci et miscellanei*. Leiden.
   (1973) *Codices Vossiani Latini*, vol. I: *Codices in Folio*. Leiden.
   (1975) *Codices Vossiani Latini*, vol. II: *Codices in Quarto*. Leiden.

Deschamps, L. (1999) 'Les citations du *De rerum natura* de Lucrèce dans le commentaire de Servius à l'œuvre de Virgile', in Poignault (1999a), 199–216.

Deufert, M. (1996) *Pseudo-Lukrezisches im Lukrez: Die unechten Verse in Lukrezens De rerum natura*. Berlin.

Bibliography

(1998) 'Die Lukrezemendationen des Francesco Bernardino Cipelli', *Hermes* 126: 370–9.

(1999) 'Lukrez und Marullus. Ein kurzer Blick in die Werkstatt eines humanistischen Interpolators', *RhM* 142: 210–23.

(2001) 'Zur Datierung des Nonius Marcellus', *Philologus* 145: 137–49.

(2002) *Textgeschichte und Rezeption der Plautinischen Komödien im Altertum*. Berlin.

(2005) Review of Flores (2002 edition), *Gnomon* 77: 213–24.

(2009) 'Lucretius', *RAC* 22: 603–20.

(2010) 'Zu den gegenwärtigen Aufgaben der Lukrezkritik', *Hermes* 138: 48–69.

De Vogel, C. G. (1959) *Greek Philosophy: a Collection of Texts Selected and Supplied with Some Notes and Explanations* (3 vols.). Leiden.

Diels, H. (1918) 'Lukrezstudien' I, *Sitzungsberichte der preussischen Akademie der Wissenschaften, philosophisch-historische Klasse*: 912–39, reprinted in Diels (1969) 312–39.

(1969) *Kleine Schriften zur Geschichte der antiken Philosophie* (ed. W. Burkert). Darmstadt.

Di Giovine, C. (1981) 'Sulla presenza di Lucrezio nel *De deo Socratis* di Apuleio', *Orpheus* 2: 114–23.

Dionisotti, A. C. (1997) 'Les chapitres entre l'historiographie et le roman', in J.-C. Fredouille *et al.* (eds.), *Titres et articulations du texte dans les oeuvres antiques*. Paris: 529–43.

Disch, H. (1921) *De Poetis Aevi Augusti Epicureis*. Bonn.

Dixon, H. (2011) 'Pomponius Leto's notes on Lucretius (Utrecht Universiteitsbibliotheck, X fol 82 *rariora*)', *Aevum* 85: 191–216.

Dolbeau, F. (1978) 'Un nouveau catalogue des manscrits de Lobbes aux XIe et XIIe siècles', *Recherches Augustiniennes* 13: 3–36.

(1979) 'Un nouveau catalogue des manscrits de Lobbes aux XIe et XIIe siècles', *Recherches Augustiniennes* 14: 191–24.

Döpp, S. (1978) 'Zur Datierung von Macrobius' *Saturnalia*', *Hermes* 106: 619–32.

Dousa, F. J. (ed.) (1597) *C. Lucilii Suessani Auruncani Satyrarum quae supersunt reliquiae*. Leiden.

Dressel, H. (1874) *De Isidori Originum Fontibus*. Turin; reprinted in *RFIC* 3 (1875): 207–68.

Duvau, L. (1888) 'Lucretiana', *RPh* 12: 30–7.

Ellis, R. (1889) *A Commentary on Catullus*, 2nd edn. Oxford.

Endlicher, S. (1836) *Catalogus Codicum Philologicorum Latinorum Bibliothecae Palatinae Vindobonensis*. Vienna.

Erichsen, J. (1786) *Udsigt over den Gamle Manuscript-Samling i det Store Kongelige Bibliothek*. Copenhagen.

Erler, M. (1994) 'Lukrez', in H. Flashar (ed.), *Grundriss der Geschichte der Philosophie. Die Philosophie der Antike*, vol. IV: *Die hellenistische Philosophie*. Basel: 29–490.

Bibliography

Ernout, A. (1924) 'Lucretiana', *BAGB* 1: 20–35.

Fabbri, R. (1984) 'La *"vita borgiana"* di Lucrezio nel quadro delle biografie umanistiche', *Lettere Italiane* 36: 348–66.

Falk, F. (1897) *Die ehemalige Dombibliothek zu Mainz*. Leipzig.

Farrell, J. (1991) *Vergil's Georgics and the Tradition of Ancient Epic*. Berkeley, CA.

Farrington, B. (1954) 'Lucretius and Manilius on friendship', *Hermathena* 83: 10–16.

(1958) 'Vergil and Lucretius', *AC* 1: 45–50.

(1963) 'Polemical allusions to the *De rerum natura* of Lucretius in the works of Vergil', in Varcl and Willetts (1963), 87–94.

Ferguson, J. (1990) 'Epicureanism under the Roman Empire' *ANRW* II. 36.4: 2257–2327.

Fernadelli, M. (1998) 'Virgilio imitatore', *Lexis* 16: 193–207.

Ferrari, M. (1972) 'In papiam conveniant ad Dungalum', *IMU* 15: 1–52.

Fiesoli, G. (2000) *La genesi del Lachmannismo*. Florence.

(2004) 'Percorsi di classici nel medioevo: il Lucrezio Bobiense. Raterio lettore di Plauto e di Catullo', *Medioevo e Rinascimento* n.s. 15: 1–37.

Finch, C. E. (1967) 'Lucretius in *Codex Vat. Reg. Lat.* 1587', *CPh* 62: 261–2.

Fischer, H. (1924) *De capitulis Lucretianis* (Diss.). Giessen.

Fleischmann, W. B. (1971) 'Lucretius Carus, Titus', in Kristeller and Kranz (1971), 349–65.

Flores, E. (1965) 'Note Lucreziane I', *RAAN* 40: 117–40.

(1978) 'Ecdotica e tradizone manoscritta lucreziana (da Pasquali a Büchner e Müller)', *Vichiana* 7: 21–37.

(1980) *Le scoperte di Poggio e il testo di Lucrezio*. Naples.

(1993) 'Gli *Astronomica* di Manilio e l'epicureismo', in Giannantoni and Gigante (1993), 895–908.

(1999) 'Lucrezio in Ovidio', in Schulbert (1999), vol. I: 35–40.

(2003) 'Su alcuni aspetti della trasmissione del testo di Lucrezio nel "400"', *Paideia* 58: 260–3.

(2006a) 'Risposta a K. Mueller, M. Deufert, M. D. Reeve', *Vichiana* 8: 117–33.

(2006b) 'Sui codici malatestiani di Manilio e Lucrezio', in L. Righetti and D. Savoia (eds.), *Il dono di Malatesta Novello: Atti del Convegno, Cesena, 21–23 Marzo 2003*. Cesena: 273–85.

Flores, E. and D. Tomasco (2002) 'Nascita dell'apparato critico', *Vichiana* 4: 3–6.

Foerster, H. (1963) *Abriss der lateinischen Paläographie*, 2nd edn. Stuttgart.

Fontaine, J. (1966) 'Le *Songe de Scipion,* premier Anti-Lucrèce?', in *Mélanges A. Piganiol* (1996). Paris: vol. III 1711–29.

Forbiger, A. (1824) *De T. Lucretii Cari carmine a scriptore serioris aetatis denuo pertractato dissertatio philologica et critica*. Leipzig.

Fornaro, P. (1977) 'Una presumibile nuova fonte della biografia borgiana di Lucrezio', *Vichiana* 6: 21–39.

Bibliography

Fowler, D. P. (1993) 'The pagination of the archetype of Lucretius' *De rerum natura*: two notes', in H. D. Jocelyn (ed.), *Tria Lustra* (Liverpool Classical Papers 3). Liverpool: 237–41.

Frank, T. (1933) 'The mutual borrowings of Catullus and Lucretius and what they imply', *CPh* 28: 249–56.

Frère, H. (1909) 'Le *Memmianus* du Lucrèce', *Mélanges d'Archéologie et d'Histoire de l'École Française de Rome* 29: 199–211.

Friderici, R. (1911) *De librorum antiquorum capitum divisione atque summariis* (Diss.). Marburg.

Fuhrer, T. and M. Ehler (eds.) (1997) *Zur Rezeption der hellenistischen Philosophie in der Spätantike*. Stuttgart.

Gabotto, F. (1891) 'Appunti sulla fortuna di alcuni autori romani nel medio evo. III. Lucrezio', *La Bibl. delle Scuole Italiane* 3: 243–4.

Gagnebin, B. (1976) *L'enluminure de Charlemagne à François Ier*. Geneva.

Gale, M. (2000) *Virgil on the Nature of Things: The Georgics, Lucretius and the Didactic Tradition*. Cambridge.

Galland, P. and A. Turnebus (eds.) (1554) *Corpus Agrimensorum Romanorum*. Paris.

Ganz, D. (1990) *Corbie in the Carolingian Renaissance*. Sigmaringen.

(1991) 'Heiric d'Auxerre, glossateur du *Liber glossarum*', in D. Iogna-Prat, C. Jeudy and G. Lobrichon (eds.), *L'École Carolingienne d'Auxerre de Murethach Remi, 830–908*. Paris: 297–309.

(1996) 'Lucretius in the Carolingian Age: the Leiden Manuscripts and their Carolingian readers', in Chavannes-Mazel and Smith (1995), 91–102.

Gasparotto, G. (1965–6a) 'Isidoro e Lucrezio I. Le fonti dei capitoli "De tonitruo" e "De fulminibus" del "De natura rerum" e delle "Origines"', *AAPat* 78: 73–130.

(1965–6b) 'Isidoro e Lucrezio II. Le fonti dei capitoli "De Arcu" (XXXI) "De Natura Rerum" e "De arcu et nubium effectibus" (limitamente all'arcobaleno delle "Origines" (XIII. 10)', *AAPat* 78: 207–38.

(1966–7) 'Isidoro e Lucrezio III. Le nubi' *AAPat* 79, 39–58; 'Isidoro e Lucrezio IV. La peste IB. Le fonti dei capitoli "De pestilentia" del "De natura rerum" (XXXIX) e "De acutis morbis" delle "Origines" (IV.5.17–19)', *AAPat* 79: 101–30.

(1967–8) 'Il Petrarca conosceva direttamente Lucrezio. Le fonti dell'ecloga IX, *Querulus, del* Bucolicum Carmen', *AAPat* 80: 309–55.

(1968–9) 'Lucrezio fonte diretta del Boccaccio?', *AAPat* 81: 5–34.

(1972) 'Ancora Lucrezio nel *Bucolicum Carmen* (XII, *Conflictatio*) del Petrarca', in *Dignam dis: a G. Vallot*. Venice: 211–37.

(1972–3) 'Il nome di Lucrezio nel Petrarca', *AAPat* 85: 293–307.

(1983) *Isidoro e Lucrezio: le fonti della meteorologia Isidoriana*. Verona.

(1991) *Petrarca e Lucrezio. Schemi e risonanze del 'De rerum natura' nelle opere latine del Petrarca*. Verona.

Gatzemeier, S. (2013) *Ut ait Lucretius: Die Lukrezrezeption in der lateinischen Prosa bis Laktanz*. Göttingen.

Bibliography

Gerlach, F. D. and C. L. Roth (eds.) (1842) *Nonii Marcelli De compendiosa doctrina*. Basel.

Gerlo, A. (1956) 'Pseudo-Lucretius', *AC* 25: 41–75.

Getto, G. (1958) 'La peste del "Decameron" e il problema della fonte lucreziana', *Giornale storico della Letteratura Italiana* 135: 507–23.

Giancotti, F. (1976) '*Aerea vox*: un frammento attribuito da Servio a Lucrezio e consimile espressioni di altri poeti in Macrobio, Servio e altri', in *Grammatici Latini d'età imperiale: miscellanea filologica*. Genoa: 41–95.

(1980) 'Il preludio di Lucrezio, il trasposizionismo e Lattanzio', *Orpheus* 1: 221–50.

Giannantoni, G. and M. Gigante (eds.) (1993), *Epicureismo Greco e Romano*. Naples.

Giesecke, A. L. (1992) 'The influence of Lucretius on the bucolic, heroic, epic, satiric and lyric poetry of the early Augustan Period' (Diss.). Harvard.

Gigon, O. (ed.) (1978) *Lucrèce*. Geneva.

Gillespie, S. and P. Hardie (eds.) (2007) *The Cambridge Companion to Lucretius*. Cambridge.

Giri, G. (1911) 'Il giudizio di Quintiliano intorno a Lucrezio', *Classici e Neol.* 7: 2–8.

Gneisse, C. (1878) *De versibus in Lucretii carmine repetitis* (Diss.). Strasburg.

Goddard, C. P. (1991) 'Epicureanism and the poetry of Lucretius in the Renaissance' (Diss.). Cambridge.

Goebel, E. (1854) *Observationes Lucretianae et criticae et exegeticae*. Bonn.

(1857a) *Quaestiones Lucretianae criticae, quibus et de codice Victoriano disputatur*. Salzburg.

(1857b) 'Lukrez und sein Verhältniss zu Horaz', *Zeitschrift für die österreichischen Gymnasien* 8: 421–7.

(1860) 'Zur Textkritik des Lucrez', *RhM* 15: 401–18.

Goebel, E. and A. Goebel (1857) 'Die schedae Vindobonenses', *RhM* 12: 449–56.

Gómez Pallarès, J. (1998) 'Catulo 1,9–10 y el proemio de Lucrecio al "De rerum natura"', *Veleia* 15: 299–314.

Goold, G. P. (1958) 'A lost manuscript of Lucretius', *AC* 1: 21–30.

Gordon, C. (1985) *A Bibliography of Lucretius*, 2nd edn. Winchester.

Goulon, A. (1999) 'Quelle connaissance Lactance avait-il du *De rerum natura?*', in Poignault (1999a), 217–57.

Gowers, E. (2005), 'Virgil's Sibyl and the "many mouths" cliché (*Aen.* 6.625–7)', *CQ* 55: 170–82.

Graevius, J. G. (1697) *Callimachi Hymni Epigrammata et Fragmenta* (2 vols.). Utrecht.

Grimal, P. (1978) 'Le poème de Lucrèce en son temps', in Gigon (1978), 233–62.

Gruter, J. (ed.) (1602–34) *Lampas sive fax artium liberalium* (7 vols.). Frankfurt.

Hadzsits, G. (1935) *Lucretius and his Influence*. New York.

Bibliography

Hagendahl, H. (1958) *Latin Fathers and the Classics. A Study of the Apologists, Jerome and Other Christian Writers*. Gothenburg.

Hall, F. W. (1913) *A Companion to Classical Texts*. Oxford.

Hall, J. B., A. L. Ritchie and M. J. Edwards (eds.) (2007–8) *P. Papinius Statius. Thebaid and Achilleid* (3 vols.). Newcastle.

Hanon, L. (1943) 'L'influence philosophique de Lucrèce dans les Géorgiques de Virgile' (Diss.). Louvain.

Hardie, P. (1986) *Virgil's Aeneid: Cosmos and Imperium*. Oxford.

Harrison, S. J. (2000) *Apuleius: a Latin Sophist*. Oxford.

Harth, H. (ed.) (1984–7) *Poggio Bracciolini: Lettere* (3 vols.). Florence.

Haupt, M. (1875) *Opuscula* (3 vols.). Leipzig.

Heinsius, N. (ed.) (1662) *Operum Ovidii Editio Nova* (3 vols.). Amsterdam.
    (1742) *Adversariorum Libri IV* (ed. P. Burman). Leiden.

Heinze, R. (1924) Review of Diels (1923–4 edition), *Deutsche Literaturzeitung n.f.* 1: 41–9.

Helm, R. (1892) *De P. Papinii Statii Thebaide*. Berlin.

Hemmerdinger, B. (1968) 'Le Boccianus perdu de Lucrèce', *Belfagor* 23: 741.

Henrichsen, R. J.F. (1846) *De Fragmento Gottorpiensi Lucretii*. Odense.

Herren, M. W. (2012) 'The Graeca in the tituli of Lucretius: what they tell us about the archetype', *WS* 125: 107–24.

Herrmann, L. (1956) 'Catulle et Lucrèce', *Latomus* 15: 465–80.

Hertz, M. J. (1851) *Karl Lachmann: Eine Biographie*. Berlin.

Heyworth, S. J. (1995) 'Dividing Poems' in Pecere and Reeve (1995), 117–48.

Highet, G. (1951) 'Juvenal's bookcase', *AJPh* 72: 369–94.

Holford-Strevens, L. (2002), '*Horror vacui* in Lucretian bibliography', *LICS* 1.1: 1–23.
    (2005) *Aulus Gellius: an Antonine Scholar and his Achievement*, 2nd edn. Oxford.

Holland, L. A. (1979) *Lucretius and the Transpadanes*. Princeton.

Hollis, A. S. (2007) *Fragments of Roman Poetry c. 60 BC–AD 20*. Oxford.

Hosius, C. (1914) 'Zur italienischen Überlieferung des Lucrez', *RhM* 69: 109–22.

Housman, A. E. (1972) *The Classical Papers of A. E. Housman* (ed. J. Diggle and F. R. D. Goodyear) (3 vols.). Cambridge.

Howe, H. M. (1951) 'Amafinius, Lucretius, and Cicero', *AJPh* 72: 57–62.

Hunger, H. *et al.* (eds.) (1961–4) *Geschichte der Textüberlieferung der antiken und mittelalterlichen Literatur*. Zurich.

Hunt, R. W. (1971) 'The deposit of Latin Classics in the twelfth-century Renaissance', in R. R. Bolgar (ed.), *Classical Influences on European Culture AD 500–1500*. Cambridge: 51–5.

Hutchinson, G. O. (2001) 'The date of Lucretius' *De rerum natura*', *CQ* 51: 150–62.

Innocenti, P. (1972) 'Per una storia dell'Epicureismo nei primi secoli dell'era volgare: temi e problemi', *RSF* 27: 123–47.

Isola, A., E. Menestò and A. di Pilla (eds.) (2002) *Curiositas: studi di cultura classica e medievale in onore di Ubaldo Pizzani*. Naples.

Bibliography

Ives, S. (1942) 'The exemplar of two Renaissance editions of Lucretius', *Rare Books* 2: 3–7.

Jahn, O. (1847) *Archäologische Beiträge*. Berlin.

Jauss, H. R. and D. Schaller (eds.) (1960) *Medium aevum vivum: Festschrift für Walther Bulst*. Heidelberg

Jessen, J. (1860) 'Lucrez im Mittelalter', *Philologus* 30: 236–8.

(1870) *Über Lucrez und sein Verhältniss zu Catull und Späteren*. Kiel.

Jocelyn, H. D. (1965) 'Ancient scholarship and Virgil's use of Republican poetry II', *CQ* 15: 126–44.

(1969) *The Tragedies of Ennius*. Cambridge.

(1984) 'The annotations of M. Valerius Probus', *CQ* 34: 464–72.

(1985) 'The annotations of M. Valerius Probus II', *CQ* 35: 149–61.

(1986) 'Lucretius, his copyists and the horrors of the underworld (*De rerum natura* 3.978–1023)', *AC* 29: 43–56.

Jones, H. (1992) *The Epicurean Tradition*, 2nd edn. London.

Kaster, R. A. (1995) *Suetonius: De grammaticis et rhetoribus*. Oxford.

Keil, H. (1872) *Exempla poetarum e codice Vaticano edita* (Progr.). Halle: iii–xv.

Kennedy, C. W. (1943) *The Earliest English Poetry: a Critical Survey of the Poetry Written before the Norman Conquest*. London.

Kenney, E. J. (ed.) (1971) *The Cambridge History of Classical Literature,* vol. II: *Latin Literature*. Cambridge.

(1974) *The Classical Text: Aspects of Editing in the Age of the Printed Book.* Berkeley, CA.

Kenyon, F. G. (1932) *Books and Readers in Ancient Greece and Rome*. Oxford.

Keus, K. and J. Clements (2004) *A Conservation Binding for the Manuscript Voss. Lat. F. 30: Lucretius*. Amsterdam.

Klepl, H. (1940) *Lucrez und Vergil in ihren Lehrgedichten* (Diss.). Leipzig and Dresden.

Kleve, K. (1989) 'Lucretius in Herculaneum', *CE* 19: 5–27.

(1994) 'An approach to the Latin papyri from Herculaneum', in F. del Franco *et al.* (eds.), *Storia Poesia e Pensiero nel Mondo Antico: Studi in Onore di M. Gigante*. Naples: 313–20.

(2007) 'Lucretius' Book II in P.Herc. 395', in *Akten des 23. Internationalen Papyrologenkongresses [July 2001]* (ed. B. Palme). Vienna: 347–54.

(2009) 'Futile criticism', *CE* 39: 281–2.

(2010) '*Lucretius Herculanensis, PHerc. 395*, and *Disegno Oxoniense 1615*', *CE* 40: 95–7.

(2011) 'The enigma of Lucretius', *CE* 41: 231–4.

(2012) 'The puzzle picture of Lucretius: a thriller from Herculaneum', in J. Z. Buchwald (ed.), *A Master of Science History: Essays in Honor of C. C. Gillispie*. Dordrecht: 63–78.

Klussmann, E. (1867) 'Arnobius und Lucrez oder ein Durchgang durch den Epikureismus zum Christentum', *Philologus* 26: 362–6.

Korpanty, J. (1990) 'De Ovidio Lucretii imitatore', *Eos* 78: 183–6.

Bibliography

Kristeller, P. O. and F. E. Kranz (eds.) (1971) *Catalogus translationum et commentariorum*, vol. II. Washington, DC.

La Bua, G. (1997) 'La "laus Cornuti" nella V satira di Persio e Lucrezio *De rerum natura* III 1–30', *BSL* 27: 82–101.

Lachmann, K. (1847) '[*Ad* Lucr. VI.970]'. *Index lectionum aestivarum*. Berlin: 3–4.

(1849) 'De Lucilii saturarum libris', *Index lectionum aestivarum*. Berlin: 3–8.

(1876) *Kleinere Schriften zur Classischen Philologie* (ed. J. Vahlen). Berlin.

La Penna, A. (1994) 'Un'altra eco di Lucrezio in Seneca?', *Maia* 46: 319–22.

Lapidge, M. (2006) *The Anglo-Saxon Library*. Oxford.

Lecocq, F. (1999) 'De la création du monde: les *De rerum natura* d'Ovide ou Lucrèce metamorphosé', in Poignault (1999a), 129–47.

Leeman, A. D. (1968) 'Lucretius superstes', *Lampas* 1: 23–44.

Lehmann, P. (1908) *Franciscus Modius als Handschriftenforscher: Quellen und Untersuchungen zur Lateinischen Philologie des Mittelalters*, vol. III.1. Munich.

(1911) *Johannes Sichardus und die von ihm benutzten Bibliotheken und Handschriften: Quellen und Untersuchungen zur Lateinischen Philologie des Mittelalters*, vol. IV. 1. Munich.

(1929) 'Mitteilungen aus Handschriften', *Sitzungsberichte der Bayerischen Akademie der Wissenschaften*: 23–6.

(1960) *Erforschung des Mittelalters: Ausgewählte Abhandlungen und Aufsätze*, vol. III. Stuttgart.

Lehnerdt, M. (1904) 'Lucretius in der Renaissance', in *Festschrift zur Feier des 600-jährigen Jubiläums des Kneiphöfischen Gymnasiums zu Königsberg*. Königsberg: 1–17.

Lenz, C. (1937) *Die wiederholten Verse bei Lukrez* (Diss.). Leipzig.

Leo, F. (1912) *Plautinische Forschungen zur Kritik und Geschichte der Komödie*, 2nd edn. Berlin.

Lindemann, F. (ed.) (1831–40) *Corpus Grammaticorum Latinorum Veterum* (4 vols.). Leipzig.

Lindsay, W. M. (1890) 'The Bodleian facsimiles of Latin papyri from Herculaneum', *CR* 4. 441–5.

(1901) *Nonius Marcellus' Dictionary of Republican Latin*. Oxford.

(1905) 'De citationibus apud Nonium Marcellum', *Philologus* 64: 438–61.

(1915) *Notae Latinae: an Account of Abbreviation in Latin MSS of the Early Minuscule Period (c. 700–850)*. Cambridge.

Lindsay, W. M. and P. Lehmann (1925) 'The (Early) Mayence scriptorium', *Paleographia Latina* 4: 15–39.

Lindsay, W. M. *et al.* (eds.) (1926), *Glossaria Latina*, vol. I. Paris.

Löfstedt, E. (1913) 'Zu lateinischen Inschriften', *Eranos* 13: 79–81.

Lohmann, W. (1882) *Quaestionum Lucretianarum capita duo*. Brunswick.

Long, A. A. and D. N. Sedley (1987) *The Hellenistic Philosophers* (2 vols.). Cambridge.

Bibliography

Lowe, E. A. (1972) *Palaeographical Papers 1907–1965* (ed. L. Bieler). (2 vols.). Oxford.

Lucarini, C. M. (1999) 'Su alcune imitazioni di Lucrezio in un capitolo dei "Florida" apuleiani', *MD* 42: 223–4.

Maas, P. (1958) *Textual Criticism* (tr. B. Flower). Oxford.

Madoz, J. (1947) 'Un símil de Lucrecio en la litteratura latino-cristiana', *Principe de Viana* 7: 3–12.

(1952) 'A simile of Lucretius in Christian-Latin literature', *Folia* 6: 40–52.

Madvig, J. N. (1834) *Opuscula Academica*. Copenhagen.

Mai, C. (ed.) (1828–38) *Classicorum auctorum e Vaticanis codicibus editorum tomi X* (10 vols.). Vatican.

Manitius, M. (1886) 'Zu Aldhelm und Baeda', *Sitzungsberichte der phil-philol. und hist. Klasse der Kaiserlichen Akademie der Wissenschaften zu Wien* 112: 535–634.

(1892) 'Philologisches aus alten Bibliothekskatalogen', *RhM* Ergänzungsheft 47.

(1894) 'Beiträge zur Geschichte römischer Dichter im Mittelalter. 14: Lucretius', *Phil.* 52: 536–8.

(1911–31) *Geschichte der Lateinischen Literatur des Mittelalters* (3 vols.). Munich.

(1912) 'Micons v. St-Riquier "De primis syllabis"', *Münchener Museum* 1: 121–77.

(1935) *Handschriften antiker Autoren in mittelalterlichen Bibliothekskatalogen, Zentralblatt für Bibliothekswesen* suppl. 67.

Marache, R. (1956) *Mots nouveaux et mots archaïques chez Fronto et Aulu-Gelle*. Rennes.

Marinone, N. (1974) 'I frammenti di Egnazio', in Varii (1974), 179–99.

Marx, F. (ed.) (1894) *Incerti auctoris de ratione dicendi Ad C. Herennium Libri IV*. Leipzig.

(ed.) (1904–5) *C. Lucilii Carminum Reliquiae* (2 vols.). Leipzig.

Masson, J. (1894a) 'Newly discovered fragments from Suetonius' life of Lucretius', *The Academy* 1169: 236–7.

(1894b) 'Traces of a fresh source of tradition regarding the life of Lucretius', *The Academy* 1155: 519–20.

(1895) 'New details from Suetonius's life of Lucretius', *JPh* 23: 220–37.

(1896) 'New data presumably from Suetonius' life of Lucretius', *CR* 10: 323–4.

(1907–9) *Lucretius: Epicurean and Poet*. London.

Matter, A.-J. (1846) *Lettres et pièces rares ou inédites*. Paris.

Mattiaci, S. (1986) 'Apuleio e i poeti arcaici', in Varii (1986), II: 151–200.

Mazzacane, R. (1984) 'Varianti Noniani di Lucrezio', *Studi Noniani* 9: 149–77.

Mazzoli, G. (1970) *Seneca e la poesia*. Milan.

Menhardt, H. (1957) *Das älteste Handschriftenverzeichnis der Wiener Hofbibliothek von Hugo Blotius 1576. Kritische Ausgabe der Handschrift Series nova 4451 vom Jahre 1597 mit vier Anhängen*. Vienna.

Bibliography

Merrill, W. A. (1905) 'On the relation of Horace to Lucretius', *Univ. of California Publications in Classical Philology* 1.4: 111–29.

(1909) 'Cicero's knowledge of Lucretius's poems', *UCPCPh* 2.2: 35–42.

(1913) 'The archetype of Lucretius', *UCPCPh* 2.10: 227–35.

(1914) 'Corruption in the manuscripts of Lucretius', *UCPCPh* 2.11: 237–53.

(1918) 'Parallels and coincidences in Lucretius and Vergil', *UCPCPh* 3.3: 135–247.

(1926) 'The Italian manuscripts of Lucretius. Part I', *UCPCPh* 9.2: 27–45.

(1927) 'The Italian manuscripts of Lucretius. Part II. Variant readings', *UCPCPh* 9.3: 47–83.

(1928) 'The Italian manuscripts of Lucretius. Part II (continued)', *UCPCPh* 9.4: 85–126.

(1929) 'The Italian manuscripts of Lucretius. Part II (concluded)', *UCPCPh* 9.9: 307–71.

Mewaldt, J. (1927) 'Lucretius', in Pauly-Wissowa *RE* 13: cols.1659–83.

Migliorini, P. (1980) 'Osservazioni di critica letteraria in Ovidio: il giudizio su Lucrezio in Am. I,15: 24–5', *Prom.* 6: 56–66.

Milde, W. (1968) *Der Bibliothekskatalog des Klosters Murbach aus dem 9. Jahrhundert*. Heidelberg.

Minyard, J. D. (1985) *Lucretius and the Late Republic: an Essay in Roman Intellectual History*. Leiden.

Mommsen, T. (1861) 'Zu den Scholien der virgilischen *Georgica*', *RhM* 16: 442–53.

Monet, A. (ed.) (2003) *Le jardin romain. Épicurisme et poésie à Rome*. Lille.

Morisi, L. (2002) 'Ifigenia e Polissena (Lucrezio in Catullo)', *MD* 49: 177–90.

Mueller, L. (ed.) (1872a) *C. Lucilii saturarum reliquiae*. Leipzig.

(1872b) 'Virgil, nicht Lucrez oder Lucilius', *RhM* 27: 184–5.

Müller, G. (1958–9) 'Die Problematik des Lucreztextes seit Lachmann', *Philologus* 102: 247–83; 103: 53–86.

Müller, K. (1973) 'De codicum Lucretii Italicorum origine' *MH* 30: 166–78.

(2003) Review of Flores (2002 edition), *MH* 60: 234.

Munk Olsen, B. (1979) 'Les classiques latins dans les florilèges médiévaux antérieurs au XIIIe siècle', *RHT* 9: 49–121.

(1985) 'T. Lucretius' Carus' in *L'étude des auteurs classiques latins aux XIe et XIIe siècles*, vol. II: *Livius–Vitruvius*. Paris.

(1987–9) *L'étude des auteurs classiques Latins aux XIe et XIIe siècles*, vol. III. *Les classiques dans les bibliothèques médiévales* (2 vols.). Paris.

(1995) *La réception de la littérature classique au moyen âge (IXe–XIIe siècle)*. Copenhagen.

(1997) 'Les titres dans les manuscrits des poètes classiques latins copiés du IXe au XIIe siècle', in J.-C. Fredouille, P. Hoffmann, M.-O. Goulet-Cazé and P. Petitmengin (eds.), *Titres et articulations du texte dans les oeuvres antiques*. Paris: 511–27.

(2009) *L'étude des auteurs classiques latins aux XIe et XIIe siècles. La réception de la littérature classique*. Paris.

Bibliography

Murgia, C. E. (2000) '"The most desperate textual crux" in Lucretius – 5.1442', *CPh* 95: 304–17.

Mussehl, J. (1908) 'Eine dublette in Buch IV des Lucrez', *Hermes* 43: 286–95.

(1912) *De Lucretiani libri primi condicione ac retractatione* (Diss.). Greifswald.

Mutschmann, H. (1911) 'Inhaltsangabe und Kapitelüberschrift im antiken Buch', *Hermes* 46: 93–107.

Németh, B. (1983) 'The death of Cotta and the date of Lucretius' *De rerum natura*', *ACD* 20: 39–41.

Nethercut, W. R. (1973) 'Vergil's *De rerum natura*', *Ramus* 2: 41–52.

Neumann, F. (1875) *De interpolationibus Lucretianis* (Diss.). Halle.

Niccolosi, L. (1946) *L'influsso di Lucrezio su Lattanzio, Raccoltà di studi di letteratura cristiana antica*, vol. II. Catania.

Nicodemo, F. (2002) 'Le presunte interpolazioni nel *De rerum natura* di Lucrezio', *Vichiana* 4: 288–312.

Nünlist, R. (1997) 'Zu den Lukrez-Buchrollen aus Herculaneum', *ZPE* 116: 19–20.

Obbink, D. (2007) 'Lucretius and the Herculaneum Library', in Gillespie and Hardie (2007), 33–40.

Ogilvy, J. D. A. (1967) *Books Known to the English, 597–1066*. Cambridge, MA.

Opelt, I. (1972) 'Lukrez bei Hieronymus', *Hermes* 100: 76–81.

Orchard, A. (1994) *The Poetic Art of Aldhelm*. Cambridge.

Orelli, J. K. von (1827) Review of H. Meyer's *Ciceronis Orator*, *Jahrbücher für Philologie und Paedagogik* 3.4: 84–91. Leipzig.

(ed.) (1833) *Eclogae Poetarum Latinorum*, 2nd edn. Zurich.

Osann, F. G. (ed.) (1826) *L. Caecilii Minutiani Apuleii De orthographia fragmenta*. Darmstadt.

Otón Sobrino, E. (1989) 'Epicuro y Lucrecio en la polémica de Tertuliano y Lactancio', *Helmantica* 40: 133–58.

Owen, W. H. (1968) 'The lacuna in Lucretius II, 164', *AJPh* 89: 406–18.

Paladini, M. (1995) 'Tre codici lucreziani e Pomponio Leto copista', *AION* 17: 251–93.

(1996) 'Il Vat. Ottob. Lat. 2834 di Lucrezio', *Sileno* 22: 281–90.

(2000) 'Parrasio e Lucrezio', *Vichiana* 4.2: 95–118.

Palmer, A. (2012) 'Reading Lucretius in the Renaissance', *JHI* 73: 395–416.

(2013) *Reading Lucretius in the Renaissance*. Cambridge, MA.

Palmerius, J. M. (1580) *Spicilegium*. Frankfurt; repr. in Gruter (1602–34), IV 717ff.

Panayotakis, C. (2010) *Decimus Laberius: the Fragments*. Cambridge.

Paratore, E. (1939) 'Spunti lucreziani nelle Georgiche', *A&R* 3: 177–202.

(1947) 'Postille lucreziane', *PP* 2: 192–208.

(1950) *Una nuova ricostruzione del "De poetis" di Suetonio*, 2nd edn. Bari.

Pascal, C. (1903) 'Lucrezio e Cipriano', *RFIC* 31: 555–7.

(1906) 'Carmi perduti di Lucrezio?', *RFIC* 34: 257–68.

(1920) *Scritti varî di letteratura Latina*. Turin.

Bibliography

Pascucci, G. (1959) 'Ennio, *Ann.*, 561–2 V² e un tipico procedimento di αὔξησις nella poesia Latina', *SIFC* 31: 79–99.

Pasetto, D. (1962–3) 'I *capitula* Lucreziani', *AFLN* 10: 33–50.

Pasquali, G. (1952) *Storia della tradizione e critica del testo*, 2nd edn. Florence.

Pecere, O. and Reeve, M. D. (eds.) (1995) *Formative Stages of Classical Traditions: Latin Texts from Antiquity to the Renaissance*. Spoleto.

Pellegrin, E. (1948) 'Le *codex Pomponii Romani* de Lucrèce', *Latomus* 7: 77–82.

Perutelli, A. (1996) 'Ifigenia in Lucrezio', *SCO* 46: 193–207.

Peterson, R. (1891) *Quintilian Book X*. Oxford.

Petitmengin, P. (1997) '"Capitula" païens et chrétiens', in J.-C. Fredouille *et al.* (eds.), *Titres et articulations du texte dans les oeuvres antiques*. Paris: 491–509.

Philippe, J. (1895) 'Lucrèce dans la théologie chrétienne du IIIe au XIIIe siècle et spécialement dans les écoles Carolingiennes: I', *RHR* 32: 284–302.

(1896) 'Lucrèce dans la théologie chrétienne du IIIe au XIIIe siècle et spécialement dans les écoles Carolingiennes: II', *RHR* 33: 19–36, 125–62.

Pieri, A. (1977) *Lucrezio in Macrobio: adattamenti al testo virgiliano*. Florence.

Pillinger, H. E. (1971) 'Tibullus I,10 and Lucretius', *CJ* 66: 204–8.

Pizzani, U. (1959a) *Il problema del testo e della composizione del De rerum natura di Lucrezio*. Rome.

(1959b) 'Versi lucreziani nel Codice Vaticano Reginense Lat. 598', *RCCM* 1: 399–402.

(1968) Review of Büchner (1966 edition), *Latomus* 27: 651–7.

(1986) 'Angelo Poliziano e il testo di Lucrezio', in Tarugi (1986), 297–311.

(1996) 'Angelo Poliziano e i primordi della filologia Lucreziana' in L. Tarugi (ed.), *Poliziano nel suo tempo*. Florence: 343–55.

Pizzolato, L. F. (1971) 'Una possibile presenza lucrezianaa in Agostino (*Conf.*, VII, 21, 27)', *REA* 17: 55–7.

Plinval, G. de (1942) 'Pour ressaisir le sens de Lucrèce (*De rer. nat.* II 42–25)', *REL* 20: 50–3.

Poggio, 'Bracciolini' (1538) *Opera collatione emendatiorum exemplarium recognita*. Basel.

Poignault, R. (ed.) (1999a) *Présence de Lucrèce*. Tours.

(1999b) 'Les citations de Lucrèce dans le commentaire de Servius', in Poignault (1999a), 199–216.

(1999c) 'Les références à Lucrèce chez Quintilien, Fronton et Aulu-Gelle', in Poignault (1999a), 177–98.

Pol, E. (1975) 'The first century of Leiden University Library', in Scheurleer and Posthumus (1975), 395–434.

Pucci, G. (1966) 'Echi lucreziani in Cicerone', *SIFC* 38: 70–132.

Purmann, H. (1846) *Quaestiones Lucretianae*. Breslau.

(1847) 'Beiträge zur kritik des Lucretius', *Philologus* 2: 66–76.

Raasted, J. (1955) 'The lacuna after Lucretius II,164', *C&M* 16: 84–90.

Rademaker, C. S. M. (1981) *The Life and Work of Gerardus Joannes Vossius*. Assen.

Bibliography

Radiciotti, P. (2000) 'Della genuinità e delle opere tràdite da alcuni antichi papiri latini', *Scrittura e Civiltà* 24: 359–73.

Rapisarda, E. (1947) 'L'epicureismo nei primi scrittori latini cristiani. La polemica di Lattanzio contro l'Epicureismo', *Antiquitas* 2: 45–52.

(1950) 'Influssi lucreziani in Prudenzio', *VChr* 4: 46–60.

Reeve, M. D. (1980) 'The Italian tradition of Lucretius', *IMU* 23: 27–48.

(1987) '*Eliminatio codicum descriptorum*: a methodological problem', in J. N. Grant (ed.), *Editing Greek and Latin Texts: Papers Given at the Twenty-Third Annual Conference on Editorial Problems*. New York: 1–36.

(ed.) (2004) *Vegetius: Epitoma rei militaris*. Oxford.

(2005) 'The Italian tradition of Lucretius revisited', *Aevum* 79: 115–64.

(2006) 'Lucretius from the 1460s to the 17th century: seven questions of attribution', *Aevum* 80: 165–84.

(2007) 'Reconstructing archetypes: a new proposal for an old fallacy', in P. Finglass, C. Collard and N. J. Richardson (eds.), *Hesperos: Studies Presented to M. L. West on his Seventieth Birthday*. Oxford: 326–40.

Regel, G. (1907) *De Vergilio poetarum imitatore testimonia* (Diss.). Göttingen.

Reinhardt, T. (2005) 'The language of Epicureanism in Cicero: the case of atomism', in Reinhardt, Lapidge and Adams (2005), 117–50.

Reinhardt, T., M. Lapidge and J. N. Adams (eds.) (2005) *The Language of Latin Prose* (*Proc. Brit. Acad.* 129). London.

Reisacker, J. A. (1873) *Horaz und sein Verhältniss zu Lucrez*. Breslau.

Reynolds, L. D. (ed.) (1983a) *Texts and Transmission*. Oxford.

(1983b) 'Lucretius', in Reynolds (1983a), 218–22.

Reynolds, L. D. and N. G. Wilson (1991) *Scribes and Scholars*, 3rd edn. Oxford.

Richter, W. (1974) *Textstudien zu Lukrez*. Munich.

Roberts, C. H. and T. C. Skeat (1987) *The Birth of the Codex*. London.

Rösch, H. (1911) *Manilius und Lukrez*. Kiel.

Romano, D. (1993–4) 'I muscoli de Entello e un'ipotesi sul primo Lucrezio', *AAPal* 14: 27–36.

Ronnick, M. V. (1995) '*Suave mari magno*: an echo of Lucretius in Seneca's Epistle 53', *AJPh* 116: 653–4.

Roos, A. G. (1847) *Dissertatio critica, continens annotationem ad Lucretii poëmatum libros tres priores*. Groningen.

Rossetti, L. (1928) 'Il "De opificio Dei" di Lattanzio e le sue fonti', *Didascaleion* n.s. 6: 117–200.

Rostagni, A. (1931) 'I primordi dell'evoluzione poetica e spirituale di Virgilio. V: Virgilio e Lucrezio', *RFIC* 59: 289–315.

(1934) 'Dalle varianti blandiniane (e dalle presunte interpolazioni in Orazio, in Virgilio ecc.) alle recensioni critiche di Probo', *RFIC* 12: 1–26.

(1939) 'Ricerche di biografia Lucreziana, II: La "Vita Borgiana"', *RFIC* 17: 113–35.

Rychlewska, L. (1954) 'Quaestiones Nonianae', in *Tragica*, vol. II. Wroclaw: 115–41.

Bibliography

(1964) 'De Lucretii exemplari a Nonio Marcello adhibito', *Eos* 54: 265–83.

Sabbadini, R. (1905) *Le scoperte dei codici Latini e Greci ne' secoli XIV e XV*. Florence.

Salmasius (1656) *Claudii Salmasii Viri Maximi Epistolarum Liber Primus* (ed. A. Clementius). Leiden.

Sandys, J. E. (1906–8) *A History of Classical Scholarship* (3 vols.). Cambridge.

(1915) *A Short History of Classical Scholarship*. Cambridge.

Sanford, E. M. (1924) 'The use of classical authors in the *Libri Manuales*', *TAPhA* 55: 190–248.

Savage, J. J. (1952) 'Quintilian and Lucretius', *CW* 46: 37.

(1958) 'Two notes on Johannes Scotus', *Scriptorium* 12: 228–37.

Scaffai, M. (2008) 'Il "topos" delle molte bocche da Lucilio a Lucrezio (e vice versa)', *Eikasmos* 19: 153–74.

Scaliger, J. J. (1575) *M. Verri Flacci quae extant. Sex. Pompei Festi De verborum significatione libri XX*. Paris.

[J. Scaliger] (1586) *In locos controversos Roberti Titii Animadversorum liber*. Paris.

Scarcia, R. (1966) 'Varia Latina V: note alla "vita borgiana" di Lucrezio', *RCCM* 8: 74–7.

Schaller, D. (1960) 'Die karolingischen Figurengedichte des Cod. Bern. 212', in Jauss and Schaller (1960), 22–47; reprinted with additions in D. Schaller (1995) *Studien zur lateinischen Dichtung des Frühmittelalters*. Stuttgart: 1–26, 399–403.

Scheurleer, T. H. L. and G. H. M. Posthumus (eds.) (1975) *Leiden University Library in the Seventeenth Century*. Leiden.

Schmid, W. (1938) 'Altes und neues zu einer Lukrezfrage', *Philologus* 93: 338–51.

Schmidt P. L. (1993) '*De honestis et nove veterum dictis*. Die Autorität der *veteres* von Nonius Marcellus bis zu Matheus Vindocinensis', in W. Voßkamp (ed.), *Klassik im Vergleich*. Stuttgart: 366–88.

(2008) '(Macrobius) Theodosius und das Personal der *Saturnalia*', *RFIC* 136.1: 47–83.

Schrijvers, P. H. (1999) 'La présence de Lucrèce dans le *De opificio Dei* de Lactance', in Poignault (1999a), 259–66.

Schröder, B.-J. (1999) *Titel und Text: Zur Entwicklung lateinischer Gedichtüberschriften, mit Untersuchungen zu lateinischen Buchtiteln, Inhaltsverzeichnissen und anderen Gliederungsmitteln*. Berlin.

Schubert, W. (ed.) (1999) *Ovid, Werk und Werkung: Festschrift für M. von Albrecht* (2 vols.). Frankfurt/Main.

Sconocchia, S. (2002) 'Su *capitula* e *indices* del *De rerum natura* di Lucrezio', in Isola, Menestò and di Pilla (2002), 51–90.

Sedley, D. (1998) *Lucretius and the Transformation of Greek Wisdom*. Cambridge.

(1999) 'Lucretius' use and avoidance of Greek', in Adams and Mayer (1999), 227–46.

Bibliography

Serrao, M. (1982) 'Influenze lessicali di Lucrezio sull'opera epica di Stazio', *Anazetesis* 6–7: 18–23.

Shackleton Bailey, D. R. (1977) *Cicero Epistulae ad Familiares* (2 vols.). Cambridge.

Shrimpton, G. J. and D. J. McCargar (eds.) (1981) *Classical Contributions. Studies in Honor of M. F. McGregor*. Locust Valley, NY.

Shuckburgh, E. S. (1888) *Horace. Epistles 1*. Cambridge.

Shulman J. (1981) *'Te quoque falle tamen*. Ovid's anti-Lucretian didactics', *CJ* 76: 242–53.

Siebelis, J. (1844) 'Beiträge zur Kritik und Erklärung des Lucretius', *Zeitsch. f. Alterth.* 99–101: 785–807.

Silagi, G. (ed.) (1982) *Paläographie 1981*. Munich.

Sinclair, B. W. (1981) 'Thucydides, the *Prognostika*, and Lucretius: a note on *De rerum natura* 6.1195', in Shrimpton and McCargar (1981), 145–52.

Sivo, V. (1987) 'Appunti sull' *"Opus prosodiacum"* di Micone di Saint-Riquier. Gli estratti del codice parigino Bibl. Naz. lat. 8499', *AFLB* 30: 217–36.

(1988) '"Fortuna" medievale di un verso lucreziano (Da Micone di Saint-Riquier a Giovanni Balbi)', *Inv. Luc.* 10: 305–25.

Skinner, M. B. (1976) 'Iphigenia and Polyxena: a Lucretian allusion in Catullus', *PCPhs* 11: 52–61.

Skutsch, O. (1985) *The Annals of Q. Ennius*. Oxford.

Smith, M. F. (1978) Review of Müller (1975 edition), *CR* 28: 29–31.

(1993a) *Diogenes of Oinoanda: the Epicurean Inscription*. Naples.

(1993b) 'Did Diogenes of Oinoanda know Lucretius? A reply to Professor Canfora', *RFIC* 121: 480–99.

(1997) 'The chisel and the muse: Diogenes of Oenoanda and Lucretius', in Algra, Koenen and Schrijvers (1997), 67–78.

(2004) 'In praise of the simple life: a new fragment of Diogenes of Oinoanda', *Anatolian Studies* 54: 35–46.

Smith, M. F. and D. J. Butterfield (2011) 'Not a ghost: the 1496 edition of Lucretius', *Aevum* 84: 683–93.

Smolak, K. (1996) *'Rectius itaque Lucretius*: zur Kritik des Laktanz an Ciceros Philosophiehymnus', *ZAnt* 45: 351–8.

Solaro, G. (1993) *Pomponio Leto: Lucrezio*. Palermo.

(1997) 'Lucrezio in Inghilterra agli inizi del secolo XIII?', *Eikasmos* 8: 241–4.

(2000) *Lucrezio: Biografie umanistiche*. Bari.

Sommariva, G. (1980) 'La parodia di Lucrezio nell'*Ars* e nei *Remedia*', *A&R* 25: 123–48.

Sosin, J. D. (1999) 'Lucretius, Seneca and Persius 1.1–2', *TAPhA* 129: 281–99.

Spengel (1851) Review of Lachmann (1850 edition), *Münch. Gel. Anz.* 33 nos. 96–8: 769–92.

Stacey, S. G. (1898) 'Über Spuren des Lucrez bei Livius', *Archir für lateinische Lexicographie* 10: 52.

Bibliography

Stephan, C. (1885) 'Das prosodische Florilegium der S. Gallener Handschrift nr. 870 und sein Werth für die Juvenalkritik', *RhM* 40: 263–82.

Stok, F. (2000) 'Fonti grammaticali del *Cornu copiae* di Niccolò Perotti', *Studi Umanistici Piceni* 20: 50–71.

Strzelecki, L. (1936) *De Flavio Capro Nonii Auctore.* Krakow.

Suerbaum, W. (1992) 'Zum Umfang der Bücher in der archaischen lateinischen Dichtung: Naevius, Ennius, Lukrez und Livius Andronicus auf Papyrus-Rollen', *ZPE* 92: 153–73.

   (1994) 'Herculanensische Lukrez-Papyri – Neue Belege für die Phase der Majuskel-Kursive eines bekannten Klassikertextes: Nachbetrachtungen zur Edition von K. Kleve', *ZPE* 104: 1–21.

Szymański, M. (2006) 'Lucretius' O, Q, L, F: doing justice to manuscripts', *Eos* 93: 132–4.

Taisné, A.-M. (1999) 'Le *De rerum natura* et la *Thébaïde* de Stace', in Poignault (1999a), 165–75.

Tangl, M. (1916) 'Studien zur Neuausgabe der Bonifatius-Briefe', *Neues Archiv* 40: 639–790.

Tarugi, G. (ed.) (1986) *Validità perenne dell'Umanesimo.* Florence.

Thiermann, P. (1987) 'Redécouverte et influence de manuscrits d'auteurs Latins classiques au début du XVe siècle', *RHT* 17: 55–71.

Thilo, G. (ed.) (1887) *Servii Grammatici qui feruntur in Vergilii Bucolica et Georgica Commentarii.* Leipzig.

Thomson, D. F. S. (1997) *Catullus. Edited with a Textual and Interpretative Commentary.* Toronto.

Timpanaro, S. (1963) *La genesi del metodo del Lachmann.* Florence.

   (1970) '*Longiter* in Lucrezio III 676', *Maia* 22: 355–7.

   (1978) *Contributi di filologia e di storia della lingua latina.* Rome.

   (2005) *The Genesis of Lachmann's Method* (tr. G. Moth). Chicago.

Tolkiehn, J. (1912) 'Lukrez und Carm. epigr. lat. 1061', *Wochenschrift für Klassische Philologie* 29: 1245–6.

Tomasco, D. (1980) 'Su Apuleio, De deo Socr. I 116,9–II 119,10 Th.', *Vichiana* 9: 166–72.

   (1981) Review of Flores (1980), *Vichiana* 10: 272–8.

Tosi, M. (1984–5) 'Documenti riguardanti l'abbaziato di Geberto a Bobbio', *Archivum Bobiense* 6–7: 91–172.

Traglia, A. (1962) *Poetae Novi.* Rome.

Traver Vera, Á. J. (2011) 'Revaluación del manuscrito lucreciano Caesaraugustanus 11–36', *Exemplaria Classica* 15: 113–21.

Trencsényi-Waldapel, I. (1958) 'Cicéron et Lucrèce', *AAntHung* 6: 321–83.

Turnebus, A. (1566) *Commentarii et Emendationes in Libros M. Varronis De Lingua Latina.* Paris.

   (1580) *Adversariorum Libri III* (collected edn; 3 vols.). Basel.

Tydeman, H. W. (1825) 'Over de bibliotheek van Isacus Vossius', *Mnemosyne: Mengelingen voor wetenschappen en fraaje letteren* 15: 260–90.

Bibliography

Uglione, R. (2001) 'Poeti latini in Tertulliano', *A&R* 46: 9–34.

Ullman, B. L. (1932) *Ancient Writing and its Influence*. New York.

(1960) *The Origin and Development of Humanistic Script*. Rome.

Usener, H. (ed.) (1887) *Epicurea*. Leipzig.

Vahlen, J. (ed.) (1892) *K. Lachmanns Briefe an Moriz Haupt*. Berlin.

Van der Valk, J. (1902) *De Lucretiano carmine a poeta perfecto atque absoluto* (Diss.). Kampen.

Van de Vyver, A. (1935) 'Micon et Dicuil', *RBPh* 14: 25–47.

Van Lommel, A. (1876) 'Opvolging der Jesuieten en hunne opvoilgers in eenige steden en dorpen van het tegenwoordige bisdom van Haarlem: Alkmaar 1608', *Haarlemsche Bijdragen* 4.

Varcl, L. and R. F. Willetts (eds.) (1963) *GERAS. Studies Presented to G. Thomson*. Prague.

Varii (eds.) (1901) *Strassburger Festschrift zur XLVI. Versammlung deutscher Philologen und Schulmänner*. Strasburg.

(eds.) (1974) *Poesia latina in frammenti. Miscellanea filologica*. Genoa.

(eds.) (1986) *Munus amicitiae: scritti in memoria di Alessandro Ronconi*. (2 vols.). Florence.

(eds.) (1991) *Studi di Filologia Classica in onore di Giusto Monaco*, vol. III: *Letteratura Latina dall'età di Tiberio all'età del Basso Impero*. Palermo.

Verdière, R. (1971) 'Lucain 7,62–65', *Latomus* 30: 723.

Vetranius, M. (1563) *M. Terentii Varronis pars Librorum XXIV. De Lingua Latina*. Lyons.

Vezin, J. (1982) 'Observations sur l'origine des manuscrits légués par Dungal à Bobbio', in Silagi (1982), 125–44.

Volk, K. (2002) *The Poetics of Latin Didactic*. Oxford.

(2009) *Manilius and his Intellectual Background*. Oxford.

(2010) 'Lucretius' Prayer for Peace and the date of *De rerum natura*', *CQ* 60: 127–31.

Voss, I. (ed.) (1684) *Gaius Valerius Catullus et in eum Isaaci Vossi observationes*. London.

Walser, E. (1914) *Poggius Florentinus: Leben und Werke*. Berlin.

Washietl, J. A. (1883) *De similitudinibus imaginibusque Ovidianis*. Vienna.

Watts, W. J. (1972) 'A literary reminiscence in Juvenal (IX,96)', *Latomus* 31: 519–20.

Weil, H. (1847) 'Ueber einige Stellen des Lucretius', *Zeitsch. f. d. Alterth.* 5: 305–12.

Weingärtner, A. (1874) *De Horatio Lucretii imitatore*. Halle.

Weinreich, O. (1918) 'Religiöse Stimmen der Völker', *Archiv für Religionswissenschaft* 19: 158–73.

Werlauff, E. C. (1844) *Historiske Efterretninger om det store kongelige Bibliothek i Kiøbenhavn*. Copenhagen.

West, D. (1969) *The Imagery and Poetry of Lucretius*. Edinburgh.

West, M. L. (1973) *Textual Criticism and Editorial Technique*. Stuttgart.

Bibliography

White, D. C. (1980) 'The method of composition and sources of Nonius Marcellus', *Studi Noniani* 8: 111–211.

Wigodsky, M. (1972) *Vergil and Early Latin Poetry* (Hermes Einzelschriften 24). Berlin.

Wilhelm, J. J. (1965) *The Cruelest Month*. New Haven.

Wilkinson, L. P. (1949) 'Lucretius and the love-philtre', *CR* 63: 47–8.

Willis, J. (1980) Review of Pieri (1977), *Mnemosyne* 33: 445–8.

Winsbury, R. (2009) *The Roman Book*. London.

Wöhler, R. (1876) *Die Einfluss des Lukrez auf die Dichter der Augusteischen Zeit*, vol. 1. Greifswald.

Woll, L. 1907. *De poetis Latinis Lucreti imitatoribus* (Diss.). Freiburg.

Woltjer, J. (1881a) *De Manilio poeta*. Groningen.

(1881b) 'De archetypo quodam codice Lucretiano', *Neue Jahrbücher für Philologie und Paedagogik* 123: 769–83.

(1884) 'De anno natali T. Lucretii poetae', *NJKPh* 129: 134–8.

(1893) 'Zur Lucrezbiographie des Borgius', *Berliner Philologische Wochenschrift* 10: 317–18.

(1895) 'Studia Lucretiana II. De vita Lucretii', *Mnemosyne*. 23, 222–33.

Wood, A. (1691–2) *Athenae Oxonienses: an Exact History of all the Writers and Bishops Who Have Had their Education in the Most Ancient and Famous University of Oxford* (2 vols.). London.

Wordsworth, C. (ed.) (1842) *The Correspondence of Richard Bentley* (2 vols.). London.

Zetzel, J. E. G. (1977) 'Lucilius, Lucretius and Persius 1,1', *CPh* 72: 40–2.

(1981) *Latin Textual Criticism in Antiquity*. New York.

Ziegler, K. (1936) 'Der Tod des Lucretius', *Hermes* 71: 421–40.

Zingerle, A. (1869–71) *Ovidius und sein Verhältniss zu den Vorgängern und gleichzeitigen römischen Dichtern*. Innsbruck.

INDEX

Aldhelm, 95, 269
Anecdotum Parisinum, 3, 100
Apuleius, 53–4, 189
archetype (of Lucretius' manuscripts), 4, 9,
    15–19, 21–8, 33, 67, 92, 94, 98,
    101, 118, 122, 124, 127, 137, 139,
    141, 149, 151–75, 177, 182, 184,
    187, 202, 205, 208, 212, 214–15,
    217–18, 268–72, 299–300
Arnobius, 57, 59, 287
Ars Bernensis, 79, 82
Audax, 77, 81, 96
Augustine, 57, 61
Aurispa, Giovanni, 41, 43
Ausonius, 86

Bartolomeo da Montepulciano, 41–4
Bede, 81, 96, 129–30
Bentley, Richard, 47, 67
Bernays, Jakob, 14–20, 22, 27, 59, 73, 113,
    309–11
Bertinianus codex, 14, 307–10
Beverland, Adrian, 307, 312
Bischoff, Bernhard, 7, 11, 204, 218–19,
    236, 246, 270
Bobbio, 11, 29–31, 218
Boethius, 86, 88
Breuis expositio, 73, 103, 264

Caesar, 49
Cannon, Robert, 307, 312–13
capitula, 3, 11, 16, 39, 119, 124, 127,
    136–202, 220, 224, 238–9, 259,
    268, 271–2, 274–85, 299–300
Catullus, 1, 48, 131–2
Censorinus, 86
Charisius, 75, 77, 83, 101, 116–17, 129–32
Cicero, Marcus Tullius, 1, 49, 53, 57–8, 62,
    112, 114, 131, 186, 189, 215, 223,
    231, 266

Cledonius, 77, 81, 87
Commenta Bernensia Lucania, 98
Consentius, 77, 81
Corbie, 9, 11, 30–1, 267
Cyprian, 61

De dubiis nominibus, 79, 82
Deufert, Marcus, 3, 22, 50, 65, 178
Dicuil, 35, 96
Diels, Hermann, 8, 11, 15, 17, 21–2, 28, 31,
    81, 101, 112, 116, 119, 129, 133,
    136, 150, 171, 182, 204, 206,
    233–4, 237–8, 242, 246, 248, 256,
    258, 269
Diogenes Laertius, 198, 201
Diogenes of Oenoanda, 69, 100
Diomedes, 77, 81
Donatus, Aelius, 74, 76, 80–1, 85, 87, 96,
    108, 287
Dositheus, 81, 96
Dungal, 4, 7, 18, 22, 24, 26–31, 143, 160,
    173, 194, 203–21, 234–6, 250–3,
    266, 272, 296–7

Egnatius, 48, 128
Ennius, 103–4, 107, 112–13
Epicurus, 1, 57, 65, 106, 182,
    196–8, 240
Ermenrich of Ellwangen, 30, 97, 100,
    287
Eutyches, 79, 82
Exempla diuersorum auctorum, 92, 264

Festus, Sextus Pompeius, 38, 46, 53–6,
    62, 87, 99, 101, 115, 117,
    242
Florilegium Sangallense, 12, 30–1, 67,
    92–4, 96–8, 100, 264–5, 287
Fronto, 52

Index

Gallandus, Petrus, 307–10
Gellius, Aulus, 1, 48, 52–3, 57, 62, 67, 94, 103, 184, 189–90, 223
Gifanius, Obertus, 110, 115, 136, 305, 310–11
Glossaria, 99, 111, 287
Greek
    capitula, 181–5, 188, 193, 197–201, 224, 239
Gronovius, Jacobus, 307, 311
Gronovius, Johannes, 40, 306, 311–12
Gude, Marquard, 12, 14, 16, 313

Haupt, Moriz, 16, 51
Haverkamp, Syvert, 12, 136, 258, 307, 311–13
Heinsius, Nicolaas, 14, 210, 258, 307–8, 310–11, 313
Heiric of Auxerre, 94–5, 100, 224
Herculaneum papyri, 5–6
Heyworth, Stephen, 171–2
Hieronymus; *see* Jerome
Hincmar, 97, 287
Homer, 102–4, 107–8, 120, 190, 287
Horace, 3, 47, 86, 95, 113, 191
Hostius, 104
Hrabanus Maurus, 1, 8, 90–1, 117, 228, 287
Hyginus, 53–4, 60, 97, 287
hyperarchetype, 23, 25, 127, 156, 163, 268–70

interpolation, 2, 20, 51, 172, 270
Isidore, 46, 73, 88–91, 96–7, 100–1, 111, 116–18, 239–40, 242, 263, 268, 287
Itali, 13–16, 18–45, 127, 136, 181, 248–56, 270, 272–3

Jerome, 1, 3, 51, 60, 69, 90, 97, 110–11, 199, 287
Julian of Toledo, 96
Junilius, 125
Junius Philargyrius, 73–4
Juvenal, 11–12, 48, 93

Kristina, Queen of Sweden, 306

Lachmann, Karl, 5–6, 8, 10, 14–20, 22, 24, 27, 30, 65, 85, 102, 106, 108, 111–12, 115, 122, 124, 126,

129–30, 133, 136, 143, 147, 153, 161–7, 171, 182, 206, 218, 233, 247, 258, 268, 271, 299
Lactantius, 46, 56–9, 61, 101, 288
Lactantius Placidus, 86–8
Lambinus, Dionysius, 9, 14, 18–20, 47, 67, 115, 117–19, 215, 243, 307–11
Leiden University Library, 7–10, 258, 260, 307, 309, 311–12
Leto, Pomponius, 34, 42, 44
Lindenbruch, Friedrich, 313–14
Lindsay, W.M., 8, 62, 204, 222, 259
Livy, 48
Lobbes, 30–1
Lucan, 3, 48, 96–8, 108–11, 132–4, 287
Lucilius, 15, 89, 106–11, 113, 115–17, 120, 130, 132, 134, 186
Lucretius, *passim*
    capitula of; *see capitula*.
    manuscripts of; *see Itali*; Oblongus codex; Quadratus codex; *Schedae*

Macarius von Busek, 8, 259, 275
Macrobius, 60, 67–70, 72, 99, 101, 103–4, 110, 117, 287
Madvig, Johan Nicolai, 12–13, 16, 20, 22, 106
Mainz, 7–8, 30, 41, 43, 222, 228, 248, 256, 259, 305–7
Manilius, 48, 223, 288
Martial, 94, 190
Martianus Capella, 85–8
Maxim(in)us Victori(n)us, 78, 81, 91
Memmianus codex, 14, 310
Memmius, Erricus, 310
Mico Centulensis, 91–2, 96, 264, 287
Modius, Franciscus, 14, 308, 310–11
Müller, Konrad, 3, 16–17, 21–2, 27–9, 33, 136, 206, 234–8, 247–9, 253, 255–6
Munro, Hugh, 6, 15, 17, 20, 22, 47–9, 107, 112, 119, 121, 258, 308, 310
Murbacensis codex, 24, 28, 30
Murbach, 24, 28–30, 93, 268

Nansius, Franciscus, 307–12
Nepos, 49
Niccoli, Niccolò, 15, 20, 39–41, 43, 251, 254–6

Index

Nonius Marcellinus, 35, 51, 60–7, 80–1, 83–4, 94–6, 101, 117–20, 131–4, 240, 269, 287

Oblongus codex, 6–8, 13–45, 203–60, 296–8, 305–9, 311–13
corrections of
corrector Saxonicus; see Dungal
O², 22–30, 35, 38, 143, 227–37, 241–2, 244–5, 247, 250–2, 256, 260, 272, 297–8, 308
O³, 7, 28, 34–9, 84, 138, 220, 227, 229, 233–56, 260, 272, 298
O⁴, 227, 256–8, 267, 272, 298, 309
O^ann·(Annotator), 220–8, 234, 247, 266, 297
rubrication of, 137, 148, 170–5, 177
Opus prosodiacum, 91, 264
Ovid, 48, 95, 132, 190

Paulus Diaconus, 55–6
Petronius, 48
Pizzani, Ubaldo, 22, 46, 98, 102, 106, 109, 111–12, 127, 306
Pliny the Elder, 1, 49, 109, 185, 188, 223
Pliny the Younger, 51–3
Plotius Sacerdos, Marius, 76, 79–81, 120–2, 128
Poggianus codex, 15, 18–45, 212, 236, 247–56, 272–3
Poggio Bracciolini, 2, 14–15, 18, 20, 24, 28–30, 36, 40–4, 248–50, 252, 254–6, 268, 287
Politian (Angelo Poliziano), 34, 37, 39, 43–5
Pompeius, 77, 80–1
Porphyrio, 47, 86
Priscian, 35, 77, 81, 83–6, 92, 96, 101, 110, 228, 287
Probus, M. Valerius, 1–4, 112
Propertius, 48
Prudentius, 61, 288
Pseudo-Acro, 86–7
Pseudo-Probus, 74, 79, 82
Purmann, Hugo, 13–16, 117, 120, 268, 310

Quadratus codex, 7–10, 13–21, 30–1, 165, 261–7, 307–13

metrical annotator of, 261–7
rubrication of, 7–9, 138, 261, 267
Quintilian, 50–2, 60, 63

Reeve, Michael, 13, 22–3, 27, 33, 35, 37, 39–41, 43–4, 210, 237–8, 245, 249, 259, 305, 307, 309–10
Ritschl, Friedrich, 13–15

Salmasius, Claudius, 40, 306, 311–12
Scaliger, Joseph Justus, 110, 115–17
Schedae, 9–19, 21, 30–1, 313–14
rubrication of, 138–41
Scholia Bernensia, 73–4, 103, 108, 124–5
Scholia Veronensia, 72–4, 100
Seneca the Younger, 49–53, 57, 62, 125, 132, 223, 231, 287
Serenus, 88–9, 223
Vatican manuscript of, 97–9
Sergius, 96–7
Servius, 48, 69–74, 81–2, 87–8, 90, 100–12, 114, 117, 119–26, 149, 182, 188–9, 231, 287
St Bertin, 9, 21, 30–1, 267, 307–11, 287
St Gallen, 12, 30, 92–4, 97, 100
Statius, 48, 50, 87, 132, 182, 231
Susius, Jacob, 312

Tacitus, 50
Terentianus Maurus, 240
Terentius Scaurus, 75–6, 80, 85
Tertullian, 56–7, 62, 87
Tibullus, 48
Timpanaro, Sebastiano, 13, 15, 17, 20, 22, 83, 269–70
Turnebus, Adrianus, 9, 48, 115, 307–10

Varro Reatinus, 15, 48, 51, 114–18, 131, 188
Velleius Paterculus, 49
Verrius Flaccus, 53–6, 129
Virgil, 3, 48, 50–1, 67, 69–75, 81, 87, 99–100, 102–9, 111, 113, 124–5, 128, 132, 231, 241
'*Vita Borgiana*', 1, 114, 116
Vitruvius, 1, 49
von Barth, Kaspar, 84, 120, 129–30, 306, 314
Vossius, Gerardus, 306–7, 310–12
Vossius, Isaac, 258, 306–13

.